Retelling a Life

ROY SCHAFER, Ph.D.

RETELLING
A LIFE

Narration and Dialogue
in Psychoanalysis

BasicBooks
A Division of HarperCollins*Publishers*

For credits regarding previously published chapters, see pp. 317–18.

Library of Congress Cataloging-in-Publication Data

Schafer, Roy.
    Retelling a life: narration and dialogue in psychoanalysis
/ Roy Schafer.
         p.   cm.
    Includes bibliographical references and index.
    ISBN 0–465–04811–0
    1. Psychoanalysis.   2. Psychology—Biographical meth-
ods.   3. Discourse analysis,
Narrative.   I. Title.
    [DNLM: 1. Psychoanalysis.   2. Psychoanalytic Theory.
3. Psychotherapy—methods.   WM 460 S296r]
RC506.S292   1992
616.89'17—dc20
DNLM/DLC   91–44125
for Library of Congress   CIP

For Rita

CONTENTS

ACKNOWLEDGMENTS

I WOULD like here to express my indebtedness to a number of major modern thinkers who have deeply influenced the conception of psychoanalytic interpretation used throughout the book and particularly in chapter 9. Listed alphabetically, not in order of influence, they are Mikhail Bakhtin, Wayne Booth, Jacques Derrida, Stanley Fish, Michel Foucault, Jurgen Habermas, Frank Kermode, Paul Ricoeur, Gilbert Ryle, Hayden White, and Ludwig Wittgenstein.

I thank my wife, Dr. Rita V. Frankiel, for her enthusiastic personal support, her confidence and patience, and her helpful critiques of the scope, organization, and much of the content of this book. Dedicating the book to her is small thanks for all she has done.

I also thank Jo Ann Miller, my editor, for her encouraging interest and guidance. And I am grateful to Susan Zurn, project editor, and Debby Manette, copy editor, for first-rate assistance at Basic Books, and to Barbara B. Frank for her secretarial care and readiness to help out.

INTRODUCTION

RETELLING A LIFE rests on the foundation of my work on action language (1976, 1978, 1983). I presented action language as "a new language for psychoanalysis," one designed to replace the mechanistic language of Freud's metapsychology. Metapsychology features an obsolete theory of mind as a mental apparatus. Yet the language of metapsychology has continued to shape much of the thinking and many of the expositions of mainstream, mostly North American Freudian analysts.

In my proposed new language for theory, I use *action* in the broad sense that characterizes much of its use in the philosophy of mind, action, and ethics. In its broad sense, action refers to far more than overt behavior; it refers as well to whatever it is that people may be said to do, and in this respect it stands in contrast to *happenings,* those events in which one's own human agency plays no discernible or contextually relevant part (for example, a rainstorm or receiving a misaddressed letter a week late). Among the things that people do is perceive, remember, imagine, love, hate, fear, defend, and refrain from overt activity. In psychoanalytic discussion, special emphasis is then placed on what people do unconsciously and conflictually (fantasize, remember, love, defend, and so forth).

Subjective experience itself is viewed as a construction of human agency. Experience is not simply "there in the mind" waiting to be found and retrieved by objective introspection. Different people tend to construct experiences of the same event differently, each for reasons of his or her own. Many of these reasons originate early in life and therefore give rise to primitive forms of emotional and cognitive experience, and these persist unconsciously and influentially into adult life. They also add individual coloring to otherwise standardized responses to the conventions of one's culture.

Actions are performed by a person, not by a "mind" or "personality" and not by "drives" or "defense mechanisms." Repression, for example, is an action of a person, and so are an angry tirade, an erotic approach to another person, and the solving of a puzzle.

Narration enters into it as soon as we take into account that, as philosophers say, actions exist only under one or another description. That is to say, we may describe the same event differently depending on our aims, such as approval or condemnation; our context, such as being among strangers or intimates; our level of abstraction, such as setting up broad categories or developing individualized accounts; and other such discursive variables. The action of projecting, for example, may be variously described as defensive, a constituent of empathy, a refusal to take responsibility, a distortion of reality, self-deception, or an early form of defining external reality. Indeed, to speak of "projecting" is already to present an action under a description; it is not an unmediated report of a fact, and it can be named differently.

In the context of narrative theory, therefore, it would be emphasized that actions are always told by someone and that each telling presents one possible version of the action in question. (It may be argued that we are never absolutely right to say that it is the "same" action when there are only distinguishable versions of it; however, that argument introduces a philosophical problem that does not bear on the present theme and so need not concern us here.)

I invoke the idea of narration precisely in connection with the inevitability of alternative descriptions. Using the term broadly, I designate as narration whatever qualifies as a telling or as the presenting of a version of an action; also, whatever qualifies as a version of a happening or an event or scene of any kind, as each of these, too, is always presented under one or another description.

In the sense used here, narratives are not made-up stories (fictitious in the established sense) with beginnings, middles, and endings. Narrating, giving an account, presenting a version, developing a storyline, telling: These terms and others like them make up the core vocabulary of the narrational approach.

It is especially important to emphasize that narrative is not an alternative to truth or reality; rather, it is the mode in which, inevitably, truth and reality are presented. We have only versions of the true and the real. Narratively unmediated, definitive access to truth and reality cannot be demonstrated. In this respect, therefore, there can be no absolute foundation on which any observer or thinker stands; each must choose his or her narrative or version. Further, each narrative presupposes or establishes a context, and the sentences of any one account attain full significance only within their context and through more or less systematic or consistent use of the language appropriate to the purpose.

Psychoanalysis is conducted as a dialogue. However much the analyst may remain silent as she or he listens patiently for suitable opportunities to define themes of unconscious conflict, the process still qualifies as dialogue, for each of the analyst's utterances and meaningful silences counts heavily in the course of the work—sometimes far too heavily owing to the influence of powerful transferences. In this dialogue, actions and happenings (for example, traumatic events) are continuously being told by the analysand and sooner or later retold interpretively by both analyst and analysand. Closure is always provisional to allow for further retellings. In many instances the tellings are nonverbal enactments: showings that are yet to be transformed into tellings. Often the analysand's responses to the analyst's interventions are themselves regarded as material to be retold (clarified, interpreted) in order to progress toward insight. Insight itself refers to those retellings that make a beneficial difference in a person's construction and reconstruction of experience and adaptively active conduct of life. Each retelling amounts to an account of the prior telling as something different or, more likely, something more than had been noted. In this dialogic way, each analysis amounts in the end to retelling a life in the past and present—and as it may be in the future. A life is re-authored as it is co-authored.

Narration has no necessary connection to literariness or self-conscious ornamentation. Although literariness (such as deliberate building of suspense, conventional poetic diction, conspicuous use of stylistic devices) may be an aspect of some narrations, matter-of-fact reportage qualifies as narration just as much as an account presented by a flowery orator.

These introductory remarks merely indicate—they certainly do not expound fully—the narrational and dialogical approach to psychoanalysis. The chapters of this book containing numerous clinical examples, will, I hope, fill in many of the major details of this approach. They should help the reader to see more clearly the usefulness of narratological and dialogical considerations in grasping the theories and practices of psychoanalysts and the diverse, often dramatic, bodily and mental phenomena to which they give rise and which, in the end, exemplify them.

Although these chapters cover a wide range of topics, they can be arranged in four parts: "Narrating the Self," "Narrating Gender," "Theories as Master Narratives," and "Versions of Practice." The parts are not altogether distinct from one another; for example, self narratives are considered throughout the book as are versions of practice and of theories (master narratives). At times the discussions confront major philosophical problems, such as those pertaining to knowledge of self and others, personal identity, and theory construction; at other times, and often, they are deeply engaged with clinical observation, interpretation, and technique.

With reference to the self, after introducing aspects of self narratives in relation to the goals, processes, and especially endings of clinical analyses, I go on in chapter 2 to argue that, for the individual subject, the self is always a narrative construction, always open to flux, and so never totally settled once and for all; on the same argument, this generalization also applies to others in a person's life—the objects so-called. Thus, unlike some other current and popular positions, my position on the self is anti-essentialist; I do not regard the self as an entity found in nature and available for detached study by nonparticipant observers. Selves are told through dialogue, in words, images, and enactments, and they are retold by observers whose narrative preferences and strategies express specific aims, values, and competencies. This first part ends with my considering narrative aspects of the philosophically thorny question of self-deception, and, with that, of defense, multiple-self theories, and other issues of concern to ego psychology, self psychology, and object relations theory.

In the second part on gender, I take up the inherently narrative nature of gender in five different, though related, contexts: the frequently masculine bias in Freud's psychology of women; sexist rhetoric in clinical discussions of impotence and frigidity and its consequences for our conceptions of heterosexual relations; problems of men and women in dealing with success and happiness; men's problems with emotionality; and disruptive aspects of power and rage in male-female relationships. In an effort to shrink the frequently emphasized gap between feminists and psychoanalysts, I emphasize the interaction between sexist factors in social reality and women's unconscious conflicts and identifications, recognizing always that the latter do not develop in ways that are altogether independent of our phallocentric social order. Clinical illustrations are distributed through these chapters.

Aspects of the third part, "Theories as Master Narratives," have been anticipated in the preceding parts; nevertheless, major and direct discussions are presented through, first, a review in modern terms of Freud's legacy; second, an examination of the role of narration in clinical as well as applied psychoanalytic interpretation; and third, a short survey of the many problems encountered by any attempt to find common ground shared by the major, competing schools of psychoanalytic thought. Psychoanalysis emerges as an array of master narratives that dictate specific and incommensurable storylines for the interpretive work of analysts.

In the final, heavily clinical part, and with the aid of detailed examples, I first take up numerous narrational aspects of the clinical interpretation of defense and resistance and the clinical uses of narrativized life experience in the past and present. Then, in an effort to clarify further my story of what psychoanalysis "is," I take up in sequence the difficulties, ambiguities, and limits of training analysis and of the attempt to differentiate analysis from its imitations and from psychotherapy. With psychotherapy now in the text, I take up next some crucial dialogic issues involved in practicing psychoanalytic therapy. And I conclude this wide-ranging story of narration in psychoanalysis by discussing "analytic love"—the analyst's sublimated love for his or her patients as it is expressed through the analytic work itself, taking my cue from Hans Loewald's several published references to this phenomenon.

A number of the chapters in this book have already been published. For the sake of coherence and consistency, I have revised that previously published material, in some instances only slightly, in others more noticeably. I have done so by cutting in order to reduce repetition; by clarification, to improve the argument; by change of terms, to coordinate the chapters; and by highlighting, to bring out the places of narration and dialogue in the argument where they had been left obscure or merely indicated in passing.

My goal was not unity at any price; however, with the benefit of hindsight, I now see considerably more coherence among these chapters, the writing of which has extended over a number of years, than I could have recognized during the production of each of them. In one way or another, these pieces are about interpretation. As I now conceive it in narrational and dialogic terms, interpretation is always a way of either telling something that has not yet been put into words or retelling something already told. In sum, we may say that it is a life that is being reworked beneficially through analytic dialogue.

PART ONE

NARRATING
THE SELF

CHAPTER 1

Self-interest, Self Interest, and the Termination of Psychoanalysis

IT is one of the enduring popular burlesques of psychoanalysis that at its conclusion, the analysand is a moral monster. Self-interested to the exclusion of all considerations of decency, tact, and mutuality, guilt-free and shame-free in unbridled appetitiveness, the analysand prowls through the world seeking opportunities for self-assertion and self-revelation. And to boot, does all this with instantly displayed and usually boring, if not offensive, insight into the self and others. In a word, this person is selfish: maddeningly and tediously selfish. So the burlesque goes.

One dictionary defines selfish as "concerned *excessively* or *exclusively* with oneself: seeking or concentrating on one's advantage, pleasure, or well-being *without regard for others*" (my emphases). Is this the business that analysts are in? Is it the analyst's mission to help people to be selfish? Is the attainment of unconflicted selfishness a criterion for successfully terminating analysis? It seems rather that that mission could bespeak only poverty of spirit on both sides of the couch.

It must be admitted at the outset that this burlesque can be properly applied to the way some people behave in the thick of their ambivalent analytic transferences. Sometimes it can be applied to analysands who have interrupted their analyses or who have completed what they or their therapist mistakenly or pretentiously call analysis or successful analysis. Additionally, the caricature may not be far from the mark in describing some people as they are when they begin analysis and as

3

they may continue to be or to seem, even if in diminished form, as their analyses make substantial progress. None of which should be surprising, and all of which should, upon reflection, give the lie to the burlesque. But the burlesque persists, and we must ask why that is so.

Analysts know to how great an extent this conventional lampoon of analysands originates in the irrational attitudes of not-so-innocent bystanders and observers. Knowing this, thoughtful analysts make it part of their job, especially as termination approaches, to help genuinely progressed analysands recognize and withstand the pressures exerted by this attack or by one of its many variants. They do so by continuing to promote insight—in this respect by analyzing analysands' denials of what they are up against and their regressive responses to it. This facilitation of insight might begin by taking up denials of an analysand's own ability to understand what prompts the hostility or the regressive shift; that they are denials is made plain by the abundance of available evidence of the burlesque's origins, and, that they are regressive shifts is made plain by the patients having more or less vigorously returned to modes of response that appear to have been worked out or given up in the course of analysis.

Let us consider, first, three outstanding origins of the burlesque: frustration, envy, and defensive insecurity. The three go together and essentially imply one another, but each can be singled out for purposes of exposition.

FRUSTRATION AS THE SOURCE OF THE BURLESQUE

Analysts know that many of those who share their lives with analyzed people prefer them as they were preanalytically. Especially those analysands who used to be inhibited, undemanding, and masochistic in attitude were liked the better for it. Once they had been good company: good losers and ever ready with the knowing looks, the sympathetic shrugs, and the self-pitying and bitter jokes that convey a sense of togetherness and passive resignation to a life that offers little and deprives one of much. Once they had been ready to make the expressive movements and to emit the sighs and groans that grease the wheels of communality. Male and female, they played the basic Woody Allen role with considerable ingenuity. Now unappreciative friends, relatives, and lovers view these progressed analysands with a sense of frustration, for they had grown accustomed to the patients' self-effacing faces. In these faces they had seen the victims of the spontaneous, provoked, or simply imagined sadistic exploitativeness of others. They are the prisonerlike faces of those who share the passive and not uncommon ideal of living unhappily in shame, guilt, weakness, helpless rage, and failure.

Progressed analysands have already understood this dynamic. They have developed that understanding largely through analysis of their own transferences, and that understanding has been crucial in whatever progress they have made. Now for the most part they no longer play these victim games as seductively, expertly, or insistently as before. With some consistency they convey a strong sense of pride combined with realistic assessments and expectations. They also convey a strong sense of self-love and self-respect combined with continued strivings for further development. By changing in these ways, they not only frustrate the desires of others, they stir up envy.

ENVY: THE SECOND PRESSURE ON PROGRESSED ANALYSANDS

Envy is the origin of the second sort of pressure that progressed analysands must withstand. Poisonous envy: Surrounding the progressed analysands like poison gas, it takes the form of little digs, malicious and too readily believed gossip about the analysand or the analyst or promising life situations, and other such efforts to spoil the goodness that analysands have newly found in themselves, in their analysts, and in the surrounding world. In response, they are tempted to, and in fact do regress—slowly, rapidly, grossly, or subtly; it is not the first time in their lives they have responded so, and, as before, they feel that their survival depends on this defensive shift. The vigilant analyst picks up these shifts in level of functioning, recognizing how in large part they are regressive responses to envy, and helps work out their connections with current real and imagined interactions with others. Imagined interactions must be taken into account, for the analysand's fear of envy and other defensive dealings with his or her own inner grandiosity and shame may lead the analysand to project envy as well as frustration and a sense of insecurity where there is not very much supporting evidence.

At this relatively late stage of analysis, that which has been imagined will be readily linked up in the analytic dialogue with two sets of factors: (1) influential infantile prototypes of envious responses by siblings, friends, parents, and others in the immediate environment, and (2) a guilty sense of the analysand's own unconscious, infantile, ruthless greed and grandiose competitiveness, intensified perhaps by comparable qualities in others. Much of the analytic work will throw into sharp relief the extent to which an analysand's progress has stimulated defensive insecurity as well as frustration and envy in others around them.

BURLESQUE OUT OF DEFENSIVE INSECURITY

Well-analyzed people are felt by others in their lives to be threats to the defensive solutions that they have come to count on. These analysands no longer consistently support prevailing neurotic compromises and no longer consistently endorse and participate in the preferred but severely compromised pleasure possibilities in the lives of these others. Out of defensive insecurity, these others may then experience the analysands' hard-earned and owned pride as nothing more than insensitive egoism, their unconcealed self-confidence as merely callous exhibitionism, and their unhampered though not exclusive attention to pursuing their own interests as ruthless exploitativeness or self-indulgence. What, they will then ask, has happened to these analysands' stoicism? Where is their ethical responsibility? Have they lost their sense of decorum? What has happened to their sweetness? Why do they not just go along in order to get along?

Adding to the problem in all three respects, progressed analysands may have reached a point where they continue in analysis not out of dire need and abject humiliation but because they want to, even if not without noteworthy ambivalence. To the extent that they do want to continue, it is because they view analysis as having added life to their lives and as fortifying them in their efforts to do the same for themselves in the future. They see analysis as having strengthened their integration and enhanced their future prospects. Now they are not so inclined to think of analysis negatively; in their psychic realities it is far less a crutch, a trap, or a life sentence than it is a release, an opportunity, a source of autonomy. Worse still, from the standpoint of these frustrated, envious, defensively locked-in others, progressed analysands may even have the nerve to say that, on balance, however arduous analysis remains, they enjoy it! They enjoy it even while recognizing ever more clearly and with expectable mixtures of foreboding and regret that the time is coming when it will no longer be in their own self-interest to continue in analysis. As one analysand said, "It doesn't get any easier, but it does get better." These analysands are experienced as threats not only to the defensive order of things but to the social order in general. Clearly, they must be stopped!

ANALYSANDS' RESPONSES TO THE REACTIONS OF OTHERS

Small wonder then that they encounter efforts to undermine their gains. Small wonder, too, that they anticipate and experience some painful loneliness as their relations with at least some of the important others in their lives become more and more estranged and less and less worth the cost to them. They sense the withdrawal of others or their own withdrawal from others, or most likely both at once; or the emphasis may fall more on disapproval on both ends of the relationship than on direct withdrawal. Analysands must feel the pressure to regress, to "fit in" once again, in circumstances like these. Terminating analysands will have many other reasons to revive problems that already have been effectively analyzed; nevertheless, it is important to the completion of the analysis to help analysands confront, in an analytic way, this kind of appeasement of others through flight from progress.

Postanalytically, too, analysands may respond regressively when they encounter the reactionary pressures I have described. And they may not see the connection for what it is, perhaps partly out of the wish to regress back to being an analysand for other reasons. In any case it is not unusual for some analysands to return for postanalytic consultation with some kind of flare-up of previously mastered problems or symptoms. Upon analysis, it may soon become apparent that these flare-ups are designed unconsciously to appease others. In analysands' fantasies, the analyst may be among those to be appeased—the analyst they have "left behind," "discarded," "abandoned," "used up," "fooled," or "surpassed" in youthfulness, success, pleasure, or what have you. Guilt may play a major part in these returns. At such times, further analysis is likely to establish that the need to appease is greatest where there had been deep-seated vulnerabilities not so much to others as to guilty reactions to the analysands' own special achievements and richness of experience. Residual fears of their own greed, competitiveness, and grandiosity may also be involved. And some of these regressing former analysands may be undergoing a variant of survivor's guilt in relation to others in their lives: not sure they deserve their gains and so fearing that what they have gained will be taken away from them. In all of this, analysts will encounter the play of transference residues, negative and positive.

Appearances may be deceiving at a time like this, for it is not necessarily true that analysands' gains are predominantly unstable. The likelihood is that, unexpectedly, their gains, their advances to higher levels of functioning and interaction with others, have brought them into new difficulties or new versions of old difficulties. It may prove that their continuing personal development after termination has evoked further manifestations of central infantile conflict and unresolved transference. It may be that, as Freud (1937b) surmised, these conflicts were not active enough or accessible enough during the main period of analysis to be worked through adequately. Even so, postanalytic work will be based on the considerable working through that was accomplished earlier, for analysts today understand that personalities are not so compartmentalized that some major issues never enter a sustained analysis in one guise or another. This newly encountered conflictual experience may, for example, center around getting married, divorcing, becoming a parent, losing a loved one, or achieving high-level success at work, no one of which can be altogether removed from infantile fantasy and its conflictual aspects. With some analytic clarification of current pressures, these former analysands may be ready to be on their way again without undergoing a second lengthy analysis. Unanalytic perfectionism on the part of the analyst may, however, dictate otherwise.

In any event, the terminating analysands' secured and enhanced self-interest must be seen as both an important asset and a potential source of new problems. The new problems appear at the interface of internal object relations and relations with others in the environment.

SELF-INTEREST VERSUS SELF INTEREST

Thus far I have been merely approaching the intrapsychic and interpersonal complexities of the enhanced self-interest of terminating analysands. I have been using the term *self-interest* in its conventional sense of protecting and promoting one's own best interests in whatever way one defines them. There is, however, another kind of self interest [unhyphenated] that we must attend to: interest in constructing, maintaining, and extending a self to which one can feel committed. This interest may be benevolent or malevolent or, as is often the case, a mixture of the two. In the progression toward termination, the balance shifts slowly but surely toward benevolent self interest. In the following text I discuss the two poles of self interest, giving some clinical examples along the way. Subsequently I attempt to show that benevolent self interest must include interest in the selves of others.

In certain respects this turn in the discussion runs parallel to Erikson's discussion of ego identity formation (1956); in other respects, as when I invoke certain aspects of Kleinian thought about the depressive position and reparation, and also when I invoke Hartmann's discussion of the testing of inner reality, I more or less diverge from Erikson. And when, in conclusion, I take up the self as one kind of psychoanalytic narrative, I shall be far from Erikson's essentially naturalistic presentation of ego identity: a presentation in which the development of identity is described as simply observed in nature by an objective observer rather than as an account delivered by a narrator from a particular psychoanalytic point of view. What lies immediately ahead, then, is consideration of the two kinds of self interest and discussion of clinical examples. Finally, I develop a metatheoretical view of this entire presentation as psychoanalytic story or narrative.

Malevolent Self Interest

The best starting point now is a focus on malevolent self interest. Certainly, analysts are extremely familiar with self-scrutiny that ranges from nagging reproachfulness to outright persecution. Typically, this harsh and painful self-scrutiny is stereotyped in content and fragmenting in its effects. Typically, those who are inclined to burden themselves with this malevolent gaze directed inward promptly do so in spades whenever they begin to experience or express benevolent self interest. Almost instantaneously at those times, they turn the benevolent narrative around into new charges against themselves, say, of smugness, overconfidence, showing off, or destructive competitiveness. By projection, they may charge others with being persecutors, and in order to externalize their own conflicts completely they may readily go on to provoke others into being persecutors.

Whatever the extent of the distortions, analysts bear in mind that, first of all, it is the patients themselves who are the malevolent critics. Primarily, they have already been doing the dirty work intrapsychically either by raising their own voices against themselves or by conjuring up the experience of hostile introjects who examine them hatefully. These are people who will not take yes for an answer. They say such things as these: "I don't want to give in to my good feelings," "I have trouble feeling depressed today," and in an apparent slip, "You've got to learn to take the good with the bad." In these cases, the self is not the party of the first part; it is the party of the worst part.

When it is done malevolently, the construction of a self is consistently restricted and warped. A self-victimizer elaborates one-sided, often grotesque fantasies about the self that, however, are presented as reports of incontrovertible reality testing. Should the analyst mistakenly attempt to argue against these reports, he or she is likely to be regarded with some suspicion if not contempt. However negative it may be, this self-portraiture does manifest sustained self interest; it is not helpful to analysis to think of this material merely as showing problems with self-esteem or fixation on passive suffering or something of that sort. Those points of view have their own important place in analysis, but they may not fill the place occupied by the recognition of a malevolent form of self interest.

The clinical examples that follow show different types of malevolent self interest, and some also indicate transition to benevolent self interest over the course of analysis. For purposes of exposition, I present these case examples mainly in terms of the single storyline that concerns us here; many other storylines were, of course, consistently noted and elaborated in each case.

Case Example

After five years of treatment, one young woman reported that she was really beginning to look at herself in the mirror in order to see what she looked like. And she liked what she saw. It was not that previously she had had no visualized self; rather, she had visualized herself as ugly. This malevolent fantasy picture was disconfirmed by her beginning to look at herself realistically, and it was the new look that was consistent with the way her friends had been seeing her all along. For the analyst, too, it seemed that ordinary reality testing would not support the extreme attributions of ugliness she had been making. Upon analysis, it seemed that a large part of the patient's previous self-narrative had been being used as one of her archaic defensive precautions against intimacy; this was one element of a masochistic strategy that she had worked out and maintained from her earliest years. Previously, she had not dared to test out that self-narrative by conventional means and to revise it accordingly. She had no reality-tested self and precious little benevolent self interest; in her psychic reality, she could not afford to have them.

As could be expected in a case like this, the analysand had grown up with parents who, owing to their own plainly apparent, severe conflictual existence, had not taken an objective and appreciative interest in the physical and emotional child she had been and for the most part had remained, both in their psychic reality and in hers. She was seeing herself through their eyes. There had been no benign parental mirror—only her parents' aversive and critical stereotypes of what she was as compared to what she should be and was failing to be, only their fixed and destructive ideals of anhedonic conformity and flawlessness. They had never framed the open-minded questions, the mirroring questions, the benevolently interested questions: What have we here? How can we respond to it genuinely? How can we help it along? Their interest in her self was malevolent. Such at least was the lifelong experience reported by this young woman during much of her analysis. However exaggerated her account of her past—and it did require important modifications later on (for these see below)—these painful details were well documented, and they were prominent influences on her development up to the present.

In her attempt to compensate for the absence of benevolent parental interest and subsequent self interest, this young woman had tried to develop a public image of flawlessness and unreachability. In this effort her subjective success was limited, but this did not stop her from persevering. Accordingly, she had precluded mirroring and caring responses by others; she had perpetuated the problem of continuing to feel that she was living among uninterested others. On his part, the analyst had shown consistent analytic interest in her through his careful and caring attention to enactments that entered into her transferences; these enactments included much oppositionalism and much displacement into the trials and tribulations of her daily existence outside the analysis. So far as he could, he had avoided showing such *un*analytic interest in her as providing her with explicit, socially conventional reassurances. As time went on, it seemed that it was his analytic interest, combined with the suitable interpretations it made possible, that was helping to bring about moderating changes in the superego prohibitions she had been enforcing, the damaging ideals she had been holding up, and the unconsciously sexualized pain that had been involved.

The patient showed these changes by beginning to take an interest in having a viable self of her own. This was to be a self that encompassed needs, appetites, sensuality, individuality, and the assets of attractiveness, intelligence, generosity, and other such benevolently conceived qualities, qualities that are a delight to behold and a pleasure to live out once the attendant dangers and despair have been reduced. It was noteworthy that these excursions into benevolent self interest were accompanied by some sexual arousal in her sessions and that this arousal regularly frightened her and stimulated regression. In my analytic experience, some sexual arousal often accompanies explicit and new self-affirmative advocacy, and it often seems to be the cause of some immediate backing off; I believe the patient backs off because feeling sexually stimulated or feeling alive in that way is itself viewed malevolently as something to be condemned and suppressed.

Concurrently, the patient began to take an interest in the actual, extremely conflicted, and pain-inducing selves of her parents. At times in her analytic sessions she even allowed herself to empathize with them; the empathy seemed genuine enough in that it was experienced without minimizing or disavowing her rage and sense of deprivation. Only then could she dare to peek into an actual mirror, even if only briefly and anxiously; that is to say, she began to tolerate peeking into the psychic lives of others with some real curiosity and even some compassion at the same time as she began to look more deeply and empathically into her own psychic life and into her face as its visible manifestation.

Case Example

The next example is that of a woman who, although she was appreciated by everyone in her field as an extraordinarily talented person, could find no way to participate in their judgment. She had grown up with a nebulous mother—an unreflecting mirror, one might say—and so had developed no adequate foundation for a benevolently affirmative self interest. This simplistic causal connection seemed to hold up, but only as one factor contributing to her problems; the final account of the origins of her problems, developed over the course of the analysis, was far more complex than that. As is usual in such cases, it was not just a question of lack of self interest; not having felt herself to be an object of interest, she had developed prohibitions against affirmative self interest. To wish for benevolent interest was bad and to feel it was bad.

This important consequence is another example of how children who grow up under adverse developmental conditions establish severe moral self-condemnations on the grounds of their deprivations and traumas and thereby play an active part in the organization of depressive and masochistic positions and in the compensatory grandiose inclinations that often go along with those responses.

Because benevolent self interest had become bad as well as dangerous, this analysand had to be consciously bewildered and troubled by the esteem she commanded in her current life. She professed not to know what all the commotion was about. She could only shrug off praise and catalog the reasons why she deserved criticism or at least no response at all. Thus, she could respond only in frightened and guilty ways to the acclaim she received. These negative responses were not just surface responses; they went deep into her—without, however, altogether replacing the latent compensatory grandiosity that had become part of her make-up, too. As she progressed toward termination, she was able to moderate all this malevolence to a significant extent and to reduce her latent aloofness.

Case Example

A third patient reported that, on looking at himself in the mirror each morning, he responded with shock and a tendency to duck out of his reflection with aversion. He was not seeing the reflection of the good-looking and capable man that, by all conventional standards, he was. We can say that, strictly speaking, he was not looking at himself or his self and in that sense was not seeing a reflection at all. Instead of seeing, he was enacting his mother's reacting with dismay to his birth and his presence in her life. And by ducking out of the mirror, he was, among other things, ducking out of her life—compliantly dying, submissively suiciding in this symbolic way. Later on in the analysis and as a result mainly of analysis of corresponding transferences, he could tolerate some benevolent self interest; then he was able to give some independent account of his mother's failure to thrive as a mother and to go on from there to experience consciously the mixture of helpful, guilty, and devastated reactions to her failure he had had when a child and to some extent still had. Earlier it had been more than he could bear to recognize and sort out these reactions and thereby to become truly able to look and see. Earlier the failure had to be his, not hers. Looking and seeing were tabooed activities.

Case Example

In the words of a fourth patient—words he was capable of only late in his analysis—"I had to be a moving target, a chameleon, a nothing; if I exposed myself even to myself, I'd be killed or I'd kill them. So I became a mush; I had no edge." By "them" he was referring to extremely persecutory and neglectful figures in his early environment, but also, to a very great extent, as shown by his transferences, to internal versions of these figures that had been greatly magnified in their destructiveness and were imagined to be lurking in the shadows of his inner world.

Although analysts do not minimize the destructive consequences of parental failures, they realize that they cannot hope to work through the problems being presented unless they also attend closely to the many ways in which the analysands, already when they were children, began creating actual failure or accentuating it in fantasy. They also remain vigilant to the many ways in which these analysands cling to the problematic consequences of these real and examined failures and the many ways in which they continuously re-create them in feeling if not in fact. Analysts focus on this unconsciously insistent, provocative, and inventive repetitiveness. They focus, too, on the veiled inclinations toward, and compromised expressions of, hateful, frightened, ashamed, guilty, and reclusive reactions. Additionally, they focus on their patients' turning passivity into activity by identifying with the real and imagined aggressors. In these ways they establish grounds to interpret the self-perpetuated inner-world battle of the malevolent self interest against the positive. Benevolence, it seems, had become the enemy.

In this complex situation, analysts face forbidding technical problems. Large parts of the existing textbooks on technique are directed at just these problems, though often in other terms. I shall not attempt to survey them here, even briefly; however, I shall mention one essential caution: Benevolent analytic self interest can be faked, consciously and unconsciously, and it may take an analyst some time to get beyond defensive pseudointerest or false-self posturing. The painfulness of primitive guilt and depression begins to act as a powerful deterrent just as soon as analysands feel the first faint stirrings of benevolent self interest. Analysands may then become quite ingenious in taking in the analyst by seeming to be wholeheartedly and progressively "in analysis."

In some instances, the analyst may become part of the problem by being all too ready to be taken in by this show of the patient's. That analyst may do so owing to his or her own fears of dealing with the extremely painful, primitively depressive episodes that the analysand must live through in order to participate genuinely. Indeed, the patient's mounting a semblance of benevolent progression toward termination may be a reparative gesture stemming from just those deep, unanalyzed depressive problems. In other words, in part, an analysand enacts in the transference a guilty attempt to undo the effects of destructiveness without dealing with the destructive wishes and fantasies themselves. Kleinian analysis has much to teach us in this connection, and I shall include some notes on that below.

BENEVOLENT INTEREST IN OTHERS

This part of the discussion is organized around two questions: Should the idea of benevolent self interest include benevolent interest in others? And is it only a matter of enlightened self-interest—self-interest in the narrow, conventional sense—to take an interest in others, that is, to do unto others as you would have them do unto you, or in other words, to work out trade-offs in which everyone gets his or her back scratched?

Trade-offs do have their place in the conduct of life, and at the termination of a helpful course of analysis, the analysand is not likely to react in ashamed or guilty ways when tacitly making some such accommodations in a context of ordinary enlightened self-interest. But it would be to leave too much out of the story of human affairs to give an account of relatedness to others *only* in terms of narcissistic utilitarianism. In particular, that account would leave undeveloped the analysis of what mediates these trade-offs and thus of what makes some of them binding, exhilarating, and successful and leaves others indiscriminate, tedious, and doomed to failure.

The evidence that accumulates as termination approaches supports an affirmative answer to my first question. Benevolent self interest does go hand in hand with interest in others. As termination approaches, analysands report ever more frequently that they have had experiences with parents and others that show that there was an unexpectedly or unremembered good side (in some sense of the word *good*) to these others and in the analysands' feelings for them. Reports of this kind became prominent even in the first and extreme case I sketched earlier—the young woman who insistently thought herself ugly. Later on in her treatment, others who had been consistently portrayed as cold, self-absorbed, competitive, or destructive began to be portrayed as acting differently. They were beginning to show benevolent interest in, tolerance of, and satisfaction with the analysand. Sometimes they even helped out: the father in a more conventional "fatherly" way and the mother, warmly even girlishly, in a conventionally more "motherly" way. They tried to help with the patient's career; to be helpful with matters of grooming, marriage, and play; to come to the rescue in a nice enough way when crises developed. They commiserated. Previously limited to monologue or muteness, they entered into dialogue. They phoned and they wrote. They shared confidences. Not always, of course, not necessarily frequently, and not always successfully, for they were still manifesting deep-seated and provocative ambivalence. Nevertheless, they acted differently enough to make a difference.

Usually it seems that analysands are not just presenting less distorted versions of these others. Nor does it seem that these others have just begun to act differently for reasons of their own. Upon analytic investigation, it typically turns out that the analysands' activities have been an important stimulus to these changes. Even though acting and responding to the positive results with much anxiety, analysands have played a significant role in bringing about these new gratifications. It becomes evident that patients are approaching parents and others in a different way: showing interest, anticipation and planning, forbearance, firmness, appreciation, and understanding. Patients are no longer so easily put off by the initially negative responses of others. Patients do not rapidly withdraw or get into a fight, nor do they provoke quarrels in order to cut off the possibility of affection, disclosure, embrace, apology, and gratitude. More than one analysand has said, "I was able to let them love me."

As these modified accounts of relatedness develop, analysts gain a sense of parents, siblings, and friends beginning to be uncovered or rediscovered and of families beginning to be reunited. Some analysands even seem to move emotionally into their family's control center while feeling at the same time that they can also let themselves be cared-for children once again or, as far as they recall, children for the first time. Also, they can do all this without denying their recognition of the fragility and potential malevolence that continues to pervade the family.

To put it more exactly: Those who seem to allow themselves to become children for the first time may actually be doing it for the third time; the first time was perhaps in their unremembered prehistory and the second time certainly in earlier developments within the transference. But even the scope of prehistory may begin to change, for often these analysands begin to bring up parallel memories of previous positive behavior by these significant others and by themselves. Earlier in analysis, these memories of very early times were either just not there or were not there in sufficient quantity or distinctness to be used to question analytically the repetitively one-sided portrayal of others. In part the analysands are now viewing past interactions in a new light and in a more rounded way; these changes in perspective should qualify as another form of recovery of the past.

Thus, as termination approaches, the life history is sometimes revised radically. Voids are filled in, stormy weather is replaced by partly sunny, and the temperature rises from subfreezing, progressing at least to the point where the ice can begin to thaw. It feels like spring (rebirth, adolescence, first love) is in the air. From the standpoint of benevolent interest, analysts can say that, in these instances, the analysands are now being benevolent enough to others to allow or even encourage them to be benevolent in return; at least these others let up on their malevolent interest, which, in the patients' subjective experience, is felt to be no small gain in benevolence. Another analysand put it this way: "I see now that if I give more, I get more," and he made it clear that he was not talking about a trade-off of gratifications so much as a generally expanded sense of pleasure possibilities in reciprocal enhancement of selves.

We may say that the analysands are helping others to feel better and do better and to feel better about doing better. And it will all have been made possible in the forge of the analysis of transference; that is where all these changes must be hammered out in whatever form is possible, that form not necessarily being the one that characterizes the restoration of relationships with others. I emphasize the greater rapidity of change in many of these cases as termination approaches, but I do not imply that changes of this sort are absent until then in any analysis that is progressing satisfactorily.

THE ROOTS OF BENEVOLENT SELF INTEREST IN THE DEPRESSIVE POSITION

I turn now to the last part of my discussion of benevolent self interest: its foundations in the depressive position as described in Kleinian psychoanalysis (M. Klein, 1964; see also Segal, 1964). At this point, the plot thickens; the benevolence is seen to be rooted in conflicts of its own.

We must picture young children as possessed by frightening and remorse-inducing destructive fantasies and unable to differentiate these from conventional reality on the basis of well-developed reality testing and consistently mature feedback from the environment. On this account, children need urgently to keep making reparation for their destructiveness; reparation must be made perhaps especially in relation to the mother, although it can certainly include many others as well. This reparative urgency is not simply a phase of early childhood; rather, it enters into our finest adult achievements in human relations and into all our cultural attainments. Further, if it is granted that the establishment of certain defensive strategies is a necessary part of civilized life, then it can be understood that these reparative needs also foster the development of appropriate defenses.

When reparativeness is well integrated into a person's character, he or she derives a sense of goodness from it. The core of the goodness, however, seems to derive not from that development alone; to a significant extent, it derives from incorporated good parenting and the child's pleased and pleasing responsiveness to it. Together, these reparative and identificatory elements provide an antidote to the poisons of greed, ingratitude, and apprehensiveness that otherwise have pervaded these subjects from childhood on.

I have already mentioned that, frequently, analysts see in their analysands a bitter struggle against allowing this goodness any play in their relationships. They see this in the transference especially. Analysands cling to hatefulness and mistrust (characterized in fundamental respects as the paranoid-schizoid position in Kleinian thought). They insist that it is only realistic to limit themselves to guardedness and coldly calculated trade-offs. They rationalize greed, exploitativeness, and ingratitude, anticipating that if they depart from this policy they will become slavish, more victimized than before, and perhaps even melancholically depressed. Fearing that they are sheep, they put on wolf's clothing. Later on, however, as they progress in analysis, they may begin to change their lines and say of others, in the words of one analysand, "They want to be friends and now I let them; I let them come along with me in my feeling, and I don't try to make them be one way or another. It's better for all of us." Another analysand said something similar: "I feel more responsible and less guilty. Before, I felt like a kid. Now Henry makes me feel good because of the way I make him feel. I don't shut it down like I used to because I felt like it was too much for me. And I love it."

It is, however, not only the Kleinians who are so concerned with the internal world. It is just that they have their own rich and useful way of conceptualizing it. Ego-psychological analysts have not lost sight of that world. In this regard I refer to Heinz Hartmann's (1956) emphasis on the testing of inner reality. Hartmann was trying to develop an adequate concept of reality testing from an ego-psychological point of view. He argued that an essential part of ego-oriented analytic work lies in enhancing reality testing in its inner-directed as well as its outer-directed aspects. In the context of my discussion, one of the fruits of the testing of inner reality is the recognition that that reality contains reparative goodness and that it is crippling or impoverishing either to deny that goodness expression or to avoid finding it in others, despite manifest appearances, assuming that it is there to be found.

Also, the testing of inner reality makes it plain that, in addition to reparativeness, patients have established powerful identifications with the parents and parent surrogates as their more or less idealized *caretakers* during early childhood. Having been building blocks of the personality, these identifications cannot be denied expression except at very great personal expense. During analysis, it may well be that, first, the transference must be opened up to benevolence and the correlated recovery of relevant but hitherto repressed memories from early childhood of the "good" side of the self and the selves of others; only then will it be possible for positive infantile identifications to be recognized, tolerated, expressed, and integrated.

No longer defending rigidly against these aspects of inner reality entails acting on them without great ambivalence and continuing to do so even when the returns are far from what might be wished for. Benevolence, as we know, is not always rewarded, as terminating analysands repeatedly discover or rediscover. Nevertheless, in many cases, to the extent that other conflictual positions have been worked through and other aspects of self interest have been liberated, it will have become clear to analysands that discriminating reparativeness and integration of feared identifications entail no great danger of being "taken over" by slavishness, exaggerated and self-injurious altruism, pure malevolence, or deep depression. Thus analysands are ready to make those second efforts when first benevolent actions are rejected or fall flat; often the second or perhaps even the third effort brings the desired result. Sustained reality testing of other selves finds the goodness, such as it is, that is available.

Progressively, it becomes established that self interest requires a person to take a benevolent interest in both the self-interest and the self interest of others, to empathize with them, enjoy them, respect them, and protect them, and to show them whatever measure of interest and gratitude is their due rather than showing only frustration, envy, and defensive insecurity. In some instances, however, it can and does become clear that in spite of all of a person's best efforts with important others (spouses, parents, old friends), the cost of keeping a relationship nondestructive is too high. When the entire effort seems at last to be futile, the best course to follow will be to limit that relationship drastically or end it.

As termination approaches, the changes I have just been describing become particularly conspicuous in the transference. Analysands may become more and more reliable collaborators and even on occasion good supervisors—that is, participants who do not regress when the analyst seems not to have acted well. Instead, such analysands tend to find a way that is neither obscure nor self-injurious to let the analyst know what is disturbing the analytic work at one moment or another. Also, as I mentioned, terminating analysands may show a stable and relatively relaxed interest in being in analysis and may take a deep interest in it. They may act appreciatively, gratefully, or excitedly, with no significant anxiety or guilt and no hypersensitive concern with being pleasing—and may do all of this without foregoing further expression, if necessary, of more dismal, archaically hostile, and sexual tendencies.

Although competitive, envious, possessive, and prurient interest in the analyst keeps coming up all through the analysis, its forms usually become much more temperate, and they do not undermine the intense and benevolent collaborative spirit that usually characterizes the final phase of analysis.

This mature self interest will be evident at the very end of a beneficial analysis when progressed analysands depart, smiling or crying or both, convinced not only of a better and truer set of storylines with which to give an account of a past life, including a past analytic life, but convinced that there are better and more truth-making sets of storylines with which to organize and conduct a life among people in the future. Analysands recognize the inseparability of self-interest and self interest and the inseparability of both from interest in the self-interest and self interest of others. For the most part it will no longer seem to serve well or to be necessary to keep saying or implying of self and others, "I don't care," "I don't dare," and "It's no use trying," and also "You don't care," "You don't dare," and "You're not trying." There are other and better stories of human relatedness to construct and tell.

CHAPTER 2

Narratives of the Self

THE concept of the self can be approached in two ways: as posing a significant problem for theory construction in psychoanalysis and as a significant feature of the self psychology of everyday life. Herein I attempt to show that the terms and the results of these two approaches need not be as different as might be expected. That is, the self psychology of theory may be shown to have a good deal in common with everyday self psychology as it appears in ordinary language, such as analysts hear from the couch. In particular, both approaches may be characterized as the construction of narratives. Grossman (1982), it should be noted, took up some of these problems under the aspects of individual *fantasy* of a self and individual *theory* of a self and considered both aspects in relation to psychoanalysts' theories of the self.

THE SELF IN CONTEMPORARY ANALYTIC THOUGHT

The self has become the most popular figure in modern, innovative psychoanalytic accounts of human development and action. Usually the self is presented in these accounts as an active agency: It is the source of motivation and initiative; it is a self-starter, the originator of action; it is the first-person, singular, indicative subject, that is, the "I" of "I come," "I go," "I will," "I won't," "I know," "I wonder," and "I do declare!" This is the self that exhibits itself and hides itself and can love or loathe its own reflection.

There is still more to the usual presentation of this active self. The self appears in these accounts as the subject of experience: It constructs and participates in an experiential world; it is the self of taste and value, impression and emotional direction; it is the sexual self, the private self, the fragile self, and the bodily self.

Furthermore, this featured active self is the central organized and organizing constituent of the person considered as a structured psychological entity. In this aspect the self is the unity, the essence, the existential core, the gestalt, and the mastermind of a person's life.

In modern times this self or some selective version of it has been called by many names: the self and the self-system by Sullivan (1940), the action self by Rado (1956), the true self by Winnicott (1958), and the cohesive or nuclear self by Kohut (1977). Additionally, it is the superordinate self of Kernberg (1982) and the self as agent of the philosopher Macmurray (1957).

Concurrently, however, this self is not always and only active. Usually it has been presented as also being the object rather than the subject of action and experience. And often, as in reflexive locutions, this self appears as the object of its own action and experience, as when we speak of self-observation and self-esteem. Moreover, the self as object is not just a reactive agency or an observed agency; it is also the ensemble of self-representations. That is, it is the core content of all of a person's ideas about him- or herself, the self-concept or self-image. In this mixing together of agency and content, there is, I believe, some serious overloading of the conceptualization of self and possibly some theoretical incoherence as well (Schafer, 1976, 1978). Despite this, modern theory has it that the object-self is impinged upon by internal and external stimulation, and as a result of this impingement, both the functional self and the represented self may be fragmented, shriveled, inflated, chilled, and so forth.

Even in a brief and incomplete introductory survey of the self in contemporary analytic thought, which is all I claim for this section of this chapter, it is mandatory to mention that this self has also been presented, at least implicitly, as a force. In one respect this force is very much like an instinctual drive the aim of which is full selfhood or self-realization; in another respect this force is very much like a growth principle that vies with or replaces Freud's (1911b) pleasure principle. I believe this obviously teleological self principle or self drive is at the center of Kohut's (1977) self psychology; there it plays just as essential a part in explanations of psychopathology and cure as it does in explanations of normal development and personality organization. And I believe there can be discerned a similar teleological thrust in Erik Erikson's (1950, 1956) "ground plan" of development and its particular manifestation in a close relative of the self, namely, ego identity.

To continue establishing the terms for a narrative account of the self, I discuss, first, the self as active agent and second, the experiential self.

THE SELF AS AGENT

It is intrinsic to any psychological theory to present the human being as an agent or actor in certain essential ways and to some significant extent (Schafer, 1976, 1978, 1983). Even an extreme tabula rasa theory must include an account of how the person who has been written on by the surrounding world and by bodily processes becomes, in turn, an author of existence. Although the person may be a repetitive and largely preprogrammed author, he or she cannot be that entirely, for there is no one program to be applied to everything identically. The person must select and organize in order to construe reality in one adaptive way or another or one maladaptive way or another. Certainly, the theorist who is advancing a new set of ideas about human psychology must be viewed as a selective and organizing agent.

An author of existence is someone who constructs experience. Experience is made or fashioned; it is not encountered, discovered, or observed, except upon secondary reflection. Even the idea of experience as that which is turned up by the introspecting subject introduces an actively introspecting subject, an agent engaging in a particular set of actions, and thus someone who may introspect in different ways and for different reasons (Grossman, 1967). The introspecting subject extracts from the plenitude of potential experience what is wanted; in one case it may be sense data and in another case a self or, as is more usual, an array of selves. Introspection does not encounter ready-made material. For these reasons, developmental theories cannot avoid giving accounts of the different ways in which experience is constructed as advances take place in the child's and adult's cognitive and psychosexual functioning. Analysts refer to this as phase-specificity.

All this has to do with the self, for in their necessarily presupposing an agent, psychological theories of the self usually equate agency with selfhood. These theories then speak of what the self does. This is a permissible move in the game of theory construction. Once agency and selfhood have been equated, however, at least two new problems will have to be dealt with.

Self or Person?

The first problem is explaining what advantage is gained by saying that a self engages in actions rather than saying that a person does. Why speak of activity at one remove from the person—from him or her or, for that matter, from you or me? Might there be some misguided need on the theorist's part to add an air of detachment to the discussion, an air that spuriously gives it an appearance of scientific legitimacy or clinical objectivity? Is it demonstrably more plausible or heuristic to say that a self can be organized and organizing than to say that a person can be?

But perhaps it is not an image of scientific detachment and of clinical objectivity that is at stake; perhaps it is a culturally reinforced need to retain in our psychologies some extrapersonal source of agency and thereby some implicit passive stance toward life. Although the self that is set apart from the person is not quite a soul or a god, it may be viewed as an idea that is not quite free of the kind of disclaiming of personal agency that most of us associate with souls and divine visitations. This is so because in adequate accounts of human action the person is retained alongside the self as a necessary activating figure.

Self psychologies retain the person in this way. They tend to exempt the "I"—the first-person pronoun, singular indicative—from the self in order to make the theories work; for the "I" is the informative witness to its own self and the source of the theorist's data. Comparably, when Freud talked of psychic structure, he still found it necessary to refer to the person or subject, for the structural theory could not do all the work; it needed a psychological being to stand behind it and to contain it, and it is that being that I call the person. In "The Ego and the Id" (1923a), for example, Freud introduced the person through blatant personification of the ego (see, for example, p. 58).

Doubling and Multiplying the Self

The second problem encountered by a psychological theory that attributes agency to the self rather than to the person follows on the heels of the first. If the theorist tries to deal with the first problem by making every effort to include the "I" within the self, then he or she is required to speak of that self as being self-constructing, self-maintaining, self-containing, and self-evaluating. That is, the theory is committed both to self as mental mover and to self as mental content, or to self as subject and object simultaneously—and thus to a self that includes itself. There occurs at the least a doubling of the self. This doubling is a feature of Kohut's (1977) self psychology: The Kohutian self is not only an experiential self, it is also a center of initiative that establishes and repairs self-experience in general and self-esteem in particular. Additionally, in order to account for the profusion of diverse tendencies that characterizes each person's life, the self psychologist must sooner or later, and more or less officially, propose the existence of various subselves (for example, the grandiose self, the true and false self). Each of these subselves is supposed to be viewed as acting as a more or less independent agent even while it is still to be regarded as part of one basic self.

What is the result of this doubling and multiplying of selves? We seem to end up with a mind that is located both *within* and *outside* its boundaries and that contains numerous little minds that are *within* itself and at the same time *are* itself. This odd turn in self theory is a sign that it is in deep trouble. It has become fluid if not weakened. In contrast, it is less artificially detached and perhaps theoretically and scientifically less pretentious to think more plainly in terms of persons constructing and revising their various experiential selves of everyday life and ordinary language. Then each person is taken to be a narrator of selves rather than a non-Euclidean container of self entities. In the next section I hope to strengthen the case for a narrative approach to the self.

THE EXPERIENTIAL SELF

I begin with a puzzle and my solution to it. The puzzle is analogous to the one where you look for hidden faces in a sketch of the landscape. Here is the puzzle: How many selves and how many types of self are stated or implied in the following account? A male analysand says to his analyst: "I told my friend that whenever I catch myself exaggerating, I bombard myself with reproaches that I never tell the truth about myself, so that I end up feeling rotten inside, and even though I tell myself to cut it out, that there is more to me than that, that it is important for me to be truthful, I keep dumping on myself."

I count eight selves of five types. The first self is the analysand self talking to his analyst, and the second is the social self who had been talking to a friend. These two selves are similar but not identical in that self-organization and self-presentation are known to vary to some extent with the situation a person is in, and in many ways the analytic situation is unlike any other in life. The third self I count is the bombarding self; the fourth, the derogated self that exaggerates; and the fifth, the exaggerated self itself. The sixth is the truthful self the man aspires to be; the seventh, the conciliatory advisor of the bombarding self, the self that advises cutting out the reproaches; and the eighth is the defended self, the one with redeeming features. As to type, there is what is presented as the actual self (whether exaggerated, reproached, or defended), the ideal self (truthful), the self as place (the one with the rotten inside and the one that can be dumped on), the self as agent or subject (the teller, the bombardier, the aspirant, and the advisor), and the self as object (the self observed, evaluated, reproached, and defended).

My answer to the puzzle introduces once again my thesis that there is value in viewing the self in narrative terms. I suggest that the analysand's experiential self may be seen as a set of varied narratives that seem to be told by and about a cast of varied selves. And yet, like the dream, which has one dreamer, the entire tale is told by one narrator. Nothing here supports the common illusion that there is a single self-entity that each person has and experiences, a self-entity that is, so to speak, out there in Nature where it can be objectively observed, clinically analyzed, and then summarized and bound in a technical definition—as if Humpty Dumpty could be put back together again. Whether the material is rhymed, brief, and cute like Humpty Dumpty, or prosy, long, and difficult like most analytic material, we analysts may be said to be constantly dealing with self narratives—that is, with all the storylines that keep cropping up in clinical work—such as storylines of the empty self, the false self, the secret self, and so on.

SELF NARRATIVES

I must point out first that it is consistent with ordinary language to speak of self *narratives*. In ordinary language, we refer to ourselves or to the self of another person in a variety of ways that derive from the different vantage points that we occupy at different times and in different emotional contexts. Implicitly it is accepted that, except for certain rhetorical purposes, there is no one way of telling it "like it is." For example, in my puzzle, it comes across as perfectly acceptable to produce what appears to be one narrative that includes a self that never tells the truth and another self characterized by other and more estimable tendencies within which self is situated the self that exaggerates. It is taken for granted, it is common practice to converse on the understanding that, whether in the role of observer or observed, a person can only *tell* a self or encounter it as something *told* (Schafer, 1983). Or, as the case may be, tell more than one self. The so-called self exists in versions, only in versions, and commonly in multiple simultaneous versions.

For example, to say "I told myself to get going" is to tell a self story with two characters, an admonishing self and an admonished self, or perhaps with three characters if we include the implied author who is telling about the admonishing. To say "Deep inside him there is a grandiose self" is also to tell a story about two selves, this time about one self contained within another. And smacking one's head after making a mistake is to make a show of punishing a dumb self. This last example also makes it plain that some of these versions of self are nonverbal. That is, they are versions that are shown in expressive movements or life-style rather than told verbally; however, showing or enactment may be regarded as a form of telling, so that it is warranted to treat nonverbal manifestations as self narratives in another form of our common language, say, as charades of self narratives.

To debunk the idea, as I have been doing, that personal experience discloses a single self-entity and that theory must include that self is not to maintain that all self narratives are inherently unstable and inconsistent; nor is it to maintain that all these narratives are on the same level; nor yet that the content of these narratives concerns only chronic flux or chaos. Many of our actions may be presented noncontroversially as differentiated, integrated, and stable, and these presentations themselves may share these organized and enduring qualities. In many instances, certain self narratives are so impressively stable in organization and content and so clearly superordinate to others that it seems a matter of simple observation to say that there must be, or we must be seeing, psychic structure. There must be nuts and bolts somewhere, we feel, or good strong glue to make it possible. But in reacting thus we are, I submit, following the good old storyline of primal chaos: This chaos is the baby with only an id to start life with, the seething cauldron of instinctual drives that must be curbed and contained by psychic structures. This is not the account of a preadapted baby in a world of prepared objects or others, the account that today seems much more adequate to express the way we make sense of humanness and its development.

Furthermore, through developmental study and analytic recon-

struction, we can often impressively claim to trace a progressive differentiation, integration, stabilization, and hierarchical arrangement of
self stories.

At the same time, however, it must be said that in daily life we seem
to have acquired an exaggerated impression of single and unvarying
self-entities. This results from our unreflective attitude toward the
heavy use we all make in our ordinary language of first-person singular pronouns and of such reflexive terms as self-esteem and self-control. Also, as we have self as agent available to us as a culturally or
linguistically well-established narrative possibility, we gain an apparently experiential conviction that we possess a unitary and enduring
self that may be experienced directly, unmediated by language and
story. Locutions such as "be yourself" and "divided self" are instances
of what I mean. Our common language authorizes us to think and
speak in terms of single, stable self-entities. And so we want to protest
that the self is not a matter of language, theory, and narrative mediation at all: The self is something we know firsthand; it is (in that mar-
velously vague phrase) the sense of self, a self we feel in our bones. I
submit that it is correct to reply that "to feel it in your bones" is to
resort to yet another good old storyline of the knowing body or the
body as mind; the "sense of self" does not escape the web of narration.

In addition, from the psychoanalyst's point of view, there are still
more and differently told experiential selves to take into account than
my first answer to my puzzle suggested. I referred only to selves that
appear to be consciously or preconsciously available at the moment.
Yet unconsciously, the analysand in my puzzle may also be regarded as
experiencing and presenting to the analyst *in the transference* a helpless
self—that is, a child-self that cannot run its own affairs and so must
appeal to a parental figure for help. Additionally, the puzzle statement
may be indicating to the analyst that, unconsciously, the speaker is
maintaining, among other experiential selves, a cruel and totalistic
moral self, a grandiose self without blemishes, and an anal self that
defiantly makes messes by lying.

I have just named only a few of the narrative retellings of the troubled analysand's self stories that the analyst may have to develop in the
form of interpretations. Even what I called his actual self may have to
be retold. For example, it may turn out that, for this analysand, his
actual self is given very little to exaggerating; he produces no impressive analytic evidence in his sessions that he does exaggerate to any
notable degree; and the significant problem may be that, fearing the
envy of others, he has suppressed the presentation of a justifiably
proud actual self and has substituted for it an unconvincing defensive

account of an outrageous braggart. The self that is claimed to be felt in one's bones could not possibly encompass all of these experiential selves, even if it could think; neither could the "sense of self" encompass all of them.

At this point, we might ask whether, in the interest of our own mental safety, we should not avoid this milling crowd of narrated selves in which we could easily get lost or trampled. Should we not instead mingle with only a few well-behaved self categories? My answer is, first, we do have available superordinate self categories, such as the actual self and the ideal self (Schafer, 1967). Second, we should be careful not to lose sight of the proliferation of selves in each person's construction of experience lest we begin to mistake our superordinate categories for entities discovered in Nature and observable without narrative mediation. In principle, no limit can be set on the number of experiential self constructions that it may be profitable to discuss in one or another context of inquiry. It is no good saying that we already have enough concepts to do the job of interpretation, for to do so is to close the book on new approaches and the new phenomena made available by these approaches. As I have argued in connection with prisoner fantasies (1983), each proposal in this realm should be assessed on its merits.

STORYLINES

Although I have alluded to the storylines of self narratives, I have neither attempted to define them nor provided examples. In this connection, however, we must ask not only "What *is* a storyline?" We must also ask "What is the relation of storyline to self-representation, fantasy, and metaphor, the three apparently germane concepts that clearly occupy more or less established or at least familiar places in analytic thought?" It is around these questions that I have organized this next section of my argument.

First, then, what is a storyline? By "storyline" I refer to whatever it is that can be used to establish a set of guidelines and constraints for telling a story that conveys what convention would certify as having a certain general kind of content. These guidelines and constraints may be derived from one or more symbols, metaphors, similes, images, themes, or dramatic scenes, or some combination of these. This storyline serves as a tool for working out ways to retell other stories in its terms, and so it makes it possible for narrators both to generate many versions of what is conventionally regarded as the same basic story and, through reduction, to create faithful repetitions of these versions out of apparently diverse narrative materials. In one respect, for example, we have the storylines of imprisonment, rebirth, and odyssey that are commonly developed in the course of analytic work.

Take, for example, the instance of using rebirth as the storyline: The analyst may understand an analysand's references to new growth, new beginnings, glowing embers among the ashes, emergence from water, revival, and so on, as references to rebirth. In other instances, analysts develop narratives of oedipal victory and defeat and of masochism: When using the oedipal storyline, analysts may take a negative therapeutic reaction in part as a frightened retreat from oedipal victory and in part as a switch to the negative oedipal position. In contrast, when using the masochism storyline, analysts may take a negative therapeutic reaction in part as a sign of powerful reluctance to give up preferred forms of compromised and painful gratification and in part as a bid for their pain-inducing, preferably sadistic response to the dashing of their own therapeutic hopes.

With this sketchy account of storyline and its uses in analytic interpretation, let us now compare and contrast storyline with self-representation, unconscious fantasy, and metaphor. In this way I hope to bring home what I mean when I speak of the storylines of self narratives and why I give storyline the central position that I do.

Self-representation

Self-representation is a concept with a complex history and current status in psychoanalysis. As one of its most relevant features, the concept of self-representation is intended to announce the writer's assumption or realization that the self, like the object, is knowable only through more or less individual, partial, or whole versions of it. These are the versions the analyst encounters or defines in the analysand's psychic reality, and they may have little to do with conventional or putatively true versions of the self.

There is nothing mutually exclusive about the concepts of storyline and self-representation. Storyline may, however, be regarded as the more inclusive concept of the two. This is so because in practice single representations are not identified and analyzed as static and isolated mental contents. Rather, they are dealt with thematically, that is, as being significant insofar as they actually or potentially play parts in basic stories of the self. For example, the prisoner storyline includes a large array of not necessarily glaring representations of the self as deprived, confined, or punished; at the same time, it includes a large array of more or less subtle representations of others as judges, jailers, or fellow prisoners. It is the job of interpretation to show that those are the representations it will be important to define more sharply and relate to one another in a thematically unified rendition of the analysand's diverse associations. Seen in this light, storyline pulls together and develops important aspects of the conceptualization of self-representations—and object representations, too.

Unconscious Fantasy

Unconscious fantasy is another concept with a complex psychoanalytic history and current status. Arlow (1969a, 1969b), in two discussions that seem to have become the standard references in modern Freudian literature to unconscious fantasy, came close to the idea of basic storyline. He took note of the aspect of unconscious fantasies he called "plot line." However, Arlow was not concerned, as I am now, with working out a narrative approach to psychoanalytic topics. He referred to these plot lines, such as Sleeping Beauty, in a way that was conceptually subordinate to fantasy, and he mentioned plot line only in passing, in a footnote (1969b, p. 47); obviously, he was engaged in making another kind of contribution.

As I see it, we must go beyond the consideration that to speak of a fantasy is to imply that we are referring to mental content organized by a storyline; we must also note that storyline has a more obvious generative connotation than emplotted fantasy does, for it is forward-looking or anticipatory. It is on this basis that storyline can more readily encompass the many variations of basic stories we conventionally recognize in daily life and analytic work. Fairy tales, too, have many versions; indeed, they have so many that it becomes unclear at what point we may no longer speak persuasively or confidently of a specific story as an unusual version of the same basic story (Smith, 1980). The same is true of any of the storylines I mentioned earlier: Odyssey, for example, which can encompass many variations, has the generative advantage and at the same time the disadvantage of unclear outer limits. In practice, it can become unclear when the analyst is forcing the same storyline on material that is extremely varied.

Metaphor

Have I been talking of metaphor all the while, and also of metaphoric entailment (Lakoff and Johnson, 1980)? Metaphoric entailment is exemplified by the basic spatial metaphor, Good is Up. This metaphor entails that, among other attributes, intelligence, good taste, and wealth are Up, while stupidity, vulgarity, and poverty are

Down. These are entailments insofar as consistency and coherence of discourse are being aimed at, which they often are. Thus, for example, very intelligent is "highly" intelligent. These few remarks on metaphor and entailment seem to suggest that metaphor says the same as story-line.

Again, however, it seems to me that storyline is the more inclusive term of the two. As I noted earlier, metaphor may establish a storyline, and what is called unpacking a metaphor is in certain respects much like laying out the kinds of story that are entailed by the metaphor. For example, "Analysis is Hell" entails the analyst being experienced as the devil. The analyst's attention to departures from the fundamental rule are experienced as the heat being put on. Perhaps in analogy with "War is Hell," the analyst's discipline is likened to Sherman marching to the sea. The stress of the analytic process becomes punishment for past sins; and so on. It is understood that the manifestly metaphoric "Analysis is Hell" is to be used as a set of latent instructions or rules for telling certain kinds of story about being analyzed. Analysts who can work through a core conflict show that they understand the narrative regulations of metaphor; they show it by their steady sense of relevance as they listen to apparently diverse communications.

A Clinical Example

There are many ways by which children are provided with storylines for the construction of self narratives and at the same time the construction of narratives concerning others. The dynamic content involved in these transactions is well known to analysts, but because that content has not usually been conceptualized in narrative terms, I should like to present a clinical example of consequential storylines and to bring it into relation with the topic of childhood memories.

The example concerns a successful, hard-driving, loveless career woman in her forties, once-divorced, who had never managed to establish a lasting, intimate, and gratifying relationship with an adequate and assertive man. From her early years on, she had been warned emphatically by her mother never to let herself be dependent on a man. That warning may be retold as having conveyed to her a number of interrelated storylines, only some of which I shall mention here.

It was being conveyed to her that as a girl and woman she was fated to be vulnerable to helplessness in relation to any man with whom she got deeply involved; further, that the only way to develop and maintain significant strength and dignity was to cut herself off from hetero-sexual love. Thus, she was being told that a heterosexual female self is a weak and degraded self and, also, that to love her father was to make herself vulnerable to this fate. In the broadest terms, she was fated to live in a world of powerful, dangerous, and certainly untrustworthy men. Although this woman had by no means renounced her hetero-sexuality altogether, she had repetitively developed and played out many versions of this set of storylines in her relationships, and ulti-mately she did so in her transference to her male analyst. Penis awe and envy, fantasies of castration and of a hidden penis, and primal scene themes were woven into the grim stories of her life that she both elaborated and enacted.

Before going any further, I should make it clear that I am not sug-gesting that her parents and others around her were the only convey-ors of storylines for her life. As I mentioned, analysts assume that the child, too, is a storyteller from the onset of subjective experience. For example, there is the storyline "I once had a penis and lost it." The usual analytic term for childhood constructions of this sort is fantasy. I have been saying that fantasy is a story and that children manufacture stories that interweave what they are told and what they imagine. There is nothing analytically new in this point except my emphasis on narration. And, of course, there is always our culture with its stock of established storylines.

To return to the analysand: An additional and congruent burden had been imposed on her explicitly during her adolescence and her early adult years by her father's admonishing her never to have chil-dren. In this way, he authorized and reinforced her own guilty, anx-ious, and defeated account of her childhood oedipal romance. This romance included in the usual way wishing to bear her father's child. Thus, from her father's side, too, she was being pressed to renounce her heterosexual femininity. In large part she was to construct stories of marriage as offering extremely limited prospects of satisfaction and fulfillment; there was little to hope for even in the ordinary marital form of displaced and matured forms of oedipal love. Furthermore, her father's admonishment could not fail to add weight to her own storyline that she was an unwanted and burdensome child who some-how was responsible for her parents' unhappiness and lack of fulfill-ment. As was to be expected, she repetitively applied and elaborated this self story in her transference. For example, the repetition began with her earliest appointments when she insisted on paying for each visit at its conclusion. It turned out that she did so in order not to be a financial burden on the analyst, and, in addition, in the terms of the storyline of dangerous dependence on men, so she would not be indebted to the analyst in any way. The storyline she was acting on was this: The only good woman is a good man; more exactly, a tough, utterly self-reliant man in drag. In effect, by paying as she did, she was saying "This is the story of my life." This enactment included some other major storylines, too, such as those touching on anality, concerns with social status, and so forth.

My intent in this summary of a few aspects of this analysis is theoretical clarification primarily rather than revision of the dynamic variables analysts customarily invoke to understand clinical phenomena. My theoretical point is that so-called self-concepts, self-images, self-representations, or more generally the so-called self may be considered to be a set of narrative strategies or storylines each person follows in trying to develop an emotionally coherent account of his or her life among people. We organize our past and present experiences narratively.

On my reading, this perspective on experience as a narrative construction is implied in Freud's final comments in his 1899 essay, "Screen Memories." There, after commenting on the "peculiarity of the childhood scenes" in that the child is portrayed as an outside observer of scenes in which he or she is an involved participant, and thereupon taking this peculiarity as "evidence that the original impression has been worked over," Freud soon concluded:

> The recognition of this fact must diminish the distinction we have drawn between screen memories and other memories derived from our childhood. It may indeed be questioned whether we have any memories at all *from* our childhood: memories *relating to* our childhood may be all that we possess. Our childhood memories show us our earliest years not as they were but as they appeared at the later periods when the memories were aroused. In these periods of arousal, the childhood memories did not, as people are accustomed to say, *emerge;* they were *formed* at that time. And a number of motives, with no concern for historical accuracy, had a part in forming them, as well as in the selection of memories themselves. (P. 322; Freud's italics)

I further believe that Freud was indicating the view, subsequently developed in ego-psychological terms by Ernst Kris (1956b) and that I am now recommending in narrative terms, that theoretical clarification of this sort *does* make a difference in practice. It encourages analysts to be aware that the life-historial material being worked with may be usefully approached as a series of tellings and retellings constructed and reconstructed over the course of development—indeed over the course of the analysis itself. In this light, what we call free association may be retold as the production of bits and pieces or even larger segments of life stories being constructed and related in the here and now of the analytic relationship.

Speaking in terms of memory, Freud said, "the raw material of memory-traces out of which it [the screen memory] was forged remains unknown to us in its original form" (1899, p. 322). I am adding that we do best to think of the raw material itself as having, to begin with, become *psychic* material in narrative form, however rudimentary the narrative. In other words, the clinical questions we put to whatever we hear from the couch are these: Of which story is this now a part or a version and for which further stories has it served or is it now serving as a storyline? With regard to the self specifically, the questions become these: Which self stories are now being hinted at or disclosed or are now in the process of being constructed or revised and for which purposes?

CHAPTER 3

Self-deception, Defense, and Narration

SELF-DECEPTION AND DEFENSE

Freudian analysts have not established the idea of self-deception as a problem with which they should be concerned. They do not focus on self-deception in their formal propositions, and they do not mention it with any frequency in their informal discussions of theoretical and clinical matters. However, some casual versions of self-deception do crop up within the clinical dialogue—for example, when the analysand says to the analyst, "My mind played tricks on me," and when the analyst says to the analysand, "You are kidding yourself."

Traditionally, analysts have taken up the phenomena presented in these self-deception locutions under the description *defense*. The idea of defense, however, is not simple and straightforward. It has been embedded in the complex, technical vocabulary that Freud introduced and dubbed metapsychology. Consequently, before considering self-deception as narration, it will be necessary to review at some length both the place of defense in traditional analytic discourse and the assumptions that secure it in this place. And this review requires a comparative discussion of defense in the mechanistic terms of Freud's metapsychology and the nonmechanistic terms of action language. In order to situate this chapter in the context of the analyst's daily practice, I refer frequently to clinical problems, practices, and ambiguities; it is in practice that the foundation has been laid for the psychoanalytic understanding of defense. At the same time, however, the complexity of the conceptual problems to be dealt with requires a measured, formalistic, unhurried mode of exposition and also some familiarity with the argument of chapter 2.

Freudian psychoanalysts take up defenses under two headings. The first is the mechanisms of defense. Included here are, for example, repression, projection, and reaction formation. The second is defense, or defensive measure, operation, or function, terms that connote a virtually limitless number of actions, any one of which may, after adequate clinical investigation, be said to be engaged in, or to have been engaged in, defensively. Included here are, for example, altruistic surrender as a defense against greed and envy, hostility as a defense against clinging dependency, and clinging dependency as a defense against hostility. The limits on what can be subsumed under this meaning of defense are set only by the analysand's inventiveness and the analyst's perceptiveness and narrative skills.

When the description *defense* is being used appropriately, the claim is made that in some sense (one analysts usually leave vague or unspecified) the subject—say, a woman—both knows and does not know that she sees, remembers, desires, believes, or feels something that she believes does or will involve her in some kind of dangerous situation, X. We cannot attribute a defense to her without attributing to her the knowledge (in some sense) that there is a danger to defend against. Further, not only is it assumed that the subject believes that because of X, she is in danger or is about to be; it is also assumed that she believes in this threat unconsciously and that she engages in defense against it unconsciously. Accordingly, she cannot be expected to explain as defensive those actions or changes of action (including reconstructions of experience) that she is aware of in this connection, such as an impulsive gesture of generosity or a flattening of emotional responsiveness. In one way or another, she will describe and explain these actions and changes of action in ways that skirt or deny their defensive employment and significance.

Freud (1926) laid out what he considered to be the four major danger situations of early childhood: loss of the love object, loss of the object's love, castration, and superego condemnation and punishment. He proposed that in psychic reality, where whatever is thought or imagined is taken by the subject to be real or actual, these dangers are the prototypes of all later dangers (even of death). That is, all later dangers in psychic reality are considered to be derivatives of these early ones and are potentially and usefully reducible to them through interpretation. In Freud's terms, when that part of the "mental apparatus" he called the ego unconsciously recognizes that one of these danger situations or one of its derivatives is developing, it responds with anxiety. Under ordinary circumstances, the ego then uses the first phase of this anxious reaction as a signal of impending or mounting danger, and it invokes one or more mechanisms of defense or defensive measures against this danger or its consequences. In one account, the ego makes this defensive move to prevent the danger situation from materializing full force (for example, it represses certain fantasies in order to curb "immoral" sexual inclinations). In another account, the ego aims to avert panicky dissolution of its own organization. The essential phases of this defensive process are passed through unconsciously, and its essential constituents operate unconsciously.

These accounts of defense require the subject to deceive herself twice (at least) as to the dangerous state of affairs, X: (1) She manages somehow not to know consciously part or all of what she knows and believes unconsciously; (2) she manages somehow not to know consciously that and how she is effecting this split between knowing and not knowing. For example, by unconsciously employing the mechanism of projection, she attributes an unacceptable hostile impulse of her own to someone else. In another defensive context, she might resort to any of the countless defensive measures that make it possible to block, divert, misrepresent, or obscure her knowledge of X. For example, by defensively exaggerated optimism, cheerfulness, and initiative, she might represent in glowing terms both herself and her experienced situation. Thereby she avoids consciously experiencing her life in the exceedingly painful terms of the profound and chronic passive-depressive mood with which she feels herself to be continuously threatened. And for this ruse to be successful, she must take the defensive measure unconsciously. To be successful, the deception must be immaculate.

I will assume from this point on that when psychoanalysts refer to defense, they are also referring (among other things) to multiple self-deceiving actions that are performed unconsciously. But when, why, and how they refer to defense requires some clarification.

DEFENSE: SOME DISTINCTIONS, QUALIFICATIONS, AND ELABORATIONS

Freud's Metapsychology

Freud (1915a), ever interested in developing a model of mind to help him explain psychoanalytic phenomena, tried in a number of ways to explain this knowing/unknowing defensive split in the subject's mental processes. (Because he did not deal with all the phenomena that today's analysts define and deal with, his discussions are not always as refined and comprehensive as would now be required. Accordingly, they are no longer as authoritative as they once were.) All of his explanations were essentially nonpsychological in that he based them on his mechanistic-energic metapsychology. That is, he based his explanations on shifts, accumulations, and expenditures of unmeasurable and qualitatively varied psychic energies (libido, aggression, attention cathexis) and on other factors that were holdovers from his earlier, neurologically conceived "Project" (Gill, 1976). Additionally, these energic explanations were, in one way or another, redundant or gratuitous (G. Klein, 1975). Subsequently, other analysts, among them Hartmann (1964), Kris (1975), Jacobson (1964), and Rapaport (1967), made noteworthy efforts to follow in Freud's metapsychological footsteps.

Notwithstanding these efforts, typical Freudian analysts in the course of their daily practice do not concern themselves with asking "How is it possible for someone simultaneously to know something and not know it?" and "How is it possible to defend and not know that one is doing so?" They just take it for granted that it is possible to effect this split unconsciously and that the split is probably present in what they hear and see in their clinical work. They do not seek a philosophically secure account of defense, and they do not justify their doing without that account. They try to pinpoint the occurrences of defensive transformations; they try to investigate their origins, their occasions, and their reasons or "determinants"; and in their own thinking perhaps, they try to sort out all the "mechanisms" involved. All this they do in order to interpret as precisely as possible the conflicts that necessitate self-deceiving actions, the compromise formations or attempted solutions that rest on self-deceiving actions, and the defense-serving characterological rigidities that must be both explained and modified for therapeutic purposes.

Wishful Thinking

Analysts distinguish between defense against X and simple wishful thinking to the effect that Y, something desirable, is the case. In simple wishful thinking (for example, in the presumably simple case of a very young child's idealization of a parent), the subject is assumed to be altogether ignorant that anything but Y could be the case. There is nothing to suggest that the subject is trying to rule out some other unconsciously known account of things (the dangerous X) owing to the intense anxiety that would be experienced should it consciously be recognized that X is, or is threatening to be, the case.

But analysts do frequently follow two other possible lines of interpretation of wishful thinking. The first is that there are complex forms of wishful thinking, as when the defense mechanism of denial is being used (for example, in a later phase of idealization, the child idealizes the parents defensively in order not to experience the insecurity that it feels upon recognizing its relative helplessness and their shortcomings). The second is that there are complex forms of ignorance, as when the subject evinces anxiety over finding things out (for example, the subject actively maintains ignorance of family secrets, an ignorance that not rarely is dispelled solely by clinical analysis of anxiety-based situational avoidances and both gaps and contradictions in remembering). Thus, in their work with adult analysands, modern analysts typically are skeptical of the idea of simple or nondefensive, conflict-free wishful thinking. In keeping with the principle that psychoanalysis is a conflict psychology, they look for defensive or self-deceiving features routinely, and usually they are not disappointed in the results (Fenichel [1941], A. Freud [1936], Schafer [1968c]).

Defense Mechanisms

With the possible exception of repression, the mechanisms of defense are not held to be inherently and exclusively designed for defense. For example, projection and introjection, which are believed to operate as malignant defense mechanisms in certain forms of psychopathology, are also presented as playing central roles in the highly adaptive process of empathy. Even though repression may never be taken to be entirely without defensive uses and consequences, it may on occasion be interpreted as being used to implement aims that are not exclusively defensive. For example, repression may help a young child bear up under conditions that otherwise would be intolerable. Later in life, this use of repression may be established by reconstructions during analysis, reconstructions according to which "forgetting" psychic wounds and their occasions seems to have been the only way to endure excruciatingly painful phases, situations, and relationships of childhood. When recounted in contexts of this sort, repression will be presented as an adaptive resource or process; the analyst then will able to anticipate with some confidence that any sudden relinquishing, relaxing, or failure of specific repressions could be traumatic or lead to traumatization. In psychic reality, the analysand appears to view these modifications of repressions in just that way and will, accordingly, approach analysis in the most gingerly or defensive manner.

It makes no sense to pigeonhole any one of the myriad activities thay may be used defensively—such as being altruistic, clinging, or hostile—as inherently and exclusively designed for defense.

Self-deception

Self-deception need not be linked to mechanistic conceptualization just because it is linked to defense. It is not necessary ever to invoke the term *mechanism* when speaking of defense. Speaking nonmechanistically, which is a linguistic option being taken by more and more analysts as they discard the model of a "mental apparatus," we can just as well put the matter in this way: In times of apparent danger, and in order to be able to function less anxiously and in a less restricted or damaging manner, the subject (not the ego) will aim to develop or restore subjective feelings of safety and confidence by employing forms and contents of thought whose nature it is to transform threatening conceptions of the current state of affairs and threatening courses of action, or both, into less threatening ones. This occurs in the case of denials, idealizations, and reaction formations. In this, the subject will be self-deceiving.

Rather than acting less anxiously, a person may, of course, act defensively in order to function less guiltily, in a less ashamed or depressed manner, or in some other less painful and restrictive fashion. These variations of affective tone and action do not alter the criteria as to what is the best way to conceptualize defensive actions.

Defense by the Analysand

Defense is, of course, defense *by* as well as defense *against*. Everything that has already been mentioned about the types and instances of defense and defense mechanisms indicates the often bewildering variety of factors the analyst must take into account. On a higher level of abstraction, defense is, mechanistically, instituted by the metapsychological "ego" or, nonmechanistically, *by* the person or agent.

Defense of the Ego

Defense is also defense *of*. The traditional Freudian analyst regards defense as defense of the ego, the adaptive "organ" or "structure" of the mind. There are many aspects of defense of the ego, and which of these aspects the analyst emphasizes depends on the specific intersystemic or intrasystemic problem he or she is placing in the foreground. Problems in the ego's relations with the id center on intersystemic boundaries; specifically, they center on protecting ego functions against the dangers of sexualization and aggressivization. The function of perceiving, for example, may be said to be excessively sexualized (invaded by the sexual drives of the id) when it is being used to implement voyeuristic aims. Similarly, remembering may be said to be excessively aggressivized (invaded by the aggressive drives of the id) when the faults and errors of others are relentlessly and remorselessly cataloged and rehearsed. Self-deception might implicitly enter this intersystemic interpretive context when, for example, although the subject defensively believes consciously that she is engaged in reading purely for scholarly purposes, the analyst is able to interpret that she is also reading sexually, perhaps mainly in order to bring herself into a sexually excited state. In another instance, she might be reading not for scholarly purposes alone, as she maintains consciously, but also and unconsciously aggressively, perhaps mainly in order to violate or destroy certain familial or general social conventions or to prepare an "overkill" critique of a hated rival.

Problems in the metapsychological ego's relations with the superego and the ego ideal center on reducing the need for self-punishment, making restitution to others, and recovering from loss of self-esteem, all seemingly in response to, or as manifestations of, the subject's painfully experiencing guilt and shame. Self-deception enters this intersystemic context when, for example, reading, ostensibly undertaken for pleasure, competition, or profit, is interpretable at least partly as an unconsciously carried out, weighty act of self-punishment or penitence (for example, as a way of forgoing certain social or erotic pleasures).

In the metapsychologically based structural theory of psychoanalysis, the ego also has organizational or intrasystemic problems of its own, and it uses defensive measures in this connection too. It may even be said to be engaged in defense against defense, as in the case of a conscious Pollyanna stance of denial that defends against projective paranoid mistrust of others. Analysts usually discuss these conflictual actions as reflecting the ego's problems both in preserving its own organization against potentially traumatic threats in the environment and in resolving the difficulties inherent in coordinating or synthesizing its multiple aims, functions, and contents. Garden-variety instances of intrasystemic problems are confronting and resolving contradictions among beliefs, values, and personal loyalties. For example, self-deception may take the form of representing oneself as being more interested in social relationships than one actually demonstrates to be the case, as when one does not, despite ample opportunity to do so, do things with other, presumably interesting or enjoyable people.

Complete analysis of significant clinical phenomena will include some reference to all the intersystemic and intrasystemic problems that have just been reviewed. Analysts speak in this regard of multiple function (Waelder, 1930) and compromise formation (Freud, 1899). Typically and repeatedly, they focus their attention on a number of such problems until they are satisfied that they have developed and worked through with the analysand the needed insights.

To emphasize that defense is defense *of* is, in part, to point again to the adaptive aspect of self-deceiving actions. However, it must be borne in mind in this connection that what an analysand may be defending adaptively might not conform to any conventional use of the term *adaptive*. For example, in a seemingly unadaptive way, the analysand might be protecting a rosy view of a terrible occupational situation; only after analysis will the analyst be able to understand that rosy view in its adaptive aspect (for example, it makes it possible for the analysand to go on working). Analysts do not use adaptation to mean conventional adjustment or conformity (Hartmann, 1953). They mean something closer to socialized survival values and the means-end relations these values imply and are used to support, any or all of which may be highly individualistic or conventionally disapproved.

Goals of Psychoanalytic Interpretation

Analysts assume that the more desperate the conditions under which defensive action is initiated, the more rigidly will the defenses be deployed. In less extreme circumstances, when defenses are being less rigidly maintained because they are less desperately resorted to, they can sometimes be modified by the subject herself. For example, in one context, the subject might notice that she is rationalizing her envy of a strong rival by thinking she is merely expressing a sense of decorum and then stop being defensive in that way. In another context, she might calm down after being upset and realize that it was because her pride had been hurt that she had been trying so hard and even arbitrarily to find fault with others in order to humiliate them and thereby, she hoped, restore her own self-esteem; whereupon she might reestablish with increased stability her usual more tolerant and less self-deceiving outlook.

Among its many potential accomplishments, psychoanalytic interpretation prepares or assists the analysand to be independently and regularly self-correcting or less self-deceiving. Through interpretation, it reduces the desperateness of the prototypic danger situations of childhood in terms of which, unconsciously, the analysand has continued to construct experience. It also familiarizes the analysand with her characteristic, hitherto unconsciously employed repertoire of defensive activities and their histories and fantasy content. It does so in order to help her recognize signs that she feels endangered and is already beginning to respond defensively in a way that now she mostly does not want. And it reduces the multiple, more or less irrational aims and emotional positions that have, over time, come to be served by these defensive activities, a development that has made them seem even more indispensable than they had seemed initially. (It does so, for example, when the need to be pleasing through defensive reaction formation against hostility has come to serve effectively other, maladaptively restrictive functions, such as gaining attention and sympathy by presenting oneself and conducting one's affairs in an overly pliable or "spineless" manner.)

SELF-DECEPTION AND NARRATION

In defense, the subject restricts what can be represented and experienced consciously, thereby excluding X, the threatening content, from her idea of . . . of what? Her self? Her personality? Her ego? Her being? Her consciousness? There is no single, correct, and exclusive answer to the question. Each of the answers I suggested is permissible, each covers a somewhat different range of phenomena, and each has had its uses within one or another philosophical, literary, or psychological framework of assumptions and concepts.

In the preceding sections of this chapter I have tried to establish the legitimacy of claiming that, for psychoanalytic purposes, what conventionally could be presented as one and the same action may be described as defense, wish fulfillment, punishment, and adaptation. The description to be used should depend on the analytic observer's aims and on the context of method and attribution of significance that has been established by, or in keeping with, these aims. For example, consider the repression that appears to have enabled the subject to endure terrible events of childhood. It might be said, *within a social-developmental context,* that that repression had been an essential means of adaptation at that time and under those circumstances. Then repression is presented not as a defense merely but as a process of adaptation as well. In contrast, *in a clinical context,* later on, when this victim's suitability for psychoanalytic treatment is being assessed, the analyst wants to emphasize the current, pathological rigidity and scope of the defensive repression that once had had that psychological survival value. Then the analyst may present that repression primarily as an extremely costly and forbidding defense.

I am applying the familiar proposition that no single designation of an action may be presented as final, definitive, exclusive, or conclusive. Narrative priority may be given to a particular description of an action only after carefully spelling out a context of aims, conventions, circumstances, and practices, or at least when there is ample reason to assume that the listener or reader knows this context very well. The description to be given of an action depends on the kind of account one wants to give of it. No action can be presented intelligibly or usefully if it is not in the context of an implicit or explicit narrative. The narrative context helps readers understand the description being employed at the same time as the description contributes to the further development and persuasiveness of that narrative account. Part-whole interactions of this sort seem to be intrinsic to informative or clarifying communication.

It may be argued that it is incoherent to refer to "*an* action" or "the same action" under different descriptions, for different descriptions present different actions. "The same action" loses all meaning or all power to constrain or verify what is being said. Yet it can be asserted that this argument does not take into account the fact that, in order to communicate at all, we abide provisionally by conventions with regard to sameness or identity. Convention provides minimal accounts of actions—for example, kissing or hitting. A minimal account makes possible the beginning of an answer to the question "Just what are we talking about?" It is only a beginning in that the minimal account does not provide an explicit and developed context in which to consider the action in any useful way. Contexts for action descriptions are established by an emphasis on motivation, pragmatic consequences, ethical import, historical circumstance, or whatever else would relate minimal descriptions to our interests. In turn, the significance of each such context derives from still larger contexts; depending on what kind of inquiry is being undertaken, those larger contexts might or might not have to be specified. Closure on contexts is endlessly deferrable.

I am not claiming that the minimal account is not conceived narratively itself, for even an extremely terse description of an action may be viewed as being the expression of a choice that is in accord with an implicit narrative design. Nevertheless, in each instance of minimal description we are left to ask: What are we to see it as and why? The regulative and generative influences of the description are minimal. We are left with many degrees of freedom—even if, under the prevailing conditions, not with total freedom. There are constraints, even though it is characteristic of psychoanalytic and some kinds of interpretation in the humanities to show that these constraints are far fewer than the conventional narrator would feel comfortable with. For example, some kissing may be retold as an attack that is close to hitting and some hitting may be retold as a sadistic form of loving that is close to kissing.

Briefly, then, I am claiming that—provisionally and always open to critical review and revision—we may speak of different descriptions of the same action, even though we can work only with the different versions of that action and in principle can never get to *the* action itself. (This is true except for certain conventionally acceptable minimal descriptions whose narrativity it is not usually to the point to consider.)

Returning now to defense: No instance of action is, therefore, to be limited in presentation only to being (1) a defense—or self-deceiving. In principle, it is always possible, and it may be more to the point, to present it also as: (2) one or more wish fulfillments, (3) one or more adaptations, (4) one or more punishments, (5) any combination or compromise of the four sets of possibilities, (6) any other description of these possibilities, combinations, or compromises, and (7) any other description of defense or self-deceiving action (for example, in some circumstances defensive reaction formation can also be presented as an instance of defensive identification).

Also, for certain narrative purposes, we might give an account of an action that contains less than we could include. For example, the accounts that analysts give in their writings are not always as complex as they could be, for an action might be considered merely under the description of a specific defense or a specific wish. That many of Freud's examples of wish fulfillment in dreams are of this optionally simplified sort may be inferred readily from the contrast between them and the examples of the complex approach to dreams he used in his work with Dora (1905a), work in which he was engaged at about the same time he wrote his dream book (1900). Simple in one narrative context, he was complex in another; indeed, there is a considerable range of complexity within the dream book itself. A similar range of complexity characterizes the interventions and the written examples of any adequate clinical analyst.

Because so much describing, relating, and explaining depends on the kind of account of action that is desired, the topic of defense and, with it, self-deception may be placed squarely in the interesting and evocative realm of narration. In this narrational realm, questions are asked that differ from those asked in Freud's mechanistic and objectivist metapsychological realm. Now, usually implicitly, it is asked: What kind of story do I as observer want to tell? What kind of story am I now committed to tell (assuming I concurrently have made the commitment to provide a consistent and coherent account) by my beginning to organize a clinical or theoretical report around a specific description, that is, as my implied storyline? For example, in using the description of *defense,* a warlike storyline is established, and in the interest of narrative consistency and coherence the writer makes a commitment to follow that storyline. Such terms as *abwehr, warding off, attack, infiltration, breakthrough, collapse, strengthening,* and *rebuilding* may be used: terms that have figured prominently in conventional psychoanalytic discussions of defense, and all of which may be said to be entailed and regulated by commitment to the same bellicose storyline. Elsewhere (see, for example, chapter 14), I have tried to show that the term *resistance* (a close relative of defense) establishes a commitment to the same adversarial storyline and that it may misrepresent or limit the technically desirable impartial and affirmative aspects of psychoanalytic practice.

I have already pointed out in chapter 2 that "storyline" is to be favored over "metaphor" and over unpacking metaphor or working out metaphoric entailments because, in my estimate, it has more obvious generative and regulatory connotations. Storyline suggests that there are a number of versions of the story that may be actualized, provided only that the storyteller observes enough of the conventional constraints (follows the "line"). These conventional constraints are not ordinarily extremely limiting, but there is usually a point beyond which attentive readers or listeners will begin to question whether a different story is now being told; for example, a consistent emphasis on experiences of relaxed pleasure in the context of giving an account of defense will be thought to be changing the story unless it is made clear that and how that relaxed pleasure is necessary to the story of defense.

Also, to favor "storyline" entails no neglect or exclusion of metaphor. Along with theme, image, dramatic scene, and expressive movement, metaphor is now to be regarded as one of the ways of introducing a storyline, one that is undeveloped or only implied. Unpacking a metaphor or working out its entailments should be regarded as making explicit its implications and defining its narrative consequences.

Consequently, self-deception may be considered a description that derives from and invites the further development of two storylines combined: *the self* and *deception*. Next I give an account of the problems raised by, and the generative potential and regulative effects of, this combination of storylines.

The Self Storyline

Let us consider the issues first from the side of the *self* storyline. Upon taking self-deception to be laying down the storyline of the self lying to itself, we encounter the same problems that reside in those accounts in which the mechanistic ego, when defending itself, seems to be deceiving itself and, equally odd in Freud's (1926) account, to be doing so after signaling to itself with blips of anxiety that defense (deception) is in order. Freud noted that the ego's deception is practiced unconsciously. As he developed his ideas, he seemed to argue that this unconscious aspect of the deception is both a necessary inference from analytic "data" (analysands give no sign of knowing they are defending) and a commonsense requirement (a deception cannot succeed if it is known to be a deception). In his studies of defense Freud proposed that he seemed to have encountered another kind of unconscious, that is, an unconscious that had *not* been repressed (1923a). With this proposition, he tried to avoid that infinite regress in explanation according to which there would have to be defenses against defenses against defenses ad infinitum. But in introducing another kind of unconscious into his model, in saying that one unconscious set of mental operations may deceive another such set, Freud was establishing another mind within the metapsychological mental apparatus. Thus, at least in this respect, a multiple-ego narrative took the place of the story of the ego's deceiving itself.

A version of this second mind or ego appears in the storyline of *self-deception*. Not that we are obliged to tell the odd and necessarily unconvincing story in which the self deceives itself; rather, we are to tell the story of one self in the act of deceiving another self. Self-deception is an event in a narrative that features multiple selves. In this multiple-self narrative, we are to present each self as able to act autonomously and at least one of these selves as able to act secretively. A story of this sort can be told in much the same way as a story of one person deceiving another. Thus, the account "I was kidding myself" differs little from "He was kidding me." The storyline's generative and regulating roles are the same. Whether the story will feature one or more persons should not affect its development. All that is needed is a pair of selves, belonging either to one person or two, each self having its own capabilities, initiatives, and reasons. If one person may have or does have at least two selves, the story of self-deception may continue unhampered. It is just that another kind of mind—actually multiple-mind—must be featured in this story. And it is not thrown into question that only one person is the subject of this story; the philosophical problem of how the identity of one person is established is not raised (nor, of course, is it settled).

As I argued earlier, there are many narratives of self, and many selves have been named to fit the tales in which they are to figure. There is the true self, false self, cohesive self, fragmented self, public self, secret self, sexual self, ideal self, and so on. There are also implicit multiple selves in the notions of self-control, self-love, self-hatred, self-esteem, and so on (Schafer, 1978). Consider, for example, the multiple selves (including the self of the speaker) in these locutions: "I won that fight with myself"; "My feelings washed over me like a giant wave"; "I can't forgive myself for showing myself off so."

Are we bound to reject multiple-self narratives? Is there any compelling reason to disallow psychological narratives featuring a proliferation of selves? The criterion of parsimony is no help in setting limits on multiple-self narratives or in excluding them altogether, for that criterion is always more treacherous to apply than seems at first to be the case. Simply to posit fewer selves or just one self is not sufficient to establish parsimony, as it may be necessary then to make many additional assumptions in order to accommodate the smaller cast of characters. Was Freud really being parsimonious when, to locate anxiety in the ego, he invoked the problematic idea of the ego's sending itself anxiety signals?

To the objection that multiple-self narratives introduce something like a demonological model to explain human action, it may be countered that at present there seems to be no other satisfactory way to provide for the following: (1) the accounts of multiple personality in which one personality observes another but not vice versa; (2) the accounts of posthypnotic suggestion, in which the subject acts as if he or she were maintaining a second, distinct self that independently complies with the hypnotist's suggestions; (3) the accounts of the subjective experience of introjects, that is, figures that seem to be in the subject's "inner world" and to observe, judge, and otherwise influence him or her (for example, a consciously experienced maternal figure that seems to operate as an independent persecutory or reassuring presence); (4) the accounts of splitting, said to be particularly prominent in so-called borderline personalities, according to which there ire distinct and totalistic "good" and "bad" selves organized around positive and negative affects and with corresponding "good" and "bad" others or "objects" (Kernberg, 1975) and, in Kohut's (1977) self-psychological theory, apparently autonomous subselves, such as the "grandiose self." We do not yet have a way to discuss these accounts that avoids altogether the use of manifest and latent multiple-self narratives. On this basis, we continue to develop multiple-self stories, like it or not. I am proposing that it is useful to consider these "phenomena" under the description of complex narratives and, further, that we should not ignore the often cumbersome consequences of using the multiple-self storyline (Thalberg, 1977).

Matters are not easier when considering the alternative storyline of a single self. Some problems arise out of a misunderstanding. Typically, those analysts who insist that there is *only* a single self, like those who employ accounts of multiple selves, do not recognize that they are making a narrative choice. Consequently, their accounts of a self that is simply *found* have a naïvely empirical tone. They seem to reify *the* self as a concrete mental entity. According to this sort of monistic view, there can be only one self (or mind, or ego, and so on) per person. Only one is demonstrable, and only one exists. The self is not a construction made by observers—that is, one way of telling about mental and behavioral actions; it is an entity in Nature that may be observed directly by the objective or the "empathic" observer, who may be the subject whose self it is. This a priori account is holistic. It establishes a narrative of basic mental unity. Typically, that narrative features the progressive differentiation and integration (except under pathological circumstances) of that one entity and also its regressive fragmentation and fluidity under conditions of stress. Additionally, this entity is presented as retaining its identity over time even though every one of its elements may change, and it is supposedly capable of regaining its mature identity after it has lost it through stress-induced regression.

In the history of the psychological study of human beings, the possibilities and the advantages of this holistic story have been developed extensively (Werner and Kaplan, 1963). It has probably been the dominant narrative in psychology. The story is very well documented. Because the story is so familiar, we are not ordinarily prepared to recognize it as a story. We do not automatically view it as just one way of telling about personality development and action. Other ways of telling about development and action, such as the multiple-self way, are brushed aside. The phrase "I am not myself today" or "be yourself" is regarded merely as a manner of speaking. Either the accounts of multiple personality, posthypnotic suggestion, and so on, are ignored, or tortuous monistic versions of them must be developed in order to remain consistent theoretically.

In my own case (1976, 1978, 1983), before I recognized the consequences of the view that we are always and only dealing with implicit or explicit narrative presentations of reality and never with reality pure and simple, I deplored the (often implicit) proliferation of selves. I saw that proliferation not only as theoretically cumbersome; I saw it also as an instance of defensively disclaimed action and of importing into theory the phenomenon that that theory intends to explain. I favored the monistic narrative.

I continue to favor the monistic narrative and for much the same reasons. However, the storyline I favor is not that of one self or one mind, but of *one person* as agent. And I propose that that person be viewed as a narrator, that is, as someone who, among other noteworthy actions, narrates selves. One person narrates numerous selves both in order to develop desirable (not necessarily "happy" but at least defensively secure) versions of his or her actions and the actions of others and to act in ways that conform to those selves. In this account, there is no self that does anything. Instead, there is one person telling stories about single selves, multiple selves, fragments of selves, and selves of different sorts, including *deceiving* and *deceived selves*. The narrator may, of course, attribute selves or self-states of these sorts to others, too, and others may (and do) reciprocate.

This single-person program seems to have an important heuristic advantage over the multiple-self program. The multiple-self narrative always allows the narrator-theorist to slip by some important theoretical problems by introducing one more self into the cast of characters; this is what instinct theorists used to do when they added to their lists of instincts new ones to deal with difficult phenomena. These ad hoc improvisations offer little prospect of sustained dialogue about self-psychological "phenomena." Additionally, a simple multiple-self choice introduces all the fruitless problems of arranging those selves that do get official recognition into some kind of stable, hierarchically organized structure. This structure is bound to be controlled or regulated by a super-self once due recognition is extended to commonly accepted accounts of large-scale coherence and consistency of functioning. In this way, the concretized monistic self returns through the back door, and we witness a failure of the entire enterprise.

To summarize, self-deception is but one instance of a set of problematic ideas that are introduced by self theories or grand self narratives. It is advantageous to regard self-deception as a story that people tell in order to present themselves or others as their own dupes or in order to make a psychoanalytic interpretation. In this story, the person is constituted by more than one self. The self-deception story is consistent with numerous other conventional multiple-self stories that are always being told by parents, friends, teachers, poets, philosophers, psychologists, analysts, and so on. By common consent, it is a story that "works": It communicates effectively and it helps construct experience. But it is only a version.

For those who do not accept this multiple-self version, the critical problem is not that of establishing one definitive, presumably nonnarrative account of what self-deception *is*. Rather, what should be examined are the origins, the occasions, the reasons, and the consequences of the variety of self narratives that may be rendered in connection with the study of what seem to be knowing/unknowing splits and corresponding reports of self experience. On this basis analysts consider the cast of self characters in the accounts people give of action as similar to the cast of characters in a dream; upon analysis this cast of dream characters gets to be retold as distributed versions of self: the self in desire, the self sitting in judgment, the self as child, the self as opposite gender, and so on.

The Deception Storyline

Let us take the following instance as an example around which to organize an examination of the storyline of deception. By all conventional standards, S.M., a teacher, derives pleasure from regularly treating his students cruelly; that is, he is a sadistic teacher. He, however, thinks that he treats his students fairly, dispassionately, professionally, and he is pained to think that he might ever have to do something in his role as teacher that any of his students might feel or any witness in the classroom might think to be cruel. His pleasure, he maintains, is in being a dedicated teacher. Surely, an ordinary observer would be inclined to say, S.M. is deceiving himself. Isn't the discrepancy of accounts as plain as can be? How can S.M. not see it?

The attribution of self-deception is, however, based on a number of unstated assumptions, interpretations, and evidential claims. Far from this deception being an unmediated perception by an "objective" observer of what S.M. is "really" doing, it is a rather elaborate construction.

The construction begins with the assumption that there is (or certainly there could readily be established) a firm consensus of informed and competent observers to the effect that S.M. is sadistic to his students. It is assumed that there exists a conventional description of that sort of conduct on the part of a teacher that fits S.M.'s conduct to a *t;* the consequence of this consensual validation is that a sadistic account is true or adequate while any other is false or inadequate. To tell it otherwise would violate our common sense of social coherence and ordinary reality. The burden of proof is not ours.

The construction continues with the assumption that S.M. knows the conventional account or is capable of using it appropriately in other situations, and does use it so, perhaps with reference to the actions of other teachers or other authority figures or even his own actions outside the classroom. It is also assumed that S.M. knows unconsciously that the sadistic account does fit his conduct in the classroom and that he will not admit this knowledge consciously to himself. We will make these assumptions if we are in possession of enough "evidence" of the following sort (in addition to S.M.'s inconsistency or incoherence in his use of "sadistic"). To the least suggestion that he is being sadistic to his students he overreacts: He protests his benevolent intentions more frequently, indignantly, anxiously, or desperately than would be expected. Also, he is impervious to rational confrontations by others that his conduct does fit a conventional description that he does accept in other contexts. Further, he behaves in a conspicuously frustrated or otherwise troubled manner when circumstance prevents his continuing to act cruelly to his students and derive pleasure from it. He exaggerates, minimizes, forgets, jumps to conclusions, contradicts himself, and so on, in ways that are not typical of him when he gives accounts of the relevant situations and actions. A psychoanalytic examination of his life history, fantasies, dreams, conduct in love, and so forth, strongly supports "sadistic" as the description that best fits his personality picture. These are the kinds of "evidence" psychoanalysts hope to obtain in order to justify attributing noteworthy sadism to some people and attributing correlated defensive measures (and self-deceptions) to them. In S.M.'s case, analysts can then say that he has a stake in not seeing himself as he is (that is, as sadistic) and latently believes himself to be; he is bound to be fooling himself.

We cannot fail to notice how obtaining this warrant and making this attribution depends entirely on the observer's adhering to conventions of description, interpretation, contextualization, and reduction of one account to the terms of another. Specifically, there are judgments to be made about types and degrees of inconsistency, competence, overreacting, imperviousness, frustration, and so on. There are other judgments to be made as to which accounts adequately con-

vey a life history and personality make-up and additional judgments as
to whether specific accounts of events fit these general ones and how
well they do so relative to alternative psychoanalytic accounts. The evidence does not consist of simple, narratively unmediated, objective
facts. What is called the evidence is, like all other evidence, theory-
laden. It is constructed in that uncertain area between what is found
and what is created, and it is that "evidence" that is used to support
reasoning which, unreflectively, is taken to be simply logical, factual,
and conclusive.

Two more sweeping assumptions go into the construction of the
deception story: First, individuals are best regarded as being naturally
and primarily truth-seekers; second, they engage in truth-seeking primarily consciously. These, however, were not Freud's (1911b) assumptions. He assumed that gratification (the pleasure principle) is natural
and primary, while truth-seeking (the reality principle) not only is secondary but is difficult to attain and sustain and is clearly a compromise with harsh necessity; it is a compromise that is entered into in
order to guarantee as much gratification as is compatible with security
or, in extreme cases, survival. Freud (1915a) further assumed that
unconscious mental processes—fluid, concrete, illogical, wishful, timeless, contradictory—are primary, while conscious rational mental processes not only are secondary but normally are merely the
fragmentary result of selective endorsement and attention. Certainly,
conscious mental processes are not in themselves the best guides for
making sense of the decisive features of anyone's cognitive and emotional development and present functioning. Thus, for Freud the
problem was not to explain social and personal incoherence; it was to
explain the attainment of socialized, objective, and coherent mental
processes. In his account, we start out with mercurial wishful thinking;
we never give it up altogether; we work out ingenious compromises,
including especially those that provide for us, in the derivative form of
social conformity and consensus, everything that we wished for so
urgently as children, such as a secure and gratifying place in a secure
and gratifying family.

For Freud, then, deception was not the preferred storyline of personal development and everyday functioning. His story goes from the
nonveridical unconscious id to the rational, realistic conscious ego. In
contrast, the story of self-deception seems to be the story of a rational,
realistic conscious ego that is somehow losing its supremacy.

Those who tell the deception story ignore the availability of more
than one convention to describe or explain a situation or course of
action. They also ignore the way some available conventions contra-

dict others, rather like those proverbs that seem to work well enough when taken singly but begin to look untrustworthy when paired with other well-working proverbs that more or less contradict them. Additionally, a sweeping consensus in human affairs is pretty hard to come by unless the issue is so impersonal and conventionalized that it is irrelevant, trivial, and uninteresting. Further still, conventions change over time, and what we regard as desirable social change often stems from gross breaks with convention. We cannot depend uncritically on convention and consensual validation in making claims about what is real or true.

Prepared with these qualifications, let us return now to S.M. If we say he is acting cruelly to his students in order to derive pleasure from doing so, we are initiating the construction of a story that depends on many other stories, among which is the story that there is an overwhelming coalition of real and safely imagined witnesses who would give a sadistic and self-deceiving account of S.M.'s conduct. This coalition would agree on the judgment that S.M.'s conduct meets enough of the criteria of sadistic action and self-deceiving action to leave little room for doubt. Further, the coalition would reject both the idea that S.M. is unmotivatedly and incompetently missing the point and the idea that he is secure in another conventional account, such as that he is trying to bring out the best in his students by holding up and strictly enforcing high standards of achievement and decorum, not being put off by their juvenile and manipulative howls and protests, and so on. They refuse to acknowledge that they might be making value judgments in the realm of legitimate and competing educational psychologies and philosophies. But would they be arguing fact or preferred storylines?

The answer I propose here is that it is the storylines that establish the facts of the case, which of these facts are to be taken as significant (for example, as evidence of sadism), and how these facts are to be situated in an account of the situations and actions in question. Like the self, deception can be taken as a storyline, and it is useful to do so. And self-deception can be taken to be a complex and coordinated elaboration of two storylines. The case of S.M. could be told differently; it often is. Owing to ambiguities that are encountered all along the line, it is not easy, though it is not impossible, to discredit alternative, nonsadistic versions of the case of S.M.

I am not proposing that any account is as acceptable as any other. Rather, I am proposing this—when we speak of true and false accounts of actions, we are positioning ourselves in a matrix of narratives that are always open to examination as to their precritical assumptions and values and as to their usefulness in one or another project. Some versions of S.M.'s conduct, such as that he is totally permissive, would depart so far from the conventions and uses of social or clinical discourse that they would founder from the start, except perhaps if they were being developed with obvious irony. Of them we say that they are false, inadequate, or illogical in any comprehensible discourse. Some accounts will be judged to be better or closer to the truth than others on the basis that they show a higher degree of consistency, coherence, comprehensiveness, and common sense than the others. But in the complex instances that concern us the most, we cannot count on incontestable proofs of superiority and we resort to, or submit to, rhetorical, ethical, and esthetic persuasiveness to decide what is better or best. Such, at any rate, is the account being used here of the way narratives of action are constructed and used.

SUMMARY AND CONCLUSIONS

Analysts deal intensively with defense in their clinical work. As defense implies self-deceiving actions, analysts have a lot to say about the when, the why, and the various forms and transformations of these actions. However, none of this gives them a basis outside a narrative project to say anything in response to the question of how it is possible in the first place for anyone to be self-deceiving. Self-deception itself is a description of action that inaugurates an explicit or implicit narrative; it lays down a complex storyline of multiple selves interacting. Like self-deception, defense, too, can be taken to lay down a storyline. Thus, it is open to examination as a term that both conforms to a version of mental development and functioning and prescribes certain ways of maintaining and extending that version. I presented the contrasting versions of defense in Freud's mechanistic metapsychology and my action language. I did so to support my thesis that it can be illuminating to approach self-deception in the terms of narration, that is, as a matter of choosing a storyline and observing such constraints as it exercises on narrators working within the conventions of how these deceptions are to be presented.

PART TWO

NARRATING GENDER

CHAPTER 4

Problems in Freud's Psychology of Women

PROLOGUE—1991

Except for a few minor changes, I have left chapter 4 in its original 1974 state. The reader who has been attending to my major argument for a narrational perspective on psychoanalytic theory and practice in part 1 (and also in parts 3 and 4) will readily see how the lexicon of narration can be introduced at key points in the argument. In contrast, I have revised chapter 5, on impotence and frigidity (originally written in 1978), so that it is more in keeping with my current narrative perspective. Chapter 5 should help the reader estimate the difference that my perspective makes in the flow and impact of my discussions of gender. Narrational considerations are more in the foreground of chapters 6, 7, and 8.

Psychoanalytic ego psychology has established as its proper subject of study the whole person developing and living in a complex world. No longer is psychoanalysis a theory simply of instinct-ridden organisms, turbulent unconscious dynamics, and the like. All aspects of development are to be seen as being profoundly influenced by learning in a context of object relations that are, on the one hand, biologically essential and biologically directed and, on the other hand, culturally molded and historically conditioned. Analysts also emphasize the clinical as well as theoretical dangers to psychoanalytic understanding represented by any simple and immediate reduction of manifest content to infantile dynamics.

On this basis, ego psychology has helped establish lively two-way interchanges between psychoanalysis and modern biology, psychology, anthropology, history, linguistics, philosophy, aesthetics, and other disciplines. Proceeding with justified caution, psychoanalysis has begun moving more freely within the history of ideas, of which it is itself, of course, a significant part. And within the history of ideas, sooner or later it comes to pass that well-established answers are found to require reconceptualization or replacement by new answers, framed to deal with different and possibly better questions.

Consequently, psychoanalysts who genuinely appreciate ego psychology will not shrug off the current great discussion of the making, warping, and exploiting of women in our society. In this discussion, fundamental Freudian propositions about psychological development are being challenged from all sides while the entire psychoanalytic enterprise is being widely discredited as the child and now the servant of the male-dominated, bourgeois social order. Simply interpreting these criticisms as militant rationalizations of penis envy being put forth by neurotic females and their male supporters is a flagrant instance of reductionism and intellectual isolationism and is equivalent to shrugging off this discussion, which, it should be noted, concerns the allegedly distorted development of men as well as women. Analysts should be prepared to rethink the concept as well as the role of penis envy in female development. This can be done without dismissing or minimizing many findings concerning its psychological importance.

My focus here is on some problems in Freud's theoretical generalizations concerning women's development and characteristics. These generalizations deal with typical conflicts and typical rational and irrational attempts to solve them. They have, of course, been of incalculable value both in understanding the varieties of female development and, through clinical psychoanalysis, in greatly alleviating neurotic disturbances in individual instances. But problems there are, and my strategy in getting at them is to focus on the type of theorizing Freud used in this connection. I examine the logic and internal consistency of his ideas; I try to sort out the preconceptions that went into the making of the theory, the empirical evidence it deals with, and the rules by which this evidence was established. Additionally, I attempt to identify the confusions between these three features of the theory. These are the theoretical features and the confusions that determine what are certified as the facts of gender, how these facts are related to each other, and whether and where there are factual errors and failures to make sense.

It is legitimate to begin by limiting the discussion to Freud alone. One reason for doing so is that much of the current criticism is directed specifically against Freud and relies heavily on allegedly representative quotations from his writings. Another reason is this: Although Freud's psychoanalytic descendants have made many major theoretical and technical advances, his basic assumptions—indeed the very mode of his thought—are still very much with us in modern psychoanalysis. Consequently, we may concentrate on Freud without being altogether ahistorical. At the same time, we must bear in mind that, over the years, Freud modified many of his ideas. We must ask, therefore, whether he modified his psychology of women.

It seems that he did. Not only did he finally emphasize how little, after all, he really understood female development (1931, 1933); he also began to emphasize, along with the vicissitudes of penis envy, the major and continuing influence of the girl's active preoedipal attachment to her mother. But Freud was not altogether consistent in making this change, for, in his final discussions of the subject (1937b, 1940), he pretty much reverted to his earlier, simpler, and patriarchal viewpoint (1923b, 1925). To put it plainly, this is the viewpoint from which Freud's propositions seem to imply that female development is both second best and second rate: second best in the experience of the girl and woman and second rate in the judgment of patriarchal spokesmen of civilization at large. Freud never did consolidate and develop a fundamental change in this regard. From this fact follow many of the problems in his psychology of women.

I discuss some major and representative problems under three headings: "The Problem of Women's Morality and Objectivity," "The Problem of Neglected Prephallic Development," and "The Problem of Naming."

THE PROBLEM OF WOMEN'S MORALITY AND OBJECTIVITY

What sense, if any, could Freud have been making when he characterized women as being less moral than men? Consider what he said:

for women the level of what is ethically normal is different from what it is in men. Their superego is never so inexorable, so impersonal, so independent of its emotional origins as we require it to be in men. . . . that they show less sense of justice than men, that they are less ready to submit to the great exigencies of life, that they are more often influenced in their judgments by feelings of affection or hostility—all these would be amply accounted for in the modification of the formation of their superego. (1925, pp. 257–258)

The Freud who wrote this passage was also well aware that many or most men manifest serious deficiencies in conventional moral rectitude. He saw this in their personal lives: Think of the men in the Dora case (1905a). He saw it in their professional lives: Consider the scandalous way in which he was treated by his colleagues in medicine and psychiatry. And he saw it in the lives of men as citizens: Recall his gloomy remarks on World War I (1915d). More than once he expressed plainly his low estimate of the morality of most people in the world he knew. Consequently, in his generalizations about women's morality, he could not have been contrasting them with *most* men, at least not in *that* sense of the word *moral.* What then was he doing?

In one respect, he seemed to be referring to a certain quality of moral rigidity characterizing men more than women. Men's moral stands seemed to him much less easily swayed by emotional appeals or so-called subjective impressions than those of women. Men seemed more consistently to affirm and abide by abstract and so-called objective principles. Although it could be argued effectively that the idea of this quantitative sex difference rests on a selection of criteria that is biased in favor of men, and so more or less begs the question, I shall bypass this issue in order to stay close to Freud's explicit line of thought, and I shall grant, *though only for the sake of critical analysis,* that this difference is real.

As clinicians, most psychoanalysts would, I think, infer from the "fact" of this quantitative difference that men have a greater capacity for isolation of affect. Like many others, Freud did estimate that hysterical proclivities are more commonly encountered in women and obsessive proclivities in men, and he did portray isolation of affect as a peculiarly obsessive mechanism (1926). Consequently, what seems to follow from Freud's generalization is that obsessive natures are more moral than hysterical ones. But that conclusion makes no sense for two reasons. One is that, although obsessives differ from hysterics in at least certain aspects of their morality, it is meaningless to suggest that it is possible to measure such differences on a single scale or indeed on any scale, for no scalar quantities are in question; obsessions and hysteria are modes of response or configurations of attitude and behavior. Instead of quantification, we would only be imposing a value judgment in the guise of making an empirical comparison. Apparently following the conventional patriarchal approach of his time, Freud was *in this sense* confusing values and observations. (In another sense, which is irrelevant here, there can be no value-free observations.)

In addition to this logical objection to the individious comparison, there is a psychoanalytic objection to be raised. Even assuming this isolation and this rigidity to be true differentiae, a psychoanalyst could never accept the obsessive as a more definite morality or a firmer one. This is so because obsessive morality is founded on reaction formation against anal-sadistic tendencies, intellectualization, irrational and savage unconscious guilt, and much devious immorality for which atonement must continually be made or that must be "magically" undone. Additionally, obsessive tendencies toward scrupulosity serve as unconscious equivalents of masturbation and torture. The obsessive model is, according to psychoanalytic understanding, a poor model of morality, indeed. And to argue on behalf of milder or more neutralized versions of this morality, we would still have to compare them with milder or more neutralized versions of hysterical morality; so the other problems I have just raised would still have to be faced. The charge of reductionism or genetic fallacy would have to be made against *both or neither* of these references to the infantile psychosexual prototypes of morality.

Thus far, Freud's quantitative comparison of the morality of men and women does not seem to stand up. Let us go on to examine it from another viewpoint. Freud also seemed to be assuming that holding to moral stands once taken, regardless of consequences in one's own personal relationships, is a sign of firmer morality, and that men clearly surpass women in this regard. There are additional grounds for entertaining this interpretation of Freud: He did think the predominant danger situation in the lives of women is loss of love, whereas in the lives of men castration is the main danger situation (1926); and since castration anxiety is considerably more narcissistically detached a concern than fear of loss of love, in that it is more remote from the immediate vicissitudes of love relationships, it provides a more impersonal foundation for moral activity. In Freud's final theory of development, this castration anxiety is the chief incentive for the renunciations and identifications that constitute the influential superego organization (1923a). Freud concluded that girls, already believing themselves to have been castrated, lack the same incentive as boys to become moral, and consequently seek solace and restored self-esteem in being loved by men and receiving babies from them (1925).

In this context Freud was clearly not appreciating two factors. One is the part played in the girl's development by the example of the active, nurturant mother who has her own sources of pride, decency, and consolation, and the other is the part played by the great variety of positive environmental emphases concerning girls and women. His attention was fixed on the decisive part played in the girl's development by one set of unconscious equations: My lost penis = father's actual penis = the baby I wish to be given me by father's penis.

Freud's conclusion seems inevitable. It is not only that women crave unconsciously to be loved, invaded, and impregnated, but that they bend their morality all too readily in order to fulfill these cravings; their fear of disapproval often overrules whatever independent sense they may have of what is right for them and others. No Freudian psychoanalyst would deny the applicability of these propositions to many segments of the significant problems presented in analysis by typical neurotic women in this culture. But surely every such analyst would affirm as well that, whatever the castration anxiety of men might have to do with superego structuralization, typically that anxiety is so unresolved, so persistent, and so intense that it continuously incites men to violate conventional morality and to do so often in an egregious manner. Consequently, when Freud cautioned against overestimating the degree of true superego formation in people in general, he must have meant men in particular.

More remains to be said about superego morality. For Freud, the unconscious infantile superego is the foundation of individual morality and establishes its character. His immediate *developmental* concern in working out his superego theory was to give an account of how and why the incest taboo is established and secured. He did not address himself particularly to the concept of reality-attuned, organized, adaptive moral codes; later on, Hartmann did so (1960). Many places in his writings suggest that Freud had some definite ideas along this line. These ideas are also implied in the dictum that Hartmann says Freud was fond of quoting: What is moral is self-evident. But in his psychoanalytic writings, he did not, as he should have, sharply distinguish between superego and moral code.

Generally speaking, the consequences of drawing this distinction have been insufficiently appreciated. One such consequence is a radical alteration of our idea of superego, for now we are able to see that superego is not morality at all, nor can morality grow out of it alone, for superego is fierce, irrational, mostly unconscious vindictiveness against oneself for wishes and activities that threaten to bring one into archaically conceived, infantile danger situations. As Freud described it, unconscious superego is mostly a demonic aspect of mind,* and as he developed this theory of it, it is his Death Instinct enshrined in psychic structure (1923a, 1930). This is the sense of Freud's conclusion that one aim of therapeutic analysis is to reduce superego influence on ego functioning (1933); by this he did not mean any reduction of morality.

This severe superego authority does generally enforce respectful observance of certain fundamental personal, familial, and societal taboos. In this respect, it is a powerful, societally oriented set of primitive prohibitions and policies of self-punishment. But Freud also demonstrated that this same internal authority may be subversive of people's achievements, their love, and even their moral codes, for, like any harsh and arbitrary authority, it continuously incites rebellion, hatred, and self-destructiveness. In its extremes, superego can even make criminals of people. Whatever superego does contribute toward eventual morality requires considerable tempering before that morality can be secured, and certainly superego cannot temper itself; it cannot become independent of its being and its emotional origins.

It follows that Freud may have drawn exactly the wrong conclusion from his developmental psychosexual theory. If, because of her different constellation of castration concerns, a girl does not develop the implacable superego that a boy does, then at least in this respect she might be better suited than a boy to develop a moral code that is enlightened, realistic, and consistently committed to some conventional form of civilized interaction among people. And perhaps that is the truth instead and the basis of another widely held view of women that Freud ignored in this connection: women as the guardians of civilized conduct and morality. I shall not argue here for or against the logical inevitability or empirical truth of either of these conclusions or of any other. Before doing so, we would have to scrutinize various types or styles of moral code—the assumptions, articulation, flexibility, scope, and applications of each—and that would be to study qualitative differences as such. Also, we would have to compare the developmental sequences of relaxing initially severe superego policies with consolidating a moral code despite initially insufficient superego formation. Clinically, analysts see both sequences. Probably no one factor or description could state the whole truth in this regard. We must

---

*I say unconscious superego is *mostly* demonic, for Freud also pointed to a benign, loving aspect of superego (Schafer, 1960). But that aspect, too, is archaic in its magical, grandiose, and absolute attributes, and so cannot amount to a moral code; like the punitive aspect, it can constitute only part of the history of that code.

remain dissatisfied both with Freud's estimate of men's and women's moralities and with his assumption that analysts may measure and generalize in this respect.

Can we be satisfied with Freud's related view that women are less objective, lucid, and acute in comprehension than men (1920b)? Here Freud was implying that, besides manifesting less superego development than men, women manifest less ego development (though when he said this, in 1920, he had not yet formulated his structural theory; but see also his paper of 1931). The derivation of this generalization is the same one I presented of Freud's estimate of women's morality: briefly, that an already castrated being's incentive for development is weaker than that of a being fearful of castration; that is to say, as it is to superego development, castration anxiety is also the greatest spur of all to ego development.

If we again agree *provisionally* that there are or may be sex differences in ego development, how are we to construe them? As in the case of morality, I suggest that these are not measurable differences in degree of development. Certainly the degree of development of single skills or functions can be measured according to the rules for applying specific scales to performances elicited by standardized methods. And certainly informal estimates of this circumscribed sort can be made, with the naked eye as it were. But, taken as a whole, such differences between men and women in ego functioning as there may be would be qualitative, corresponding to *modes* of functioning rather than to *amounts*. Contrary to Freud, there can be no final authority on the question of whether one mode of functioning is superior to another, for the question makes sense only in a context of values. Modes may be described, and different modes may be contrasted, but only a taken-for-granted patriarchal value system could lead to Freud's unqualified statement about women's relative mental incompetence.

Furthermore, there are contradictions to be noted. For example, if women are, as Freud believed, more intuitive and keenly empathic than men, are they not thereby manifesting another *kind* of acute comprehension? The difference then would not lie in acuteness at all, but in the judge's estimate of worth. Additionally, there hovers over all these considerations the major questions of whether or in which respects these differences do exist, and, if they do, whether they are inevitable or are enforced or at least exaggerated by methods of rearing and educating boys and girls differently in and for a phallocentric world.

There is also the hard question posed by wide individual differences *within* the sexes.

Here I should point out that Freud's feminist critics are close to Freud in a fundamental sense. Freud, too, presented the world as phallocentric, though he had in mind the world as it exists in psychic reality, whereas his critics are referring to the actual formative and normative environment. And yet, what of it? Let us grant the primary or tremendous importance of psychic reality. Then we would expect it to shape the comprehension of social reality, to constitute a significant part of the social reality we encounter in the form of other people, and, historically, to determine much of the content and organization of social reality—to all of which real adaptations would have to be made. Consequently, the child's sexual identity would be defined by that "complemental series" of inner and outer influences that Freud regularly invoked in his developmental propositions. A one-sided approach to reality cannot stand up to close inspection.

Additionally, Freud relied heavily, in his final theory of ego and anxiety, on the idea of the infant's prolonged helplessness and the consequent importance of the environment, both as it really is and as it is in psychic reality; this idea entails the recognition that external reality and psychic reality shape each other. In this light, Freud's more thoughtful feminist critics may be viewed as exploring the following questions concerning sexual identity: To what extent does societal indoctrination shape psychic reality and regulate the development of skills, attitudes, and ideas and values about oneself in relation to others? And how are any such societal influences mediated by family roles, schooling, and the actualities of later existence as well as by anatomical-physiological differences between the sexes? These questions are not alien to Freudian inquiry, especially when it is informed by ego-psychological adaptive considerations. What is problematic is the patriarchal bias in Freudian conceptualization and emphasis, a bias involving taken-for-granted models of masculine and feminine roles in our society.

In some early and illuminating Freudian papers on female sexuality, Karen Horney (1924, 1926, 1932, 1933) identified patriarchal bias in the then-existing psychoanalytic literature on the sexes. However, her mode of thought—that of the authoritative scientist laying down definitely the properties of a species—continued the patriarchal tradition of formulating sweeping generalizations about the sexes. It is unlike the nonpatriarchal mode of that exciting and evocative mixture of observation, impression, discovery, perplexity, and reservation that we encounter throughout Freud's case studies and clinical papers, that part of his *oeuvre* which, patriarchally, Freud seemed to regard as merely his "novels" or preliminary scientific data (I might say, in his terms, the feminine side of his work). Here I can only allude to the idea that phallic prototypes and values play major roles in traditionally esteemed modes of knowing used alike by many women and men.

We must conclude that Freud's estimates of women's morality and objectivity are logically and empirically indefensible. In large part these estimates implement conventional patriarchal values and judgments that have been misconstrued as being disinterested, culture-free scientific observations.

THE PROBLEM OF NEGLECTED PREPHALLIC DEVELOPMENT

Because Freud tried to account for women's personality characteristics and problems mainly in terms of the phallic phase, he neglected to assess adequately prephallic development. It is necessary to put this problem in theoretical perspective before coming to the problem itself. Accordingly, I first discuss in some detail certain general features of Freud's theorizing that seem to account for his having based so much of his theory of psychosexual development on anatomical genital factors.

The fact that Freud adhered to a biological, evolutionary model for his psychology (Schafer, 1970b) led him to neglect, in his theorizing, and thus in his comparative views on men and women, prephallic development. His model requires a teleological view of the propagation of the species (see, for example, Freud, 1933, p. 131). That is, it requires the assumption that individual human beings are destined to be links in the chain of survival, and this assumption necessarily implies that genital sexuality is the culmination of psychosexual development. In turn, that idea necessarily implies that anything else is an arrest of development and so must be, in some sense of the so-called natural order of things, unnatural, defective, or abnormal. Accordingly, pregenital pleasures, being nonprocreative, belong at best to foreplay in adult sexual life; otherwise they are perversions. And homosexuality, being similarly nonprocreative, is to be viewed not as an alternative to genital heterosexuality but as a so-called inversion. In this entire line of thought can be observed the operation of an implicit but powerful *evolutionary value system*. According to this value system, Nature has its procreative plan, and it is better (healthier, more normal) for people to be "natural" and not defy "the natural order." The propositions are not neutral.

Here is one of the great ironies in the history of psychoanalysis:

Even after Freud gave up the idea of an instinct of self-preservation and in general deemphasized his ideas about very specific instinctual drives, he continued to think along similar lines in some respects and, in so doing, contradicted his major clinical observations and conclusions. Clinically, even as early as his "Three Essays on the Theory of Sexuality" (1905b), he had come to realize that genital heterosexuality is a difficult, imperfect, more or less precarious achievement, and that this is so because it is a psychological task as well as a biological eventuality. Biology provides chiefly the stimuli, especially the insistent, pleasurable, and potentially painful stimuli of bodily needs and the sensuous zones; it is experience in human relatedness that defines and emphasizes specific aims and objects. The attainment of genital primacy is therefore very much a matter of the child's learning certain lessons about sexual pleasures and dangers and its developing some type and degree of mastery of both of these. Because of the child's immaturity, this learning and striving for mastery will involve many animistic, illogical, unrealistic, and symbolic infantile mental processes; these processes, usually ignored or underestimated by the revisionist schools of cultural analysis, are among the phase-specific features of early psychosexual development. And this learning will be very much under the influence of bodily experience in the context of some caretaking presence. But however crude it may be, it *is* learning.

In effect, Freud had shown that for human beings there is nothing inevitable about propagating the species. This was truly a revolutionary discovery! Because we know only societies that, owing to various combinations of need and tradition, are geared for creating children, we tend to take it for granted that procreativity is a central and inevitable aspect of human beings, as of other animals. It need not be argued here that, in crucial respects, human beings differ fundamentally from other animals, and it was Freud's clinical contributions that made it possible to realize in how many ways and how insistently societies steer children from their infancy toward procreative male and female roles. However imperfectly, we are continuously preparing children in our society to become fathers and mothers in nuclear families. Freud also showed, and especially emphasized, that, from the standpoint of the child, this indoctrination impinges on, and to a large extent is understood in terms of, the child's own wishes to be in the procreative role; these are wishes based on the child's identifications, rivalry, love, infantile fantasies, sensuous desires, and other variables familiar from clinical work. But there is no sense of assuredness among the members of our society that the child's own procreative wishes would or could by themselves finally establish their own primacy; and so, implicitly and explicitly, we plan the child's psychosexual development. We try to turn out men and women who will aspire to have children in nuclear families, too, and who, in turn, will prepare their children to continue this pattern and will think it good and natural to do so and live so.

Although it is fruitless to speculate about how children would develop in this respect if left to their own devices, we are able to consider the place of learning in procreative genitality because there are other and real types of control situations. For instance, in our society we often observe children and adults who have been indoctrinated by parents to hold ideal conceptions of sex roles other than the traditional procreative ones. These are the psychologically masculinized daughters and psychologically effeminized sons. Moreover, procreation is not an inevitable consequence of the pleasure of sexual excitement and orgasm; nor is hetersexual genital intercourse the only route to these pleasures.

Considerations such as these highlight the centrality of learning in the human being's movement toward procreativity. Consequently, we need not and should not assume a self-fulfilling instinctual drive toward propagation of the species. Nor is it logical to argue that some drive of that sort has to be operative, even though it is not amenable to our isolating it and studying its action; if it cannot be studied, we have no right to speak of its existence or to build it into the foundation of our developmental theories, as Freud did. That it might have a place in preliminary or informal speculation, which might then lead to significant discovery, is another matter altogether. I have discussed logical problems in psychoanalytic theory elsewhere (1972, 1973a, 1973b).

Finally, with regard to *unlearned* influences on psychosexual identity, it must be noted that Freud never really integrated his references to constitutional differences in the strength of masculinity and femininity with his psychological propositions about sexual development. Furthermore, he did not—indeed, could not—demonstrate that he regularly encountered these differences in the neurotic people with whom he was working. He just assumed their existence.

Thus, it is one great consequence of Freud's discoveries that psychoanalytic explanations may no longer presuppose any natural or preestablished culmination of human psychosexual development. Another consequence, a corollary to the first, is that psychosexual outcomes other than reproductive genitality are called illnesses and arrests in development *only from the standpoint of the values and associated child-rearing practices common to the dominant members of a society.*

In speaking of perversions and inversions and their cure, we are operating in the realm of societal value systems concerning taken-for-granted evolutionary obligations; we are not operating in any realm of biological necessity, psychobiological disorder, or value-free empiricism. There is no established relation between these value systems and psychoanalytic insights, though there may be between these value systems and religion or existential choices. None of which is to deny, of course, that clinical psychoanalysis can and does often greatly reduce profound and painful conflicts in these areas, or that it may be legitimate or even inescapable to define illness in terms of value systems. But analysts should know that this is what they are or may be doing.

The argument may be pursued by emphasizing Freud's helping us to understand the socially widespread intense revulsion toward, and derogation and persecution of, so-called sexual deviants. He showed that these violent reactions are founded on three factors: a degree of precariousness in the heterosexual genitality attained by most nondeviant people; a greater or lesser dread common to these people of succumbing to modes of gratification that would disconfirm their heterosexual genitality; and some readiness on their part to project their repudiated desires onto others and then persecute them. This *precariousness* expresses various unconscious fixations on, and regressions to, homosexual and pregenital pleasures, and this *dread* and *persecution* reflect the intense, partly incorporated social pressures against adopting these deviant sexual roles. These pressures have, of course, impinged on the child's archaic fantasies of pleasure, destruction, castration, loss of self and others, and loss of love and security; and they have been understood in terms of these fantasies and gained much of their great power from them.

Along the same line, Freud helped us to see through and beyond our society's many hypocritical moralistic attitudes toward pleasure of all sorts and its usually excessively confining sense of decorum, especially with regard to sexuality. But this understanding of sexual development and sexual attitudes must be predicated on the proposition that human sexuality is indeed *psycho*sexuality. The concept psychosexuality excludes a sexuality of blind instincts culminating in propagation of the species, as in nonhuman organisms (though even for them this simple statement is no longer really acceptable); and it excludes a sexuality simply of erotic techniques and orgasmic adequacy. Psychosexuality means mental sexuality, that is, a sexuality of meanings and personal relationships that have developed and been organized around real and imagined experiences and situations in a social world.

Freud disregarded this consequence of his own revolutionary clinical discovery. He persevered with the biological, evolutionary model and value system. Just as his doing so greatly confounded his metapsychological theorizing (Schafer, 1976), it limited his clinical view of development prior to the phallic phase; thereby it interfered with his developing an altogether satisfactory developmental psychology of girls—and of boys as well. The fact that psychoanalysts, in following Freud, tend to regard and name these early phases the *pre*genital and *pre*oedipal phases betrays the relevant bias and limitation in traditional thinking.

In Freud's major systematic statements, he repeatedly indicated that real mental development begins and is crystallized during the time of the passing of the Oedipus complex, which is the very time when the foundations of procreative genitality are being decisively laid. For example, Freud spoke of the ego as at best a rudimentary organ before this time. Also, he seemed to underestimate the influential fantasies of incorporated parental figures and other "presences" that seem to abound during the very early years and to persist to some extent thereafter. Further, Freud held that it is not only the superego structure which is established during the resolution of the Oedipus complex, but the structured and structuring ego as well (1923a); for only then, on the strength of its new identifications and the desexualized energy now available to it for sublimated activity, does the ego begin to function as an organized, independent, and influential agency.

In his structural theory of mental development, Freud provided no fully adequate and integrated treatment of the acquisition of language, habit training, oral and anal fantasy life, consolidation of narcissism, rudimentary character formation, and many other early factors. Despite his tremendous discoveries concerning just these prephallic factors, Freud still put the phallus, oedipal fantasies, castration anxiety, and procreation in the center of his developmental theory. And yet we can only begin to comprehend the development of the phallic phase and the Oedipus complex and the possibility of their coming to any resolution whatsoever on the basis of considerable prephallic ego development (Schafer, 1968b).

This centering on ultimate procreative genitality explains some of the imperfections of Freud's psychology of women. The essential point may be developed through consideration of Freud's having pretty much taken for granted the girl's catastrophic response to her discovering the anatomical difference between the sexes and her basically implacable envious attitude thereafter. Freud was remarkably incurious about the background of these reactions. He did refer (almost in passing, it seems) to speculative ideas put forward by others concerning the girl's being primed to respond thus catastrophically by prior losses of breast and feces; otherwise he was silent. Similarly, with regard to the danger situations of loss of love object and loss of love, which precede the era of castration concerns, Freud's comments remained schematic as well as isolated from considerations of the girl's intense reaction to the anatomical difference.

We encounter the same problem even in Freud's major revisionary efforts of 1931 and 1933. Although there he stressed the pregenital girl's activity, her mother's "sexual seduction" of her through bodily ministrations, the girl's natural ambivalence toward her mother and her struggle with her over masturbation, he did not present these variables as the foundations of the castration shock. These variables remained isolated. Soon they would be superseded by the beginning of the "feminine [phase] to which she [the girl] is *biologically destined*" (1933, p. 119, emphasis added). Here there is no sense of developmental continuity.

To mention only one more problem: Freud was too quick to favor the designation *penis envy* for the complex array of feelings, wishes, and fantasies of which penis envy is, after all, only a part, though often a most intense and consequential part. Here the influence of Freud's phallocentrism can hardly be overlooked.

Insofar as it is the hallmark of psychoanalytic investigation, and particularly of Freud's thinking, that it always presses its questions further and further in the interest of establishing the fullest understanding possible of the particularity of response on the part of individuals in specific circumstances, especially when these reactions are intense, disturbing, profoundly formative, and enduringly influential, it is all the more remarkable that at this point Freud asked virtually no more questions. It is as if it is sufficient just to know that girls assume they are phallic in the way boys are and that they pursue active as well as passive aims until the terrible time of revelation, mortification, and envy. But it is *not* sufficient. The psychoanalytic clinician as well as theorist must remain curious and so must go on to ask: Why *is* the girl so mortified and envious? Her mortification and envy are not explained by the fact of her simply seeing the difference; nor are they explained by her having previously maintained unchallenged her assumption that she and the boy are anatomically alike.

To begin to answer the question at all satisfactorily, we must assume that, before the time of mortification and envy, it was already terribly important to the girl that there be no differences between herself and boys. And to make that assumption is to land smack in the middle of so-called pregenital mental development. At this point, this phasic location can no longer seem quite so *pregenital*, in any case. In effect I am arguing that we cannot have a simple, self-evident *shock theory* of the girl's mortification and consequent penis envy. That the girl reacts this way indicates that she is already heavily invested in and worried about genital comparison and intactness. Freud's consistently restricted view of these developments is evident in the way he contrasted to the boy's initial "irresolution and lack of interest" the girl's response to having to face the anatomical difference: "She makes her judgement and her decision in a flash. She has seen it [the penis] and knows that she is without it and wants to have it" (1925, p. 252).

The problem of the readiness for castration shock is not the whole of the difficulty. In their quest for particularity of explanation, psychoanalysts must also ask about the apparent precariousness of the girl's self-esteem in the face of the genital discovery, however and whenever it is made. Indeed, in Freud's theory this precariousness is presented as so great that the collapse of self-esteem in the context of the castration fantasy is held to be a decisive and permanent influence on the woman's entire mental development and organization. As Freud was to put it much later on, penis envy was the "bedrock" of her neurotic problems (1937b). But, again, where are Freud's questions in this regard? It was he, after all, who taught us how to establish through psychoanalysis the historical background and the complex determination of psychological trauma.*

Even after making allowances for due restraint on speculation, it may still be argued that Freud was in a logical and methodological position to at least raise these questions about the girl's readiness for mortification and envy and the precariousness of her self-esteem. The answers, about which I have more to say later, would have to center on the girl's relationship with her mother during the first years of her life, and they would establish the profound importance of this relationship throughout the remainder of the daughter's existence—as of the son's. *That Freud did not raise these questions seems to be in large part an expression of his being preoccupied with the organs of reproduction, in consequence of his commitment to an evolutionary model and value system and a patriarchal bias.* Freud neglected to a noteworthy degree two interrelated psychological variables, one the manifestations of mind prior

---

*Methodologically, *at the time he was writing,* Freud was wise not to press his questions too far. He cautioned against formulating propositions concerning mental processes during the earliest phases of development, for the relevant data from clinical work were, at best, extremely fleeting, fragmentary, and ambiguous, and it was primarily through analytic work proper that his developmental propositions were framed and tested (1931).

to the time of the phallic phase and the Oedipus complex, the other the powerful role played by learning in the development of sexual attitudes, roles, and subjective experience. Far more than it should have, anatomy had become Freud's destiny.

Anatomy and reproduction, and anatomy and mind: The links were forged. Despite Freud's keen awareness of early mental functioning, he developed no *psychological* way of taking it into account. Mostly he biologized the early mental processes by relegating them to instinct, instinctual energy, processes, and principles, such as the pleasure principle, the primary process, and the repetition compulsion; and he viewed each of these as seeking to gratify its own aims in its own way. Thereby he anthropomorphized them, that is, reintroduced psychological propositions by the back door of biology (Grossman and Simon, 1969; Schafer, 1976).

A psychological approach to the prephallic period must center on the girl's primary, mind-formative, certainly intensely and complexly physical, and ultimately indestructible relationship with her mother. Freud, however, was mostly concerned to explain the girl's turning *from* her mother *to* her father as lover and sire of her children. In this effort, he portrayed the girl as having simply turned against her mother and, together with that, against her own identification-based active orientation and her clitoris. But, to be consistent with psychoanalytic propositions and findings, the girl and, later, the woman must be seen as being in a profoundly influential, continuously intense and active relationship, not only with her real mother but with the idea and imagined presence of her mother, and with her identification with this mother; she must also be seen as integrating her clitoris firmly into her sexuality. Whatever the girl's narcissistic vulnerability at the time of the castration shock, it would have its history and find its meaning in this matrix. Although Freud approached this consistency in some of his later papers, he did not achieve it.

Freud's value-based interpretation of his investigations is further evidenced in a limitation of his approach to the problem of the analysis of transference. Typically, he construed the transference he had observed as being based on the ambivalent tie to the father of early childhood. Even in his 1931 paper, in which he was reconsidering his psychology of women and beginning to emphasize the importance of the pregenital relation to the mother, he suggested that it would be *female* analysts particularly who would be the ones to work out the child's early relation to the mother. Thereby he continued to neglect the essentially androgynous role of the psychoanalyst in the transference; for the male analyst this means his female as well as male identity in this central aspect of his work. There is little evidence that Freud was alert to or impressed by maternal transference to the male analyst—or, for that matter, by maternal countertransference on the part of the male analyst.

It is not inaccurate to say that Freud tended to neglect bisexuality, even though that concept and the relevant observations are such central elements in his theory of development. This neglect is evident in his discussions not only of transference but of resistance, ego and superego formation, and other topics as well (Schafer, 1976). He was preoccupied with the father's position in a way and to a degree that stunted his conception of the mother's status in the family and thereby her stature in his theory. Again, for his theory of development, the important thing was to get the girl to become *feminine* and ready to receive love and babies *passively* from an active man, thereby to continue to propagate the species. For this, Freud thought he needed a sustained phallic perspective. But that perspective is not inclusive enough for his own psychoanalytic discoveries.

THE PROBLEM OF NAMING

Now we must consider how such designations as feminine, passive, and active behave in descriptive and explanatory propositions. This is the problem of naming.

To designate is also to create and to enforce. By devising and allocating words, which are names, people create entities and modes of experience and enforce specific subjective experiences. Names render events, situations, and relationships available or unavailable for psychological life that might otherwise remain cognitively indeterminate. Consequently, whether something will be an instance of masculinity or femininity, activity or passivity, aggression or masochism, dominance or submission, or something else altogether, or nothing at all, will depend on whether we consistently call it this or that or consistently do not name it at all, hence do not constitute and authorize its being. Similarly, to the extent that we link or equate such names as, for example, femininity and passivity, we exert a profound and lasting formative influence on what it is said to be like to be feminine or passive. Logically, there is no right answer to the questions of what is masculine and what is feminine and what is active and what is passive. There are no preconceptual facts to be discovered and arrayed. There are only loose conventions governing the uses and groupings of the words in question. And these conventions, like all others, must manifest values.

For example, in our society we often merge words pertaining to social values such as status and so-called breeding with words pertaining to sexual identity. To be a lady in the sense of a fine lady and to be feminine may be set up as equivalents, with the consequence that a woman who does not act ladylike, according to a certain conception of that word, may be said to be not feminine. In this instance, not feminine might mean rude, loud, socially too forward, sexually too adventurous, intellectually too serious, or cosmetically too casual or vivid. Thus, to say that a woman is not feminine is often a way of saying that she does not act or look as a woman "ought to" act or look. An additional part of this poor lesson is the implicit idea "She is bad." In this way, verbal conventions that implement value judgments are passed off as simple and unequivocal facts—and are so learned by children (Hartmann, 1960).

Clinical psychoanalysts have much occasion to observe and modify the disturbing influence of cultural, familial, and individual conventions regarding the valuative use of words or names and of their groupings and equations, especially in the case of words pertaining to sexual identity, aggression, and personal worth.

In this third and final (and all-too-brief) section of my discussion, I concentrate on one strategic problem of naming: how Freud used the words *active* and *passive* in relation to the words *masculine* and *feminine*. Freud showed some awareness in this regard—that he was using and devising verbal conventions. In one place he said, "Maleness combines [the factors of] subject, activity and possession of the penis; femaleness takes over [those of] object and passivity" (1923b, p. 145). In another place he said, "We call everything that is strong and active male, and everything that is weak and passive female" (1940, p. 188). Except for his reference to the penis—which, being an empirical rather than a defining proposition, is out of place in the first statement—Freud seemed to know that he was not making empirical assertions about how women really and necessarily are. In many places he even insisted that women come in all kinds, as do men. What he wanted was merely a suitable rubric for such personal characteristics as weakness and passivity. The names he chose were masculine and feminine (or male and female), and so, within this verbal convention, a woman is masculine to the extent that she is active and strong, and so on (see, for example, 1933, pp. 114–117).

Whatever our criticisms of this choice of names, such as that it both implies and enforces a derogation of women, it seems thus far that Freud was proceeding logically. In fact, however, he repeatedly lost his bearings and did not keep definition distinct from observation.

Freud's logical sophistication did not stop him from making all sorts of conventional patriarchal statements about what women are actually like and should be like (for example, submissive to their husband's authority). Such statements suggest that all kinds of "right" answers about sexual identity are being dictated by a pair of biological principles—the masculine and the feminine. Freud's repeated remarks about constitutional strength of masculinity and femininity reveal this to be so.

This same confusion can be traced in the course of Freud's chapter entitled "Female Sexuality" (1933). What was masculine and feminine, like what was moral and objective, seemed to be self-evident to him. His attempt at definitional rigor succumbed to this complacency. For Freud, then, feminine comprised passive, submissive, and masochistic; it meant the willing object of the man's biologically natural sexual and aggressive activity. This thesis must have seemed to Freud a scientific way to guarantee the continuation of the species. Looking back, we can see now that it served the continuation of the patriarchal social order, which, in his theories at any rate, Freud seemed to take uncritically as Reality. To put it another way, Freud assumed there to be normative links between, on the one hand, female-feminine-passive-submissive-masochistic and, on the other hand, male-masculine-active-dominant-aggressive. If this is so, a change of any one term would necessarily imply a change of all the others linked to it.

In trying to explain how women get to be as they allegedly are, particularly in terms of their attempts at resolving their penis envy, Freud made many fundamental and grand discoveries. Nevertheless, he was begging the question in at least two different ways. One was his presupposing that in fact women get to be *essentially* passive, submissive, and masochistic. The other was his presupposing that it is their psychobiological *destiny* to get to be as he said they are. Consequently, he worked with a simplified view of women, and he paid scant attention to the questions whether and to what extent girls are continuously being seduced and coerced into being "that way" by members of a society committed unconsciously, if not consciously, to guaranteeing that outcome.

Much of the argument turns on the meaning of passive. For Freud, masochism is the passive complement of sadistic aggression; submission is the passive complement of dominance; being loved, of loving; being looked at, of looking; and being impregnated, of impregnating (see, for example, Freud, 1915b). If all these passivities add up to femininity, we had better be clear about how Freud was using the word *passive*. The trouble is that Freud was not clear or consistent in his use of that word. At times he was even self-contradictory. First of all, he confused phenomenological passivity with passivity in the eyes of the psychoanalytic observer of behavior (Schafer, 1968a).

A clear example from psychoanalysis is the so-called fate neurosis in which, phenomenologically, a person repeatedly experiences him- or herself as the unfortunate passive victim of circumstance. At the same time, the psychoanalytic observer of behavior sees the person in question as actively bringing about his or her own misfortunes, say as symbolic castrations for incestuous wishes or as abandonments that are punishment for unconscious oedipal triumphs.

Second, when Freud generalized about women's passivity, he neglected such factors as unconscious identification with the partner in any significant relationship. Yet he had been the very one to establish the importance of these factors through his psychoanalytic method. In this connection, for example, the masochist is understood to be also unconsciously identifying with, and thereby vicariously enjoying the activity of, the sadistic partner. To this I must add that moral masochists, at any rate, not only actively seek out and provoke the abuses they seem to suffer passively but use their suffering to torment others.

Third, Freud repeatedly demonstrated how extraordinarily subtle and complex the interweaving of active and passive themes can be in any one person's life. From this fact it follows that one-sided or simple characterizations of any significant project as active or passive hardly makes sense, once a given person and situation is known well enough. Yet Freud was not deterred from generalizing on the basis of such simplistic characterizations. Again, he dealt inconsistently with his own discoveries and conceptual perspective.

Perhaps most fundamental to the analysis of this problem of naming is that, in many crucial instances, the decision whether to speak of behavior or of aims or attitudes as active or passive is like the decision whether to say of a certain glass of water that is half full or half empty. For example, to be exhibitionistic a person must find a real or imagined audience and show him- or herself off, which is to be active; and it is to be looked at, which is to be passive. Another example: To be loved is to be passive, and yet there are so many ways of getting to be loved and of receiving love, all of which are forms of being active. One more example: Does the penis penetrate the vagina or does the vagina receive the penis? Here I should point out that, immediately after the sentence I quoted earlier in this section, in which Freud grouped subject, activity, and possession of the penis as the referents of maleness, he went on to say "The vagina is . . . valued as the place of shelter for the penis; it enters into the heritage of the womb" (1923b, p. 145). Can a human place of shelter be passive? Can a womb be passive? To put it in terms of persons-in-relation, which are the proper ones, we must ask whether it makes any sense to say of a woman engaging in sexual intercourse that she is simply passive and whether it makes any sense to say of a caretaking mother that she is simply passive. Although Freud raised this last question (1933, p. 115), he did not draw its consequences for his general theory.

That Freud was not prepared to think about mothers very far is, as I noted earlier, evident from how little he said directly about them and about relationships with them, and, correspondingly, how little he said about how they appear in the transference, the resistance, and the formation of the ego and superego systems. Additionally, in his writings he showed virtually no sustained interest in their subjective experience—except for their negative feelings about their own femininity and worth and their compensatory cravings to be loved and impregnated, especially with sons. Consequently, Freud dealt with the feminine trends in men chiefly in terms of the two factors of castration and "passive" homosexuality, and he failed to consider in depth and systematically what more is entailed by being a woman and feeling like one in our society and how it might be different under other conditions. It seems that he knew the son, the father, and the castrate in himself and other men but not the daughter, the mother, and the woman.

To return to the idea of a fine lady: There is a Victorian precept that in sexual relations "a lady doesn't move." The modern psychoanalyst has to recognize this role not as passivity but as a desperate form of activity: a drastic inhibition required to play this inactivated part. The inhibiting may be carried out unconsciously and supplemented by conscious aversion, and the groundwork for this behavior would have to have been laid in early childhood, but it is activity nonetheless, at least as much as anything else is. It is from Freud particularly that we have learned about this unconscious activity. Yet although Freud the clinician was ever alert to the many forms unconscious activity takes in the lives of women, Freud the theoretician, when dealing with the development of sexual identity, named this inhibition passivity and made it the crux of femininity.

CONCLUDING REMARKS

Freud was working within a nineteenth-century biological-medical tradition that was not of his making. He merely applied and extended the conventions that constituted that tradition which was marked by a fusion of mechanistic and evolutionary modes of thought and patriarchal complacency. It based itself on ruling principles of nature, such as activity-passivity and masculinity-femininity, and other broad generalizations designed to take nature by the throat. Additionally, it was a tradition of belief in the idea of value-free empiricism and of pride in the achievements of the utterly objective scientist, and so was philosophically too immature to appreciate what is better established today: the pluralistic, relativistic, linguistic, and inevitably valuative aspects of the various forms of knowledge. Against these odds, Freud's achievement is all the more impressive. Nevertheless, at this historical moment we are obliged to identify and clarify the problematic aspects and limitations of Freud's contributions to the psychology of women. Much remains to be said on this subject and on the correlated subject of the fear that haunts the lives of men, pervading their relationships with women as well as with men: the fear of being second best and second rate themselves.

CHAPTER 5

The Phallocentric Narrative of
Impotence and Frigidity

IMPOTENCE and frigidity, whether actual, imagined, or anticipated, are two of the most pervasive and abiding concerns of men and women. And there is hardly another human concern that is so imbued with irrational thinking. As a rule, impotence and frigidity are taken to be failures of the worst kind. Esteem for oneself and others rides precariously on sexual performance and one's idea of what this performance signifies. Some who live in the shadow of these concerns desperately avoid sexual intercourse and even social relations, while many others desperately keep proving to themselves or to the world that they are not impotent or frigid or that they have no reason to fear being so. These concerns with impotence and frigidity also disrupt relations with friends of the same sex, owing to the shame, bravado, competitiveness, and plain dishonesty to which they ordinarily give rise. Moreover, through displacement, men and women manifest these sexual concerns in other areas of life, such as physical, occupational, intellectual, and social fitness and worthiness. Although these areas seem far afield from sexuality, unconsciously they are more or less invested with sexual significance. In the end, there may remain few aspects of life that are not haunted, unconsciously if not consciously, by these concerns.

Psychoanalysts have learned a great deal about direct and displaced expressions of these actual, fantasied, and anticipated disturbances. Simply describing the phenomena in question and summarizing what has been learned about them would require a series of books, not only because there is so much to cover but also because psychoanalysts differ among themselves as to what it is most important to describe and explain and how to do so. But as I want to do a different job than that, I devote the first and introductory part of this chapter only to some well-established descriptive and explanatory highlights.

Mainly in this chapter I want to show how phallocentrism may be discerned in the conventional ways observers construct the narratives that define and appraise the phenomena in question. These narratives feature discriminatory ascriptions of personal agency that conform to the traditional sexist ideas of what it is to be a man and a woman or of the differences between the masculine and the feminine. In that way they bias our observations of sexuality from the first, perception never being divorced from our master narratives.

It is beyond the scope of this chapter to focus on sexual relations other than heterosexual genital intercourse.

PSYCHICAL IMPOTENCE AND FRIGIDITY

Nothing will be gained for present purposes by agonizing over strict clinical or descriptive definitions of impotence and frigidity; no one attempt can be successful because the narrative possibilities that yield up these definitions are so numerous. It is, however, important, for reasons that will emerge, to avoid importing into our definitions presuppositions about ability, capacity, achievement, success, and failure.

In the main, *impotence* refers to the absence or disappearance of a penile erection or the absence of ejaculation during a man's ostensible attempt to perform the heterosexual act fully. When used more loosely, *impotence* may also refer to premature or minimal ejaculation and to partial erection, in which descriptive respects the notion of *degree* of impotence seems to be appropriate. Those instances of impotence that have clear organic etiologies need not concern us here.

Freud used the term *psychical impotence* to cover all instances of psychological origin, but also and mainly in a narrow sense to cover the far more common instances of *selective* impotence. Selective impotence refers to a man's being limited to completing the sexual act with only certain types of women; typically these are "degraded" women in relation to whom the man may exclude tender, affectionate, and respectful feelings. Of these men Freud (1912a, p. 183) said, "The whole sphere of love . . . remains divided. . . . Where they love they do not desire and where they desire they cannot love." Selective impotence is the form most frequently encountered in clinical practice, particularly if we take account of the fact that it is observed as an intermittent phenomenon just as often in relation to one woman, perhaps the man's wife, as it is in relation to a type of woman.

As customarily used, *frigidity* refers to a woman's lack of sexual desire, ardor, and pleasure in sexual intercourse; it may include conscious aversion to the act. We may speak of *degrees* of frigidity. Corresponding to the man's difficulties with erection and ejaculation are the woman's vaginal tightness and dryness, which, because they usually occasion pain and fear of pain during intercourse, further decrease her sexual arousal and increase her aversion to the act. The term *frigidity* is used by some to refer to the regular absence of orgasm. What Freud said about psychological impotence in the narrowed sense applies, with appropriate changes, to frigidity: Psychological frigidity refers commonly to selective frigidity, whether it is with one type of man or with one man at different times. If nowhere else, this selectivity is likely to be evident in the excited and orgasmic masturbation that is often practiced by otherwise frigid women.

Freud (1910b; 1912a, p. 183) observed the following of the restricted sexual activity of the selectively impotent man: "It is capricious, easily disturbed, often not properly carried out, and not accompanied by much pleasure." The restricted sexuality of the selectively frigid woman shows the same features.

Through Freud's investigations and those of generations of analysts after him, it has been established that a multitude of factors must be taken into account before an explanation of individual cases of impotence and frigidity can be claimed. There is no one, simple, causal explanation for it and no one, simple account of the reasons for it. Indeed, it may be said that there is no significant aspect of personal development and existence that cannot sometimes figure as a condition of, or reason for, these disturbances. Foremost among the factors emphasized by Freud is the unconsciously maintained incestuous significance of the sex act. In cases of impotence and frigidity this significance is enlarged, unduly threatening, and dealt with by splitting the person's affectionate and erotic feelings and directing only the latter toward "degraded" or otherwise unsuitable persons. For the man, unconsciously, there is also the interfering influence of the castration anxiety associated with his oedipal rivalry with his father. For the woman, there is in addition the unconsciously imagined shameful fact of her castration, her mixture of longing and bitterness with respect to her frustrated wishes to bear her father's children, and her envious, appropriative, or destructive attitude toward her partner's penis.

Further, the disturbing influence of exaggerated, unconsciously maintained homosexual attachment to the parent of the same sex—the inverse or negative Oedipus complex—is often carried into heterosexual relations, rendering them threatening and unsatisfactory on that count, too. Disruption may stem as well from special concerns with the so-called voyeuristic and exhibitionistic aspects of sexual intimacy. These aspects usually originate in infantile observations or imaginings of the primal scene, that is, the parental coupling. They are likely to involve fear of, and shame at, exposing or viewing sexual excitement and confronting the imagined damage and threatening potential of the female genitalia.

Today psychoanalysts realize more than ever that, in addition to oedipal and genital influences, *preoedipal* or *pregenital* influences also figure significantly in the heterosexual life of a man or a woman. To the extent that the preoedipal is a disturbing factor (it need not be so), a person may, for example, unconsciously view the sex act as devouring and persecutory or excrementally dirty and explosively destructive. Disruption may stem from the imagined unacceptable requisites of cruelty and suffering in sexual activity. The sexual disturbance may then serve to protect the partner and stave off guilt. Confusion associated with early and unstable phases of the differentiation of the self (or ego) from others in the environment may be the occasion of a person's greatly fearing that he or she will lose both the self and the world through increasing intimacy, mounting sexual excitement, and orgasm.

From one case to the next, analysts attribute different degrees of importance to these and other, usually unconsciously operative factors. In some cases, some of these factors may be present with no obvious disruption of sexual performance and no dissatisfaction. In fact, often it is found that for certain people, some of the frequently disruptive factors are necessary features of sexual performance and satisfaction. In some instances of this kind, such as those involving staged cruelty and suffering, analysts speak of perversions. Freud numbered these so-called perverse features among the many "conditions for loving," grouping them thereby with the splitting of feelings and persons that I mentioned earlier. In these instances, analysts are likely to have occasion to interpret enactments of impotence and frigidity in areas of life other than the directly sexual. However, it is more often the case that these "perverse" features retain the status only of unconsciously elaborated and repudiated fantasies, and that they act as disturbers of the sexual peace rather than as overt "conditions for loving"; simultaneously, they may disturb the peace of working and conducting other aspects of a person's life. In many cases an analyst's weaving a web of interpretation of these consciously repudiated perverse fantasies goes a long way toward reducing or eliminating both direct impotence and frigidity and displaced or symbolic versions of them in work and elsewhere, particularly as they get to be enacted in the transference.

Before concluding this introductory survey, I must mention two more sets of common observations. First, many men and women carry through the sexual act on the strength of conscious fantasies they construct during its performance. Typically these fantasies involve someone other than the actual partner and sometimes they exclude the self as well, or instead. Also, these fantasies often represent relations that are not copulatory and may not even be sexual by ordinary standards; for example, threatening or adventurous interactions or situations may serve the purpose. And the fantasy during heterosexual activity may be homosexual. Recourse to fantasy as a condition for sexual loving is so common that I hesitate to speak of it as merely disguising impotence or frigidity. But in psychoanalysis, the hypothetical ideal has usually been total involvement in the immediate personal relationship—that is, in the actual erotic and affectionate interactions through which it is manifest. This is what psychoanalysts mean by *geniality*. With reference to the ideal of genitality, therefore, intercourse based on conscious fantasies falls closer to masturbation than to loving sexual relations, and so it may mask impotence and frigidity of considerable proportions. Also short of the ideal are the many instances of sexual intercourse that are simply not very satisfying; it is not unusual for men and women to feel pent up and to masturbate not long after "completing" these sex acts, as if they must meet their conditions for loving in the isolation of fantasy after the act rather than in the physical closeness during it.

The second addendum is this: On close analysis it often emerges that the actions of a person's partner have been playing a key role in the person's own impotence or frigidity. What has been getting in the way may be, for example, some subtly conveyed lack of ardor or tenderness or some aversion or rage. But analysts will not be content to stop asking questions once a strong case has been made for the existence of this kind of disturbing factor. Analysts will go on to try to understand why the analysand has chosen and stayed with that kind of sexual partner or why he or she has refrained from taking steps to improve the situation, or why the designated patient has not even noticed consciously the partner's provocation.

Relationships of this kind are unconsciously imbued with meaning of many kinds; typically they serve certain purposes rather than being plain bad luck. To the extent that this is so, the actions of the sexual partner imply choices of a person's own. As a rule, it takes two to make a chronic sexual problem. However, what will be decisive finally is not the partner's overt behavior in itself, but the way it fits and confirms the analysand's unconsciously maintained infantile imagoes, such as that of the abandoning mother or prohibiting father. In this light, the relational sexual problem gets to be seen as a route to what is centrally and anciently conflictual for the individual; and following that route, with the invaluable help of transference analysis, will contribute to alleviating that problem, for it will rest on a frank reconsideration of the person's lifelong human predicaments rather than on the technological adjustments of his or her sexual conduct that may be effected by sex counseling.

PHALLOCENTRIC NARRATIVES OF SEXUAL PERFORMANCE

The extended connotations of the words *impotence* and *frigidity* make it clear that a masculinist conception of heterosexuality is built into our thinking about heterosexual activity. "Impotence" means lacking in strength, force, drive, or power; it is a word specifically suited to describing a person as agent. "Frigidity" means extreme coldness; it is a word specifically suited for describing a milieu. Together, the words entail the proposition that in sexual relations a man is acting in a milieu. It is implied that there is only one agent. Although a milieu may be said to have effects, it cannot be said to act. Only people act. It follows from this pair of designations that the woman is by nature an inactive or passive object: If frigid, she is an unsuitable object; if ardent, she is a suitable object. Strength, force, drive, and power are not for her; nor are intent, initiative, interaction, and control. And in the same vein, the properties of milieu are held to be alien to the man's nature. The words lay down a host of potential storylines, all of them imbued with phallocentrism.

Of the various ways open to me to tell this phallocentric tale, I have chosen to make extensive use of the figure-ground terminology of perceptual organization. According to the conventional terminology for sexual performances, the man—especially his penis—is the figure in the sexual act; the woman—especially her vagina—is the ground. In figure-ground relationships, it is the ground that sets off the figure and never the other way around. The figure imparts some properties to the ground; visually a gray ground becomes whiter if it contains a very dark figure and becomes blacker if it contains a very light figure. It is also possible to say that the ground imparts some properties to the figure; for instance, a dark ground makes a light figure look whiter and a light ground makes a light figure look darker. Although reciprocal influences are exerted by figure and ground, this reciprocity does not obviate the fact that one is figure and the other ground.

According to the master narrative established by the words *impotence* and *frigidity*, a man may arouse a woman sexually without thereby establishing her as a figure in the sexual act and certainly not as *the* figure of the act. Instead, he will have changed the temperature of his milieu, and it will be a change that sets him off all the more as figure through his enhanced and confirmed potency. In clinical work it is often observed that a man's anxiously striving to bring his partner to orgasm has less to do with concern for her as a person and more with self-centered confirmation of his being a potent figure or agent acting on an object. Sometimes men use impregnation for the same kind of self-reassurance.

The figure has definition, boundaries, articulation, structure, prominence, and impact; it is that which is seen as such; it is what is looked at; it shows itself by standing out; it is remembered. The ground or milieu is amorphous, unbounded, unarticulated, unstructured; it is seen only through what it does for or to the figure; it is necessary for the sake of something else; it is modest, recessive, anonymous, set back or behind; it is not remembered, at least not for itself. Thinking along similar lines, Virginia Woolf likened the woman to the flattering mirror that shows off the man. From the standpoint of writing, the woman is the page on which the man writes his story of power. Thus, the phallocentric tale of what it is woman's nature to be and what she ought to be, if she is to be feminine, corresponds closely to the correlated terms *milieu, object,* and *ground.*

This sexist idea is shared by the mass of men and women, and it covers much of the conventional role of motherhood as well. Typically, male chauvinism or phallocentrism is the condition of both sexes, even if not equally so in every respect. When I say *sexist,* therefore, I am not referring only to men; nor am I referring only to its crudest forms. Elsewhere (see chapter 4), I have tried to show how sexist thinking influenced for the worse Freud's formulation of his otherwise profound, though partial, insights into the psychology of women.

The ground receives and incorporates the figure; the figure intrusively occupies the ground. The woman receives the man who intrudes into her. As the child is told, Daddy plants the seed in Mommy. The man has sexual drive; the woman sexual appetite. Consequently, the woman who assumes the prerogatives of the figure, as conventionally described, can expect to be viewed by others as aggressively masculine or as hostile to men or competitive with them. In psychoanalytic work, we often observe that, unconsciously and *in part*, a woman of this sort *is* attempting to depose the ruling man and be a man herself and, more specifically, to acquire symbolically a penis for herself by taking it away from the man. One familiar clinical instance of seizing the conventional male prerogative is encountered in the sexually tantalizing, exhibitionistic but frigid woman who, unconsciously and totally, equates her body and its sexual prominence and influence with the phallus. For her, the male's arousal is ground to her figure.

FANTASIES OF THE VAGINA DENTATA AND THE PHALLUS AS BREAST

The fantasy, shared by men and women alike, of the vagina dentata—the mutilating, castrating, devouring vaginal mouth—is frequently found to play a major part in impotence and frigidity. In the man's case, the fantasy of being unmanned by this vagina is in large part a way of wishfully projecting what he wishes: to turn into a woman, *for men envy women, too*. In the fantasy, the frightening female organ will do to him what he secretly wishes to bring about, even while fearing that outcome. Alternatively, the vagina dentata fantasy may be the man's way of regressively retreating to the imagined ultimate milieu: the mother's womb or the postnatal, pregenital configuration of the mother's holding arms and lap, nourishing breast, and smiling face. By such imaginings, the man hopes to merge into the ground and become one with the passive object. Thereby he will exist only through or in an indefinite other; no longer will he be required to be a person in his own right or to deal with another figure in its own right. Never again will he be alone. Perhaps thereby he will also avoid that brute annihilation of the woman as person that he unconsciously believes to be the consequence of his having to be a rapacious figure in the sexual relationship.

On the woman's part, the vagina dentata fantasy is a typical correlate of the unconsciously maintained fantasy that she has been wronged and humiliated by having been denied a penis or by having had it taken away from her, and of her having accordingly adopted an envious, rivalrous, castrating attitude toward the phallic, rapacious man. Implied in this retaliatory orientation is her wishing to become, or become once again, an assertive figure or agent. Analysts differ among themselves in how they rank order penis and power. As an assertive figure, the woman will have definition, structure, visibility, power; she will count as a person. But at the same time, in one of those unconsciously conflictual or paradoxical actions, her dentalization of the vagina may well also imply a regressive movement, specifically a returning to the role of the biting infant at the breast.

The breast enters the fantasy in this way: Psychoanalysts have defined a widespread, if not universal, fantasy in which, unconsciously, penis and breast are equated; and correlatively, semen and milk. These equations are especially salient in the analyses of those people who have centered their sexual interest in fellatio fantasies and practices, no matter whether they have done so in an overexcited, repulsed, or paralyzed fashion. Much gagging and vomiting of psychological origin can be attributed in part to a person's engaging in these fantasies conflictually and unconsciously.

This equation of breast and penis implies that the shadow of the mother has fallen on the penis and on the man whose organ it is; accordingly, the sexual act is, unconsciously, oral as well as genital. The equation of breast and penis undercuts the idea that sexism and phallocentrism are synonymous, for the bodily presence or absence of the penis as penis is now only one part of the story. Psychoanalysts would generally agree that the breast-penis equation is a lasting monument to the influence of the mother who necessarily both feeds and deprives. For this reason, figure-ground relations may be said to start at the breast and to remain there to a considerable extent. The denial of this pregenital substratum serves the defensive needs of both sexes, and in my opinion it has also served the defensive and conformist needs of many psychoanalysts of both sexes. I shall return to this point shortly.

In one of his last major contributions to the topic of femininity, Freud (1933) finally acknowledged the enduring primacy of this maternal figure in the lives of women. However, he did so only in a limited context: He ascribed many of the difficulties women have with their husbands to their importing into the marital relationships unresolved problems with their mothers; not just that they are identified with their troubled mothers, but that they unconsciously set their husbands up as unsatisfactory mothers. They establish maternal transferences to their husbands. Had Freud taken a more general view of the matter, he might have gone on to emphasize the positive potential of this same transference. A woman can, and often does, find a good mother as well as a good man and father in her husband, and to that extent has a richer and more gratifying relationship with him. Carrying this narrative line a step further, we may say that a man's integrated and balanced identification with some kind of good-mother image contributes to the warmth, generosity, and stability of his heterosexual relationships; the intent of this kind of female identi-fication in a man is not primarily self-castration.

Sexism, whether blatant or unconsciously insidious, denies these insights and opportunities to men and women. Even more so does it deny the positive paternal potential in a woman's being the figure in relation to a man. There is little or no reference to this factor in the psychoanalytic literature. Most analysts seem to be content to stop at the idea of the phallic woman as *woman;* they view that imagined fig-ure primarily in relation to castration anxiety; they dwell on people's unconsciously needing to reassure themselves that there is no anatom-ical difference between the sexes and thus no imagined castration to fear and no irreparable genital damage or deprivation to come to terms with. Useful as this view is in many cases, it is too narrow in that it does not encompass the idea that the phallic woman also contains the fantasized and perceived paternal potency, authority, and person-hood. Insofar as a woman's activity and authority is unconsciously por-trayed as masculine or phallic, it implies the father's potency in action. In relation to this potency, a man may become unconsciously passive, objectified, feminized, but he just as well may be paternally supported in being manly. For the man, both are consummations devoutly to be wished for as well as feared.

THE SUBJUGATION OF THE MOTHER

The significance of the infantile fantasies of the phallic and pater-nal mother and the vagina dentata cannot be overestimated in consid-ering impotence and frigidity. Of equal importance is the mutual envy that exists between the sexes with its correlated wishing for and fear-ing the imagined castrated status. These contradictory representations and orientations pervade unconscious fantasizing. But the earliest, pregenital phase of psychological development involves other great problems that contribute to the personal and social issues with which we are here concerned. One particularly important issue is the diffi-cult, stressful, and unstable differentiation of oneself as an active fig-ure—a person—in relation to the caretaking and terribly powerful

maternal figure. Through reconstructive analysis of dreams and transferences, which is paralleled by psychoanalytic child observation, it
appears that the young child imagines loss of individuation to be a
kind of devouring engulfment or annihilation that is perpetrated
either by the mother or on the mother. It is a fantasy that, paradoxi-
cally, is experienced both excitedly and with shuddering horror—as is
the castration fantasy.

This archaically conceived struggle for and against individuation
seems to remain a lifelong project. Although some people continue
this struggle more conspicuously, erratically, and anxiously than others, the fact of the struggle must be taken into account in any effort to
understand problems of gender identification and its role in relations
between the sexes.

In the case of girls there is the later problem—the first to have been
securely established in psychoanalytic interpretation—of the struggle
they carry on anxiously and guiltily against their rivalrous oedipal
identification with the mother; this is the identification by means of
which a girl hopes, unconsciously—though often consciously—to take
the mother's place with the father. This later problem appears differently in the case of the boy. For him it is necessary to devalue the oedipal mother as one way of moderating his desiring to win her and his
fearing that he will be inadequate to the task of winning her or satisfying her sexually. For the girl and boy alike, and both preoedipally and
oedipally, the mother, far from being the ground or the passive object,
emerges experientially as a gigantic figure to contend with and come
to terms with. Speaking of the problems of the female writer in *A
Room of One's Own,* Virginia Woolf (1924) recognized this phenomenon when she said, "A woman writing thinks back through her
mothers." She would not have been wrong to say this of men, too, and
not only when writing, for mothers continue to influence eating,
dressing, loving, giving lectures, and so forth.

One of the important vantage points for viewing analytic data, then,
is the one that looks squarely at the developing person's struggle for
individuation and for an independent sense of adequacy, wholeness,
safety, power, and worth. In this struggle, it seems to the child that the
imposing figure of the mother, which is the prime representative of
womanhood, must be cut down or cut up in order to be subdued or
made manageable. She must be rejected, derogated, set apart, or consciously ignored. Here then is a set of powerful, unconsciously maintained reasons why, later on, both men and women are ready to
participate in the socially reinforced discrimination against women, or
at least to assent to it passively. For the same reasons, however, this fig-

ure must also be protected or repaired with special care—often by idealization, often by the person's own enslavement.

Critics of our sexist society find much to support their position in the fact that many or most mothers have more or less accommodated themselves to this state of affairs. These are women who, consciously, have given up aspirations of their own other than serving as a favorable ground or flattering mirrors for their husbands and children; they have neglected their own competences and potentialities of other sorts; they are disillusioned and discouraging figures who depend for self-esteem on defensive idealizations of them and enslavement to them. Today, many thoughtful young women scorn their conventionally sexist mothers and women of their sort. They regard them as wives who have declined into domesticity. They are disturbed, unconsciously even more than consciously, by their inevitable and lasting identification with these mothers. Although they seek desperately to escape, deny, or cancel out this identification, they make the effort so totally that they are bound to fail, achieving rather a radical discontinuity in their sense of themselves. Moreover, they cannot grasp the full meaning of that attempt at disidentification unless they take into account the problems, dating from infancy, of individuating from the archaic mother-figure and establishing a two-person relationship with her. They must also take into account the problems posed by the oedipal mother imago and the disillusioning mother imago of later phases of psychosexual development, and additionally they must see what they have gained by their identifications with her and what they can and do still value.

Thus, even though a demoralizing figure, the mother is still maintained as a forceful presence in the woman's own life. She is a figure to be reckoned with in her subjective inner world. The subjugation of women, in which women play a part that is more complex than that assigned in simple feminist theories of social reinforcement for male advantage, is also the subjugation of the powerful mother-figure of childhood. Unconsciously, it can get to seem that a woman's (a man's, too) life depends on that subjugation and the social world seems organized to lend its support to that project. Reparatively, that subjugation, of the mother-figure is given the appearance of adoration.

It is not sexist, as some radical feminists claim, to spell out, and work with, these insights into the relations between the sexes. It is sexist to maintain that the disruptive dramatization and proliferation of these familiar fantasies are altogether unmodifiable, that is, are simply and totally built into human development and have nothing to do with a social reality that encourages and reinforces them in countless ways and does so also for male advantage. It is sexist to think that a girl would naturally, totally, and permanently feel inferior and envious simply because she lacks a penis. It is sexist to say that nothing can be done about the reinforcing social reality, and even more so to assert that nothing should be done about it. Those feminists who have been making the developmental and social distinctions I am making—and there are some—are, I think, in a better position to attack both the societal and the therapeutic problems, for they have a more intimate knowledge of the enemy, within and without.

THE WHOLE PERSON

Developing the narrative further, we must go on to consider next what it means to be a whole person. From the standpoint of narrative action, what makes a person whole? I am referring now to an ideal definition, recognizing that in life and at best we approximate our ideals only intermittently. One of the fruits of effective personal psychoanalysis is that the analysand affirms this ideal and on the average lives closer to it than before the analysis.

A whole person is the one who acts, the agent. A whole person acts knowingly without profound reservations about the fact of acting, and so acts with presence and personal authority and without anxiously introducing serious disclaimers—such as the claim of being passively moved by natural forces, by the mind, or by a split-off self. In sexual relations, as elsewhere, a whole person acts the role of agent while refusing to deny personhood to the sexual partner, and accepts it as a psychological fact of life that *there cannot be only one whole person in the relationship*. In contrast, those who engage in extreme fantasies of omnipotence, such as paranoiac patients, implicitly sacrifice their own personal wholeness while denying that wholeness for others. Those who are thoroughly egocentric make the same double-barreled assault on self and other.

Guaranteeing the personal wholeness of others entails a readiness on a person's own part to serve on numerous occasions as object, ground, or milieu in relation to them, for they, too, must be given scope to exercise and confirm *their* personal agency and wholeness. A good conversation exemplifes what I am referring to: Can there be good conversation with only one person communicating in words, sounds, and gestures? Here we encounter the phenomenon of the *reversible* figure-ground relationship (the Necker cube, the Rubin vase/two profiles, and so on), and we come to the problem of changing the terms in which we understand the relations between the sexes.

We know that adamant rebellion does not change the terms of a problem with authority; the terms remain the same except that they have now a minus sign placed before them. Nor does a rigid role reversal change the terms of a problem. The miser who becomes a spendthrift, the mouse who becomes a lion, the homosexual woman who acts more like the stereotypical man than most men and the homosexual man who acts more like the stereotypical woman than most women: None of these has changed the terms of the problem; each is attempting to achieve what has been called in psychoanalytic discussion a change of content without a change of structure. A flip-flop is only a change of content; it accepts the structure of things as they are. Money, majesty, or macho remain the important structuring factors. Analysts have learned to be wary of such changes when, as often happens, they observe analysands abruptly and dramatically reversing their characteristic patterns of manifest action.

Traditionally, a fundamental change of the terms in which a problem is defined has been called a structural change. With regard to sexism, however, the change of terms that is called for is not limited simply to changing by conscious decision that which is to be designated *masculine* and *feminine* or *active* and *passive;* nor is it limited to consciously reallocating the prerogatives of the two sexes. Changes in both of these respects, though important and possible, depend for their force on a necessary and consequential change in the idea of a whole person who can enter into reversible figure-ground relations with others as co-agents.

A whole person allows the reversibility, in a relatively conflict-free fashion. He or she refrains from insisting on being only agent or object, only figure or ground, only active or passive, or only masculine or feminine, as conventionally defined. The reversibility is itself a form of action in that both refraining and allowing are actions. A whole person is neither threatened by reversibility nor incapable of enjoying either position in a relationship. The mutuality or reversibility of being a person not only matters more to a whole person than conventional ascriptions of masculine-feminine and active-passive; to a considerable extent, adopting the idea of persons-in-relation renders the other ideas unwelcome interferences in the business of living. Sometimes the reversibility includes projecting one or the other side of a person's bisexuality into the partner and enjoying it there: the man projecting what he regards as his feminine side or his masculine side; the woman, the same.

It must also be remarked that the reversibility, once established securely, no longer entails the threat or experience of loss of personhood. The reversible figure-ground model implies different and concurrent modes of agency; the tension between the alternating figures is essential to the phenomenon.

None of what I am saying discounts differences in degree and style of reversibility; for to state an ideal is not to prescribe absolute uniformity in its realization. To those who would cry *"Vive la différence!"* thinking of the pleasures of heterosexuality, I can only point out that nothing in my argument minimizes the different and complementary conformations, roles, and pleasure possibilities of male and female bodies; if anything, my argument should go some way toward enhancing the possibilities of loving unanxiously, unconflictedly, inventively, and without drastic confusion of stereotyped roles.

Consider, for example, the burden of always being pleasing, which weighs on most women in our sexist world and contributes to their masochistic and depressive proclivities. This burden of being first and foremost a reassuring milieu can be lifted and replaced by the pleasurable option, open to both sexes, of pleasing others of either sex—and of displeasing them, too, especially but not necessarily when it is in a good cause. A change of this sort—not a change to unmitigated hostility—is difficult to achieve; among other things, it means coming to terms with the incorporated, terribly powerful mother of infancy and of the oedipal period, the figure who ordinarily is felt to be hidden behind the ready smile and yielding empathy and who, it is hoped, is pacified and controlled thereby. Psychoanalysis facilitates this change while affirming that infantile tensions are never overcome entirely and that they increase their influence at times of crisis.

"GOOD," "BAD," "CAN," AND "CAN'T"

Some other changes in the terms of the problems of sexuality and sexism that can be accomplished through psychoanalysis concern narratives of the good and the bad, the innocent and the guilty, the safe and the dangerous; under a different and crucial aspect, these changes concern narratives of success and failure. The proper understanding of these changes depends on narratives of personal relations that do not obscure the range of agency or action.

Modification of the idea of the good and the bad, the innocent and the guilty, and the safe and the dangerous can for the most part be subsumed under the traditional psychoanalytic heading of modification of the superego. This modification is said to relieve the ego of the pressure to be as defensive as it may get to be in relation to the varieties of sexual desiring and other action. This is a familiar and crucially important chapter of psychoanalysis and will not be summarized here.

Suffice it to say that the analysand may come to accept it as an inescapable part of being a whole person that a person continues to be, in some measure, an orally receptive and biting baby, an anally sensuous and dirty baby, and a bisexually incestuous young child who is identified with both parents and desires each of them erotically. Through analysis, these continuities may get to be seen as the inescapable heritage of growing up human, which means developing into a person in the context of a family and a society composed of men and women. It also means growing up with a male or female body that has its own pleasure possibilities and vulnerabilities; moreover, it means reclaiming one's own body from the internalized parental figures, making it one's own by asserting the right to decide on its uses in sexual relationships, and enjoying the pregenital residues in lovemaking. This set of modifications typically has the effect of reducing the unconsciously maintained dominance of many of the infantile carryovers that have been most disturbing in a person's relations with a partner. These carryovers have remained disturbing because they are the ones that have been most anxiously, guiltily, and uncompromisingly fragmented and repudiated and so have never been mastered, integrated, and put to good use.

As superego condemnation diminishes, what once could only be desperate adventures, engaged in surreptitiously or in fantasy or else sternly prohibited, now become possibilities of play. The sexual act as a whole becomes a possibility of play. The claim that this is so is in no way incompatible with the claim that sexual loving is also a possibility of intimacy of the most serious kind. Play and seriousness are themselves freed from the trap of either/or judgments. These either/or judgments bear the mark of a person's own archaic, unconsciously enforced superego categories. As Freud noted (1921), this type of moralistic enforcement is frequently increased in scope and severity upon marrying and having children, for these are transitional actions in connection with which people often consolidate further their identifications with the conventionally prohibiting parental imagoes. If these imagoes are particularly forbidding, problems of impotence and frigidity may increase from then on, and so may sexist attitudes. Advancing into middle age is, I would say, another transition that favors shifts toward sexual conservatism.

Changing the narratives of success and failure at sex—the storylines of making it or not making it—comes under another aspect than does modification of superego identifications. What it requires is a new appreciation that, in the most fundamental psychological sense, impotence and frigidity are not failures at all. Here we arrive at the importance of correcting, by analytic working through, presuppositions that we are dealing not with actions but with abilities, capacities, or achievements—with cans and can'ts. Like other symptoms, impotence and frigidity are more correctly and profitably retold interpretively as complex actions corresponding to complex psychological situations. Even though their final manifestations are physical and physiological states of muscular, circulatory, and secretory unpreparedness for the complex sex act, these manifestations are appropriate features of the intentional actions and situations they unconsciously imply. They are not happenings—events to be suffered passively: So psychoanalysis teaches or tells in its narratives of sexual behavior; so it interprets to the analysands the problems of impotence and frigidity

To put what I mean concretely: If, for example, unconsciously, one partner in a marital sex act is fleeing a scene of incestuous sexuality, that person is neither in a marital sexual situation nor moving more deeply into it, nor is anything happening to a passive victim; unconsciously, that person is fleeing. Similarly, if, unconsciously, one partner in a sex act is tightening up mentally and muscularly in order to avoid an orgasmic anal explosion, an imagined eventuality that will make a mess or be destructive and in either case threaten loss of love and painful shame, that person is not to any appreciable degree interacting erotically and genitally with another person, nor is that person an unfortunate passive object; unconsciously, that person is holding in. And if, to give one more example, a man is doing all he can not to show himself off or see the other, owing to the still influential prohibitions or shame connected with infantile exhibitionism and voyeurism, then he is hiding his body and his excitement, or he is blinding himself or imaginally turning his back on his lover, and in either case hardly qualifying as a lover himself; far from finding himself out of it, he is unconsciously making sure to be out of it.

Whatever the explanation, it is psychoanalytically wrong to tell it as a story of failure. In the psychoanalytic narrative, the impotent or frigid person is doing exactly what is right to do under the unconsciously defined, fantasized circumstances that count the most at that moment. When those circumstances are sufficiently understood, no plausible alternative account is available. The storyline of failure makes sense only with respect to some inaccurate *conscious* idea of what kind of situation a person is in and what he or she wishes to do in it. That limited conscious idea precludes insightful change.

In contrast, the implicit or explicit action narrative makes insightful change possible: change, not success; change through recasting the fundamental terms of the problem. Accomplishing any such change in the social realm will require overcoming or mitigating the societal seduction of boys into uneasy representatives of pure masculine force and of girls into demoralized representatives of pure feminine milieu. What is required is a social psychological theory of the narrative seduction of children. That theory would, however, have to take account of what clinical psychoanalysis and child observation have established: the eagerness and the frightened acquiescence with which children participate in these seductions owing to the thrilling and terrifying features of their infantile fantasy life. In the light of this new, complementary seduction theory, we may hope to reclaim many disclaimed sexual actions and thereby to help people be whole, responsible, reciprocally related persons. Although that kind of recla- mation work might in time do a lot more than enhance pleasurable, consummated sexual relations, it can at present help diminish much needless sexual frustration and humiliation.

CHAPTER 6

The Idealization of Unhappiness and the Pursuit of Failure

PSYCHIC suffering is more than the motive for analytic therapy. It is the problem for the therapy as well, in that the analysand has probably established psychic suffering as a fixed and necessary feature of his or her mode of living. Upon analysis, entrenched suffering often turns out to be, unconsciously, a compromise formation with multiple and contradictory constituents, meanings, or functions.

Usually discussed as masochism, entrenched suffering must in each case be analyzed in terms of themes or storylines. These themes are more particular than would be suggested by the abstract term *masochism*. These particular themes or storylines serve as organizers of interpretations. Inevitably, more than one such organizer must be applied to any one analysand's material. Few of these organizers are mutually exclusive. In the present context, they include (in traditional terms) an extravagant ego ideal with respect to which the self must always fall short; a severe superego with respect to which every pleasure must be paid for with painful guilt and self-destructiveness; and the sexualization of suffering itself, that is, suffering as what Freud (1915c) called a "precondition for loving."

In this chapter I propose two organizing themes or storylines of entrenched suffering: the pursuit of failure and the idealization of unhappiness. As well as making some general clinical remarks, I offer brief and partial case summaries that illustrate some of the major meanings of, or functions served by, failure and unhappiness. Finally, I remark on what appears to me to be a relative difference between the sexes with respect to the pursuit of failure and the idealization of unhappiness. In this connection I take up some implied fundamental problems in the theory and the psychoanalytic interpretation of unconscious mental processes.

GENERAL CLINICAL REMARKS

Typically, those who suffer from repetitive failure and chronic unhappiness present themselves dismally as afflicted or victimized. Upon analysis, however, the reported failures prove to have been pursued at least as much as they have been the result of inescapable adversity. Similarly, the unhappiness frequently proves to have been self-inflicted at least as much as it has been an expression of the inescapable miseries of everyday life. It is the unconsciously arranged and perpetuated portions of psychic suffering that the analyst should clarify and modify through interpretation. Freud (1920a) made essentially this point in his discussion of the fate neuroses.

Certainly our analysands do not simply bring all their unhappiness on themselves. But even when the analyst makes due allowance for sheer adversity, of which there is usually more than enough in everyone's life, there is ample room for him or her to show neurotic analysands not only that they are being inappropriately self-blaming for this adversity but are adding to the adversity itself, thereby increasing the failure and unhappiness being reported. It is a distinguishing feature of psychoanalytic work that emphasis is placed on unconscious activity of this sort. This feature of the work is actualized through the analyst's paying close attention to psychic reality, particularly as it is discernible in the here and now of transference and defense. In this context, "psychic reality" refers to the private, largely unconsciously maintained, infantile meanings of success and failure and of happiness and unhappiness. The term also refers to the way in which the analysand repetitiously uses these archaic meanings to construct current painful experience. Experience is always to be regarded as constructed rather than simply introspected. Transference and defense demonstrate the construction of experience in the analytic situation.

THE PURSUIT OF FAILURE

Freud (1916) approached some major aspects of the pursuit of failure under the heading "Those wrecked by success." That the phenomena to which Freud referred are widespread may be asserted all the more confidently if we take into account the wreckage associated with the mere anticipation of success and also if we allow that being wrecked may be a matter of degree, as in the case of neurotic mediocrity. Freud also noted that commonly, though usually unconsciously, analysands fear "getting well" as a form of success, that is, success as analysands. Consequently, we may recognize that what Freud (1923a) called the negative therapeutic reaction, which in varying degrees also bedevils analytic work, is a variant of being wrecked by analytic success or the prospect thereof.

In his explanations, Freud typically emphasized the unconscious oedipal triumph signified by worldly success and the guilty self-punishment for this triumph that is signified by the ensuing personal and occupational wreckage. However, the pursuit of failure is far more complex than would be suggested by Freud's typical focus on oedipal dynamics, even though we can only be impressed by the interpretive success of that focus throughout the history of psychoanalysis.

Strictly speaking, the characterization of certain people as being wrecked by success is made descriptively; that is, it is made from the standpoint of the outside observer rather than from the standpoint of the subject's own psychic reality. Looking on as outside observers, we are limited to considering dramatic overt instances, such as the depression that follows on the heels of a long-desired promotion or the panic that follows on the consummation of a long-desired love relationship. Descriptively, the subject appears to be a passive victim of achievement. In contrast, working within psychic reality, analysts seek to establish in each instance just what constitutes success and just what constitutes being wrecked by it. The individual, subjective, mostly unconsciously maintained conceptions of success and failure are not always what convention or common sense would lead us to expect.

This divergence from commonsense expectation is not surprising once we take into account that, as a rule, people are more or less unconsciously conflicted with respect to their goals in life. Due to this conflict, what is success from the point of view of one set of aims is failure from the point of view of other aims that conflict with them. Freud (1900, p. 604) established this principle in another connection, that of pleasure, when he observed that what is pleasurable for one psychical system may be painful for another. In the terms of the structural theory he developed later on (1923a), he had in mind particularly those instances in which id gratification conflicts with the ego's defensive and adaptive aims and the superego's archaic moral aims. Thus, analysts view symptom formation, for example, as combining pleasure and pain as well as success and failure. In this perspective, a subject cannot be a passive victim of achievement; unconsciously, the subject has made failure a project and frequently has become ingenious in achieving it. As one analysand once said, after having crystallized insight into his artful and unrelenting pursuit of failure, "If I put ten percent of this energy into really succeeding, there is nothing I could not achieve."

Failure as well as success must be looked at in the same complex and superficially paradoxical way. From the standpoint of psychic reality rather than conventional reality, failure may represent more than painful defeat or punishment. For example, failure may also represent the triumphant fulfillment of archaic moral aims in opposition to infantile libidinal aims; similarly, it may represent the triumphant fulfillment of a person's ego aims of reducing psychic pain to a minimum by withdrawing from situations of worldly success that threaten to bring on intolerable anxiety or guilt. Consequently, analysts must keep on asking: What is the failure in success? and What is the success in failure? It was in this vein that Theodore Reik (1941) emphasized the concept of victory through defeat in his analysis of masochism.

I have organized my case examples of the pursuit of failure largely around pathological formation of the ego ideal, as the ego ideal is an essential component of character structure. Success and failure cannot be discussed psychoanalytically without considering it. However, for reasons advanced and developed elsewhere (Sandler, Holder, and Meers, 1963; Schafer, 1967), I prefer to speak of the ideal self rather than the ego ideal. Traditionally, the ego ideal has been tied too closely to superego theory, and so it does not adequately take into account the primitive wishful, defensive, and adaptive aspects of ideal formation along with its archaic moral aspects—that is, its id and ego aspects along with its superego aspects. It is easier to take account of antisocial, utilitarian, or primitively wishful ideals when working with the concept of ideal self. I use that term to refer to a guideline for activity rather than to denote an active force or agency in the mind.

Identification, too, must be seen as central to the development of the ideal self, provided that we take into account the fantastic, infantile elaboration of the idea of the person with whom the child is identifying. Ideals are often based on identifications with figures who, in conventional terms, are far from moral or well sublimated.

Case Example

Consider a young man whose ideal self features being an under-achiever. That underachievement was his ideal was established only after analytic exploration of his trials and tribulations in school, at work, and in the analysis. In his psychic reality, to be an underachiever was to conform to the role his family appeared to have assigned to him early in his life. This role warded off envy and disparagement by his siblings; it also earned parental love in the form of his father's compassionate help when, but only when, the boy was in trouble. Typically, feelings of being a "good kid" were associated with lack of achievement and steady self-disparagement. His self-esteem rode on his being an underachiever. Thus, disturbed formation of his ideal self had to be counted as a major variable in his repetitive pursuit of failure. Erikson (1956) discussed similar phenomena in terms of negative identity formation.

To present this young man's problem as one of a disturbed ideal self is not to ignore the castrating oedipal defeat that was entailed by his meeting negative ideals. Nor is it to ignore his conflictedness with respect to the negative features of his ideal self, for it also became obvious that he had not entirely renounced his positive oedipal strivings and other, more positive ideals associated with them. In self-contradiction, he also rebelled against the negative ideals he maintained unconsciously; however, owing to the painfulness of acting otherwise than self-destructively, he could not sustain his rebellion. In his analytic sessions, for example, he could hardly finish a sentence in which he said something that was even slightly positive about himself; he had to interrupt with self-criticism.

Thus, for this young man, failure was also a success of a kind, while being a success was also a failure. In his transference, he mostly worked energetically to invite the analyst's compassionate help by presenting himself as stupid, ineffectual, and desperate. And while consciously he professed to be ashamed of himself for his inadequacies, it developed over the course of the analysis that, unconsciously, he was being a "good kid," was feeling like one, and was expecting the analyst to be pleased with his failures and his need for help.

Case Example

In another instance, one of the dominant ideas of success was based on the analysand's having unconsciously identified with an asocial and antisocial gambling father, a man who had had more than his share of worldly success and worldly failure. The son felt most alive and manly when he was working alone, recklessly and unnecessarily at the brink of failure. He felt most feminine and castrated when he had to work within a group and when he was a loser. Being an isolated loser was a position he unconsciously desired and feared simultaneously.

Case Example

A third young man's pursuit of failure served unconsciously to protect the self-esteem of his apparently weak, unsuccessful father. But this unconsciously repetitive activity also served other important functions: In one way, it amounted to rebellion against his father's demands on him for a conformist type of dedication to success; in another way, it amounted to compliance with his family's general tendency to romanticize emotional distress. Emotional distress was a condition of being interesting, and the setting of this condition appeared to be based on the powerful sadomasochistic pattern of family interaction. Thus, for him, failure was a way of being sadistically and masochistically lovable as well as defiant. In contrast, being successful in a neutral and well-organized way was to invite painful exclusion from the family drama and from the opportunity for oedipal thrills and perhaps ultimate victory.

Case Example

Yet another young man had identified himself with a pretentious, egoistic father in a way that could only lead to failure in his own conventional undertakings. With this paternal identification, the young man had to be intolerant of his own limitations; he had to be a pretentious, self-undermining poseur himself. At the same time, however, in going to extremes he was enacting an angry mockery of his father. Additionally, he was not challenging his father on psychically real oedipal grounds. The real challenge would have been to be a solid, sincere, aesthetically sensitive achiever of the sort that he knew his unhappily married mother responded to romantically. Thus, for this young man to be manly in character and not castrated psychosexually was tantamount to repudiating his identification with his father, and this we know to be a difficult feat for any man under any conditions. Analysts should not be misled by analysands' consciously and vehemently asserted aim of disidentifying with paternal models—or for that matter, maternal models as well. Consequently, this young man could repudiate only partially this damaging paternal identification. Moreover, not only was the father an achiever in his own right, whatever his pretensions, but, as always, there lay in the background of these derogated images of the pretentious father the unconsciously maintained imago of the powerful phallic father that the analysand had developed during the years of very young boyhood. This is the omnipotent, idealized father who, in psychic reality, is never seen in all his complexity, conflictedness, insecurity, and limitation.

The powerful primordial father should never be forgotten. Analysands tend insistently to represent only the scaled-down father of later periods of development. They hope thereby to get the analyst to accept these shrunken representations as psychically accurate and complete. These derogated representations also have their place in personal development—they, too, are psychically real—but the analysis of the pursuit of failure, as of so many other problems, depends on getting beyond these limited and later representations to the early father imago. The primordial father is always sexually powerful enough to overwhelm, satisfy, and impregnate the mother and to castrate the oedipally rivalrous son. He can handle anything. But this primal father is not just a threatening figure; he is also a latent source of a strong and successful ideal self. Only the analysis of transference and defense enables the analyst to get securely beyond the later, problematic, consciously asserted, derogated representations of the father and thereby to tap into developmental strengths that have been given no secure place in the analysand's character structure.

More now about this pretentious young man. Early in his analysis, while he still consciously idealized his father, he felt that he could never be as cool, witty, literate, and daring as his father. He promptly engaged in a similar idealizing of the analyst, and he elaborated an extravagant, superficial identification with him. His self-esteem shot up with his analytic pretentiousness. Consequently, he was hardly approachable through analytic interventions. This father-son repetition in the analytic relationship was his initial transference, and at the same time it was obviously his initial major form of defense. Technically, therefore, it was necessary to conduct some close and patient examination of contradictory ideas and feelings concerning the idealized father of later and disturbed phases of development. This preliminary work outside of transference and defense was necessary to show the analysand that, as a son, he also felt betrayed, enraged, and despondent, and that the ideal self he was playing at was flimsy, exhausting, and painful. This phase of the work required some forceful confrontations on the analyst's part. Only subsequently could the more fundamental aspects of transference and defense be taken up analytically and a similar account of his relationship to the analyst be developed. This work opened the way to an analysis of the influence of the primordial father imago, and thereby it opened a way to alternatives to being a success only at failing.

As I mentioned, I organized the preceding examples largely around disturbed development of the ideal self; however, during analysis, the pursuit of failure gets to be organized around many other themes as well. For one thing, there is the obvious problem of warding off envy. Of the many variants of envy that could be elaborated in this connection, I want to emphasize especially the psychically real envy directed by one or another parent at the child's promise and attainments. I refer here to the envious father who feels less well endowed and less attractive to his wife than his son and to the envious mother who feels less feminine, less competent, and less attractive to her husband than her daughter. The promising or successful child faces the threat of experiencing some form of unconsciously maintained, envious, filicidal desire and sabotage. In these settings, any strong positive emotional response of the nonenvious parent is experienced as threatening in its incestuous implications.

Thus, it is not only that too much harm seems to be threatened by one parent's envy, but that too much gratification of the most problematic kind seems to be threatened by the other parent's positive response. In instances of this sort, we are probably always dealing with fantastic infantile parental imagoes resting on a fragment of good reality testing. Technically, the analysis may be blocked if the element of reality testing is totally ignored; at the same time, the analysis may miscarry if only reality testing is emphasized while the infantile fantastic elaborations are ignored. It is a delicate and taxing problem to sort out and balance these factors.

Before I move on to idealized unhappiness, I should mention other organizing themes. For example, success presents the danger that unconsciously maintained grandiose ideas of the self will be experienced consciously. Kohut (1971, 1977) had some significant points to make in this regard. Some analysands experience significant and even panicky disorientation of an incipiently manic or paranoid sort once they dare to recognize and assert their own special achievements or the special talents that are implied by these achievements. During these moments of truth, they may convey a sense of loss of reality and contact with others, sometimes even a sense of being crazy. Body-image distortions may occur. Consequently, they retreat in panic from these recognitions and assertions, and they do so repeatedly until their frightening fantasies, expectations, and reactions are more fully defined and worked through. Here, too, issues of reality testing must be taken into account, now in relation to adequate appraisals of the self.

In my view, this crisis of narcissism is not resolvable in terms of Kohut's self psychology alone. Self-psychological considerations may help gain access to fear of a latent grandiose self and of patent exhibitionism, but, as a rule, this crisis of narcissism also seems to imply the oedipal crisis that served as Freud's central organizing theme. The crisis may also imply a disruption of a preoedipal symbiotic tie or a disturbing sense of merging with the grandiose imagoes of the parents of very early childhood. Annie Reich (1953, 1954, 1960) was among the first Freudians to show a keen attentiveness to the mix of oedipal and preoedipal factors in these narcissistic crises.

To continue with self-psychological themes, sometimes the path to success seems to be blocked unconsciously by the fantasy of irremediable deficit or defect. Ideas of deficit and defect do often seem to refer to mothering that was not "good enough" or empathic enough. But that this deprivation seems to have taken place does not mean that there is no network of oral, anal, and phallic-exhibitionistic fantasies or fixations, and of defenses against them, that have served as latent sources of the idea of having been damaged by poor care. However important parental empathic failure may have been, it does not preclude the central presence of fixed and pervasive ideas of being damaged and of many infantile wish fulfillments and defenses. If the analysis is not confined to self-psychological issues, it often does prove a useful next step to reinterpret the unempathic mother, for example, as the fantastically exaggerated, powerful, and retaliatory oedipal rival or the rejecting or unsatisfied oedipal and preoedipal object. It may turn out that it is oedipal threat and defeat or preoedipal abandonment or torture that have been giving their apparent force to the ideas of defect and deficit.

An individual may use these ideas of being crippled to cope with problems of bisexuality: The male may so use psychic castratedness; the female, the repudiation of phallic aspirations. In addition, the idea of a defect may be used unconsciously as a malignant phallus or breast to triumph over the world, and in this way it may represent victory exhibitionistically and omnipotently snatched from the jaws of defeat (see, for example, Shakespeare's *Richard III*). I have argued elsewhere (1983) that some analysands may use unconsciously maintained and elaborated ideas of being imprisoned or empty in the same way that others use ideas of being damaged or defective.

Whatever the case, to those in hot pursuit of failure, conventional or analytic success inevitably means giving up a lot. For this reason, analytic accomplishment may be an occasion at least for painful mourning and more likely for periods of painful depression. In psychic reality, what is lost is the mother's breast (however bad), the secret penis, the omnipotence, and so on, that make up the fantastic assumptions on which character is based. The acutely distressing aspects of success and failure are primarily infantile in origin rather than contemporary. Certainly any contemporary success of a conventional public sort does give rise to many new problems of personal synthesis and interpersonal relationship, and those problems are not to be ignored. Yet all these new stresses and strains derive whatever devastating force they have from being construed unconsciously in the terms of infantile attachment, loss, seduction, defeat, damage, and other dangers. For those who appear to be wrecked by success, there may be much of value that is hidden among the ruins.

THE IDEALIZATION OF UNHAPPINESS

Here I lead off with a few case examples of the idealization of unhappiness and the implied construction of an unhappy ideal self.

Case Example

A woman in analysis made the following slip of the tongue. Intending to say that upon having been confronted by a threatening situation, she had experienced cold chills going down her spine, she said, "Cold thrills went down my spine." This woman had a lifelong history of attempting to relieve others of their unhappiness by absorbing it into herself. Unconsciously, as many women in our culture seem to do, she incorporated their unhappiness and suffered for them. In so doing, she felt that she was being a good girl, that is, kind, compassionate, supportive, undemanding, even self-sacrificing. From a young age, she had done this to an extreme degree with all members of her family. This Christlike role, itself a kind of excellence for her, also supported and restored good feeling to the others involved. It certainly had this effect in her fantasies, although as the analysis proceeded, evidence accumulated to suggest that often her family members were most comfortable with her when she was unhappy. The consequence of her incorporating the unhappiness of others in her family was that she could then more easily idealize them as secure, kind, compassionate, and supportive to her as a girl and later as the woman with whom we are here concerned. In her psychic reality, she gained love and importance by being unhappy, and by this means, too, she added worth to her idea of herself. In line with analytic expectation, she attempted to play this role in the transference: If she could not perceive some discomfort or distress in the analyst for her to incorporate, she invented it; thus, it was part of her transference that she was protecting or healing the suffering analyst by suffering herself and thereby reaching toward her ideal self.

Technically, it was necessary to interpret this chronic unhappiness as being designed unconsciously to enhance her own self-esteem at the expense of the analyst, as earlier it had been at the expense of her family members. The strategy also had to be analyzed as an attempt to love and be loved by an idealized figure, albeit through suffering. Additionally it emerged that, unconsciously, she also enjoyed punishing others by being miserable to the point of being inconsolable. Her idealization of unhappiness was, in its relation to others, an ambivalent or conflictual strategy. The various gratifications she achieved through this strategy rendered it extremely difficult for her to contemplate or undergo change. Signs of improvement were conducive to dramatic negative therapeutic reactions; that is, she lost analytic ground whenever she began to feel better.

Her slip of the tongue in substituting "thrills" for "chills" pointed to a sexual masochistic theme for which there was other evidence, including extensive and exciting fantasies of abuse and humiliation. That it was *cold* thrills pointed in two directions. On the one hand, "cold" pointed to that aspect of the unhappy ideal self that was ruthlessly self-serving, envious, and competitive and that was cold in the everyday sense of a "cold heart" or "cold person." On the other hand, "cold" pointed to her defending against consciously experiencing the erotic heat of her masochism (see, for example, Freud, 1919) by maintaining instead a sexual coldness in her relations with others. Indeed, this woman had been described by a friend as a come-hither spinster.

Thus, her idealization of unhappiness could be retold analytically in terms of sexuality, aggressiveness, defensiveness, adaptation (at least in the family setting of her childhood), and archaic morality. Morality was involved because, unconsciously, she not only lived her love life and hate life through suffering, she also secretly paid for living out her ambivalence by suffering even more painfully.

Case Example

Another woman made a similar slip of the tongue. Intending to say how heavily burdened she was by her mother's negative attitudes, she said instead, "I am so heavenly burdened by her." In this woman's psychic reality, she had experienced the best parental caretaking when she was most discontent and self-disparaging, and she had experienced the worst combination of neglect, disparagement, and envy when she was effective, enthusiastic, and proud. It had seemed to her during her development that she was supposed to be an object of contempt, and she had concluded that it was presumptuous of her to think or speak well of herself or to do well by herself. Thus, in her analysis, as was true in the case of one of the men discussed earlier in the section on the pursuit of failure, she could not sustain a positive self-narrative. Typically, right after she would begin a positive narration, she would break it off, calling it silly, irrelevant, offensive, bragging, or boring. She would then go on immediately to groan over a flood of humiliating associations, or she would bring up memories of personal disasters for which she was responsible, or she would at great length detail problems with respect to which she was helpless. Sometimes she never even began the positive story. Sometimes she just switched from one type of narrative to the other without transitionally derogating what she had just been saying. Occasionally she would, as it were, break in on herself indignantly, saying, "Who do I think I am anyway?"

Unhappiness was what others wanted and, through identification with her parents, it was what she now wanted for herself. It seemed that her ideal self was an unhappy one. She felt rotten when her story was positive, and she felt desirable, estimable, and secure when it was negative. During the analysis she became aware that she expected the analyst to prefer, if not require, this unhappy self.

In one respect, her "heavenly" burdens were the alleged personal defects that guaranteed that her parents would be accepting, attentive, and consoling caretakers. In another respect, the word *burdens* referred to the infantilizing and disparaging parents themselves, along with her identification with them. As always, many other influences of an unconscious nature were also involved in the construction of this unhappy ideal self.

Case Example

In another instance, an ascetic, spartan, self-absorbed, and mute unhappiness seemed in large part to be a young woman's way of appealing to a father who, it seemed, lived his life in just that way. Her unhappiness was also a way of identifying with him. As a girl, this woman had gained his companionship and admiration by modeling

herself on him. As a woman, she regulated her own self-esteem in the
same way. Unconsciously, for her, this mode of existence was also a way
of being defiantly and proudly masculine, for in her psychic reality she
could escape from humiliating femininity through masculine inaccessibility. It is by no means unusual to encounter this father-daughter
configuration in analytic practice—again, however, as part of a larger
complex of factors.

In the three cases I just summarized, it was possible to see that these
women had also defined constituents of conventionally positive ideal
selves. There was a good deal to suggest that they had been exposed to
many influences that could only have been conducive to their developing more positive ideal selves. Consequently, they could only experience with great distress the consciously miserable ways in which they
were constructing their current lives. It was with reference to these
positive ideal selves that it became meaningful, if not imperative, for
these women to throw their unhappiness into question and to undertake analysis. But for the most part, once they were in analysis, they
kept these happier ideal selves secret; they found it very difficult to
present and sustain them consciously. One reason for this difficulty
was their struggle against identification with a devalued mother figure
(Greenson, 1954). In this struggle, they were repressing the early,
active, caretaking, and powerful mother figure. It was a case of throwing out the primary mother with the bathwater.
    At the same time, however, there was, as usual, a good deal in their
self-stories to suggest that the widespread victimization of women in
our society, the discrimination against women and their brutalization,
not to speak of the many subtle forms of seduction of women into
debased roles, had all played significant parts in these women having
taken in, developed, and rigidified the unhappiness that they subsequently had come to idealize. But, as this development is not equally
conspicuous in, and disruptive for, all women exposed to these inimical social pressures, it seems that we must still give considerable weight
in our explanations to infantile fantasy and other early developmental
influences. An adequate discussion of these issues would require a
lengthy treatment in its own right, some of which I have offered elsewhere (see chapters 4, 5, and 7).
    Suffice it to say here that no amount of analytic interpretation of
the unconsciously active, repetitive, idealizing search for suffering
implies any preconception or conclusion that, after all, women simply
bring their unhappiness on themselves. With our current understanding of all relevant factors, this idea of women is untenable as well as

damaging. Furthermore, the deidealization of unhappiness that is often accomplished through psychoanalysis tends to bring with it an increased readiness to develop what are, for these women, lively critiques of our sexist world and adequately assertive means to resist and combat the seductions into suffering with which they are constantly surrounded.

CONCLUSION: REMARKS ON PSYCHOANALYTIC INTERPRETATION AND NARRATION

When I discussed the pursuit of failure, I drew my examples from analytic work with men. When I discussed the idealization of unhappiness, I drew my examples from analytic work with women. The selection of cases reflects my impression that the theme of pursuing failure is relatively more conspicuous in analytic work with men, while the idealization of unhappiness is relatively more conspicuous in analytic work with women.

But what does it mean to say that one theme is more conspicuous in certain cases than it is in others? Does it mean that I simply find it to be so in the same sense that one finds more snow up north and up high? Or does it mean that I employ a certain theme more actively in work with one sex and another theme in work with the other sex? By raising these questions, I am introducing into our considerations a major issue in psychoanalytic epistemology. The issue is one of deciding whether what Freud (1915a) called the unconscious and what he described as its contents are discovered or created, encountered or imposed, found or made. Freud can be quoted on both sides of this thorny issue. Elsewhere (1981, 1983) I have attempted at some length to develop a case for regarding "the unconscious" as both found and made; more exactly, for regarding it as the product of dialogue or as a co-authored text produced and progressively revised by two members of the same narrative and interpretive community. I shall not review the details of that discussion here, nor shall I review similar discussions by others (for example, Ricoeur, 1977).

I introduce this epistemological issue for two reasons. One is to be able to assert that the two themes—the pursuit of failure and the idealization of unhappiness—are not mutually exclusive. Few psychoanalytic themes are; hence the frequent invocation in analytic discussions of the concepts of overdetermination and multiple function. For the most part, the examples I have presented under one heading could have been presented under the other; indeed, both themes were developed in all of the cases mentioned, even though to different degrees.

My second reason for introducing the issue of whether "the unconscious" is found or made is implied by my use of the word *theme*. As I said in my introductory remarks, I am using the word *theme* in the sense of storyline or narrative organizing principle. In following this usage, I am making the following assumptions. Analytic therapy is a process of constructing by analytic means life histories that have been dominated by the analysand's own unconscious mental processes. Histories are narrative constructions, each history being controlled by storylines. The historian chooses the storylines that make sense in the narrative and interpretive community of which he or she is a member. In the course of analytic therapy, as in the course of all historical work, more than one history can be constructed, and usually more than one is. It requires several basic themes at least to help retell a life story adequately along analytic lines.

To say that this work requires narrative choices is not to say that the analyst's lines of interpretation are sheer fabrications or are selected at random. It is to say that what we analysts accept as the facts of current and past reality are necessarily rendered in the terms of one or more themes that serve as our controlling guidelines for inquiry and formulation. In this way, and only in this way, do facts acquire significance for the analysis. The significance of facts is established by and within a context of questions and methods that are consistent with a set of narrative choices. These choices are usually called theories (see also chapters 9, 10, and 11).

Taken together, all of these assumptions make it possible to understand that the nature and content of unconscious mental processes have been defined variously by alternative schools of psychoanalysis. In the same way, though to a lesser degree, these processes are defined variously by the members of any one school of psychoanalysis.

I believe that my relatively greater emphasis on the idealization of unhappiness by women does capture an important feature of the psychology of women in our society. At the same time, however, I must grant that this relatively greater emphasis is also a consequence of my having actively developed that storyline, among others, in my work with a number of women and of my having found it useful in helping them analytically to lead what were, for them, better lives. A similarly constructed conclusion applies to the pursuit of failure undertaken by many men. Thus, in this chapter I have been as much describing some aspects of my way of working analytically as I have been describing phenomena that should be available to any other analyst and that could be of some social significance, pertaining as it does to the prevalence of manifest depressiveness in women. The discipline of psychoanalysis would be advanced were more analysts to present their conclusions as both findings and creations, in this way getting beyond fruitless, naïvely objectivist, or empiricist arguments over the so-called facts of the case.

CHAPTER 7

Men Who Struggle Against Sentimentality

SENTIMENTALITY often turns out to be a key issue in psychoanalysis. And when it does, it is likely to come up in the context of a man's noisy or quietly desperate struggle *against* sentimentality, both his own and that of others. Those men who engage in this struggle regard sentimentality as a serious fault to be corrected or a great danger to be avoided. Typically, they do not recognize the potential of the phenomena they subsume under sentimentality for adaptive uses and consequences. I am referring particularly to men who present themselves in analysis as aridly obsessional, icily narcissistic, lovelessly depressive, brutally phallic, or psychopathically superficial. In other words, more than a few men, though by no means all or all to the same extent.

We analysts cannot fail to appreciate the fact that these men have grown up in a context of parents and others who have extreme and conflictual values of their own with respect to sentimentality and who, in one way or another, have tried to pass on these values and conflicts. Nevertheless, we cannot view the antisentimentalists' self-presentations simply as a matter of having been socially conditioned and forced into conformity. Geared as we must be to facilitating personal change, we do not view the child simply as a blank page to be written on by a pack of like-minded authors. We consider it more important to develop an understanding of how antisentimentality has figured in each child's attempt to resolve conflictual issues centered on sexuality and aggression and how it has been comprehended in the individualized terms of the typical unconscious fantasies of early childhood.

Usually, analyzing the struggle against sentimentality helps open the gate to a wide variety of repudiated but developmentally significant and even valuable strivings. Among other things, successful analysis of large-scale versions of this struggle leads to greater clarity about, and tolerance of, issues of gender identity, to more intense and stable relationships with others, to a fuller subjective sense of being alive in a social world and in a worthwhile way, and to a more continuous, inclusive, unembarrassed narrative of the analysand's own complex life history as a boy and man. In contrast, analytic impasses may develop when the analyst neglects to look into the lifelong activities that have gone into an analysand's conspicuous antisentimentality, or when the analyst fails, despite the best of efforts, to make headway against it.

For these reasons, an analytic discussion of men who struggle against sentimentality has implications not only for the general psychology of men, in which respect, for example, it will bear on what often seem to be their deficiencies of empathy and their fears of self-disclosure, dependency, and intimacy. This discussion also has important technical implications concerning both the analysis of defense and transference and the analysis of diverse aspects of emotional experience in general (Schafer, 1964). Additionally, certain significant countertransference issues may come to the fore in the course of analyzing this struggle, a topic to which I turn later on.

SOCIETAL CONCEPTIONS OF SENTIMENTALITY

Tastes and mores vary among individuals and social groups, and they change over time and with changing historical and personal circumstances or contexts. Consequently, the narrational boundaries of sentimentality are not clear or stable, and the common attitude toward sentimentality is not always predominantly or exclusively positive or negative. It seems that there can be no single, simple, satisfactory definition of the word, no definition that is timeless and value-free, and no such precise definition will be attempted here. At the same time, it can be said that a decidedly masculinist bias seems to pervade the uses of the word, as if somehow "feminine" should be central to its definition.

We cannot be satisfied with the dictionary that defines sentimentality as "excessive emotionality," for we must go on to ask: Who decides what is excessive and why or according to which values and ideals and in which circumstances? Usually, it is men who have decided, particularly men in power of some kind, those who are all the more likely projectively to empty their unwanted emotionality into women and powerless men and then to hold them accountable or to condescend to them, gallantly or otherwise.

Sentimentality has been and continues to be compared invidiously to autonomy, power, genuineness, rationality, and masculinity. Sentimentality tends to be linked to childishness, weakness, irrationality, victimization, failure, insincerity, and womanishness. Consequently, it should come as no surprise that the struggle against sentimentality often occupies a strategic position in the clinical analysis of men in our society. Today sentimentalism is also under ideological attack by some feminists: Alert to the social seduction of women into being sentimentalists and thereby becoming more easily exploitable by men as well as by other women, notably by their mothers, they view sentimentality as a trap.

SUBJECTIVE REFERENTS OF SENTIMENTALITY

To which features of emotional responsiveness do male analysands allude when they appear to be setting themselves against being sentimental? Commonly, these men subsume under sentimentality (or some key word, storyline, or image equivalent to it) being tearful, nostalgic, enthusiastic, thrilled, awed, or infatuated; also, yearning or pining for someone or being playful in an exuberant or silly way. They say such experiences are not rational or that they themselves have no reason to feel that way. They wish to avoid any suggestion that they are naïve or immature; they dread being labeled maudlin or self-indulgent; they cringe before the possibility of seeming foolish or womanly. Embarrassed or ashamed, they cover up, minimize, or attempt to dispel any incipient feelings and expressive behavior of these sorts. They fall silent; they speak with heavy irony or self-mockery; they become irritable, listless, or circumstantial. Alternatively, when faced with their own sensitivity, they quickly profess a hopeless attitude. One representative member of this group lamented, "What good does it do?" before he continued in an increasingly anxious manner to convey both a fear of falling apart if he unchained his sensitivity and a suspicion that the analyst was seducing him into a weakened position.

It is, however, always to be borne in mind that, in individual cases, only selected areas of sentimentality may be proscribed. For example, a man may tolerate sentimentality with respect to his feelings for women or mothers specifically but not for men or fathers, with respect to sadness but not exuberance. In these instances, it will be important to analyze the man's principles of selective response.

REGRESSIVE ASPECTS OF SENTIMENTALITY

A virtually inevitable storyline in this narrative of analyzing the struggle against sentimentality is this: struggle against regression. As regression is a term that can cover many different processes and phenomena, its application should always be individualized, for each male analysand will have his own configuration of specific regressive dangers. Although the main dangers I take up cannot be neatly distinguished from one another, considering them under separate headings can be useful to keep track of the varied emphases we encounter in doing analytic work. My headlines are these: daydreaming, being a baby, identification with the mother, anality, and latency-age boyishness.

Daydreaming

Daydreaming is a complex compromise formation that may be understood fully only by implementing the principle of multiple function (Waelder, 1930). It is not simply a means of erotic and egoistic wish fulfillment, as Freud (1908a) suggested. To one degree or another, it must also be retold in defensive, moralistic, and adaptive terms. But whatever relative weight we assign to these various components, however pleasant or unpleasant the daydream, and however manifest or latent its essential features, it tends to have a decidedly sentimental aspect. It is sentimental in the way it depends on simplistic idealizations and so is replete with naïve, even melodramatic renditions of success and failure, good and evil, safety and danger, and gratification and deprivation. Daydreamers are not hard-nosed; they are not engaged in cool and complex appraisals of self and others or of past, present, and future situations. Their daydreams feature illusions and do not represent the highest level of adaptive functioning of which they are capable. Some daydreamers are taking a refreshing holiday from external reality. Others are beating a hasty retreat from it. All are approaching life sentimentally.

For example, the analysand daydreaming longingly about the analyst over the weekend is sentimentally engaged in idealization, bracketing out the recognition that analytic life with the analyst is often disagreeable in various ways and so setting aside the ambivalence that inevitably pervades the analytic relationship. Similarly idealizing are those daydreams that feature persistent nostalgic longings for the family of their childhood, for in cooler moments, analysands recognize that this family was a source of much suffering. The case is the same when analysands are regularly thrilled by the praise of a superior whom they fear, scorn, or mistrust, and when they weep over a kind word said by a friend who, it is realized upon sober reflection, does not really understand that well or care that much.

Analysands who struggle against sentimentality are wary of what they regard as the undermining effects of daydream idealizations. In their eyes, the simplifications of daydreaming undo the unrelenting realism or irony and the absolute autonomy that they have worked so hard to achieve and on which their feelings of invulnerability and worthwhileness seem to depend. Consequently, they fear and condemn their regressive daydreaming; they want no part of illusion-fostering and illusion-filled emotionality. And because their negative attitude may have had significant adaptive consequences during their earlier development, such as fortifying them against never-ending traumatic disappointments, they may buttress their antisentimentality with painful reminders of grim alternatives.

Being a Baby

Very often, men imagine sentimentality to be a shift of functioning in the direction of being a baby. Babies are vulnerable to merging into others or, a bit later and analogously, melting mindlessly into symbols such as the home or the flag. In this context, sentimentality means being passive, helpless, yielding, or surrendering. These men fear that they will lose touch with reality and expose themselves in naked emotionality to violation, derision, and abandonment. The orality of this regressive move is suggested by the common link between sentimentality and being a sucker and swallowing things whole or, more euphemistically, lacking refined taste. These analysands find it frightening to seek comfort, as by weeping or pleading, or to accept help when it is offered, no matter how painful or terrifying reality may seem to them at the time. In their daily lives, they may deny their wives and children any chance to "mother" them, and in their analyses they repeatedly rebuff the analyst as a real or imagined benevolently "mothering" figure.

Identification with the Mother

For these men the regressiveness of sentimentality usually involves increased emphasis on intolerable identifications with their mothers. In their sentimental moments they feel womanish or perhaps girlish. On this basis they sense that a threat of homosexual responsiveness lurks behind their image of the sentimentalist. They sometimes claim to document this connection by referring to the blatant sentimentality that characterizes certain aspects of the gay community (for example, certain prominent figures in the entertainment world). The regressively intensified identification with mother may pertain to any one of a number of developmental phases: the mother as witch or smothering breast; the sick, suffering, raped, or castrated mother of the primal scene as envisioned by the phallic-oedipal boy; the mother as degraded woman (such as prostitute).

In one of its aspects, a desperately increased emphasis on rejecting this sentimentalized identification may serve defensively to assert masculinity. But it is not the masculinity of the primal father conceived as an indomitable, castrating phallic force. Freud (1921) described the primal father as the early and awesome ideal figure, a figure whose heights a person can never hope to reach. By implication, he is a figure with respect to whom, both fearfully and wishfully, a person is always something of a softy, a soft touch, a pushover, even a willing slave, in effect a castrate and sexual partner. Men live in the shadow of this figure, and for some it is a very long shadow.

In another of its aspects, an overemphasis on the danger of maternal identification may unconsciously accomplish a hostile and anxiety-relieving caricature of the mother whose emotionality, whatever its nature, stands for both her castratedness and her frightening castrating tendencies. And in a third aspect, this overemphasis may imply struggling against the wish to return, via identification, to a dyadic relation with mother from which father and siblings are excluded, that way to have her forever. What is lacking in these instances is the fearful male's recognition, tolerance, and moderated integration of the androgynous implications of a freer emotionality. What is present instead are some scattered attempts at compromise of subjectively irreconcilable extremes. But because he is convinced that those compromises can never be stable or satisfying, he must continue to aim for a totally one-sided result. This exclusionary emphasis on male gender often serves mainly as a screen for significant pregenital issues. I have already mentioned orality; anality, to which I turn next, is another such major pregenital issue.

Anality

The master psychosexual narratives of psychoanalysis lead the analyst to expect that anal ambivalence will be found to play a particularly important role in men's struggles against sentimentality. For it is a well-established interpretation of long standing that people in general and particularly those who are emotionally disturbed, construe emotionality in the terms of anal fantasy (see, for example, Brierley, 1951, chap. 2). They deal with emotions as with fecal matter—that is, both as dangerously sadistic expulsions or explosions and as shameful, dirty, messy incontinence. These ubiquitous fantasies are encountered in especially clear form in obsessional settings. We need not depend on the clinical analytic method to develop support for the claim that this equation is ubiquitous, for there exists an abundance of concordant anal jokes, colloquial sayings and metaphors, insults, rituals, myths, and fables of every kind. "I feel shitty" is a representative instance.

Thus, being well defended against sentimentality is unconsciously equivalent to having a clean diaper, while unrestrained sentimentality is like "crapping all over the place." "Crapping all over the place" is likely to express as much vigorous and torturing defiance as passive, erotic letting go and opening up. The "tight-assed" person is not sentimental, while the sentimentalist is a sentimental "slob."

In this context we encounter the well-known unconscious links between conventional femininity and passive anality; for example, to be masculine is to be impeccably toilet trained, as clean as an astronaut, as controlled as a drill sergeant. As one male analysand put it, when reflecting on the anal fantasy implied in his antisentimentality, "It's like denying I have an asshole."

Masculinist bias is plainly evident in the sphere of anality. "Don't be an asshole" conveys this bias. Implicitly, it is women who are "sentimental assholes." It is, by the way, not unusual for women to share this unconscious stereotype (as they do so many others) and, on this basis, to feel masculine once they stop being "sentimental assholes" and dare to maintain their dignity against all the seductions and assaults that are conducive to their behaving otherwise.

In the analytic relationship, a man's antisentimentality is likely to involve not only his enacting sadistically defiant constipation and his fearfully contemplating the possibility that analysis will reveal that his true sexual interest is in passive femininity and homosexuality. It may involve as well his attempt to seduce the analyst into performing symbolic anal rape in the form of pressing confrontations and interpretations of his defensive dealings with emotionality; perhaps he can seduce the analyst to make direct demands on him for emotional output, this amounting to the "analytic enema." Consequently, it is more than likely that working out and working through the anal meanings or uses of antisentimentality in the here and now of the analysis will render the entire realm of emotional experience more accessible to expression, understanding, and integration. Here I include such potentially adaptive phenomena as the release of strangulated grief, the spilling out of exhilarated exhibitionism, playfulness, and tenderness, and the bursting out of proscribed temper tantrums, competitiveness, and pride.

Before leaving the psychoanalytic storylines of anality, we must take account of feces as gift and, through the equation of feces and emotion, of emotion as gift. It is common to observe withholding of emotion as a means of inflicting feelings of deprivation and undeservingness on others. Withholding is also a means of denying that a person has needs that the other is satisfying; the antisentimentalists are very uncomfortable with the idea of being "dependent" on anyone for anything. They prefer the isolation of imperviousness and aloofness: Nothing "mushy" about that!

Latency-Age Boyishness

Boyishness plays a significant role in men's sentimentality and their struggle against it. I refer particularly to the emotionality of latency-age and prepuberty boys and to their play and playfulness. Under favorable developmental conditions, boys in this phase of development are passionately serious and passionately playful, often simultaneously so or in rapid alternation. They are not unduly threatened by latent homosexual and other such aspects of their functioning in this emotional way, and they are resilient when they have gone to extremes or when their experiments have turned out to be too exciting to be tolerated.

The man who struggles against sentimentality defensively introduces significant discontinuity into the life history potentially available to him. He does this by trying to renounce whatever limited boyishness he once enjoyed or suffered, as the case may be. He gives the appearance of having bypassed his boyhood. He presents himself as being unable to play or as too vigorously segregating work from play. For him, there is no play in work, and there is strenuous work in play. He participates in analysis in the same way. It is unthinkable to be simply playful before the analyst or with him or her. He would never entice the analyst into playful interaction. Those playful interactions that can and do take place are not tolerated well. He tends to be stodgy and humorless. A shared laugh is something to be coped with, and it may be used to discredit the analyst. At best, he substitutes telling jokes dryly for having open-ended fun. He has no heroes, just as he has no chum or buddy to comfort him or share experiences with him. He is set against the boy he has remained in his psychic reality, just as he is set against the woman, the toddler, and the baby.

LIFE HISTORICAL BACKGROUND

What kind of life historical background seems to be the matrix of this revolt against boyishness and all the other variables I mentioned earlier? I can summarize one family drama that in some cases seems to have contributed to the development of vigorous antisentimentality; however, I cannot claim that this drama is universal or that it sufficiently explains this particular outcome. But I do find some support for my account in a paper on tearfulness by Wood and Wood (1984); they present an account of a man's struggle against tearfulness that includes, in addition to phenomena of the sort I described earlier, some of the features of development I am about to describe.

In broad outline, it seems that, as boys, a number of these men had to cope with a disappointingly unresponsive and uncomforting mother, a woman who seems to have been depressed and also embittered and rivalrous in her relations with men and boys alike; further, they had to cope with an obsessionally rigid or narcissistically aloof, competitive father who regularly debunked his young son's enthusiasms and identificatory strivings for both closeness and autonomy. One analysand would imagine his father's voice saying "schmuck" or "good boy," depending on the waxing and waning of his own sentimental responses during the analysis. This is reminiscent of Kohut's (1977) emphasis on the damaging effects on healthy narcissism of unappreciative mothers and of fathers who do not tolerate well their being idealized and taken as models by their sons.

One of the functions that gets disrupted under those developmental conditions is what Hartmann (1956) discussed in another context as the testing of inner reality (see also chapter 1). Hartmann emphasized that it is misguided to equate rationality only with the testing of external reality. He argued that, from the analytic point of view, inner reality, with all its archaic, irrational, volatile, and otherwise extreme features, is as important a part of reality as whatever is of moment in the surrounding world. Here lies the response to the analysand's defensively despondent question, "What good does it do?" The good it does is to increase the analysand's readiness consciously to recognize and participate in his inner reality and to empathize with himself in that sphere (Schafer, 1964). On this basis, he may achieve what growth and mastery he can where that is needed. Because analysis helps people to view inner reality in this light, it gets to seem neither a horror to be avoided nor a disease to be cured; rather, it is a world to be transformed in its most shaky and disruptive aspects and to be enjoyed as it is coped with. To this consideration I might add another: Unconsciously, "inner reality," along with whatever else is "inner," no longer tends to be equated so readily with femininity, filth, and infantilism.

COUNTERTRANSFERENCE

What kinds of disruptive countertransference arise in the course of analyzing men who struggle against sentimentality? Here much depends on the analyst's relations with his or her emotionality in general and sentimentality in particular. We can expect that analysts who are still waging battles of their own either on behalf of sentimentality or against it will be especially prone to disruptive countertransferences in this sphere. They will identify too much or too little with one side or the other of their analysands' positions on affective experience. Subtly or obviously, they will devote themselves to ridding the analysands of their "diseased" sentimentality or their "unpleasant" antisentimentality rather than trying to understand why this or that mode of response has been favored. They may use an analysand's emotional experiences to immerse themselves vicariously and more comfortably than they could otherwise in experiencing the feelings they have difficulty tolerating and enjoying in their own lives. Alternatively, and with the help of projection, they may combat their own sentimental tendencies by a rigorously skeptical analytic approach to their analysands' sentimentality; on this basis they may neglect the developmental potential and relevance of sentimental responsiveness and thereby limit their own analytic effectiveness.

These departures from the neutral analytic attitude may be characterized metaphorically in terms of some of the psychosexual issues
that were mentioned earlier. For example, orally, the analysand may
be put on starvation rations or drowned in chicken soup. Anally, the
analyst may be constipatedly clean, insistently enema-giving, or diar-
rheic with empathy. The countertransference may be homosexually
seductive or castrating in a this-is-our-song atmosphere or rationalized
as advocacy of the reality principle in an atmosphere of macho imperviousness. And so forth. In these respects it is well to recall the Scylla
and Charybdis of analytic work sketched by Fenichel (1941): too
much need on the analyst's part for volatile affect or too little tolerance of it.

The neutral analyst, the analyst who maintains the analytic attitude,
will be enough at peace with his or her own sentimental tendencies to
be able to participate through trial identifications in both the regressive features of the analysand's sentimentality and his antiregressive
struggle against it. The analyst will not participate in this empathic
way in order to implement or enforce any particular value other than
the health-value of knowing reality inside out, as it were, for it is this
kind of knowledge that helps the analysand work out less costly and
painful solutions or compromises than those with which he came into
analysis. In other words, the analyst's technical ideal is neither to conduct an analysis sentimentally nor to turn analysands into sentimentalists. It is rather to find ways to provide for sentimentality a better
understood and less threatening place in the analysand's range of
responsiveness and awareness. The analyst's ideal is an even-handed-
ness in this realm as in all others (Schafer, 1983).

POSTSCRIPT

Of the many storylines I could have addressed or developed further
but did not, I should like to mention two. One is the sadistic potential
of the struggle against sentimentality, that component of the struggle
that may be used to block empathy with others and to deny them their
own emotional intensity and scope. The other storyline tells of the
problems that may come up with particular force when an antisentimental male works with a female analyst: such problems as the transference conviction that the analysand is in the hands of an
infantilizing, effeminizing, or incestuously seductive mother. In that
context, the analysand uses the fact that the female analyst pays the

least bit of active attention to emotional experience in the most defensive way to confirm the reality of the danger of regression and of all that regression means to him in analysis. I have noted versions of these problems frequently in the course of my supervising women doing analysis.

CHAPTER 8

Women Lost in the Maze of Power and Rage

THEMES of aggression and power pervade the accounts we hear in our daily work as analysts. Sometimes the stated or implied emotional violence is cold, as in the cruelty of prolonged withdrawal into silence; sometimes it is hot, as in burning rage and envy. Commonly, the analysand is presented in these narratives as the sufferer, perhaps reactively angry, perhaps passively resigned, but in any case victimized and in pain. And commonly, the exploration of these accounts of emotional violence seems to find its destination in the complex dramas of the analysand's family of origin. It is inappropriate for the analyst automatically to regard these painful accounts as altogether unreliable, for up to a point they are likely to enrich the treatment with useful information.

In order to work analytically, however, the analyst must also anticipate, and go on to establish, that much more is involved in the analysand's suffering than having been victimized by her or his family's unmistakably cruel or otherwise disturbing exercises of power. What is that "more"? It is likely to include the analysand's having become, over the course of development, either a seducer of sadism or, through identification, a ruthless wielder of power and a cruel victimizer of others, often in the most subtle way; or, as is true in many cases, both at once. Once the treatment is under way, the analyst gets to be included among those others who are to be seduced into cruelty and/or victimized themselves. Those analysts who can moderate the resulting countertransferences will not fail to note the ways in which these analysands feel frightened and penitent about resorting to masochistic and sadistic strategies. That is, these analysands may be understood to be pursuing this course of action unknown to themselves and in an acutely conflicted manner. Implied in this conflicted course of action are hidden loving kindness, desperate self-protection, and adaptedness to a history of family relations that required violent and perverse orientations to self and others. These orientations were the prerequisites for the patient feeling that she or he belonged and was not an outsider furtively looking in and not an object of derision.

Further, the analyst will recognize in each analysand's productions the activity of cruel internal objects. These are imagined internal figures or introjects that have been created chiefly in two ways: first, by the projective identifications perpetrated on, and accepted by, children whenever parents use them in an attempt to rid themselves of their unwanted bad parts or characteristics, and, second, by the sequence of the child's projecting his or her own cruel fantasies about others onto the others and then incorporating the bad figures that result from these unhappy creative efforts. In these fantasies, these incorporated cruel internal objects will finally fill so much of the "inner world" and so far establish an atmosphere of hostile surveillance and persecutory retaliation, much like an army of occupation, that in part they will stimulate continuous efforts at expulsion into or onto others (on an anal model, usually). Those who enter analysis as adults repetitively replay the painful interactions of their early lives and early fantasies; this they do in direct or inverted form, both with the analyst and with others in their current lives.

In this chapter I present a psychoanalytic summary of work of mine and some male supervisees with one such group of analysands. In this instance, "psychoanalytic" refers to work organized chiefly around both Freudian and object-relational analytic descriptions and interpretations of analysands' past and present lives, lives now being repeated in interpretable form in transferences and evoked countertransferences.

THE ANALYSANDS

The analytic work to be explored took place with a number of successful career women. Although these women seemed to be different from each other in many ways, the ones with whom I am here concerned shared a proclivity to get into painful relationships with narcissistic and sadistic men. The manifest content of these relationships showed them to be simply and extremely masochistic: These women seemed to lose the high level of cognitive, administrative, and social skills and the resourcefulness and poise that they typically manifested in their work; instead they became helpless, blindly repetitive, self-accusatory, and emotionally labile, seemingly addicted to their victimization, very often unaware of their rage at the way they were being treated, deficient or at least erratic and ineffective in their self-assertiveness, and greatly restricted in allocating responsibility for their interpersonal difficulties to anyone but themselves. All power seemed to have passed from their hands.

Typically, these women worked long hours in institutional settings, and it was mainly there that they developed their love and other significant social relationships. Not rarely, the love relationships were with older men, married men, or both; if not that, they were either with men on the rebound from broken marriages or disturbed love affairs or with men who, it seemed on reflection, could well have been married long ago but somehow were not, a fact that could have served as a warning but was ignored.

As a rule, these men were portrayed as hard-driving and highly successful, capable of being charming and of serving as helpful mentors; however, they were also ruthlessly critical, exploitative, and unfeeling. Even as colleagues, they were said to act like members of a club that excluded women from membership. These men made sure to look supercritically at the work contributions of any women, no matter how outstanding or profitable, to delay rewarding them with recognition and advancement in the institutional hierarchy, and to subject them to the harassment of sexist attitudes, language, and other provocations.

When they became the lovers of these women, these men rarely accepted responsibility for misunderstandings or hurts. Instead, they expected the women to accommodate to them and be available to them on short notice, even while they showered their victims with criticism for self-interest, unresponsiveness, and similar sins. And after the relationships ended, sometimes particularly after they ended, they found ways to harass and further torment their victims. It seemed then that they were determined to undermine the self-confidence and reality testing of these women and, more than that, to undermine their sense of having an ethical or moral center. Sometimes in these narratives, it seemed as if the men were engaged in brainwashing of the sort carried on by O'Brien, the torturer and soul-murderer of Winston Smith in George Orwell's novel *1984*. Moreover, the women went on clinging to their ex-lover tormentors, rationalizing their behavior as motivated by hopefulness or loneliness or as still trying to settle the score, perhaps aggressively but perhaps only reparatively.

Although I have presented no more than a composite picture of these entanglements, I believe that, sooner or later, each of these women presented one or another combination of its details convincingly, even if in an obviously one-sided manner. And yet, with respect to all of this apparent abuse and exploitation, consciously they characterized themselves primarily as failures rather than enraged victims and primarily as buffeted about by unkind, arbitrary fate rather than as driven uncomprehendingly to repetitions of being insulted and injured. These women were in a maze from which they could not find their way out.

Analysts cannot fail to be impressed by the declines in the level of functioning that are evident in the repetitive, self-abasing, and hopeless relations these women maintain with one man or, in some cases, with a series of men, in the painful confrontations they insist on reexperiencing, and in the prevalence of depression over rage or even enlightened self-assertion in response to the patent cruelty they describe at such great length and with so little variation. It therefore seems fully warranted to conclude that there is a lot more there than meets the eye and the ear.

On this understanding and after an appropriately careful initial screening, psychoanalysis was recommended as the treatment of choice. Apparently understanding of as well as accustomed to the long, hard grind of achievement, these women seemed quite ready to accept that recommendation. They agreed to the analytic procedure as the necessary disciplined approach to resolving their basic problems. Once the work was under way, however, they seemed mainly to want and often demand comfort and counsel rather than self-understanding. As befit the circumstances, they wanted directive help in gratifying their desires for love, marriage, family, personal dignity, and a career with recognition, for in their own eyes they were good-hearted women in dire straits, eager to be shown their mistakes, ready as ever in their high-achiever roles to go on learning how to perform excellently. In this respect they hardly made the most superficial distinctions between work and analysis. From this shift of emphasis alone, it could be inferred that preoccupation with the trials and tribulations of these current relationships served in one respect as a flight from the inner world of conflicted longings and in another respect as a clinging to an implied self-concept of the helpless infant, the good little girl in need of guidance, or the "victim."

ON WRITING ON THE THERAPY OF WOMEN:
A CRITICAL PERSPECTIVE

I believe that those who write on the psychological therapy of women are obliged to give some account of how they view the historical/cultural conditions affecting the development of girls and women in family life, school, love, and work. Because these writings touch on the general psychology of women, they must somehow convey perspectives on the place of women in the world. Inevitably those perspectives will have political and ideological implications and consequences, some of them of great social significance. If this much is granted, it follows that these writings must also include some discussion of expectable countertransferential issues in the therapy of women; this is so because the author's social viewpoint is bound to contribute both to shaping the phenomena being reported and to the meanings and significance being attributed to them. Like any other countertransferences, those in question here, if attended to, will be potentially useful in both the therapeutic interaction and the reader's understanding. However, if they are screened out by defensive measures, they will limit and may even damage the treatment and the proper understanding of its text once it is written up. Certainly the close reader might not agree that my account of this work conforms closely to the analyst's stated intentions; nevertheless, these intentions are bound to play significant roles in the treatments being reported, so that there is something to gain, even if not everything, by every author's stating his or her position frankly.

Further on countertransference: I recognize that any discussion of countertransference may be overwrought or imbalanced to the point where it enacts unresolved or uncontained countertransference issues; however, it does not follow from this recognition that the mere calling attention to the play of historical/cultural factors in countertransference is itself a sign of countertransference. Indeed, I would venture to suggest that it is not only defensive but politically as well as analytically reactionary to argue that this kind of attention necessarily manifests countertransference, as if it were possible to elude completely the issues of culturally rooted countertransferences. Modern analysts are obliged to take these factors into account. Accordingly, before going further with my discussion, I shall summarize my perspective on the place of women in today's world, without completely neglecting some psychoanalytic insights that seem to me fitting in this context. I reserve for the next section my main comments on countertransference.

My summary is too brief to do justice to the complex issues being addressed; however, a comprehensive discussion would be so long and wide-ranging that it would overshadow this chapter's primary purpose and theme. Although brief, this summary is part of my effort to break with the now-discredited convention of writing as if it were possible, in areas of weighty social controversy, to be an utterly disinterested, value-free psychoanalytic observer of mental and behavioral phenomena. We may no longer claim that these phenomena are "out there in Nature," phenomena with a fixed essence waiting to be discovered and univocally described once and for all by an objective investigator.

To get now to the point. I believe that much of our social order has been arranged and is controlled by men whose attitudes toward women may be described as discriminatory, demeaning, and exploitative. I also believe that many high-achieving men may be characterized accurately as seductively manipulative, self-centered, and at least implicitly hard and cruel in their social relationships. Correlatively, the women here under study face in their work and their social lives great odds in occupational and social settings that too often neglect and even oppose their interests. These settings are continuations of the ones in which they grew up: gifted girls whose giftedness encountered at best highly ambivalent welcomes. In this respect, I believe the reality testing of these women was seriously compromised in their families and their surroundings, in that they had finally organized so much of their perception and feeling along the lines of depressive self-blame and low self-esteem.

Nevertheless, too much about these women's considerable assets and achievements would have to be ignored to settle quickly for the correct but limited social-psychological perspective within which they appear to be merely disadvantaged members of a sexist society. Although I agree that they are that, I would also emphasize that, in the sense most immediately relevant to psychoanalytic *therapy,* the maze in which they were lost was made up of the twists and turns and dead ends of their unconscious mental processes. These were the winding, entangled paths along which they distributed all the sado-masochism and all the dreams of omnipotence that flourished in the course of their growing up in their disturbed and biased family settings and social environment. Collaborating unconsciously with their persecutors seemed to be part of their lostness, and also part of their unconsciously devised strategy. That this was so became evident once these women began to benefit from the insights developed during analysis, when they found that in many instances they could renounce some habitual self-destructive courses of action, take previously inconceivable corrective or protective actions, and go on to enjoy more assertive and happier kinds of relationships and subjective experiences. They also found that they could elicit more respectful and warmer attitudes and actions—"bring out the best" in parents, siblings, and all those with whom they lived their lives at home and at work. It is not easy to apportion weight to the factors involved in these changes: decreased distortion, decreased provocation, and increased social poise and adroitness, together with efforts to "please" the analyst in the transference. There is, however, little reason to think that individual personal changes of any of these sorts can significantly and promptly reduce the general male chauvinism that continues to surround women in our society.

In these cases, although it would have been confusing and counterproductive to focus the analyses *exclusively* on the origins and dynamics of the women's unconscious, self-injurious collaborationism, it did seem helpful to elucidate as far as possible the complex part they had played and were now playing in their own *manifest* victimization. (For reasons that should become clear, I emphasize the word *manifest*.) It is on the results of this work of elucidation that I now focus. I do so despite my recognition that, to some of those concerned with these social-psychological issues, it will seem politically naïve or offensive to take this tack; to them it may still smack of blaming the victim. In my view, however, which I take to be the usual psychoanalytic view, treatment does not apportion blame; rather, it seeks to clarify the complex structure of tragic human situations in such a way as to facilitate the personal changes that could lead to the alleviation of neurotic suffering. In neurotic suffering, the social pathology of sexism plays its part mainly in the most indirect and elusive ways; and the victimizers, too, must be understood, both analytically and social-psychologically, as themselves victims of countless generations of every form of rage and power. Of more immediate consequence, however, is the recognition that, as a rule and tragically, chronic victims begin to participate in, and even to long for, further victimization, and themselves become victimizers of others as well.

THEIR MOTHERS

The principal clues, though not the only ones, leading to understanding the vulnerabilities and conflicts of each of these gifted women were established in the course of analyzing the relationship each one unconsciously maintained with her mother. By "her mother" I refer not to the mother as she "really" was, for, as modern historians acknowledge, the one and only "real" version of a piece of history can never be re-created. Rather, I refer to the mother of psychic reality— the figure the daughter constructed and experienced in an inevitable mix of fantasy, misunderstanding, and consensually verifiable fact and memory. Many negative aspects of this psychically real mother were repressed, and those that were not were denied or suppressed in the mother's physical presence; in the analysis, however, many of these negative aspects were readily described in the course of the analysand's complaining of always being victimized by her mother, even in her physical absence. Significantly, these complaints were regularly accompanied by, or followed by, guilty reactions, although often these reactions were repressed or projected.

Interpretively, it was helpful to accept for some time the analysand's stated or implied experience that the internal object was operating with a force of its own, that is, as an introject or what would be better named an imagined presence of shifting or uncertain location (Schafer, 1968b, chap. 4); only later in each analysis did it become both possible and desirable to interpret the patient's reviving this imagined figure in stressful situations, investing power in it through fantasy, putting it into operation, and then submitting to it. That is, ultimately this introject had to be analyzed as one of those quasi-delusional symptoms that are by no means restricted to the seriously ill or the so-called borderline cases.

To maintain some focus, I concentrate on two themes in the daughter-mother relationships. These two themes seem to be two sides of the same coin; at least they stood out as allied themes in the analytic work with these women. The themes are damaged self-esteem regulation and unconscious ambivalent identification with the dominating and intrusive mother. Before proceeding I must emphasize that although the mothers appeared to be demonic figures much of the time, they emerged over the course of the work as figures with noteworthy vigor, strength, color, and other assets on which the patient had built some of her own assets and to which the patient could relate in the search for a viable relationship with this most difficult, ambivalence-intensifying figure.

The mothers of these women tended to be extraordinarily intrusive, controlling, and critical. They were so ruled by shame that they were fanatically preoccupied with keeping up appearance. At times their preoccupation seemed to be barely in touch with reality, riddled with contradictions, and inevitably fragmenting in its approach to people and situations. Always on the lookout for flaws, these mothers would constantly and tactlessly raise questions not only about clothes, boyfriends, and physical appearance, but also about intellectual and cultural interests, need for solitude and privacy, and you name it. In their controllingness, they set up powerful barriers to any overt engagement with father, thereby limiting the daughter—of course, with the father's participation on the basis of his own unconscious conflicts—mainly to the daughter-mother relationship. Indeed, they used this one-on-one or dyadic strategy in the family to the point where they disrupted alliances among children, if there were others, or between the child and friends.

Usually, as it emerged, these mothers had themselves been victims of mothers even more mentally disturbed or disturbing than they were. Their own self-esteem was in ruins, and, in their conduct, they seemed to identify a good deal with their persecutory mothers. Persecutors in one perspective, they were victims in another, and links in a chain in a third.

On the face of it, these mothers so occupied the minds of their daughters—the analysands—that it seemed at first that the daughters had been blocked from setting up their own ego ideals or ideal selves; blocked, that is, from what traditionally would be called structure-building and direction-setting internalizations. When in love, the analysands did present themselves manifestly in just that way: so dependent on the affirmation of their lovers that they had no source of self-esteem of their own. Often their fathers had been compliantly, submissively, and self-defensively sidelined in the family, blocked from showing whatever fragments of interest and appreciation, normal fatherly seductiveness, and power and ideals they had available within themselves. Such factors might, if evidenced, have compensated to some extent for the mother's deprivations and depredations.

These daughters brought forth these growth-blocking experiences to account for how crushed they were by the callousness and abuse of their lovers and by the ultimate collapse of their love relationships. Without the love of their lovers, so they claimed, they felt they were nothing, even though they said they knew that, objectively, it was not so. At fault for all of this was primarily the invasive, overoccupying mother and only secondarily the sidelined father. It seemed that the analysands' development into a full-fledged positive oedipal phase had been severely limited; in the positive transference to their male analyst, after some initial pseudo-oedipal moves, these patients approached the entire realm of intimacy with a man with much guilt and anxiety and great readiness to regress. Freely felt love for a man seemed to add a new dimension to their lives that was simultaneously thrilling and threatening.

FURTHER COMPLICATIONS

These allegations and implications seemed to be true as far as they went, but they did not go nearly far enough. A host of other factors were defined as the analyses proceeded. For one thing, the constant love and appreciation of others were needed not simply for love's sake alone or for generalized intimacy or consolation, but also and mainly to drown out, refute, or show up the persecutory mother-presence.

Second, there were complex, unconscious phallic fantasies at play. In one respect, in her psychic reality, the high-achieving, good-girl daughter was serving as the compensatory phallus for a castrated mother, an arrangement that seemed to be designed to take care simultaneously of the castration fantasies of them both. In this respect, then, the daughter no longer seemed to be merely a passive tabula rasa completely covered with the mother's derogatory inscriptions. In a second and related respect, the daughter as upwardly mobile star proved to be arrogant and disdainful in relation to both parents and to men and, unconsciously and correlatively, the proud embodiment of an upwardly mobile penis—that is, an erection: someone who, or something that, would omnipotently subdue others, if necessary even through guilt-provoking tears and protestations of misery, and who would be furious and vengeful if turned back or away, though perhaps at first only feeling misunderstood and doubly betrayed. All of which is to say that a good deal of so-called inner structure could be ascribed to the patient: specifically, a grandiose self-image that involved identificatory participation in both the overwhelming force and the defectiveness of her apparently despotic mother-presence.

In both respects, therefore, each of these women was not so lost in the maze as she seemed on first telling. Indeed, it seemed to become clear and understandable that, in her transferences to the male analyst, the very idea of "truly" yielding to a man—that is, yielding at or close to what she felt to be her inner emotional core—was anathema to her. And in this additional respect, bound as she was to her mother, she seemed to take a stance toward men modeled on her mother's toward the father.

Again correlatively, the analysand's being a high achiever in the occupational worlds that traditionally are bastions of male authority and privilege was based in part on the phallic fantasy that she was in fact "one of the boys." Consequently, when she encountered professional barriers, her outrage and grief were based as much on her unconsciously imagining that she, along with her mother, was being castrated. Also involved were three other factors: those situational elements that repeated her disappointment in her father's relative inadequacy as protector and his emotional unresponsiveness; those elements that repeated the ultimate inaccessibility of her mother, for whom her occupational superiors, male or female, were stand-ins; and those elements that stemmed from powerful social traditions inimical to the well-being of women in love and work—the traditions that from early on convey and reinforce the tendencies of men and women to equate power and penis. Thus, these patients were up against much powerful destructiveness, both in their inner world and in their manifest daily life, the two realms being, as always, inseparable from one another.

Three more factors are significant aspects of these daughters and mothers. The first factor is the evidence that these analysands seemed to maintain loving, intimate, and enduring relations with at least one other woman. Although these relationships were usually in full flower before analysis commenced, they began to be used defensively in relation to the transference. They diluted the transference, for often the friend was the first to hear about significant emotional experiences and the first consultant on meanings and conceivable courses of action; the analyst was made to feel that he was merely one consultant among others, one who was even at a disadvantage, being neither an old and intimate friend nor a woman. He was put in his place by being displaced, as the father had been. This defensive use of friends could also be seen as acting out that part of the ambivalence felt toward mother that was loving, appreciative, and dependent while directing the split-off aggression toward the minimized analyst. This enactment also protected the patient from the dangers of attack and engulfment by the mother that would, she felt, surely result should she become totally involved with mother and show both sides of the ambivalence directly to her.

The second additional factor in the mother-daughter context is the deadening effect on emotional experience that could be traced largely to the mother's critical and possessive invasiveness. These mothers and mother-presences were experienced as constantly pulling the rug out from under the spontaneous enthusiasms of their developing daughters. The enthusiasms ranged from girlfriends, boyfriends, teachers, clothes, and makeup to intellectual interests and creative endeavors. These mothers had a devastating way of being unresponsive when they were not directly inflicting shame, guilt, or anxiety on their daughters, thus making them doubt even more their spontaneous feelings. As they grew older, these daughters came to inflict this affect-destruction on themselves. In this, they were identified with their aggressor-mothers. The identification served to lessen the shock of coming up against attack in the external world when unprepared for it and then impulsively reacting to an intolerant or unresponsive mother or mother surrogate and facing the consequences. The defensive strategy was peace at any price.

More than defense, however, the identification helped preserve an exclusive, totalistic tie to the mother; anything less was felt with terror to be a totally severed relationship such as was felt every time the mother failed to respond positively to her daughter's signs of growth and separate identity. Because the mother's influence continued to limit the range and depth of her daughter's investment in other relationships, the daughter lacked a developed context that would support a definite and affirmed identity of her own. Without the mother, the daughter would be alone and would be a nothing.

Consequently, when in treatment, these analysands backed off from excitement and the possibility of somehow getting excited. They were careful to maintain their own and their mother's rigid controllingness. But they were alive enough to sense the resulting deadness, which lowered their self-esteem further, even though, in self-contradiction, they also valued deadness as a barrier against the transference relationship. In one respect the analyst was put in the role of the persecutory mother; in another, that of the weak father; in a third respect, however, by consciously disclaiming their own aliveness, the analysands seemed to want to put the analyst in the role of the one who argued for life, liberty, and the pursuit of happiness, while they took the part of the other side of their ambivalence and clung to their controls and defenses and thereby to their invasive mothers and their identification with them.

Technically, the analyst had to do his best to maintain the fine balance between, on the one side, blindly accepting this projective identification laden with anxiety and guilt and, on the other, lapsing into a subdued, hands-off countertransference. Much of the time the important intervention was pointing out the analysand's attempting to create this no-win position for the analyst to occupy.

In addition to using women friends to split the transference and the ambivalent clinging to emotional deadness, I mention as the third additional factor *reparation*. In being the phallic completion of the crippled mother, the mother who herself had been wounded into cruelty by her own mother as well as by men and society, the daughter was healing her. She was making her mother whole, realizing her mother's many unfulfilled dreams through being a good-girl, high achiever. In that reparative role, it could not be acceptable to enter into a deep love relationship with a man experienced as such, for to do so would be to abandon her own mother, cripple her once again, and empty her out and depress her beyond what the analysand could bear. In this respect, love and guilt combined to reinforce the analysand's need to be omnipotent, in this context omnipotently reparative. However much each woman suffered in love and however abjectly she conducted herself outwardly in her heterosexual affairs and even in the workplace, in her psychic reality she carried power into the maze that was her life.

COUNTERTRANSFERENCE

The maze in which these women seem to stay lost is the maze of human tragedy, so much of which is necessarily beyond independent conscious reckoning. Consequently, progress in analysis is slow and painful, the work is arduous for the analyst as well as the patient, not every such patient gets deeply into treatment or continues it, and not every one of them emerges with the same types and amounts of gain. In my experience, however, analysis of the complex, androgynous, multivalent merger with the mother as it takes place in a sexist world often can make a significant adaptive difference. For the analyst, the work requires eliciting and dealing with much rage on many levels of functioning, with much manipulative and vengeful exercise of power, often enacted in the subtlest ways, and also with much maternal transference that sometimes is quite hostile and grandiose and sometimes blissful and only seemingly purely heterosexual.

This work requires much analysis of the countertransferences peculiar to working with acutely suffering, abused but powerful, successful, and exceptionally well-endowed women. For example, analysts may have the countertransference response of letting themselves be sidelined emotionally as the father had been all along, while at the same time, and still like the father, being the recipient of furtive and feebly erotic positive oedipal gestures and responses. Another example is analysts' countertransference response of wanting to assert their own force against the formidable latent power and control of these women—that is, not to feel the analytical equivalent of the "castrated wimp" stereotype or like the obligingly sidelined father—and to resort then to directiveness, emphasis, or more and more interpretation. Another countertransference features analysts' wanting to prove by shows of respect, support, warmth, and so on that they are not the narcissistic persecutory mother or a sexist male stand-in for her; also, that they are there to protect rather than neglect and to bind up wounds rather than inflict them or suffer them. This countertransference may touch at the center of the reasons why a person has become an analyst in the first place, and it is all the easier to rationalize if he shares the outlook on sexism in the world that I presented earlier.

Yet another countertransference may induce declarations of support for the patient's angry view of men and our sexist society. But this move will only make it harder to analyze the distortions and provocations that the patient has come to rely on defensively and through identification with the aggressor; specifically, it will obscure the play of these factors in the transference.

Sexist abuse and discrimination seem to be best dealt with as clear-cut trauma would be: acknowledged and used as an occasion to explore the unconscious meanings, all the pain and possible gratification, and all the fixation and resiliency unconsciously associated with that trauma. Of particular value is the demonstration to the patient of how she constructs the transference both to repeat and to repair the sexist traumatization. To proceed analytically in a less searching manner would be to join manifestly and countertransferentially an alliance with the abused analysand, a move that would leave in place the disturbances of reality testing and of self-enhancing adaptation. Thereby the analyst would be allowing the crucial, unconsciously maintained conflicts I have summarized to continue to limit the patient's mastery of problems and resumption of personal, autonomous development.

As always, every other kind of countertransference may be at play in these cases. I mention here only a few more, each of which inevitably narrows the analyst's interpretive range. Analysts may remain on only one psychosexual level, such as the oedipal or preoedipal or just the anal. They may stress only the positive (heterosexual) oedipal at the expense of the negative (homosexual) oedipal. They may focus too much on negative transference, in these cases on the woman's destructive, envious, castrating desires, thereby minimizing or dismissing her struggle against loving, admiring, idealizing, and submissive tendencies (in my experience as supervisor, a common countertransference). Also, analysts may disembody or desomatize the psychosexual factors and refer only to autonomy, dependency, trust, control, empathy, and the like, thereby playing down concretely oral, anal, and genital feelings and fantasies. (In this chapter, as I was not attempting a complete coverage of the analyses that were carried out, I did not go into these matters; anyone familiar with psychosexual theory can easily fill in the bodily referents of many of the major developments reported.)

THESE WOMEN IN LOVE: A BRIEF SUMMARY

Returning now to these women in love, or more usually desolate among the ruins of "love affairs," it seemed that their lovers, like the bulk of the other men they worked with, combined features of their mothers, their fathers, and the masculinized selves or body parts that they had projected onto these men. Their desolation and their excruciating pain combined oedipal and preoedipal features. It was *oedipal* in its (1) repetition of failure with father and confirmation of castrated status, all high achievement to the contrary notwithstanding; (2) providing positive oedipal gratification through playing the seductive but aim-inhibited role of the wonderful little girl; and (3) providing negative oedipal gratification in the sexualized union with mother. It was *preoedipal* in the centrality of the primitive merger with mother that unconsciously was played out in heterosexual relationships. With the undoing of that merger went loss of both the mother and her love and consequently the collapse of their joint grandiosity. In this light, much of their clinging to these men, much of their tolerance of criticism, demand, and abuse, involved repetition of the early projective-introjective relationship with mother, the seductively cruel, pregenital love relationship of early infancy. It was preoedipal, too, in the early guilt and reparativeness directed toward the damaged mother. Thus, their way of being in love with men could be viewed in its preoedipal aspects as helping them keep in check overt expressions of their multileveled omnipotence, rage, envy, and guilt, and at the same time obscure their relatively retarded individuation and engenderedness. All in all, their painful and costly victimization in this sexist world was therefore not without its rewards in defensive security against anxiety and guilt and in unconscious pleasure.

CONCLUSION

Although I believe my account of descriptive features and developmental and dynamic factors to be the valid outcome of helpful work with one subset of analysands, I do not claim to have laid out the necessary and sufficient conditions for a well-circumscribed disorder of living. Many of the factors I mentioned have turned up in the course of clinical work with women who presented themselves as the crushed, ineffectual victims of manifestly powerful, vain, and persecutory mothers. Also, some high-achieving women seem to attach themselves not to the sadistic-narcissistic type of man just described but rather to men they experience as passive and crippled on the surface, rather like the weak father and the handicapped mother, even though not lacking furtively sadistic and narcissistic tendencies of their own. The women who make this kind of object choice may have experienced less criticism and more idealization during their development. Further, the kind of pairing I have described may be encountered in relationships between men, between women, and in reverse form between men and women. And finally, I fully recognize that the intimate relationships of high-achieving women need not be deeply troubled at all. I have written here only about most of those who have come for analysis and seemed to show this one of a number of possible patterns of disturbance.

Whatever the limits may be on the generalizability of my report, it can, I think, be useful to clinicians in following the twists and turns of the unconsciously maintained mazes of power and rage in which women can lose themselves as they try to make their way effectively in our sexist world. Psychoanalytic work on this kind of tragic situation is of particular moment in our modern era of critical reexamination of relations between the sexes. For the female patients, it seems to increase the possibilities of a liberated and fulfilling existence in the inner world and in society. And for all those who engage in critical inquiry, it may increase their range of understanding.

PART THREE

THEORIES AS MASTER NARRATIVES

CHAPTER 9

Reading Freud's Legacies

PSYCHOANALYTIC DISCOURSE AND MODERN CRITICAL THEORY

To give a reading of Freud's contributions and their development up to the present is to face the future as well as the past. Ostensibly, those who write or speak on Freud direct attention to the recent and remote past in order to develop an objective account of a legacy and perhaps to suggest what has been done with it. In this effort, however, they cannot hope to be simply descriptive. Like it or not, they are prescriptive at the same time, for, inevitably, they chart a future for psychoanalysis. I say so because I believe that all accounts of psychoanalytic history, however conventionalized they may be, are bound to place certain matters in the foreground, relegate others to the background, and ignore still others. On this understanding, historical accounts have to be imbued with their authors' value judgments. The narratives indicate what the authors hold dear, and it is through this implementation of values that they prescribe a future. In effect, the historian will be saying, "This is what psychoanalysis should be," and in the same breath, two related prescriptions as well: "This is the best way to talk about psychoanalysis," and, "This is the way to be or become a psychoanalyst."

If this much is accepted, then it can be added that the mode of telling prescribes-allegiance to a particular discourse. A discourse is constituted in part by interlocking modes of establishing values and formulating and challenging truth-claims and in part by the practices that, it is believed, legitimize this discourse and are in turn legitimized by it. Therefore, to say of a discussion of Freud's legacy that it expresses one's aspirations for psychoanalysis is also to argue on behalf of specific values, truth-claims, and practices. This, then, must be true of the reading of Freud's legacy that I shall be presenting. Although my reading obviously owes a lot to familiar discursive traditions in our field, it also draws heavily upon what may be called twentieth-century Enlightenment.

I present this account because I want to convey my version of how we might try to situate Freud in the discourse of contemporary intellectuality. Intellectually, Freud was a child of the Enlightenment that dates roughly from the late seventeenth century, and we would, I think, all agree that it was in the context of the development of that Enlightenment that he tried to be up to date. In this "official" aspect of his effort, he provided a rationalistic, empiricist, objectivist account of his methods, the findings based on them, and his conclusions. He presented himself as working within the prevailing axioms and conventions of discourse of the natural sciences of his time. He also drew heavily on the content of what was, for him, contemporary psychology, anthropology, philosophy, archaeology, philology, and other disciplines, all of which were cast from the same epistemological and methodological mold.

In this discourse, language is taken unreflectively as a transparent medium of communication. It is not regarded as bound to person, time, place, culture, or specific conventions. Consequently, Freud did not regard the version of it he used to report his psychoanalytic work as having evolved in such a way as to express and serve primarily the interests of the white, male bourgeoisie of the Western world. Freud viewed language as a transparent and sufficient medium that is, however challenging its content may be, in harmony with the established order of things and what he called its "self-evident" morality.

But the terms of modern critical thought are not the terms of this earlier and still widely endorsed Enlightenment. In the newer context, language occupies center stage in theoretical thinking and research. Language is seen as that which makes the world that it tells about. Moreover, it makes this world through implicit as well as explicit dialogue; that is, it functions and has functioned always in a social context. Language now is a variable and not a constant; it is a message in the guise of a medium, a set of perspectives rather than a clear glass window on the world, an ideological process rather than an essence, a specific cultural net rather than a universal mode of exchange.

Additionally, it is an instrument of power to be wielded for good, as in therapy (usually), or for bad, as in racism and sexism. Therefore, I think it appropriate to try to situate Freud for our time, that is, amid the multiple perspectives made available by contemporary critical theory. Although my effort is incomplete, sketchy, and highly contestable, it conveys my allegiance to the idea of psychoanalysis as a discipline with an ongoing life.

To focus on the language of psychoanalysis requires paying particularly close attention to its dialogic nature. Equally important is the recognition that the practice of psychoanalysis is rooted in dialogue between analyst and analysand, between analytic teacher and student, and between colleagues. As so much is a matter of interchange, we may say that through dialogue psychoanalysis keeps coming into being. All the more reason to establish a dialogic context for this presentation.

To develop this context, let us consider first dialogue in relation to the general history of ideas. Progress in any discipline has always depended on continuing dialogue. Continuing dialogue over conflicting aspirations and truth-claims helps refine our notions of importance; our methods, samples, and arrangements of data; our logical tools; our conclusions; and always the rhetoric we rely on to make a case persuasively. Through dialogue, we also learn better how the opposition makes its case. Learning that, we then try to find common ground; failing that, we begin to develop more persuasive arguments for our point of view. In the process, once the questions being asked are modified, the answers will be framed differently, and even the subject of inquiry may be changed to whatever now seems to be more urgent or more fruitful than its predecessors. Goals are never set with finality. And taking into account all those contemporary dialogues aimed at connecting as well as contrasting the different perspectives associated with race, gender, and social class can only add further to the sense that the history of ideas, of theory and practice, is always in flux.

From what has already been said, it follows that the history of psychoanalysis should be written, read, and taught from this dialogic point of view. To give one example of the movement of dialogue: In reaction to changing times and interests, based in part on extensive philosophy-of-science debates over the problems of traditional metapsychology and in part on the widening scope of analytic perception and practice, which has been increasing the influence of Kleinian object-relational thought, we have been witness in the course of one generation to a spectacular change. Specifically, most psychoanalysts have shifted their discussions away from refined elaborations and critiques of the theory of psychic energy and the energic underpinnings of psychic structure; further, they have even been moving away from rigorous debates over the idea of structure itself and the explanatory value of structural concepts (Schafer, 1988).

The current trend seems to be to use the term *structure* descriptively. Used in this way, structure merely refers to whatever the observer pieces together into stable patterns of motives or modes of experience and overt conduct that are relevant to the thesis being developed. Implicitly, structure is no longer treated as a fixed essence of things waiting to be discovered, and analysts no longer are so preoccupied with the question of how it is ever possible for structure to come into existence, develop, and remain stable.

Instead, increasing numbers of analysts seem to find it more engaging and worthwhile to join dialogues that feature object relations and self experience and corresponding refinements in theoretical and technical conceptions of early development as it is reflected in the experience of transference and countertransference. In these dialogues, they weigh a variety of approaches to understanding and modifying psychopathology of every sort, and they emphasize particularly both the development and the disruption of their empathizing with archaic motives, fantasies, anxieties, and defensive shifts of orientation and experience.

Earlier I mentioned the need for persuasive rhetoric. Because rhetorical issues figure prominently in what follows, I should explain what I meant. If all cases are made through implicit or explicit dialogue, each case can be developed adequately only if its insecure or assailable aspects are recognized, explicitly confronted, and either persuasively justified or artfully dodged. In any event, the success of an argument depends to a noteworthy extent on rhetorical adroitness. Rhetoric is, however, not something people choose to use; every way of speaking or writing is subject to rhetorical analysis, and every way may be used more or less adroitly. Emphasizing and exploring how this is so is a conspicuous part of the linguistic turn in the recent history of ideas.

Consider this rhetorical perspective on psychoanalytic language: Much of the psychoanalytic literature is written in a drab style. I suggest that this style is a specialized and conventionalized rhetorical attempt to be persuasive. It attempts to be persuasive by creating an image of the writer as a reliable member of the Old Enlightenment: a neutral, value-free, countertransference-free, well-trained scientific observer; a genderless, raceless, classless expert delivering a monologue that gives all the appearance of having been stripped of rhetorical ploys. In part, this image is designed to instill a false sense of security in the reader. "Trust me," it says. And unquestioning trust is badly needed in many cases because it serves to blind the reader to two obvious difficulties that arise in connection with the detailed deterministic explanations usually featured in psychoanalytic publications.

The first difficulty is that those deterministic explanations cannot stand up to the simplest of *traditional* scientific tests, if indeed any such test can even be formulated. This difficulty arises because the testing of psychoanalytic propositions calls for a quite different approach to corroboration. The second difficulty is that the deterministic accounts do not satisfy the fictitious standard of perfect authorial disinterestedness, for usually it is easy to show that their author is trying hard to win readers over to his or her conclusions by more than the content and logic of the "findings" being reported. That *more* is a self-conscious rhetorical effort to be persuasive, and it is felt to be required because others working in the same area have either already presented persuasive arguments for other underdetermined conclusions or soon will.

I want to add an interpretation of defense to this account of the drabness of much psychoanalytic rhetoric. I suggest that this conventionalized drabness is an attempt to deny that there is much about Freud's creation of psychoanalysis, and thus of his legacy to us, that can be characterized as a triumph of vivid and masterful rhetoric. Freud wrote psychoanalysis: He wrote it in the teeth of powerful scientific opponents, and he wrote it persuasively. Consequently, in reading him, we cannot separate his content from what is widely acknowledged to be his powerful and beguiling, and sometimes even beautiful, style. Freud's winning language is now known, however, to have covered a multitude of shortcomings in his arguments. I can say so in this more enlightened and permissive period of psychoanalytic history without being thought to deny the least aspect of Freud's creative genius. Other writers on psychoanalysis, even those most closely identified with Freud, use their own rhetoric and so create more or less modified versions of the discipline.

My general point is that there is no absolutely specific and static Freudian essence. Nothing lies beyond any one writer's rhetoric and thus beyond the realm of implicit and explicit dialogue. Consequently, in order to assess properly each and every version of psychoanalysis, one must read it as a document situated in a personal context that in turn is linguistically situated in a historical and ideological context of dialogue.

FREUD'S MULTIPLE LEGACIES

All this said, how shall we begin to approach more directly the large topic of Freud's legacy? I begin by proposing that we give up the idea that there is just one legacy to sum up and assess, for in a world for-ever constituted anew through continuing dialogue, there can never be only one theoretical or technical legacy. There can only be lega*cies,* linguistic legacies, legacies that are theoretical through and through. Freud's texts will remain open forever to alternative readings and writ-ings: scientific, literary, and cultural. In time, the absolutist writings and readings on theory and technique, with which we are so familiar and which still are published in official analytic journals, will become a thing of the past. Already they come across to some of us as narrowly doctrinaire and authoritarian if not old-fashioned bravura perfor-mances. In the perspective of the modern Enlightenment, it must be Freud's readers and Freudian writers who continuously co-create Freud's legacy. This they do by how they read his texts and by how and what they write. As the readers and writers change—and they do change—Freudian psychoanalysis changes.

Further support for this elevation of reading and writing can be mustered by any survey of single topics in the analytic literature, for it requires no strain to read each such segment of our literature as a bat-tlefield of competing, incompatible, and newly triumphant claims concerning what Freud said, meant, intended, or laid the groundwork for. One example is the ongoing dispute over Freud's general orienta-tion to psychoanalysis that is based on the assumption that there is a single best or correct way to translate Freud from one language to another: Was he scientific or humanistic? Does *Ich* mean "ego" or "self" or both? Another example is the often-repeated, authoritarian recommendation on how to settle disagreements: "Back to Freud!" When that recommendation is made as a simple absolute rather than as a prod to keep up one's reading of Freud, it suggests wrongly that anyone could hope to read Freud in an absolutely selfless, value-free, culture-free, nondialogic way and thereby reach not only the right answer for the moment but the one and only true Freud. "Back to Freud!" is perhaps the greatest rhetorical ploy of all. The advisor is say-ing "Back to *my* Freud; repress the rest."

What is the basis of these interpretive wars? It is not only that Freud was not always perfectly consistent or explicit in his creative work. Nor is it just that the rhetoric through which he created and conveyed his contributions ranged from the highly tentative, uncertain, apologetic, and ingratiating all the way to the virtually dictatorial, and ranged as well from the rigorously and mechanistically scientific all the way to the free-flowing and evocatively humanistic. Nor yet are these interpretive wars based solely on what is commonly recognized to be the influence of personality, training, and experience on the way readers read Freud and new writers write Freud. There is more to add to this list of undeniably important factors.

Here I discuss only one additional set of factors: those related to power. The adversarial readings and writings I have referred to have been based to a significant extent on both the *general* history of changing organizational conditions within the psychoanalytic movement and the *specific* history of official policy regarding the programming of meetings, the publication of articles in the analytic journals, the making of referrals to colleagues, and the selection of candidates. In these respects, it seems as if, at any one time, power has played a major role in deciding the truth about Freud's legacy. And this power has not always been attained and maintained through intellectual and clinical accomplishment and consensus.

It should come as no surprise that the play of power within organizations of analysts has figured importantly in the intellectual and professional history of psychoanalysis: The exercise of power is always with us as human beings. Psychoanalysis is no exception to this general principle, and the principle need not stimulate despair. In this regard it is not only hopeful but interesting that, necessarily, shifts do occur in the conditions of power and in the modes of its employment. These shifts are the result of dialogue that cannot be silenced. And correlated with these shifts are shifts in the intensity of the surveillance, discipline, and punishment of those who oppose or disregard the doctrines that the powerful try to enforce. It is these shifts that enable changes to be established in what has been taken to be important and true. Consequently, it may be said that the changes in power will always play an important role in the flux that characterizes the truths and the values of psychoanalysis. Consideration of Freud's legacy cannot be split off from the history of power.

Witness, for example, the relatively recent growth of interest in the preoedipal period, a period that was once not to be made too much of. With that growth of interest has come progressive articulation of the concepts of mothering, parenting, and selfhood; an ever-more insistent emphasis on understanding early aggression and early stages of guilt in treating extreme cases; and also special attention to preestablished adaptation, the acquisition of language, and early modes of cognition. Another example is found in the many competing and as yet unstable but terribly important modifications of what has been represented as the psychoanalytic truths about women and the importance of those truths for the general theory of psychoanalysis. Not one of these changes has taken place outside the arena of power; each has had to be fought for, and some are still being fought for and often fought over as well.

Power in new hands; power diffused and wielded differently; surveillance relaxed; professional discipline and punishment themselves under extreme suspicion, not to mention their curtailment by actual or potential intramural strifes and even lawsuits: These changes have allowed and fostered an altered set of facts of life in contemporary psychoanalysis. One new feature of today's freer psychoanalytic life is the tolerance, both genuine and feigned, of multiple and competing claims about what psychoanalysis is. Another feature is that, far from being considered monolithic, each contemporary school of psychoanalytic thought may be heard more accurately as a din of voices in argument over readings. No longer is it possible to claim legitimately to be presenting an exclusive, purportedly final or unarguable account of Freud's legacy.

I suggest that this pluralistic view of Freud's legacy, this view that there can only be legacies that are forever subject to change, is itself one of Freud's legacies. Although it is my impression that Freud always wanted to be in control of the development of psychoanalysis, I believe, too, that he also wanted his discipline to be open to challenge and improvement through revision. Even if he often seemed to want to be the absolute judge of proposed change, if not the prime originator of it, in his role as dedicated scientist, he recognized that in order for psychoanalysis to qualify as a science, its propositions should be forever on trial. Certainly he continually reviewed his own formulations and changed them. But in his wanting to have the last word, he revealed that he did not always live up to his own ideals, for it is one consequence of the open-minded scientific attitude that he espoused so well in other respects that there never can be a last word. No one ever can have the last word, because no investigator or writer can control history. Certainly no one can ever end it. No one can stop the ongoing dialogue. Any one language has its limits. Power and prestige have their limits. Closure will elude us forever.

No one can even dictate how a name is to be used. Freud, contrary to his wish, could not even own the word *psychoanalysis* for long. Although one may regret, as I do, the extreme diffusion of meaning of "psychoanalysis" in today's world, we cannot hope to halt or reverse it. Diffusion has already gone so far that, whenever "psychoanalysis" is used, we must wonder just what it refers to. In my view, the history of psychoanalysis has reached a point where it has become futile to argue over whether this or that and nothing else is the true or real psychoanalysis. Now it makes more sense to argue that only this or that specific idea or practice conforms to the version of psychoanalysis to which one is committed as author, teacher, thinker, or practitioner, or that it conforms to the version of it that a certain group of respected peers consider to have the longest and strongest tradition behind it or the greatest heuristic power. Today we must always be prepared to argue the merits of our chosen position. It was not always so, or so plainly a matter of choice of what to value and wish to transmit to the future. We must accept the idea that psychoanalysis is not property: It belongs to no one in particular. On this view, much controversy in psychoanalysis can be seen to be no more than pointless and history-blind debate over ownership.

FREUD IN THE HERE AND NOW

We cannot afford to neglect the transformations that take place in the dialogues that transmit psychoanalysis from one generation to the next. This consideration alone would compel us to regard Freud's legacies as ongoing processes. We may say that these legacies continuously come into being; they are constantly in transition; they do not remain identical to themselves. Or we may say that for every generation, Freud is always here and now, never there and then.

I suggested earlier that transmission of ideas occurs through a process that may be called a dialogue between Freud and his readers and writers. I want now to add that, phenomenologically speaking, in this dialogue Freud may be said to be constantly talking back to his readers. I have in mind the Freud who is always here and now. His constant presence is felt by those who keep restudying his texts without being locked into an infantile transference to him or to their teachers. They find that the texts are so rich that, as readers, they must continuously correct and supplement their earlier readings. The texts even provide reminders of how Freud paved the way toward analytic ideas that keep on being put forward as new, as truly modern, even as revolutionary and superior alternatives to his ideas. In saying this I am not implying that Freud knew it all, nor that he could have known all that he did know in the same way a modern analyst knows it, nor yet that he would approve of much that is now commonly accepted by those who call themselves classical Freudian analysts. Amazingly, however, there is a Freud who is felt by serious students to be holding up his end of a lively and invariably refocusing conversation.

This inexhaustible and zestful readiness for continuing dialogue with his changing readers is another of Freud's legacies. That there is a Freud who can be always present to us is attributable to his having written in a way that steadily invites the continuation of dialogue. In his welcoming aspect, he stands above many of his influential followers, specifically those whose tone suggests that we are being told what's what rather than being prompted to consider what's next. It is only in this processive and dialogical sense that the admonition "Back to Freud!" can have a nonauthoritarian modern meaning, the meaning that it is in the nature of the work never to be done.

FREUD'S TRANSFORMATIONAL DIALOGUE

Engaging as this contribution to dialogue may be, Freud made a far more fundamental one. I venture to claim that out of Freud's genius issued an altogether new form of dialogue. He made it possible for therapists and patients to engage in consequential forms of transformational dialogue that had never existed before. He showed therapists how to do things with words to help revise radically their patients' hitherto fixed, unconsciously directed constructions of both subjective experience and action in the world: to use words to change lives in a thought-through, insightful manner. No one before him had done anything as profound, comprehensive, skillful, basically rational, and effective. Of the many possible ways to describe this monumental achievement, I submit the following. Freud's clinical dialogue alters in crucial ways the analysand's consciously narrated presentation of the self and its history among people by *destabilizing, deconstructing,* and *defamiliarizing* it.

Before proceeding further, note that it is arbitrary to discuss these processes in sequence, as if they are logically and temporally distinguished; however, my account will, I think, be clearer if I describe each process somewhat differently and invoke each in a somewhat different context. Think of it as using different windows to look into the same room and never seeing things quite the same way. Also, although much communication goes on nonverbally, it is conventionally accepted that a *psychoanalytic* therapy requires bringing significant issues into verbal dialogue—psychoanalysis as the "talking cure."

To achieve the destabilization, deconstruction, and defamiliarization of the patient's narratives, the classical psychoanalytic dialogue uses the free-association method; frequent sessions for continuity; and sessions that last for most or all of an hour so that time is available for each day's dialogue to develop, double back on itself, seemingly cancel itself out, or otherwise enter into the larger treatment process. The classical psychoanalytic dialogue also features the interpretation of defenses against full expression and felt interaction. And with the help of the mixture of the "regressive" and "progressive" phenomena it elicits, it reconstructs the way in which the history of these defenses and their motives is grounded in the typical subjective danger situations of early childhood.

Because the life narratives with which the analysand has come for treatment are more or less stabilized by these defenses, the invaluable analysis of defense, insofar as it is effective, necessarily *destabilizes* them. The process destabilizes both the established stories of guilt, trauma, neglect, misunderstanding, and blissful, unambivalent love, and the stories that seem merely to have been put together spontaneously in the thick of the ongoing analysis. The patient develops a new slant on lives that have been lived and that are expected to be lived; at the least, the versions of lives that gain importance are far more complex, less rigid and one-sided, and more tragically and ironically constructed (Schafer, 1970a).

What now of *deconstruction*? The analysand's narratives are deconstructed through the analyst's steadily focusing on first, their internal contradictions, their being founded on displacements, condensations, and marginalizations, and their erasures of expectable, emotion-laden crucial life experience; and second, the hidden hierarchies of value in taken-for-granted polarities such as male-female, active-passive, and dominant-submissive. Psychoanalytic deconstruction brings out particularly the contradictory or otherwise incoherent types of overt and fantasized relationship that the analysand tries to develop with the relatively neutral and relatively opaque figure of the analyst. This deconstructive handling of transference clarifies the complex, unstable, and conflictual nature of the analysand's enduring attempts at self-definition and relationship. The analyst also takes up many paradoxical reasons for repetitious enactments of these often quite painful transferences. In principle, though for practical reasons not always in practice, nothing is taken for granted about any version of self, relationship, or reality in general.

Contrary to popular stereotype, however, deconstruction is not a lofty name for destructiveness and disillusionment. Psychoanalytic deconstruction makes possible new and sounder construction, in particular the construction of more fulfilling narratives of lives in progress. The analyst uses the analytically defined elements of narrative incoherence to begin to *retell* the analysand's presentations and to bring the analysand into the process of retelling, now in the terms of unconsciously developed and maintained conflict and taken-for-granted or well-rationalized compromise formation. At the same time, the analyst and analysand together construct *a* history for what Freud called the analysand's "conditions for loving," a phrase to which many of us today would want to add "conditions for hating" and "conditions for playing dead or empty." (It is to take account of narrative variation among analysts that I say *a* history, not *the* history.) Among the virtues of the new constructions are their being both more confident and more provisional than those they have replaced.

Certainly, any dedicated deconstructionist would approach even these new and provisional analytic narratives with an eye to their incoherent and contradictory elements. Being the kind of method it is, deconstruction accepts no self-exclusionary limits on its application. It recognizes that to develop its position it must use the very language whose basic coherence it regularly challenges. But here the therapeutic goals of the analytic dyad intervene: Analyst and analysand make a judgment, based on shared health values, that any attempt at further change at this time might create more problems than benefits or might just lack adequate momentum; it may also be judged that the patient is in a more or less adequate position to continue the work of analysis independently, as the need arises and to the extent necessary. At this point, the joint work of deconstruction and new construction comes to an end.

There is more, however; specifically, the *defamiliarization* accomplished by the analytic dialogue. In the therapeutic interaction, the analyst begins to retell insightfully, roundedly, and empathically much that the analysand initially has told and is telling naïvely, abjectly, seductively, or aggressively, and, in any case, defensively. By introducing new or revised or unexpectedly interdependent storylines as major amendments to the analysand's narratives or as supplements to them, the analyst begins the process of defamiliarizing them and here, too, engages the analysand in the process. The nature of life history changes; its variables and its conceptions of time and place, of process and progress, and of relevance continue to change. As the patient's sense of the "timeless unconscious" develops, established accounts of present circumstances and future prospects also become less familiar.

Secretly or obviously, the analysand always approaches with great trepidation these new ways of making history and the new versions that result from them. Consequently, much working through always remains to be done, both during the analysis and after its conclusion. Insightful mastery is achieved through the kind of repeated defamiliarization and working through that psychoanalysis alone is capable of effecting. With the sense of real life as an ongoing process, the patient is prepared to accept the fruits of these labors as always open to further modification.

In the foreground of these retellings is, as I have emphasized in several chapters, the figure of the analysand as an active party to bringing about much that initially is or was experienced in passive, frequently victimized terms. In this respect, the dialogue helps the analysand shift toward some form of assertive and responsible psychosexual and psychosocial maturity. In other respects, however, as in the case of hitherto denied or minimized trauma or abuse, the analysand remains no longer defensively omnipotent; now the patient is better able to accept that in many respects she or he has been, is, and will be more or less passive, helpless, needful, or yielding. In the latter respects, analysts often observe a beneficial reduction of grandiose inflations of self-esteem, guilt, independence, and imperviousness.

Freud taught us to see the action in apparent inaction and accident, but he taught us, too, how much of our sense of power and control is illusory, is compensatory fantasy that denies and reverses the powerful and sometimes dire necessities of the body. He showed us that we share with others in our world a great amount of helplessness over our life cycles. In this, as in all of his psychology—a psychology of unconscious conflict and necessary ambiguities and paradoxes that pervade human experience and action—he introduced a modern tone into our conceptions of tragedy and irony; after Freud, our understandings and narratives of human existence could never be the same. We may add this legacy to all the others.

DIALOGUE IN THE INNER WORLD

One outstanding feature of the analytic dialogue is its showing by interpretation that, both in the past and in the present, dialogic experience is never limited to two people present to one another physically. Far from it. Through analysis the analysand is able to develop and tolerate accounts of the dialogue that no longer feature exclusively or predominantly abstract tendencies, general patterns, habits, socially defined traits, and social existence defined only in the conventional terms of behavioral social interaction. Instead, the crucial analytic versions tell of a multitude of voices rising from his or her own imagined inner world as well as a multitude of inner-world voices that, by perception or projection or both, the analysand locates in the analyst or others in the surround. Ideally, analysis brings it about that this concordant and discordant chorus of voices is no longer obliterated or muted by repression and other defenses and no longer mislocated by projection. Once it can be heard clearly, it is accessible to sorting out. Each influential voice may then become clear enough to be traced back to early experience in real or imagined relations with others; at least, its power is reduced because it is recognized for what it is. Thus far I have spoken only of voices, but, of course, other powerful sensory images of the inner multitude, some of them purely kinesthetic, are often presented eloquently.

Particularly significant for the analytic narrative are all those fantastic, libidinal and aggressive, body-centered, emotion-laden elaborations and misunderstandings that young children regularly introduce into their experience of their relationships and then elaborate further over time. The sorting out of these features and sources is rendered especially difficult and time-consuming by the interplay of introjective and projective processes that, according to the analytic retelling, characterizes the analysand's unconsciously carried-out construction of experience both in the past and in the here and now of the analytic relationship. In other words, the interpenetration of inner and outer worlds and past and present worlds is extensive, often subtle, and regularly fluid, and its analysis can never totally eliminate ambiguity.

THE CENTRALITY OF PSYCHIC REALITY

These inner-world phenomena make up a large part of another of Freud's great legacies, specifically, his idea of psychic reality. That idea embraces much more than what is conventionally meant by subjectivity and its individual variations. In psychoanalysis, psychic reality begins with that conventional notion and goes on to include the analytically essential idea of unconscious fantasy that features all those twists and turns encountered in dreams and their interpretation.

Psychic reality refers to still more than that. It refers as well to individually different and persisting wishful but conflictual and compromised modes of *constructing* new experiences on all levels of development. It emphasizes how, unconsciously, people make and remake their own subjective experience, how they do so continuously—that is, when awake as well as asleep—and how, at later stages of development, they may have to exaggerate the weight and impact of their preserved accounts of early experience. Thus it is that they may be said to live in a second reality.

This second reality lies beyond conventional reality. In it space, time, and identity are in constant flux and disarray, so that then and now, there and then, no and yes, disturbing and insignificant, I and thou, all coexist, mingle, or change places; all may be reversed or fragmented or otherwise isolated from conventional rationality. Freud's dialogue centers more and more on this powerfully influential second reality. The dialogic chorus of voices is heard mostly there. The multitude of images resides there. The transference and defenses live in it. Dreams and screen memories portray it.

We do not dismiss as irrelevant or altogether inconsequential the "first" reality—by which I mean not one that necessarily originated earlier in time but one that is conscious, rationally organized, impersonal, and adapted to convention. For clinical purposes, however, it provides only a shrunken account of the analysand's mental activity and so is limited in its therapeutic usefulness. It is the largely unconscious second reality that emerges as the chief locale or scene of effective psychoanalysis.

THE SELF-REFLEXIVE DIALOGUE

Freud's new dialogue may be characterized in yet another way; it is a supplementary way in that this characterization rests on all that has come before it. It may be said that Freud developed a therapeutically consequential dialogue that, to a very large extent, is about itself. Basically, it is self-reflexive. However much the dialogue refers to other matters, such as past life history or current problems in work, love, and self-esteem, again and again it takes a self-referential turn. The focus necessarily and productively shifts to what was said or left unsaid in the analytic relationship and how it was or was not recounted, and when, why, and on what understanding. The focus also shifts to how each development is encased in a set of hopeful and fearful fantasies. Further, it shifts to the ways in which the formal features of the verbal and nonverbal dialogue may be construed either as attempts to remember and communicate with the analyst through enactment much material that has been deeply repressed or as attempts to introduce new material in order to refute or confirm interpretations already in play in the analysis. These formal features may even be construed in both ways: repeating the old *and* introducing the new. In any case, these communications are made mostly unconsciously.

There are, however, many ways in which a dialogue could be about itself; it is the *psychoanalytic* way that Freud devised and developed to a considerable degree, the way that I have been reviewing, that seems to me to be essential to the dialogue's therapeutic and transformational potential.

FREUD AND FEMINISM

It remains to take up briefly what I consider to be another of Freud's great legacies: his contribution to the further development of feminism. If we are to situate Freud in contemporary intellectual life, then we must consider him in relation to the profoundly influential, relatively recent revolution in critical theory that has been sparked by feminism.

I claim Freud for feminism even though it is now plain that he shared and implicitly endorsed much of the bourgeois sexism of his time. Among other things, he was dismissive of feminism itself. On the other hand, however, he was at least able to begin to transcend his biases in his more specifically psychoanalytic propositions. His curiosity and creativity did not stop at the borders of the mentality of the men he studied. However imperfectly and at times even woundingly he did it, by attempting to present women as fully human, by reversing the tendency to marginalize them, he participated relatively early in this century's process of restoring to them aspects of worth and dignity equal to those of men. This he did not only through the very fact of his studying women in their psychological development, dilemmas, and psychological ailments, but also through his clarifying the anxiety-ridden, conflictual basis of male sexuality, including the anxiety and aggression toward women that men express in their simultaneous fear, idealization, and degradation of them. This psychoanalytic "humbling" of men could not but elevate women to the level of fellow creatures. Freud did all this for women in the same way that he laid the basis for a deeper understanding of the prejudices against, and the mistreatment of, children, Jews, people of color, foreigners, the sexually unorthodox, and all the others included in the list of suspects usually rounded up for discriminatory treatment by the traditional white male community, whose world this Western one pretty much still is. A wonderful legacy, indeed! It is a legacy of liberating and humane ideas and a legacy of incredible boldness of vision and persistance.

FREUD AND THE HUMANITIES

In summing up I am impressed with the extent to which Freud's creation is rooted in the humanities. Freud was not prepared to consider any such possibility. He did not consider the humanist-existentialist aspect of his work suitable for theoretical purposes. Instead, he simply took that aspect for granted as a component of both clinical empathy and his novelistic feel for the language and the events of clinical work. For theory he turned to the scientific models of his day: Newton, Helmholtz, Darwin, and others in their line. These were men who had concerned themselves with the grand concepts of force, energy, structure, and mechanism; also with biological survival, adaptation, and evolution. They had taken for granted the account of the scientific observer as a totally detached, objective figure. In their tradition, Freud tried to construct the grand metapsychology that would establish psychoanalysis as a respectable empirical science.

Although it is historically and psychohistorically understandable, a number of eminent commentators have said that Freud's effort manifested misunderstanding of his own creation. Psychoanalysis did not follow the established models—not as a therapy, as a method of investigation, or as a theory of the human mind. It can even be claimed that Freud misunderstood the place of psychoanalysis in the roster of disciplines; for although it was, as he claimed, a psychology, psychoanalysis required a conceptual and methodological framework that did not then exist within psychology and is still kept in the margins of academic psychology. There were no frameworks anchored in relativistic, contextualistic epistemologies. Existential, structuralist, poststructuralist, and hermeneutic turns in the history of social thought had not yet been taken. Analytic and phenomenological philosophies were not available to help map out the linguistic and experiential realms in which psychoanalysis travels. Unavailable or unknown to Freud were modern explorations of the narrative, rhetorical, and dialogic nature of human communication and its role in the coming into being of differentiated self-object relations. In sum, the language of Freud's creation had to wait for the development of twentieth-century thought. He could have brought to bear the teachings of Nietzsche and thereby could have developed a more modern preliminary understanding of his work as deconstructive and narrative and so on; but he did not do so and later disclaimed any knowledge of these teachings—somewhat disingenuously, it seems, according to modern scholarship. On the other hand, it has taken generations of modern thought to see clearly just what Nietzsche was beginning to set forth, so that it is, I think, going too far to require Freud to have been on the cutting edge of the philosophical thought of his time, or even beyond it.

Ahead of his time in so many respects, Freud tried to be of his time—what else could he do?—and so he misunderstood himself. But in being ahead of his time, he facilitated some of those developments he would have needed to understand himself better, to be adequately understood by others, and yet to remain clearly open to continuing revision of those understandings.

That it is acceptable for more than one legitimate and arguable reading of Freud's achievement to exist was itself virtually unforeseeable and unthinkable in his time. Today we are better prepared to tolerate, if not accept, the pluralism that is the ground for my claim that we can speak of Freud's having provided more than just one legacy. By the same token, we are readier—at least intellectually readier—to accept the idea that our current readings of him will, in time, be superseded. We can, however, maintain some confidence that newer readings will not be modeled on the laboratory sciences or on simple evolutionism and organicism. The nineteenth-century versions of empiricism and naturalism are no longer dominant at the frontiers of the human disciplines. Doctrinaire adherence to the last century's narrow discourse and restrictive methods of proof no longer reigns supreme in psychoanalysis.

In conclusion, we may say that Freud invented a new discipline. Its roots and its branches extend into many realms of knowledge, and experts in every one of these realms—psychology, biology, history, anthropology, literature, and many others—may legitimately develop for their own purposes specialized perspectives on psychoanalysis, specialized applications of it, and specialized critiques of it. Nevertheless, psychoanalysis seems destined to withstand total appropriation by any one discipline. In this sense it will always belong only to itself. Fundamentally, it answers only to itself. Although Freud could not fully appreciate the gigantic magnitude and the special requirements of the texts he left for our perusal, he gave us tools and values that have helped us to appreciate those texts more than he ever could or did. It is for us to attempt to specify just what he bequeathed us.

CHAPTER 10

The Sense of an Answer: Clinical and Applied Psychoanalysis Compared

CRITICAL theorists in the humanities often enter into dialogue with psychoanalysis, taking note of both the bearing of their contributions on psychoanalysis and the uses they have found for interpretive precedents already established by Freud and other psychoanalysts. Although these dialogues vary with the critical theory or antitheory being espoused and the particular writer espousing it, they usually throw into question some or all of these psychoanalytic precedents.

Unlike these critical theorists, most clinical psychoanalysts (certainly most American psychoanalysts) continue to ignore these intellectual developments. To understand this difference of interest, it is not enough to make allowance for difficulty in the way of psychoanalysts combining close study of the work of critical theorists with their typically substantial amount of clinical practice, reflection on that practice, and efforts at psychoanalytic scholarship. Even when interested, analysts are daunted by the vast scholarly output of critical theorists and the great diversity among them. Analysts must struggle hard even to begin to understand the interdisciplinary excursions of the critical theorists, even harder to establish a preferred position of their own, and hardest of all to dare to join the conversation.

But no matter how daunting it is, never has it been more urgent for analysts to join these interdisciplinary conversations and confront (or confront anew) the epistemological and methodological presuppositions that ground, pervade, and control their own principles and practice of interpretation. Critical theorists have been arguing that all interpretation is inherently ambiguous, inconclusive, contestable, internally at odds with itself, blinding or repressive as well as illuminating, and dependent always on a specific context that is, however, infinitely revisible in scope and criteria of relevance. No less than the security of psychoanalytic interpretation is at stake. Consequently, psychoanalysts imperil their own discipline when they avoid dealing with what seem now to be the inescapable problems that inhere in finding things out, knowing them, understanding them, and communicating them—if it makes sense any longer to continue to refer to these activities as different from, and independent of, one another. And it is well for analysts to remember in this connection that those critical theorists who have explicitly or by implication questioned the grounds of psychoanalytic interpretation are not so much their enemies any longer as they are scholars studying the problems of *all* interpretation.

Simultaneously, it is incumbent on practicing psychoanalysts to contribute to interdisciplinary dialogues by writing about the way they arrive at and convey interpretations—what I call the sense of an answer. Their contributions are needed to offset a particular and growing problem: Typically, the interdisciplinary dialogues feature close readings of *selected fragments* of Freud's writings—usually, it seems, his *early writings,* as if only at the outset was Freud a true Freudian. In fact, however, Freud's writings and the received versions of them put forth by many later analysts no longer represent or control the practice of analytic interpretation to the extent that critical theorists often assume. By not recognizing this fact, theorists effectively deny psychoanalysis a history and so a future as well. It is a denial that can be only in the service of (in the eyes of psychoanalysts) an unconvincing economy, authority, and success of critical discussions of psychoanalytic interpretation.

Thus, what is lacking in the interdisciplinary realm are historically grounded and detailed versions of *modern* psychoanalytic work. How these versions relate to early Freud—or even to late Freud—is a subtopic in the history of ideas and therapeutic practices and is itself marked by considerable controversy. In this context, critical theory should live in the present; more exactly, it should not misrepresent the distant past as the dominant present.

As I see it, then, this chapter requires a section written from the standpoint of contemporary psychoanalytic practice, only then to be followed by a main text that searches for points of connection between this practice and the ongoing dialogues of critical theorists.

In the next section I present some workaday examples of clinical and applied psychoanalysis together with some comparative commentary on them. A fuller exploration of the common problems of these two types of analytic endeavor is presented in the section entitled "The Sense of an Answer." These common problems can be used to develop a livelier and broader context for considering psychoanalytic interpretation in relation to contemporary criticism than is now available.

Illustrations in the first section are sketchy. I set forth only enough to raise questions for my main text. First I present a conventional Freudian interpretation of part of the story of Snow White. After that I discuss two pieces of clinical analysis, one featuring interpretation of some prominent personality characteristics of women whose mothers appear to have been beset by severe narcissistic problems and the other featuring interpretation of the rhetoric of severely narcissistic men undergoing psychoanalysis. Instead of interpreting a fairy tale, I could have used psychohistory, psychobiography, analysis of the creative process, or some other familiar application of psychoanalysis. I hope that, by the end of this chapter, the reader is ready to grant that the fairy-tale illustration has served adequately as a point of entry.

SOME VERSIONS OF PSYCHOANALYSIS

Snow White

In the familiar version of the story of Snow White, she is sentenced to death by a vain mother-figure who wishes to be the fairest of all. Sentence is pronounced after this sinister stepmother has been told by the mirror on the wall that Snow White is fairer than she. Snow White is depicted as her innocent, passive victim.

Interpretation

This is a defensively disguised presentation of the daughter's positive (cross-gender) and aggressive oedipal aspirations and tribulations. This girl envies her mother's queenly feminine role, attributes, and sexual opportunities. In her wishful reality and by dint of considerable projection, she transforms her mother into a wickedly vain, envious, and vengeful woman who thinks nothing of destroying her own "innocent" flesh and blood. The supernarcissistic stepmother is now the split-off bad mother and the punitive maternal superego who, because she is greatly feared as well as loved, is useful to the daughter in strengthening the repression of her dangerously rivalrous oedipal wishes. Thereby, both the control of the daughter's aggression and the future of her relationship with the mother, whom she also loves and depends on, are assured, and the appearance of the daughter's passive innocence is maintained. At the same time it is unconsciously understood by the reader, who cannot but be oedipally guilty to some extent, that Snow White deserves to be punished for her rivalrous and matricidal impulses. There is no fooling the superego; like Jimmy Durante's nose and like the Shadow, it knows.

Freudian clinicians are familiar with this kind of life-historical narration by patients. Even when they allow, as Freud did, that many mothers do compete enviously and punitively with their daughters, they claim to know, or they confidently expect it to emerge, that in these narratives they are encountering a mixture of reality-tested and imagined object relations that have been given shape and content by the conflict of what traditionally they call instinctual drive derivatives and restraining superego and defensive structures. And with respect to the immediate clinical situation, they know (they say) that in these narratives they are encountering a blend of disclosure, warning, and resistance in the already forming transference. In these cases, sooner or later, analysts are prepared to "uncover" by interpretation some version of the core unconscious fantasy or storyline of Snow White. They have a sense that they have *the* answer to the question "What is wrong?"

But this sense of closure is not incontestable, for an object-relations analyst, one who more or less follows the lead of Melanie Klein (1964; see also Segal, 1964), hovers over the Freudian analyst, saying that that is not it at all; in fact, the Freudian analysis of Snow White is pretty superficial. Really, it is an obvious case of the daughter's projection of the aggression of the Death Instinct. The destructive daughter envies the mother's breast or goodness (her apple); envy leads by way of projection to spoiling the good breast (a queen with a poisoned apple); and the greedy incorporation of that now-bad breast results in the symbolic murder of the daughter by the evil introject. Snow White is a fairy-tale version of a universal unconscious fantasy that may have little to do with the attitudes and conduct of real mothers. The fantasy's principal source is in the paranoid-schizoid position of the first months of life. Only secondarily, if at all, does it involve actual experience with figures in the external world, and only in a tertiary way does it involve the Freudian Oedipus complex of a much later and less deeply anxious and guilty phase of development.

To complicate matters further, a self-psychological follower of

Heinz Kohut (1977) points out that neither the Freudian nor the Kleinian has been attending adequately to Snow White's experience of her narcissistically disturbed mother. This is the mother who does not or cannot provide that gleam in her eye—of appreciation, admiration, confirmation—that is essential to the daughter's growth of a cohesive self, a self with the impetus and direction provided by vigorous and defined aims. By looking only in the mirror—that is, at her own self—this mother consigns Snow White to the dead—to the realm of those with stunted, fragile, joyless, and inert selves. It is a case of the mother's poisonous lack of empathy and the daughter's arrested development and aimlessness.

What is one to do in this crowd before the analytic mirror? What should I do? Should I pick one line of interpretation, blind myself to the others, and declare that now I have the answer? If I did that, I would be deciding, on some combination of theoretical, temperamental, and professionally opportunistic grounds, to adopt a doctrinaire form of the identity of a Freudian, object-relations, or self-psychological analyst. Should I say instead "All of the above" and not worry about the intrinsic confusions of eclecticism? More than a few psychoanalysts do that, in a way that is evidently insecure, just plain flashy, or intimidating in its intellectual omniverousness and anal-retentiveness—or is it phallic exhibitionism or grandiosity? Perhaps I should just steer clear of applied analysis altogether and regard it as an inconsequential, inappropriate, inconclusive, hurtful and debased form of psychoanalysis. Or perhaps I should (as I have) involve myself in comparative analytic thinking-through of these three systems of thought—and maybe others as well? But if I did that, what ground would be left under my feet? Where could I find the authority for my work? How would I know what was real? How could I defend myself against the criticisms of colleagues? How might I arrive at the sense of an answer?

For many years I did mainly restrict my interest in any form of applied analysis, which I regarded as, at best, a poor relative of clinical analysis and something of a freeloader. Of late, however, my reading and my own clinical and theoretical efforts have led me to realize that I have been avoiding some serious issues that go to the heart of understanding the nature of any kind of psychoanalytic interpretation, and in this chapter I am beginning to try to correct the error of my ways.

Do I mean, as I just said, issues pertaining to *any* kind of psychoanalytic interpretation? Is it also difficult to understand the nature of *clinical* interpretation, and is the difficulty so much the same as the one I just brought up in connection with Snow White? I think so, and I am going to continue to try to persuade you that this is the case.

Severely Narcissistic Mothers and Their Daughters

The narcissistic mothers I have singled out for consideration are those who may be described as malignantly devoted to stunting not only their daughter's development of sturdy self-esteem but their capacity for satisfying relationships with their fathers, siblings, other girls and women, and the male sex in general—in other words, with everybody. These mothers are divisive in everything they do. They use the dyadic or symbiotic strategy of divide and conquer for all it is worth. Some of their daughters rebel through promiscuity, eating disorders, addictions, geographical flight, or some combination of these. Others—the ones I am concerned with here—stay and submit. In the main they become "good girls" and remain "good girls" of the latency-age type. They are reticent, easily embarrassed, and sexually and socially naïve, inhibited, and easily overstimulated. They are much like Snow White, except perhaps in some scattered, furtive, and rebellious sexual episodes that they themselves do not understand or take responsibility for. To the compassionate observer, they are the innocent victims of their mother's depradations, and the accounts of these depradations come across convincingly as so relentless and heartless that they may cause even the experienced clinician to wince or choke up on hearing about the horror of it all, a horror that includes witnessing the daughters' continuing attempts to idealize or at least defend these mothers.

How may we interpret psychoanalytically the life-historical narratives presented by these daughters? The Freudian view would have us say something like this. These daughters are conflict-ridden with respect to the libidinal and aggressive wishes that enter into their narcissism and object-relatedness. Out of anxiety, guilt, and shame they are hiding behind repressions, and they are yielding ambivalently to something between a severe maternal superego and a persecutory introject. They yield by becoming obedient, oedipally sexless, latency-type girls as well as, on a deeper level, passive, innocent, preoedipal infants. An additional factor is related to the positive libidinal strivings of these daughters: In living out their own fantasied castration by the phallic mother, they are able to identify with their fathers, whom they see as castrated victims of these mothers. Thereby they are able to adopt a partly gratifying androgynous position in the ostensibly simply horrible mother-daughter relationship and to cling to it tenaciously.

Or should the accounts of these daughters be interpreted, as earlier I interpreted Snow White, in the object-relational or self-psychological mode? At least in the schematic fashion I have been following, it would not be difficult to develop these alternatives—breasts both poisoned and made poisonous by the daughter's projections, glares rather than gleams in the maternal eye, and so on. How to decide? How to choose or synthesize? How to define oneself as analyst—as a being in the world, or in any world? How to tackle such large theoretical issues? Or should we as analysts try?

Can these analysands say anything to help analysts decide? Conventional psychoanalysts say they can and do; we have only to listen closely to analysands and be guided by what they say. Each school of psychoanalysis claims to be fairest of all in that it presents itself as based on listening that is far more acute, empathic, and rigorous than its rivals' modes of listening. But do psychoanalysts simply listen to analysands? If so, and despite large areas of agreement among themselves, why then do psychoanalysts disagree with one another so often and so strongly? Could it be that each of them is just interpreting the life-historical narratives of analysands in the same way he or she would interpret Snow White, that is, in an applied way and with ready-made interpretations? Could it be that analysts approach analysands as sets of stories to be retold in terms of the storylines provided by preferred analytic theories? These unsettling questions do not go away just because analysts repress or disavow them.

The Rhetoric of Narcissistic Men

Narcissistic men do not take readily or kindly to the analyst's interventions. They say, "I never thought of that," as if the first order of business is to determine who comes up with the ideas, or, if not that, to announce surprise that anyone else would have something of interest to say about them. Also, in response to the analyst's interventions, they say, "That could be," in a tone that suggests that they are going to weigh each puny intervention on a very grand scale of judgment before reacting to it. Often they repeat the analyst's interpretations some time after they have been made, not only as if they themselves have been the first to think them but as if they should be admired by the analyst for their achievement. They cannot hear or retain what the analyst says if he or she interrupts, speaks at any length, or develops a point along a line they have not initiated and authorized. They treat the analyst as something of a bore, with "bore" being defined, as in the old saying, as someone who is an expert in your own field. Often these narcissists say, "I don't know what this means" and "I can't figure that one out"; never once do they allow themselves even to think of asking the analyst for guidance or interested participation. In these cases, it seems for a long time that the analyst can aspire to be nothing beyond the status of a minor and intrusive expert.

What is the psychoanalytic meaning of this rhetoric? Are these men enacting in their transferences feeling castrated by their vain, competitive, and controlling fathers? Are they also victimized by their own pathological ego-ideal formation, a development that is attributable to the impossibility of their ever satisfying vain fathers who cannot take genuine pride in themselves and who undermine their sons by their ruthless competitiveness? Are these men also repetitively enacting in their transferences the life-historical story of how they had to develop defensive grandiosity in order to deal with the helplessness and hopelessness they felt in relation to their nebulous, masochistic, and ungiving mothers, the kind of women who are more than likely to be married to men of their fathers' type? And are they simultaneously enacting their full retreat from their oedipal desires for these mothers who, typically and obviously, are unhappy, isolated, and sexually unfulfilled in their marriages? Are the grandiose aspirations of these men being played out in spectacular feats of rhetorical and other control and controllingness that inevitably reek of anal sadism? Is their anality intensified by submissive wishes to be the castrated recipients of the love of their unreliably involved but idealized fathers? These men's narrations of their childhoods, their dreams and slips and defenses, their struggles with guilt and shame, their responses to Freudian interventions: All are likely to bear out these interpretive conjectures concerning the psychoanalytic import of their rhetoric.

And yet, to indicate only one alternative view, we could say that, in their rhetoric, these men are manifesting Kohut's disorders of the self as well as any analysand could. They are deprived and traumatized by mother and father alike of developmentally crucial empathic mirroring and holding up of attainable ideals. They have been forced into the compensatory construction of grandiose selves. In the analysis, they use their power of control to protect their fragile nuclear selves against further traumatization by the analyst who might make interpretations ill-suited to their inner experience and tolerance. Anal sadism is present as a by-product ("disintegration product") of their disturbance of self and not as a central dynamic. They are not so much conflicted as deprived, wounded, frightened, and self-protective. On this view, each of these men must use this rhetoric in order to survive with whatever self he can muster and to keep it on hold for that improbable future occasion when it might be safe to let it begin to grow. How well this self-psychological account fits these men, how warmly the less damaged of them will begin to receive it as time goes on, and how amply they will confirm it with more life-historical narratives of the same sort, provided that these interpretations are imparted to them slowly, perceptively, and empathically, and provided, too, that they are allowed to appropriate the interpretations in their own characteristic way for as long as they need to.

Again, we seem to have to confront the necessity of making a difficult choice. With regard to each clinical group, I have been applying the language and logic of different theories to roughly the same or similar descriptive phenomena. In each case, however, it could be said that it is as if I have been interpreting a story in a book or that I have simply been retelling one story in the terms of another. What is clinical here and what is applied? The disturbing questions of knowing and knowledge are present in clinical as well as applied practice. The sense of an answer eludes us. To get any further, we must, I think, take up questions of first-person speech, statements of intention, and the nature of the psychoanalytic dialogue and its interpretation. This I do in the next section.

THE SENSE OF AN ANSWER

Do psychoanalysts accept and rely on the authority of first-person speech? Does the pronoun *I* spoken aloud carry special weight in establishing the authentic presence of the speaker? Are the analysand's first-person locutions sufficient or even necessary for purposes of both grounding and verifying the analyst's interpretations? Is it essentially through what the analysand says aloud in the first person that the analyst arrives at the sense of an answer to analytic inquiries? If, in response to an intervention, the analysand says "That's not what I meant" or "That was not the result that I intended," is the psychoanalyst then required to revise the intervention? Is closure guaranteed by the analysand's assertions?

These questions may seem pointless to those familiar with clinical analytic work, as the obvious answer to each is no. Familiars know that, for one thing, speech may be inauthentic in its being deliberately or unconsciously misleading, incomplete, or biased. They also know that a good deal about what is in fact the case, according to conventional judgment, is communicated nonverbally through expressive movement, silence, and certain forms of acting out, and also communicated obliquely in narratives about others. And they know, too, that any of these other communications may contradict what is being or has been asserted explicitly in the first person by the analysand.

Additionally, familiars accept the conclusion Freud (1937a) reached in "Constructions in Analysis": An accumulation of indirect responses of various sorts, such as slips, dreams, reminiscences, and transferences, may add up to proof that a reconstruction of early experience is valid even though the analysand has produced no certified memory of that piece of personal history. And finally, these analysts know that at extreme moments in any one case, or as a rule in certain extreme cases, the analysand may be present in body but psychically absent or incommunicado. Thus, first-person speech is inherently problematic. To a noteworthy though lesser extent, this conclusion also guides ordinary social intercourse, where hearing is not always believing.

And yet it has been said, and it has often been implied, that there is all the difference in the world between clinical and applied psychoanalysis for, in applied analysis, "there is no patient to talk back." To refer to the patient who talks back is, however, to imply some debatable presuppositions. First, it implies that in doing applied analysis, analysts can have their own sweet way with the material at hand because that material is utterly passive and because there are no criteria for verification of applied analytic interpretations. Consequently, if the analyst is clever, applied analysis will be easy and safe to do. In contrast, so it is argued, the clinical analyst, confronted by first-person assertions and responses, cannot both do a good job and escape the rigors and deep experiences of clinical work. On this view, applied analysis is more like a flirtation, a rape, or a forced feeding than a total, interactive, and caring relationship. Additionally, reference to the patient who talks back presupposes that clinical interpretation is simply empirical, inductive, objective, and verifiable by known and independent criteria within the psychoanalytic dialogue; in contrast, applied analysis is a derivative and speculative enterprise that is parasitic on the clinically well-grounded theory of psychoanalysis. Thus, in the absence of a patient who can talk back, applied analysis is merely a monologue, not a dialogue with built-in, scientifically sound verificational feedback. It is lower in the hierarchy of psychoanalytic practice.

In making this case for back-talk, analysts are according a special place to the analysand's spoken words. They are granting much authority to the analysand's saying yes and no and to the confessions, disclosures, rememberings, and shocks of recognition that the patient delivers with the presumed authenticity of first-person speech. Indeed, analysts do often grant this same authority to their analysands when, in order to make their own written arguments more persuasive, they simply quote them to prove a point; it is common for an analyst to write, "As this patient put it so well . . ." and to follow with a quote whose unexamined "eloquence" is intended to put the finishing touches on an argument and establish the sense of an answer. For example: "Now I know that there was poison in Mother's kindnesses" or "It is better to be a star in the gutter than an undistinguished workhorse." In each case, that analyst is speaking or writing as if "that says it all." Not only is there a sense of *an* answer; this is *the* answer.

Evidently, then, analytic thinking about speech, interpretation, and verification presents inconsistencies or paradoxes. Something vital seems not to have been thought through. The comparisons of clinical and applied analysis that follow are intended to deal with this difficulty, and they involve some clarification of the theory of psychoanalytic interpretation, the relation of theory to practice in psychoanalysis, and the criteria of proof and truth that are customarily invoked in psychoanalytic work. Although what is offered adds up only to a small selection of observations, critical remarks, and suggestions, I do not believe that the consequences for our understanding the nature of psychoanalytic interpretation will be small in scale.

PSYCHOANALYSIS AS TEXT INTERPRETATION

For present purposes it is useful first of all not to take for granted any sharp commonsensical boundary line between clinical and applied analysis. Let us rather assume provisionally that there is only one psychoanalysis and that its practice encounters a variety of problems the nature of which depend on the details of the specific content being defined within the specific context being established. The methodological step I am urging requires us to concentrate on sameness rather than difference, congruence rather than divergence, interpretation in general rather than particularized versions of it. This is a psychoanalytic world without parasites or freeloaders. Taking this methodological step should help us begin to see clearly what clinical analysts have in common with those critics and critical theorists who, in recent years, can be said to have been having a love affair with psychoanalysis. Are these critics and theorists just being reckless romantics, frustrated creative writers, or emotionally deprived academics looking for thrills in applied analytic work, or are they (many of them), as I believe, engaged in fundamentally sober, even if often evidently ambivalent, common cause with clinical analysts?

Earlier I questioned the authority of presence in speech. I referred there to misleading as well as constructively communicative aspects of speech, silence, and other nonverbal actions in the analytic situation. At that point, I was already implying a perspective on the analyst at work, specifically that he or she takes everything in the analytic situation as a text that requires interpretation or that might, by suitable interventions, be developed to the point where it is enough of a text to yield to a psychoanalytic interpretation. Ordinarily, the analysand's professed intentions, while they must count for something, do not by themselves settle any question of analytic meaning or significance. Like any other text presented to the world, the analysand's text does not remain in his or her control. Once uttered or enacted, it becomes public property in the world of psychoanalysis and part of that world's possible histories. The analysand's declaration of intention is itself very likely to be taken as a text—for example, as defensive rationalization, a false lead, or a gesture of appeasement.

At most then, the analysand is used as a consultant on his or her utterances, and the consultation is itself considered to be further interpretable text. For the most part, this consultation is not carried out under the aspect of privileged opinion or insight; it is carried out by way of the analyst's interpreting the analysand's further free associations. Thus, the analyst treats the analysand in the same manner that many literary critics treat authors—with interest in what the analysand says about the aims of his or her utterances and choices, but with an overall attitude of autonomous critical command rather than submission or conventional politeness, and with a readiness to view these explanatory comments as just so much more prose to be both heard as such *and* interpreted.

Now, there is nothing psychoanalytically radical about this view of psychoanalysis as a form of text interpretation. In one respect, I am merely restating an analytic truism. The truism holds that, for purposes of developing insight through interpretation, we cannot rely simply or directly on manifest content or what is readily available consciously to the analysand. For instance, we do not interpret, let alone accept at face value, manifest dream content or accept the analysand's direct dream interpretations as conclusive communications about aims and meanings; similarly, we do not take the manifest wishfulness of a daydream as an unmediated or uncompromised expression of a primal wish. In another respect, I am only restating Freud's criteria for the verification of reconstructions: Verification is established by an accumulation of indirect or implicit responses, *the kind of responses that become evidence only upon interpretation, further analytic dialogue, and further interpretation.*

To take clinical analytic work as text interpretation is to establish the analyst as an influential co-author of the analytic text that is being interpreted. The text, in other words, is never fully delivered to the analyst; rather, it evolves out of the analysand's and the analyst's inter-penetrating contributions. Increasingly, the two of them inhabit the text of the analysis; at times it seems that "cohabit" would be a better word for it. Cohabitation is what follows from throwing into question manifest content, including manifest avowals of intent and other such "explanations." In the end, the text and its interpretation are not alto-gether distinguishable. If, as I claim, I am merely restating psychoana-lytic truisms, analysts should not find it difficult to grant this much about their work of interpretation. Yet many or most analysts still balk at accepting the ideas of text analysis and co-authorship when they are stated this baldly. It may seem to them to undermine their sense that *the* answer exists *in* the material and is to be *uncovered;* the latent lies *under* or *behind* the manifest; psychoanalysis is *depth* psychology; and so on.

To agree that analysts interpret interpenetrated or cohabited texts is to accord to constructivism and its corollary, perspectivism, an essential place in psychoanalysis and to put into permanent question the traditional psychoanalytic claim to the status of an empirical, inductive, objectively observational science. Constructivism and per-spectivism are theoretical positions on what we can and should mean by "reality" or on the sense in which we can "know" reality. In con-structivism, the world we claim to know objectively is not given directly to perception and reason. Rather, reality is constructed according to rules; these rules, though usually implicit, are ascertainable through critical study, no matter whether they are known as such to the subject or not. People follow these rules in observing or making observable whatever it is that they go on to say is in the real world. Broadly viewed, these rules are pretty much the same among members of the same culture and historical period, although the selection, compre-hension, and application of the rules are more or less individualized. Hence the cultural diversity within conformity, or the conformity within diversity, that we generally acknowledge and more or less accept. The result is not reality plain but a perspective on reality or, more exactly, *reality by means of a perspective.*

According to this epistemological position, there is no coherent, sense-making way to approach a text. Indeed, there is no way to say what the text is that is to be approached, other than to construct re-ality by means of a particular perspective and to use consistently the language that manifests this perspective. However vulnerable the per-spective may be to deconstructive demonstrations of its incompleteness and inconsistencies, and however much it may overlap other perspectives, it is distinguishable from them by criteria that are accepted by some segment of the critical community. On this basis, most members of the psychoanalytic community take Freudian, self-psychological, and object-relational perspectives to be different.

To present perspective in narrational terms: A perspective is made up of more or less coordinated sets of storylines that allow us to state in a comprehensible way what are being counted as relevant and significant facts. These sets of storylines also imply the special appropriateness of certain methods of fact-finding and indicate how best to use them. And the narratives they generate also enact the kinds of organization of facts that are to be considered legitimate, important, cohesive, and complete.

Instead of the terms *constructivism, perspectivism,* and *narration* or *storyline,* often other words or phrases are used to grapple with the same issues of knowledge of reality or how to arrive at the sense of an answer; these include *paradigms, models of the mind, leading metaphors,* or just plain *theory.*

Freudian theory specifies and authorizes certain technical methods for eliciting and defining certain phenomena and then organizing them serially and hierarchically within increasingly abstract levels of conceptualization and clinical generalization. Additionally, Freudian theory requires that all of this be done differently from the way analysts of other schools do it. For the sake of consistency, coherence, and completeness, and for the sake of a sense of Freudian identity, this requirement of difference has to be met. Self-psychological theory, for example, is very different from the Freudian: The self-psychological theory has no instinctual drives or primary stages of infantile psychosexuality; it has little or nothing in the way of defense or resistance, internalized object relations, and tripartite psychic structure. The phenomena elicited or defined by means of the self-psychological perspective are dependent on the unique integration and limitation of the technical procedures that it authorizes. Self psychology is rule-governed as is Freudian psychology, and the rules are different enough to establish its identity.

ANALYSTS AS CO-CREATORS

For the most part, in what follows I employ the Freudian perspective on constructing the psychological reality of human beings. More exactly, however—and to establish my general thesis this point cannot be overemphasized—I can remain only within one such perspective, namely, my own version of the Freudian perspective, as that is all I can reasonably claim to have. Other Freudian versions of the Freudian perspective differ from mine, with its definite object-relational coloring. This heterogeneity explains why at their meetings conventional Freudians continue endlessly to schedule panel discussions and symposia devoted to traditional concepts and problems, such as the meaning or nature of transference and acting out. It also explains why they disagree with one another at conferences and in their evaluations of colleagues and trainees. Conventional Freudian texts vary to some extent from one analyst to the next. Conventional analysts develop more or less different versions of the basic Freudian storylines of infantile psychosexuality, aggression, anxiety, guilt, self-esteem problems, danger situations, maturation, and so on. Consequently, interpretation is needed just to say what is essential to Freudian thought, and no one interpretation is the final one. We cannot avoid confronting the extent to which our assertions are saturated with perspectivism and constructivism.

If analysts co-create analytic data, if analytic observations make sense and attain significance only within a perspective, and if only by analysts' following, each in their own way, some more or less systematized and coherent set of basic storylines, then there can be no successful defense of the traditional Freudian image of "the analyst." In this image, the analyst is a straightforward inductive empiricist, an objective and independent clinician who simply observes what analysands set forth and draws the inevitable conclusions. Interpretation, then, is indistinguishable from inevitable conclusion and final closure. This image is, however, merely one of a number of possible images of the analyst, and to some analysts it has already become a joke. It depends on blindness enforced by anxiety before authority. That image may now be seen to be a naïve, precritical or unreflective representation of the analyst; it may also be seen to be a coercively repressive and anti-intellectual representation. It is the image found in the implicitly authoritarian rhetoric of what may now be regarded as the old school of Freudian analysis.

More important to note, however, is the more or less subtle way that image is presented in the polemical presentations made by members of *every* school of analysis. The fairest of them all: analysts who can still tell us confidently in each instance exactly what is what. They seem never to have heard of, or taken seriously, constructivism and perspectivism, visions or versions of reality, heterogeneity and self-contradiction at home as well as abroad. They stand for the image that all but some of the youngest analysts have grown up on, and so there is still widespread reluctance among analysts to put this image up in their intellectual attics along with self-preservative instincts, psychic energy, and certain sexist psychoanalytic generalizations that trivialize women in relation to men.

On the basis of the preceding discussions, it would be just as warranted to recommend viewing clinical analysis as a form of applied analysis as to continue viewing applied analysis as parasitic on clinical analysis, for clinical work is thoroughly, even if inconsistently, regulated by theory. Clinical interpretation makes manifest a prescribed perspective; it has its method, its language, and its own preferred sets of storylines. True, psychoanalysts present it as a plain fact that clinical analysis often facilitates personal change for the better, in whatever terms best suit the individual case. As an engaged clinical Freudian I would not contest that presentation. But the further claim is then made or implied that for this reason psychoanalysts occupy some position that privileges them to make and follow their own laws of knowledge and to ignore the history and current status of general theories of interpretation.

In contrast, I am arguing here that clinical analysis is not a thing apart and that nothing specific follows from presenting effected personal change in this way. That change is not an independent or unambiguous variable; rather, it is part of the initial conception of what analysis is. In other words, change alone cannot be used to validate clinical interpretations, for the final account of change, far from being theory-free, is shaped and presented in the terms of the methods, the storylines, and the interpretations of one or another psychoanalytic perspective. Each perspective, theory, or paradigm presents change at least somewhat differently. Owing to its regulative effect on technical practices, each perspective seems to bring about somewhat different types of phenomena, with theory-specific implications, that can be taken to indicate change for the better. This is why debate between schools of analysis over their relative effectiveness are never resolved and may be unresolvable, even if still worth debating for the clarity of systematic thinking they stimulate.

It is perhaps easier to see how the analysis of very young children may be regarded as a form of applied analysis. In that kind of analytic work, play and other behavior, much of it nonverbal, can be grasped and used analytically only by bringing to bear, on this less-than-ideal type of material, analytic theory that has been worked out much more thoroughly in the analysis of adults. The quality of being applied is also not too difficult to see in analytic approaches such as the old-fashioned kind of Kleinian and the cruder kind of Freudian and self-psychological approaches, in all of which we encounter tedious sameness in the occasions and contents of interpretive intervention. In the old-fashioned Kleinian case, we see particularly what other analysts regard as an overabundance and excessive depth of theory-dictated interpretation of rather limited amounts of material.

Hardest of all of the cases to see as applied (at any rate, hardest for me) is modern and subtle, though still theory-laden, Freudian clinical analysis and modern Kleinian analysis (see, for example, Joseph, 1989), which has relatively greater tolerance for prolonged ambiguity and freely wandering association and sustained interest in eliciting rather than imposing fantasy material, explores more fully spontaneous shifts of subjective experience and memory, and has greater interest, however ambivalent, in new theoretical possibilities.

What now can be said of that presumably privileged person, the patient who talks back? A case has already been made for the assertion that talking back does not encounter a passive, yielding, unquestioning analyst. Yes and no, right and wrong, yes but, not quite, that's off the wall, and so on: Analysts can always and do often take these responses by analysands as further analytic material. They try to do so in the thoughtful and artful way that Freud (1937a) began to outline in his paper on constructions in analysis and that he often illustrated in his case studies and clinical examples. That is, analysts can try to find some analytic interpretive way to assess the relevance and coherence of these responses by analysands and thereby convert them into evidence bearing importantly on interpretations that have already been made.

For example, a male analysand promptly forgot an interpretation that explained why certain repressions of previous analytic interpretations had been occurring. The interpretation was this: By his forgetting, he was acting out a fantasy of defectiveness. The analyst then transformed his forgetting this interpretation of his forgetting into further evidence in support of that very interpretation, and at that moment the analyst was transforming it into evidence in the crucial context of the transference. Subsequently, the analyst was able to construct the more developed interpretation that the analysand was enacting the fantasy of being castrated into defectiveness by the analyst's cutting interpretations.

An analyst with a different perspective might have transformed this forgetting of interpretation into something else. Kohut, for example, might have made it into evidence for two traumatizing effects: first, of the interpretation of repressive defense and the implication that the defectiveness was only a fantasy, contrary to the subjective experience of the analysand, and, second, of the implication that the analyst knows better than the analysand the truth of the analysand's self-experience. All these interpretations, being exceedingly unempathic, must have led to some further fragmentation of the analysand's fragile self and thereby to his inability to retain or retrieve the latest interpretation. Briefly, according to Kohut, the analyst's interpretation might be considered more of an assaultive rejection and devaluation than anything else, and the self of the analysand would be felt to be iatrogenically traumatized and fragmented.

Another example is that of the analysand who became very angry in response to an interpretation. The analyst used that response, along with other factors, as evidence that the interpretation's correctness was threatening to the patient and that this threat was being warded off by anger. In this instance, however, the anger could have been interpreted differently, even if still in keeping with the general Freudian perspective. It could have been argued that the anger showed the interpretation to be premature or that one of the effects of the previous interpretation had been to lift the repression of anger itself. And the angry response could have been interpreted in still other ways according to other analytic perspectives (for example, the interpretation was superficial or unempathic, therefore frightening or disappointing, and therefore angering in either case).

My examples are intended to suggest the extent to which evidence is created by analysis. Contrary to the empiricist-analyst's view, I believe that evidence is not served up on a platter, nor does it reach out to grab one by the throat. Although it is easy to note back-talk, it is difficult to prove unassailably or reach a firm consensus on just what it is that is being said. Psychoanalytic claims about what is being said and why (insofar as these are distinguishable) are essentially contestable.

Lest it seem that I am presenting the analyst as completely closedminded once he or she has made an interpretation, I must point out that interpretations are often and appropriately offered conjecturally; the analyst delivers them in a way that implies that alternative, supplementary, or revised possibilities of interpretation are still open to consideration. The ideal analyst is well prepared to defer having arrived at the sense of any answer at all or at least to revise conjectures already tendered.

Let us return to more direct comparison of applied and clinical analysis to deal with another sense in which we can consider the statement that only in clinical analysis is there a patient who can talk back. In this other sense, the patient can talk back by showing change for the better, change for the worse, or no change at all, however each is defined in the specific case. For ease of exposition, I deal only with change for the better; this discussion should be readily applicable to change for the worse and no change at all without my spelling out those applications.

In connection with talking back by improving, it can be argued that, after all, analysis is a therapy; its goal is to help the analysand improve. In contrast, an artwork does not require therapy, and the goal of applied analysis is not so much to change the artwork for the better as to help its audience understand it and appreciate it better. Properly considered, the artwork does not talk back. But this argument is unhelpfully simplistic in that it does not do justice to the process and the results of both therapy and applied analytic projects, and it misconceives the relationship between an artwork and its audience.

I have already mentioned that there always has been and probably always will be room for controversy among analysts concerning the changes brought about by analytic therapy. Analysts would generally agree that among the forms of what they call resisting, there are flights into health, manic defenses, and transference cures, all of which may create false impressions of resolution of conflict and disappearance of symptoms in a lasting way. The analyst may therefore disagree with the analysand when the latter insists that things have improved greatly as a result of deeper understanding. The analysand's first-person testimony cannot be decisive in this respect.

Furthermore, analysts are likely to differ with one another in the way they apply such concepts as transference cure to a series of suggestive cases where more data are available than the analysands' explicit first-person testimony and the testimony of the treating analysts. And even when all analysts agree that there has been change for the better, they could not be expected to be unanimous about the degree of such change, nor would every one of them be likely to describe the change and explain it in precisely the same way, especially if they belong to different schools of analysis.

For example, conventional Freudians do not usually accept the benefits of self-psychological treatment as true psychoanalytic results, seeing them rather as the benefits of supportive psychotherapy or as transference cures. Self psychologists are quite ready to redescribe and reexplain the benefits of Freudian analysis in the terms of self psychology; they portray many of these benefits almost as accidental byproducts of good intentions hampered by poor technique based on poor understanding.

Furthermore, many of the changes in question are not measurable at all, for how can we measure subtle yet highly important improvements in the patient's quality of life, the patient's vision of reality, and his or her adaptation-enhancing integration of personal life-historical narratives? Upon reflection, therefore, it cannot be convincingly argued that talking back through recovery is a reliable and unambiguous feature of clinical analysis.

Turning now to the side of the artwork—say, a poem—we may question the flat assertion that applied analytic interpretation of a poem is not therapy. Following analytic interpretation of the poem (or for that matter following any other competent interpretation of it), the reader may better experience the poem's structural unity, richness of meaning, and potential impact, within the perspective provided. For this reason, we may legitimately say that the poem has become more alive and integrated, that it has been rendered available to enter into a more developed relationship with the reader, something more on the order of a mature, mutual, and modifiable relation of whole persons than one that features narcissistic aloofness and inaccessibility, schizoid weirdness, limitation to sexual organs, or something on that more disturbed and disturbing order. It would be arbitrary to insist that in consequence of interpretation only the reader has changed, for it can be argued that the poem changes with the reader as the reader becomes more expert. It is no longer the same poem. There is no determinate text of the poem. Markings on a page—the last resort of the anticonstructivist—are not the poem. The markings do not by themselves make a statement; they do not demand to be read or understood in only one way; they do not even sound.

On this basis, we may speak of interpretive recuperation or recovery of the poem. This idea is not new to literary criticism. Many of today's critics accept the proposition that a poem exists within the individualized relationship between it and the audience. Although their accounts differ in certain respects, they do agree that in necessarily interpreting in order to read at all, the reader becomes a co-author of the text. In making this argument, they have supplied the inspiration and background for my earlier argument that the analyst may be considered a co-author of the analysand's text. If, with the help of "applied" psychoanalytic understanding, along with other forms of understanding, the reader of the poem is better prepared to approach it as a particular kind of artwork than he or she might have been otherwise; if, in other words, the reader is an integrated and competent member of one or more definable interpretive and narrative communities and on this basis can draw on their conventions and observe their standards, then we might say that, in being psychoanalytically informed, the reader has been helped to bring about change for the better in both parties involved in the relationship. Among these features that are shared by psychoanalytic and other readings are the mixture of conventionalized and individual narrative and interpretive approaches and the therapeutic consequences of the work.

Furthermore, the artwork may be said to exert therapeutic influence on its critically prepared audience by introducing it to restorative perspectives on reality and restorative opportunities for subjective experience and understanding not previously available to it. Freud learned from Homer, Shakespeare, and Company, just as he made it possible for them to become more than they had ever seemed and for their audience to learn still more from them. Independent cases can be made for Freud's perspectival finding what was there to be discovered in literature, for his having re-created literature in his own image, and for a continuing interpenetration of and tension between both of these; and the same can be said for his contribution to the utterances of analysands.

There are those, however, who might still want to argue for an essential and hierarchical difference in favor of clinical work. They would point out that in clinical analysis talking back by changing for the better is a more important achievement. It is more important in that it concerns human welfare directly. Going further, they might also point out that in clinical analysis, but not in applied analysis, there is professional obligation to bring about this change.

Yet clinical analysts are not obliged to get good results, however those are defined. The clinical analyst fulfills his or her professional obligation by trying conscientiously to help bring about good results. Any feeling of obligation beyond that of making a good effort should generally be viewed as disturbed and disturbing countertransference involving some combination of guilt, overidentification with the patient, rescue fantasies, defensive grandiosity, and so on. And on their part, critical interpreters of an artwork have their own scholarly and technical obligations, too, even though the nature and extent of these are always being debated.

As to which kind of recovery is more important, that of a patient or that of an artwork, there is no way to adjudicate the issue except in terms of values or ideology that are not intrinsic to the psychoanalytic project. Clinical psychoanalysis does not prescribe the health values that it abides by once it begins by mutual consent; psychoanalysts do not properly exhort the general public to be in analysis. Moreover, we cannot hope to encounter universal agreements one way or another in this realm of judgments of importance.

Consequently, it is essential to reject the argument that the patient's talking back through recovery (or through personal disruption or stasis) distinguishes clinical analysis from applied analysis. At the least, it is warranted to reject that argument in its absolute, extreme, and unarticulated form. If we do not let ourselves be coerced by tradition into attending only to differences, if we focus on sameness as well as difference, we can see that clinical and applied analysis have in common co-creation and interpenetration of interpretable texts or of texts-as-interpretation. Clinical and applied analysis emerge as versions of one psychoanalysis, with no clear-cut parasitic relationship of one to the other. Both amount to the same work carried out under varied conditions. Clinical and applied analysts sink or swim together.

Although my conclusion is what earlier I recommended as a provisional assumption that could help us get on with the discussion, I maintain that I am not back where I started. Although I have not attained the sense of an answer, I have, I think, changed the sense of the questions that have arisen about applied analysis and stirred up some parallel questions about clinical analysis as well. But, of course, readers will not take my word for any of this, for they have been re-creating this text from the time they started reading it. They will have been developing their own sense of an answer to my arguments and will perhaps have decided that it would have been better if I had formulated other questions and other answers.

CHAPTER 11

The Search for
Common Ground

IN the contemporary psychoanalytic setting, where, as I showed in the preceding chapter, we are faced with considerable diversity of theory and practice, it can seem a most desirable goal to seek out some common ground on which all parties are standing and to maintain a sense thereby that all analysts, of whatever persuasion, are members of one basic discipline: psychoanalysis. But a search for common ground should be based on a shared and well-developed understanding of why it is a good thing to do, why it should be a rewarding thing to do, and how to go about it in a sound way. For, to begin with, a heterogeneous group of analysts would already have to be standing on some common ground before the idea of common ground could be discussed usefully. And in order to try to establish that preparatory common ground, the group would have to take up numerous issues of a linguistic, methodological, and ideological nature. Instead of any coming together, however, analysts continue to perpetuate a mixture of misunderstanding, ignoring, misrepresentation, and overeager rejection or accommodation, and instead of any systematic approach, they rely frequently on sheer assertion presented as argument and on much hasty and often severe supervisory critiques of the reported clinical work of respected colleagues.

The following remarks are intended to begin a systematic discussion of the issues. Although brief and incomplete, they do center on the thorny, if not impassable, way leading to useful discussion of the goal of common ground.

LINGUISTIC CONSIDERATIONS

In the clinical setting we must not be beguiled by manifest content. Upon searching the literature on the topic of common ground, we encounter another kind of ambiguous manifest content, namely, the words that make up technical and theoretical vocabularies. For example, consider the words *analyze transference*. These words must be taken as manifest content; both are treacherous words, treacherous because analysts of the same and different persuasions use them in association with too many different conceptions of childhood development; of psychopathology; of repetition and its basis, functions, and modes; of the uses of countertransference in defining transference; of the so-called real relationship with the analyst; of appropriate kinds and degrees of analytic activity; and so forth. This diversity of usage is all too evident in analytic writings, case conferences, and supervisory work. We must similarly regard as treacherous such other key words as *resistance* and *regression*. Consequently, to agree that analysts analyze transference, resistance, and regression amounts to little more than agreeing that they use the same words for whatever it is that they do do.

Words take on meanings through the practices in which they are used. Linguistic practices either presuppose contexts for words or try to establish these contexts as they go along. Thus, "transference" cannot be exactly the same word in the contexts of different clinical reports, for close inspection may show that in each case it has been placed in a different network of meanings. Instead of identity of meaning, there may be only family resemblances, if even that. We might have to stand very far back from individual propositions and practices to give mere family resemblances the appearance of identity and then lay claim to having searched out common ground.

For example, it could be regarded as certain that many clinical presentations manifest the analysis of transference in that they try to establish disturbing manifestations of past relationships in the present analytic relationship. And yet the conclusion that here there is common ground could be drawn only if we overlooked marked variations in clinical procedures and phenomena. Furthermore, after claiming common ground in the analysis of transference, what could we then go on to say? To what use could we put that claim? With so many specifics overlooked, the claim could not guide clinical work, nor would it be intellectually stimulating. Indeed, once familiar with details of the different schools of analytic thought, we could easily adopt the position of any one clinical case presenter and argue forcefully that when working from all other positions, we will be pursuing the analysis of transference in such a way as to make it less rather than more available to the patient's emotional experience and thus less available to relative resolution through insight. But where exactly would those critiques get us? Starting from any other position, we could arrive at another totalistic conclusion that repudiates the first.

It is, however, possible to point to some common ground. It is common ground not so much in the sense desired by those concerned with professional unity, but rather with respect to features that psychoanalysis shares with *all* investigative and interpretive disciplines. And it is to those features that I now turn.

METHODOLOGICAL CONSIDERATIONS

We can make more use now of the idea of manifest content. How do analysts transform manifest clinical content into useful analytic material? They do so by giving it a context or new context, thereby establishing and understanding it as something different from, or more than, it seemed at first. They derive that new context from what they have already defined and understood analytically about the patient's past and current life and the treatment relationship. Ideally, they get to understand both of these as presenting different versions of the same problems, for then the analytic versions of past and present problems in life and in analysis interpenetrate; having interpenetrated, these versions become virtually interchangeable in that fluid time/space of analytic accounts of unconscious mental functioning. In this aspect of the analytic method—the making, breaking, and remaking of contexts—there is *common ground* among the different schools of psychoanalysis. But, as modern literary studies show, to give only one interdisciplinary example, this ground, far from being peculiar to psychoanalysis, is a feature of all interpretive disciplines.

Also, an analyst's revisionary contextual work on clinical content is necessarily controlled by his or her theoretical orientation. Consequently, analytic understanding in the clinical setting can be the outcome only of a dialogue between analyst and analysand in which what the analyst comes prepared to look for both sorts out and shapes whatever is subsequently "found" or "presented." That understanding cannot be the report of a detached, uninfluential, and uninfluenced observer. The contexts provided for understanding in the dialogue convey the point of view of the analyst's theory. Through their engaging in what may be called spoken and unspoken dialogue, analytic interpreters do shape their observational data. *Common ground* again.

This interaction of observer and observed is widely recognized to be a feature of all investigative and interpretive disciplines.

Moving on to another set of methodological considerations, it must be emphasized that the analytic literature includes reports of analyses that are not closely comparable in detail, cultural setting, the nature of the clinical problems addressed, or the phase of analysis covered. Further, in these reports analysts seem to be working in rather different styles. For instance, they vary in how closely they stick to interpretations of the here-and-now transference and countertransference and how much regard they show for the analysand's defensive needs. These variations are evident within the analytic schools as well as between them, with the result that reports of clinical phenomena and interpretations cannot be compared with one another except in the most tentative or preliminary way.

Another methodological problem stems from the recognition that analysts write differently. It should be realized that, in reading case reports, analysts are not examining full analyses in anything like a direct fashion; rather, they are sampling written narratives of brief segments of analyses. Even when the published sample of process notes is quite detailed, much will have been left out or reduced in the interest of producing a followable, time-limited, thesis-specific, written narrative of an analytic process. Therefore, the reader would do well to resist developing the illusion that he or she can hope to draw definite and productive conclusions. That illusion would be comparable to the family myth, the myth about the family to which all family members subscribe in order to gain a conscious sense of interpersonal harmony and personal integration even though it will be to the detriment of their individual minds and hearts.

Much in the written report depends on whether, for both personal and professional reasons, the writer has aimed mainly to do a good job of representing his or her school of analysis as different from other schools or has chosen mainly to conform to the unifying aims of establishing common ground. In either case, the writer will have been writing with a systematic bias. Consequently, it is hard to assess precisely, fully, and with conviction the representativeness of every clinical report, however fine it may be as a clinical document.

I maintain that the contexts and aims of writing do so influence what gets to be written that single reports cannot serve as strong evidence for important conclusions. Here, too, in respect of limited representativeness of single case reports, divergent psychoanalytic approaches share *common ground* among themselves and with other disciplines.

Representativeness is a theme that helps us identify still more *common ground:* No school of theory and practice is so thoroughly thought through, integrated, monolithic, and binding on its members, none so static and controlling, that any one report issuing from it can be considered hard evidence of all of the school's principles and procedures. Moreover, each approach cannot avoid generating a set of potential limitations on its application and results, and each set of limitations will develop differently in specific clinical instances. As a consequence, there is continuing debate *within* schools over the representativeness of individual clinical reports. Unfortunately, the debates often turn away from the difficult methodological problem of representativeness and become judgments of the quality of this or that piece of work: "Inferior!" "Not real analysis!" or "Good job!"

IDEOLOGICAL CONSIDERATIONS

Ideologically, the search for common ground seems to me to imply a generally conservative value system in that it turns attention away from the creative and progressive aspects of the struggles between different systems of thought and practice. We may refer to conservatism with all due respect to the ostensible progressive intentions behind the search for common ground. Analysts know all too well that intentions and consequences are not the same thing.

My attribution of conservativeness is based on my belief that, in the realm of ideas and the practices in which they are realized, it is conflict that makes us both wiser and more creative. Sublimated aggression does have its wonderful uses: As well as being useful in defining the pros and cons of other approaches, it fosters adventurousness and constructive self-criticism, the kind of criticism that is required to do pioneering work and to recognize in one's own position those elements of incoherence, inconsistency, and incompleteness that stem from unexamined presuppositions and undefendable leaps of faith. The history of ideas shows that, sooner or later, in every system of ideas and practice, new frontiers will be defined and new problems internal to established positions will get to be identified and fought over. *Common ground.*

Ideologically, by valorizing the search for specifically psychoanalytic common ground, we are implying that differences are regrettable and should be leveled. Knowingly or not, we are then aiming for a single master text for psychoanalysis and an end to its history, and what could be more conservative than that? It is a high price to pay for the sense of professional unity. The progressive way—and obviously this is my contestable ideological preference—is to give up on the idea of a single master text and instead to celebrate and study differences and to continue to grow, as the field of psychoanalysis has grown, through unsettledness. Analysts should work with the sense that *their differences reveal all the things that psychoanalysis can be even though it cannot be all things at one time or for any one person.* The alternative is the blindness of conformism.

This progressive value is often deplored as one that leads to the chaotic relativistic situation in which anything goes, both technically and interpretively. But against this argument I would point out that, just like the members of other humanistic disciplines, analysts have been living with diversity for a long time, and it is abundantly clear that every major school of thought, every approach, every set of value-laden practices, has its own traditions, standards, and means of maintaining relative order as it matures. Also, whatever its problems, each psychoanalytic school of thought and practice has had things of value to teach about understanding and helping patients analytically.

PART FOUR

VERSIONS OF PRACTICE

CHAPTER 12

Another Defense: "First, the Bad News"

CLINICAL analysts often encounter a mode of behavior that may be designated "*first*, the bad news" and included among the narratives of defense. That narrative of defensive operations is the *clinical* subject of this chapter. After describing its typical forms of appearance during the analytic process, I present, first, an extended case example and then an account of the defense's manifestations during the termination phase of analysis. The theoretical implications of this material are reserved for a concluding section of this chapter.

The phenomena that may be redefined and organized by this narrative are certainly familiar to any experienced therapist. Many of these phenomena have already been taken up in the analytic literature, frequently under such therapeutically useful headings as negative therapeutic reaction (for example, Freud, 1923a, and Loewald, 1972), masochistic character (for example, W. Reich, 1933), and seduction of the aggressor (for example, Loewenstein, 1957). Under these headings we find references to the variety of efforts that analysands make, primarily unconsciously, to work up some anger, dispel some good feeling, produce a major or minor crisis, or even plunge themselves "mysteriously" into some depression or anxiety while they are on their way to the analytic session, in the waiting room, entering the office, or getting on the couch. Not only do they then present themselves as "bad news," they report and dwell on bad news at great length: their failures, disappointments, exacerbations of symptoms, and so forth. In each case this behavior is likely to be stereo-typed and repetitive. The analyst learns, if only by fits and starts, not to get drawn into these self-presentations and these discouraging details as such; for often, and especially as progress is made in the analysis, it becomes apparent during each session that the news of the day as well as the emotional state of the newscaster are just not that "bad." The repetitively gloomy beginning soon seems to be serving the function of throwing a pall over the analyst and thereby blinding him or her to what may be called, in contrast, "the good news." In this one of its aspects, "first, the bad news" seems to be a defensive manipulation of the countertransference.

To the nonjudgmental analyst, of course, it is not a matter of bad-ness at all, except perhaps in those first flickers of countertransference that indicate the action of the defensive manipulation. With reference to the analysand's psychic reality, however, it may be described as a case of "first, the bad news."

Case Example

My example is taken from the analysis of a young married woman of British origin. I have just returned from a week's vacation. During my absence, she began a new job. She also took an examination to qualify for advanced specialty training. Prior to the week-long break, much analytic time had been spent attempting to understand the intensely anxious way in which she was anticipating these two events. Connections with the transference, including those pertaining to the week's interruption, had been pointed out whenever possible. In the first session after my return she does not refer to my absence, and she alludes only vaguely and in passing to some uneasiness about having enjoyed the past week. She refers neither to her experience in her new job nor to how she had performed on the qualifying examina-tion.

Saying that the details of various events are "nagging" at her, she goes on to dwell on the ups and downs, mainly the downs, of her per-sonal relationships. In the midst of this account of her week, she lets drop again a hint that she had had some "great" times, but she then goes on to accentuate further only the negative, and she does so with considerable and mounting bitterness. She recounts in great detail how she attacked her husband for devaluing her as a marital partner and a woman; however, despite much circumstantial detail, she pre-sents no specific or persuasive evidence in support of her charges against him. She succeeds in coming across as demanding, intolerant, and "nagging," particularly in relation to her husband. Although she throws in the remark that, on the basis of our previous work, she knows that she is criticizing him for "faults" that are hers, she does not slow the accelerating attacks on him.

On my part, I begin to respond silently with some countertransference, starting to wonder glumly whether the analysis of her presenting problem of depressiveness and inhibitedness will only eventuate in her becoming remorselessly vindictive. At this point, however, I realize that she is, so to speak, once again beginning to cast a spell over me. Under this spell, with which I am familiar in this analysis, I can no longer listen empathically or remember adequately; instead, I am moved to say something critical and thereby enter into a complex sadomasochistic interaction with her. By "something critical" I refer not to criticizing her in the conventional sense but to pointing out some problematic aspects of her account that I could know in advance she would take only as criticism.

Realizing all this, I begin to remember better. I recall once again that this mode of self-presentation has always been typical of the way she begins her sessions and that it used to be typical of her sessions from beginning to end. I also remember that it has deep roots in preferred patterns of interaction within her family. I recall, too, that recently she has been attempting to shift within her sessions from this "nagging" initial self-presentation to collaborative thoughtfulness. Often, though not always, when making these shifts she has used my comments late in the sessions reflectively rather than continuing her earlier pattern of treating even what I regarded as my most neutral or empathic comments simply as abuse or misunderstanding. In short order and with some chagrin I realize that in this session I have been observing an expectable regressive response to my week-long absence.

After much airing of her grievances, she reports a dream. In the dream she is chasing her husband with a cricket bat but ends up embracing him in an enfolding manner. To the bat she associates vampire and thinks of the subsequent enfolding as being demanding and possessive to the point of being devouring. To her husband's fleeing from her she associates to her sense that he has been trying to avoid a fight and that her attacks on him have been pressured, as if she has been clinging to them, as if she has been trying to drive him away. At this late point in the session, apparently continuing the reversal of her regressive "welcome," a reversal that was signaled by her dropping hints of good times and by her bringing up the dream and being prepared to give some associations to it, she changes her tone to her new-found thoughtfulness, and she asks me what I make of all the material of the session. Up to this point, I have been silent.

I decide to answer by taking up two factors: her defensive avoidance of manifest links to the transference and her unconsciously active, stereotyped attempt to seduce me into a sadomasochistic counter-transference response. I say to her that she feels distant to me today, as in her making no mention of my absence and no mention of the new job and the examination on which we had spent so much time before I left. Not only distant from me, however, but acting as if she has been trying to get me to feel distant from her and dissatisfied with her as someone who is making no progress, as simply a "nag" who will not even tell me about her great times during my absence. She then acknowledges that she had come to this session wanting to tell me "the good news" but had felt embarrassed and didn't know why. She adds that during the past week she had been for the most part unusu-ally generous toward her husband, and playful, too, bringing him a bunch of presents, some of them "silly." She had been pleased by this change in her behavior. She says she feels embarrassed to tell me this. With even greater embarrassment, she then confesses that for a change she had even felt hopeful about herself and had thought that she might be "well" before long. The session ends with her expressing concern that she had wanted to exclude the good news and establish hostile distance between us.

It seemed to me then that a collaborative atmosphere had begun to be reestablished; however, taking into account that this change had occurred only in the safety of the end of the session, and that it had been accompanied by much embarrassment and some guilt, I could only view it as a beginning. On her part, she had by no means given up her defensive use of "first, the bad news," and on my part, I had by no means made all the interpretations that were possible. For the time being I had limited myself to what, on the basis of previous experience with her, I thought that she could hear and use productively in this conflictual context.

Looking now at this session from the standpoint of the traditional tax-onomy of defense, it is evident that in addition to repression and avoidance, she had made much use of projective identification, dis-placement (from the transference), and reversal of passivity to activity in the form of identification with the aggressor. And taking into account the induced, manifestly negative, incipient countertransfer-ence, it may be added that, more subtly, she had made a powerful

attempt to reverse active sadism to passive masochism through seduction of the aggressor. What had helped me to advance the analytic
work with this analysand from its earlier manifest phase of "bad news
only" was my continually clarifying to myself how heavily she had been
relying on this combination of defensive strategies for most of her life.
It had helped me to sort out, reorganize, and then interpret what otherwise would have remained forbidding and impenetrably confusing
manifest content. For the most part, however, it had not been useful
to point out her defensive strategies as such; interventions of that sort
usually served only to intensify manifestly negative transference
responses.

What then could be taken up with her? Here, as I do not plan to
embark on the history of the analysis, I merely summarize the major
lines of interpretation that had proved useful up to this point in the
work. Implied in her nagging, provocative orientation was her unconsciously fantasizing a masculine-phallic identity for herself. Not only
did this identity alleviate her sense of humiliation, it played a central
part in her complex preoedipal and oedipal relationships with both
parents.

Unconsciously she had been struggling against identification with
her mother. She portrayed her mother as unmotherly, repelled by
instinctual expression on every psychosexual level, moralistic, snob-
bish, pretentious but unproductive, virtually anhedonic and unresponsive to exuberance, a stereotype of British propriety and snootiness as
befit her socially insecure, upwardly mobile, provincial background in
a blatantly class-conscious society. This struggle against identification
contained the analysand's own strong aspirations to become a loving
and sensual woman and to avoid her mother's allegedly barren existence. Unconsciously she experienced the forbidding imago of her
mother as a major obstruction to realizing these aspirations, and she
expressed her submission to this imago in her hating herself for maintaining these aspirations and in her hating me for pointing out anything that increased her awareness of them.

But, as would be expected, she had also assigned a central role to
her unconsciously maintained father imago. She experienced her
father as being exceedingly uncomfortable with her whenever the positive and mutual oedipal temperature in their contacts began to rise.
At those moments, and often to forestall them, he would become withdrawn, irritable, hypercritical, and taunting in an anal-sadistic manner. Thus, for her, to be demonstrative, loving, and sensual only drove
him away; more exactly, it incited him to engage her in sadomasochistic intimacies instead. Over the course of her development she had

largely accepted his regressive terms; she had herself become an active initiator of sadomasochistic interaction with him. Quarreling was the currency of the realm. There lay her positive oedipal desires, and in her analysis she repeated these seductions endlessly in her paternal transference, just as she repeated her struggle with her mother in her maternal transference.

In this perspective, it could be understood that while in one respect her defensive strategy of "first, the bad news" was designed to drive me away, in another respect it was intended to engage me in a regressively debased positive oedipal interaction. Additionally, her defensive strategy repudiated her maternal identification and compensated her for her sense of humiliation; at the same time it played out that aspect of her maternal identification that promised to reproduce her mother's unhappy marriage in her own marriage as well as in her transference. She had to make the analysis and her marriage as joyless as the home in which she grew up.

Consequently, in the session I reviewed, she could not eagerly or demonstratively tell me about her great times. She anticipated that if she did tell me, she would lose me as the positive and accepting oedipal-level father I was just beginning to become for her; she would also lose me as a good mother, an alternative to the mother she had experienced, a figure I was just beginning to become for her as well. I would be pushed into contempt for her if she reported the generous, silly, fun times with her husband and if she manifestly welcomed me back with enthusiasm. She was protecting her newfound joy in her marriage and in her analysis. Her way of welcoming me back was to bat me around. And batting me around also expressed her intense oral deprivation, her wanting to suck life from me, which also meant incorporating my penis, thereby reinforcing her guilty view of herself as a devouring person.

Clearly then, in this case, "first, the bad news" was as much a matter of wish fulfillment and punishment, as much a matter of object-relatedness and adaptation as it was a matter of defense. In short, it had to be understood as a compromise formation, and bit by bit it was possible to interpret it to her in all its complexity as just that. But in order to get to this point, and in order to work this compromise through methodically, it was necessary to rely in my own thinking on the taxonomy of defensive strategies and transformations. It was also necessary to approach this compromise first as a defensive measure: This taxonomy and this emphasis on defense helped the two of us, as long ago it helped Anna Freud (1976) and her analysands, to become expert witnesses of the reenactment of a family drama that was being repetitively played out in the analytic relationship; it seemed to help lay down the storyline that could, finally, make a therapeutic difference in a potentially blocked analysis.

AT TERMINATION

A special version of "first, the bad news" is commonly encountered during the termination phase of analysis. In that phase we often see regressive shifts that seem to erase previous successful analytic work: Symptoms flare up, crises develop in good relationships, self-destructive behavior increases, and the transference in general assumes some of its most negative forms. All of which, to be sure, indicates difficulties with the pending separation and the need for working through issues of separation and loss. Here we shall be concerned with the way in which "first, the bad news" enters this picture.

Often the resurgence of regressive material appears at the beginning of the analytic sessions. In such cases, if the analyst either simply waits out these gloom-making reports and behaviors or with the help of a few judicious analytic interventions raises some questions about them, the analysands begin to tell and show that, in fact, they are themselves capable of significant resilience. They have, for example, already self-analyzed the regressive shifts, or they have limited the damage and taken steps to repair it; they show that they are not actually helpless, castrated, symbolically suicidal, or what have you. The session-opening gloominess is in part an attempt to seduce the analyst into a guilty and reparative countertransference; if not that, then it may be a seduction into a countertransference in which the analyst is to feel abandoned in response to the analysand's reversal of felt passivity to active withdrawal.

In some ways, this resort to "first, the bad news" resembles the adolescent's resorting to externalization of one part of a conflict over emancipation by provoking conflict with parents, in this way showing them to be unworthy of continued love and desire. In the case of the adolescent, this defensive shift probably involves an attempt to expel the incorporated parent, as if to show that all that has existed previously was a purely external relationship. The case may be much the same with respect to the analyst at termination.

In general, the regressive move is most usefully approached as a defensive measure. To a great extent, the improved patient cannot sustain that move and either gives away the game in upbeat dreams and parapraxes or gives signs of being in a good mood that contradicts much of the negative content. Sometimes the analysand just switches gears during the session. For example, in one case a dream was apparently reported in full as follows: *He was preparing to buy a $75,000 house that was quite broken down.* The analysand's associations led to the total cost of the analysis, which in fact was more than $75,000; 75,000 was also three-quarters, and that suggested that his life was three-quarters over, even though he was only in his thirties, a calculation related to his depressed parents' emphasis on their physical decline after the age of forty; three-quarters also stood for an incomplete analysis, and that implied disappointment in the analytic results. Only after this part of the work did the analysand go on to continue the dream report as follows: *He had rejected that house and he took one that was handsome, with lots of glass so that he could look outside and not be trapped in a wreck.* It was apparent then that the analysand had been setting up the analyst to fall into a gloomy mood.

In a sense, the patient in this example was showing rather than telling "bad news." Other ways of showing rather than telling include falling back on characterological rigidities that have been extensively analyzed and significantly modified prior to the agreement to move toward a termination date; also, increasing lateness or more frequent absences, the adoption of a "cured" bonhomie, and so forth. One analysand reverted to long, circumstantial, emotionally arid reports of daily events; fairly regularly, however, this analysand spontaneously began, within each session, to question this repetition and to understand it as a way of warding off the emotional experience both of mourning the analysis and of celebrating its achievements. As before, this analysand was trying to dull me and subdue any excitement or grief I might be feeling in order to keep us both in a state of being remote from one another, tightly controlled and protected; in this there was much repetition of anal-obsessive and oedipal prototypes.

Another analysand with massive guilt problems in relation to a fragile and overattached father found it necessary to resort to her characterological form of "first, the bad news" in order to reassure me that she was not about to abandon me and leave me stranded and depressed. She began being once again her "old self," that is, a good girl displaying her suffering and emphasizing how much she needed external supplies; it was she, however, who soon brought out this concern for me and who recognized it as a familiar defensive transference.

In another case, a female analysand resumed procrastinating in concluding certain significant and positive life changes, and she returned to secret forms of masturbation that we had analyzed as enactments of androgyny, specifically of having a phallic vagina that had no room for, or need of, a man's penis. Thereby she was denying both the value to her of her male analyst and, in her psychic reality, his potent analytic phallus and also her readiness to move on to a fulfilling relationship with a man of her own. In this instance, "first, the bad news" was a castration of the analyst and a return characterologically to the androgynous and ineffective boy-girl role she had played in relation to her father. All of which stood in marked contrast to many other experiences and activities of a more mature sort that she soon mentioned with an independently arrived at sense of self-contradiction and rapid insight into her responding defensively to our terminating.

On the whole, however, I would say that the most pervasive manifestation of "first, the bad news" is the one that accompanies felt progress *throughout the analysis.* In these instances, it is always a question of what is gained by apparently just submitting to the fear of getting well. What danger situation is being avoided by that submission? I have discussed this phenomenon in other connections as an attack on the analyst's empathy (1983), a fear of success or idealization of unhappiness (chapter 6), and in other ways as well, each of which will be found to have a complex inner structure, but each of which may yield to analysis only when recognized as a form of defense. As with my extended clinical example earlier in this chapter, there are different ways to tell this story of defense and so there are different stories to tell, each of which has its truth-value and therapeutic value. The choice among them, although never absolutely certain, is often guided by more or less subtle cues in the patient's associations.

THEORETICAL DISCUSSION

I have been discussing "first, the bad news" as a defensive operation, measure, or strategy. By using these terms I have attempted to illustrate several interrelated theoretical points. First, I have been highlighting psychoanalysis as a narrative enterprise, as Anna Freud (1936) did, though only implicitly, when she discussed identification with the aggressor and altruistic surrender as defenses, and as others have (for example, Bibring and her co-workers, 1961). Specifically, I have been presenting under the aspect of defense a number of complex configurations that include wish fulfillment, self-punishment, and adaptive efforts. Presenting these configurations under the aspect of defense clearly is an example of choice of narrative. Each defensive story of this complex type can be told differently: for example, as a compromise formation, as an illustration of multiple function, as an enactment of transference-countertransference fantasies that are briefly actualized through the patient's resort to considerable projective identification, or as the partially regressed expression of an intense bisexual oedipal transference.

Second, unlike Anna Freud's narrative, however, mine does not revolve around the assumption that there are "mechanisms of defense" that, in response to "anxiety signals," influence the workings of the "mental apparatus." Making that assumption and using those terms exemplifies adherence to Sigmund Freud's metapsychology, his mechanistic language for theorizing about mind and method, particularly as developed to its high point in "Inhibitions, Symptoms and Anxiety" (1926).

Elsewhere in this book (see chapters 9 and 10) I have characterized the metapsychologically developed theory of Freudian psychoanalysis as a master narrative with its distinctive storylines and rhetoric. My storyline of defensive operations is based on my previous work on action language and narration. On that basis I present the interpretable events of the analysis as actions of the analysand and the analyst, and I take up defense in the same way that I take up transference, countertransference, and repetition—as things people *do*, as the performances of agents.

Thus, the somewhat fanciful title of this chapter and its clinical focus should not be taken as a neglect of theory. In the context of psychoanalysis as a narrational project with both theoretical and clinical aspects, I present this chapter as an example of theory *in* clinical work. In this narrational context, no further theorizing is called for. A further step into a metatheory of some sort implies wrongly that clinical accounts are unprocessed "data," prescientific aggregates of observations, still to be refined into truth. That hierarchization seemed necessary to the Freud who remained faithful to his nineteenth-century scientific training and aspirations; it should no longer seem necessary to us one hundred years later.

CHAPTER 13

Psychic Reality, Developmental Influences, and Unconscious Communication

T HE distinguishing feature of clinical analytic interpretation is its emphasis on psychic reality. That is, interpretation centers on the personal meanings that analysands ascribe, especially unconsciously, to events and actions in the past and present. Typically, these unconsciously ascribed meanings are organized in repetitive fashion around infantile conflicts, fantasies, and modes of thought and feeling. But interpretation deals not only with psychic reality. It is more exact to say that it involves a complex, subtle, and shifting distribution of emphasis on psychic reality, developmental influences, and unconsciously communicated messages. In this chapter I attempt to clarify some of the issues that arise in connection with this shifting distribution of emphasis.

To make the issue concrete, I focus specifically on how analysts take their analysands' representations of other people and how they deal with these representations in their interventions. By "other people" I refer to people other than the analyst and analysand, those whom the analyst encounters only through what the analysand says concerning them. I do not, however, neglect to consider how representations of other people are related to the analysand's self-representations and representations of the analyst. Representations of other people provide a good test case for the analyst's understanding and uses of psychic reality in relation to developmental influences and unconsciously communicated messages.

While what I lay out may seem to some readers obvious or customary, even elementary, I am not aware that the topic has already been
dealt with in quite the way I deal with it. Much of my discussion is
devoted to clinical instances and technical practices. I lead off with
the analyst's primary focus on psychic reality alone; later on I amend
that somewhat puristic account.

VIEWING REPRESENTATIONS OF OTHERS AS PSYCHIC REALITY

Usually (though some analysts would argue that it should always be
so and others that it should be so only on occasion), analysts do not
take analysands' representations of other people for granted. They do
not hear them as reliable, valid, complete, factual statements. Instead,
they take each statement about other people as a communication that
bears on each analysand's psychic reality. This communication may be
taken to be a narrative account of the analysand's subjective experience of these others. If so, it may be examined for what it tells about
the analysand's unconsciously conflicted self—one or another of them
(see chapter 2). Analysts may also take this communication as a displaced reference to an analysand's experience of the analyst, that is, as
an unconsciously disguised manifestation of transference. In still
another way it may be taken as a form of remembering the infantile
past through selectively emphasized current experience. Or, finally, it
may be taken as a projected reference, as in a dream, to some aspect of
the analysand's unconsciously repudiated self-experience. Analysts may
take representations of other people in any combination of these ways.
    Consider, for example, the content of such commonplace state-
ments as "My father is old." Apparently, this is a simple statement of
fact. But instead of taking it as simple fact, analysts approach each such
communication as a possible reference to unconsciously conflictual
subjective experience and as possible displacement, life-historical background, or projection. In order to take it in any of these ways, analysts
must first assume the following to be true. The allegedly factual world
provides a plenitude of facts to speak of, and there is nothing
inevitable about what the analysand selects from this plenitude and the
narrative versions of these facts that he or she constructs. That is, the
selective principles are not totally self-evident and beyond interpretation; rather they are interpretable expressions of the analysand's current conflictual position in the analysis. They say something about both
the content and the mode of construction of the analysand's psychic
reality in the here and now. They are facts without life or significance

until they have been redescribed and given a context in the analysis. They have to be transformed into psychoanalytic facts.

Taking the representations of other people in this way, analysts promote a number of technically desirable consequences. These include, first, keeping open the possibility that over the course of analysis these representations will be revised and further revised through subsequent reversals of content or attitude and through filling in and the introduction of greater complexity. Greater complexity opens the door to interpreting the multiple functions served by representations of other people. Thus, the "old father" may get to be represented later as youthful, perhaps as competitively so, and unconsciously as murderously so. And from this later vantage point, the earlier "fact" stated simply as "My father is old" may be viewed as a defensive denial or reversal.

As a second desirable consequence of not taking any representation of others for granted, analysts avoid adopting an authoritarian or even authoritative position that they are experts on people and situations outside the analytic situation. Being cautious in this way, analysts are less likely to become dupes of an analysand's unconscious and defensive strategies or countertransference manipulations and are thus less likely to enact a role in the patient's fantasies, such as that of the omniscient conscience.

As a third advantage, analysts maintain neutrality by not taking sides in the analysand's conflictual situations. Were analysts to take any representations of other people as adequate or final, they would interfere with achieving a balanced appraisal of psychic reality. In accord with the principle of multiple function, a balanced appraisal features empathic appreciation of the analysand's needing unconsciously to work out complex compromise formations. In the long run, analysts' open-minded stance with regard to representations of other people testifies to their neutrality and interpretive competence even though, in the short run, the analysands may use it to attack analysts as unempathic and offputting, if not suspicious, or as taking sides with "the opposition."

How do analysts achieve these and other desirable effects on the analysis? One way is by indicating in those interventions touching on representations of other people that their comments are directed not at these others as such, but at the analysand's experience or version of them. They indicate that this experience or version is open to examination as a statement about the analysand's psychic reality. For instance, analysts say, "As you see her," "What you particularly want to emphasize about him," "The thing that stands out for me in your account of your father," and so on. Sometimes going further, analysts say, "You seem to be trying hard to limit me to seeing your mother as having no redeeming features, and I wonder why you need to do that," or "You have been bringing up many details that suggest you see your father as corrupt, even though you continue to insist that he is trustworthy, but for some reason you still do not acknowledge that other view of him," and so on. Analysts might go still further in some instances, saying, for example, "You describe her as if she is an erect penis," or "You make him sound like a fart."

In none of these instances do analysts simply speak out on what the facts are concerning these other people. If the analysand is threatened, hurt, or offended by this restraint, it indicates to the analysts that some defensiveness or transference problem needs to be taken up. Analysts may do this by pointing out the insecurity implied in the analysand's upset, and by going on to question the urgency with which the analysand is trying to get them to accept some version of another person in a way that is absolutely closed to exploration, interpretation, and revision.

Early in analysis, however, or during periods of crisis, it may seem to analysts that the best way to advance the analysis is to refer to other people without qualification—to speak, for example, just as the analysand has been doing, say of the father as being simply "withdrawn." As long as analysts do not get hooked on that unqualified representation, there will be opportunity later to introduce qualifications, saying, for example, "You felt he was punishing you by withdrawing," or "You felt you had driven him away." Usually this sequential accommodation is unnecessary, for ordinarily it is possible to be both tactful *and* noncommittal from the start. This can be accomplished by tone of voice alone, though it is risky to rely on implied messages; or by such prefatory remarks as "From what you say" and "If that is the case" may be used in passing. Or analysts may refer from the beginning to the father's "withdrawn aspect," to the impact of the father's "apparent withdrawal," or to the times when the father could only be "experienced as withdrawn." In general, it is better for the subsequent elucidation of the analysand's psychic reality if analysts do not use these early or crisis-based representations without some sort of qualification.

WORKING OUTSIDE OF PSYCHIC REALITY

But—and this is a big but, for here I begin to amend my puristic description—analysts do not always work within the confines of psychic reality. We see this in the reports of their work. We see it in statements, for example, that the father *was* withdrawn or sadistic, the mother *was* narcissistic or psychotic, the spouse *is* masochistic or depressive, and so on. And we see it in published interpretations of analytic material that are based on analysts' having taken certain representations of other people as certain, true, objective, factual. It would not be going too far to assume that these analysts have made comparable statements in the analytic dialogue itself; often, analysts explicitly report that this was so. Our next problem then is to fit this evidence into our schema of neutral, judicious, consistent analytic attention to psychic reality.

As a first step in dealing with this problem, we can acknowledge that, taking the analysis as a whole, analysts need not fastidiously qualify every remark touching on other people. There are three conditions under which unqualified interventions may be made with sufficient analytic security. The first is when the analysand is well into the analysis and has repeatedly and spontaneously demonstrated a reliable enough recognition that the focus of the work is on psychic reality. This means that pluralistic accounts of other people are the order of the day—and of the night, too—regardless of how "factually" things may be formulated moment by moment. The second condition is when the functions served by certain representations of other people in the analysand's defensive operations and transference have been repeatedly and productively analyzed. Analysts have gained confidence in these analysands' collaborative sense that it is important to grasp psychic reality. And analysts have gained confidence in their own grasp of these analysands' psychic reality as well. On this basis analysts do not need to be as analytically circumspect every moment; in particular, analysts are not as likely to be so concerned at that time with the hazards of countertransference, and so, appropriately, will feel free to make shorthand references to the characteristics of other people.

The third condition is when it seems that further entry into psychic reality requires the analyst to adopt a less detached or reflective manner, as with some schizoid patients at certain times. Then, analysts may refrain from introducing qualifying remarks and instead enter into a partial facilitating regression with the analysand to dreamlike acceptance of his or her narrative portrayal of other people. During these regressive excursions, analysts must remain alert to their own inclinations to become too insistent, enthusiastic, or vehement when referring to other people, for these inclinations may lead to disruptive expressions of countertransference, and they may stimulate destructive acting out. For example, simply to say "Your husband is taking advantage of you" or "Your partner in business is out to get you" might well stimulate destructive acting out.

Even when all these conditions have been met, however, analysts take a giant step away from psychic reality whenever they draw conclusions as to what these other people are really like or what they really did or are doing now. In taking this giant step analysts shift from a consistently genetic approach to a developmental-environmental-functional approach. The modern foundation for systematically understanding this shift was laid by Kris (1956b). The genetic approach focuses on the analysand's phase-specific, psychosexual fantastic constructions of reality, such as those Freud described in "Three Essays on the Theory of Sexuality" (1905b), "On the Sexual Theories of Children" (1908b), and many other papers.

In the genetic approach, analysts listen to representations of other people as to the manifest content of a dream. This way of listening is what I described earlier in my "puristic" account. In contrast, the *developmental-environmental-functional approach* (referred to as *developmental* for the sake of brevity) takes for granted certain biographical data concerning the analysand's early or current environment, the people in it, and the events that took place in it or are now taking place in it. Also taken for granted are events in the analysand's own bodily environment of a maturational or accidental nature. In this approach analysts listen to representations of other people as to a case history rather than as to a dream. Additionally, they listen in the role of diagnostician of cognitive functioning—its level, organization, and deformation.

The analysts' shift in mode of listening from the genetic to the developmental might not be readily apparent. For example, it might not seem to have occurred when an analyst continues to emphasize the primary importance of ascertaining what the analysand has made of these "actual" people and events. But this appearance is deceptive, for the analyst's viewpoint is that he or she knows what really happened or is now happening elsewhere in the analysand's life and is attempting merely to understand its elaboration or distortion in memory or report. The parents *were* obstructive, the husband *is* being withholding or guilt-provoking, and so on. What is the justification for analysts taking this stand outside psychic reality?

Taking this stand is justified, first of all, by the analysts' diagnostic estimate of the general adequacy and integrity of the analysand's cognitive activity. When this estimate is relatively high, analysts are more likely to ascribe some truth-value to reports of past and present actions performed by other people. Truth-value can be ascribed even when it is obvious that the representations of other people are being narrated in a way that is not altogether reliable—that is, when they involve defenses and transferences, as indicated by gaps, inconsistencies, glaring displacements, and apparently inexplicable emotionality. Nevertheless, analysts might still extract from these narratives that, for example, a boyfriend abandoned the analysand in a certain way or a girlfriend said she resented the analysand in a certain tone, and even that this action or tone was characteristic of this other person.

Analysts require some ground to stand on in order to make analytic sense of what is being reported in the analysand's associations; they cannot suspend judgment about everything. In this connection, analysts establish this ground by stepping outside psychic reality and making diagnostic judgments of cognitive functioning. In making these judgments analysts rely on versions of common human situations and cause-effect relations that are so highly conventionalized that they serve as standards of good reality testing, sound judgment, and adaptive functioning. Although there is always room for disagreement over these standards, for analytic purposes they are taken as generally applicable. At the same time, however, as I said, analysts are prepared for subsequent narrative revisions of what, for working purposes, it seemed safe or useful to accept as factual at an earlier or stormier time in the analysis.

A second justification of analysts' taking a stand outside psychic reality on the factuality of certain representations of others is their judgment that these representations meet the criteria of narrative good fit. Analysts use these criteria in piecing into analytically meaningful patterns various accounts of another person's actions. It would be a worthwhile task to attempt to spell out fully these criteria of good fit and their basis, but here I can mention only a few things.

As to their basis, criteria of good fit derive partly from conventional common sense or an analytically refined version of common sense, for analysts' idea of what hangs together in a story is founded on more than psychoanalytic understanding; it rests as well on conventions of coherence that are shared by analysts and analysands as members of a community of understanding. In addition, these criteria are based partly on analysts' empathic responses that have not yet been clearly conceptualized in the analysis. And they are partly dependent on the same kind of interpretive analytic synthesizing analysts use in making coherent sense of everything that is being produced by analysands in the analytic situation. In this last regard we must also bear in mind that even the coherence of an analysand's narratives of self-experience (for example, as "worthless") are not routinely taken for granted; they, too, require revision and synthesizing by analysts. For example, "I feel depressed" may refer more to anxiety than depression, particularly when an analysand fears to make an urgent request of an analyst.

One kind of good fit is based on a particular kind of correspondence or consistency. On the one hand, there are the analysand's versions of her or his actions in dealings with other people. On the other hand, there are accounts of the analysand's actions in the analytic situation itself that have already been jointly developed, provisionally accepted, and worked with. When these two sets of accounts correspond or are consistent with one another, a criterion of good fit has been satisfied—for example, a certain regularity of mistrustful reaction whenever the analysand encounters kindness.

Another kind of good fit is also based on correspondence or consistency. On the one hand, there is an analyst's conception of the analysand's problems and their developmental-environmental contexts. On the other hand, there are generally accepted analytic propositions about the way in which problems of this sort come into being or are strongly reinforced during development. For example, reports by the analysand of a father's sadism or passivity or a mother's narcissism or psychotic behavior are likely to be accepted as having truth-value when they conform both to developmental propositions concerning the effects of such parents on children and to the analyst's grasp of the analysand's problems. In accord with clinical theory, analysts accept certain developmental propositions as true and use them as tools to assess the extent to which reports of early "objective" reality correspond to or are consistent with the phenomena of the individual analytic interaction. For example, an analyst who is confident that the analysand is extremely schizoid will not accept glowing accounts of all early family relationships. These developmental propositions are not highly specific, but they do serve to set up some leading expectations. In relying on these propositions, however, analysts have temporarily stepped outside the psychic reality of the individual analysand in order to reenter it later with greater understanding.

In addition to estimates of cognitive functioning and of narrative good fit, there is a third warrant for analysts to draw conclusions about other people. This one, too, lies outside the psychic reality of an individual analysand. Analysts may be satisfied that an analysand is portraying others in a well-rounded way. This does not mean that analysts assume everyone in the world is equally well rounded in personality makeup; rather, they assume that there are analytically complex factors at work in everyone. Well-roundedness of representation is not always prominent early in analysis. In the beginning, other people are likely to be presented as simply good or bad in their natures and in their influence, or else they are presented as unpredictably totally good or bad. As a rule, only later on in analysis do representations of other people get to be well rounded. Then the representations convey some recognition on the part of the analysand that the actions of these others are complex, involving conflict, unconscious meaning, and compromise formations. We may say that, as a result of analytic work, others come to be portrayed as having their own interpretable life histories. This kind of narrative change may be tracked especially well in characterizations of parents.

Analysts do, of course, encounter some would-be superanalysands, those who deliver well-rounded representations of others from the start. These superanalysands will have to move from their judicious, well-balanced narratives of others to ones that are less defensively air-tight and involve highly emotional simplifications before they can develop more wholly felt and convincing accounts of these other people. Whether any of these sequences occurs will depend on developments in the analysis of defense and transference.

Analyst can be sure of the truth-value of the now-complex representations of other people to the extent that equivalent and similar complexity characterizes an analysand's *representations within the analytic situation* of self and of the analyst. Again, therefore, correspondence and continuity play a major part in assessments of truth-value. And when this point is reached, analysts are able to shift freely and productively between comments on the analytic relationship and comments on the analysand's other relationships in the past and present.

The fourth warrant for the analyst's speaking of other people without qualification is the last I shall mention. As an analysis progresses, the analysand behaves differently in the analytic relationship. Some of the changes are based on worked-through insight. Concurrently, the analysand reports change or lack of change on the part of others in their reactions to the analysand's different mode of relating to *them* (see also chapter 1). Analysts are now in a better position to assign truth-value to these reports of variation or lack of variation in others' reactions. Analysts give evidential weight particularly to those reports that indicate a developing awareness of the ways in which the analysand is bringing about a *range* of variation in others: bringing out the best and the worst in them, their strengths and understanding, their symptoms and destructiveness. At this point, others are no longer being presented to analysts in a self-justifying way as completely static or unpredictable ahistorical entities. This principle of changed action and reaction holds even when others are reported in terms of

personal extremes, such as unyielding passivity, depression, or mistrust. But as a rule it is impressive, as an analysis progresses, how many
additional dimensions or features of other people do get to be
brought out or made more definite by the analysand's analytically
altered modes of interpersonal activity. And they need not all be
benign features.

Analysts do not use all such changes in the representation of other
people as a basis for saying "Now you see the world for what it is," for
then they would be playing the arbitrary and condescending role of
expert. Rather, analysts say or imply something like this: "These
changes make certain things clearer about the way you needed to perceive and control others in order to fit them into this or that fantasy
or to repeat this or that relationship from your childhood." Analysts
may also use the changed narratives to raise fresh questions about the
content and construction of the analysand's psychic reality. But still
analysts are able to do so only after some temporary or oscillating
departures from a position inside the analysand's psychic reality.

An important aspect of this shift from the genetic approach to the
developmental, or from the psychic to the "actual," must be noted in
order to develop further our understanding of the place of psychic
reality in analytic work. The shift entails a second shift of emphasis
from unconsciously constructed fantasy to *unconsciously carried on communication and reality testing.* Analysts do not doubt that such communication and its implied reality testing go on in every relationship.
Taking these processes as fact or assigning truth-value to them is a
necessary step in making the unintelligible intelligible through interpretation. We are able to say, for example, "You recognize how much
your mother always wished you were a boy and not a girl." Freud recognized unconscious communication as one of the foundations of the
analytic method as well as of the formation of the superego.

Consequently, in assessing representations of other people, analysts
view the analysand as picking up messages being sent unconsciously by
these others. In the present context, the messages that are picked up
unconsciously deserve special attention. (Those that are picked up
consciously or preconsciously may be important, but they present no
special problem to interpreting analysts as they are more clearly presented as perceptions by the analysand.) For example, analysts may
infer from certain representations of the mother that, unconsciously,
the analysand has picked up the message that she wishes the
analysand had never been born. Similarly, analysts may find it credible
that the analysand has unconsciously picked up the message from
father to mother that he would like to kill her or fears being castrated

by her. Likewise, analysts may believe in the developmental "truth" of certain primal-scene representations; this may be the case when the representations seem to condense genetically based anal-sadistic constructions *and* unconsciously recognized, "actual" sadomasochistic pains and pleasures in the parents' relations with one another. And when an analysand's dream indicates unacknowledged recognition of an analyst's seductive or cruel countertransference, the understanding of the dream must include reference to what has been unconsciously communicated by the analyst and registered accurately, though unconsciously, by the analysand. We deal here not primarily with psychic reality, but with reality testing of "actual" communications.

Yet it does not follow from these points that, in this connection, analysts must shift the focus away from psychic reality more than temporarily. It remains essential that there be analysis of how and why the analysand elaborates further these results of unconsciously seeing, hearing, and understanding. In other words, analysts soon return to asking what the analysand makes of the analyst's seductiveness or cruelty, if these types of countertransference are in question. But even with all due regard for psychic reality, in the analysis analysts must step out of psychic reality somewhat in order to determine what that other person—in many instances the analyst him- or herself—is "actually" doing or feeling.

The word *actually* must always be put inside quotation marks, for there is always more than one analytically useful, realistic version of the observations in question. For instance, in the countertransference example I just mentioned, seductiveness and cruelty on an analyst's part are not necessarily mutually exclusive as realistic versions of any one countertransferential action. At one time the version to emphasize may be seduction; at another time, cruelty; while later on the analyst or analysand may include both accounts of the analyst's countertransference in a complex narrative. The complex narrative might emphasize the analyst's fear of the analysand's sadism and consequently his or her dealing with this fear through disarming efforts of an erotic or aggressive nature.

I am trying to bring out that analysts always employ a pluralistic view of what is real or actual (see also chapters 4, 5, and 6). The events in the analysis, like all other events, are available only in versions of them, and no one version states a significant fact in all its aspects. No one statement exhausts the so-called fact. Each version given by analyst and analysand is understood to serve certain functions in certain contexts, and thus gives rise to certain consequences rather than others. There is no nonnarrative set of facts for analysts to present with absolute authority. However, there are, as I mentioned earlier, some versions of events that are so highly conventionalized or consensually validated that analysts routinely use them as criteria of what is "real" or "actual." In principle, relying on convention in this way is not a mistake. Consequently, there are times when analysts rightly speak of what is "actual" or "factual" in connection with indications of unconsciously communicated messages and unconsciously performed reality testing. But, as I said, we should mean "actual" only in quotation marks, that is, within a commonsense or psychoanalytic convention of a binding sort.

With these perspectivist or pluralistic considerations in mind, we may return more judiciously to the immediate topic. It is important to pay the closest attention to what is unconsciously communicated and reality-tested outside the analysis and in the analysis itself. Regarding why the analysand engages in this communicative activity only unconsciously, analysts must assume that if an analysand has invested the cognitive functions being used with conflictual meaning of an erotic or aggressive nature, he or she regards that activity as dangerous. In other words, when the analysand has sexualized or aggressivized these functions, so that to use them in certain ways is to create a psychically real infantile danger situation, the analysand views that activity as fraught with danger. In psychic reality, reality testing may mean, for example, sexual peeping, seeing what is forbidden; and giving voice to the results of reality testing may be mentioning the unmentionable and so may mean rebellious and destructive attacks on parental authority or potency. Of course, the specific content may be the problem far more than the cognitive functions being used.

Also, by engaging in this activity and representing its results only unconsciously, analysands may be setting up analysts: Now analysts are the ones who are smart enough to see the "truth" and brave enough to state it explicitly, and so they continue to deserve being idealized by an analysand; or now analysts assume an analysand's guilt over reality testing by being the ones to state the "facts" and are to be blamed for that; or perhaps analysts will now be expressing some "truth" that corresponds to one side of an analysand's ambivalence, which the analysand can then vehemently refute as an "external" imposition. In these highly defensive contexts, it is always a question of who becomes the narrator as well as what the content of the narration will be. It should therefore be apparent that ignoring these unconsciously designed defensive maneuvers may seriously impede the analysis. Ignoring them may, for example, greatly limit analysis of self-castration and guilt in the transference.

In this connection, we should recall what Kris (1956a) emphasized when he discussed the theory of interpretation and insight. Kris emphasized in a most important way the analysand's preconscious preparation of material and the implicit demand for interpretation that is thereby established. What he did not emphasize, however, was that the implicitness of this preparation and of this demand might itself have to be interpreted as a sign of a defensive move within the transference. The analysand's psychic blindness to what he or she knows may be unconsciously manipulative as well as defensive.

Analysts frequently shift their focus of listening from the psychic reality of the analytic situation to what is "actually" happening in it, and then back again to psychic reality. Without this shifting or oscillating, the analytic work may become unbalanced. Analysts' ideas about what is "actually" happening play a vital role in defining transferences and defensive operations and thus in empathizing. I have been alluding to the need for analysts to oscillate between the genetic and the developmental perspectives in order to do well-balanced analytic work. This need to oscillate is evident, for example, in analysts' optimal handling of analysands' reactions to vacations. On the one hand, the vacation must be taken as an "actual" interruption, and sooner or later the psychic meaning of this event must be explored. Psychically, it may be an abandonment, a rejection, a flight, an exclusion from a tempting primal scene or orgy. On the other hand—that is, when analysts do not lose sight of psychic reality in its fullest sense—the "actuality" of the vacation's entailing separation or interruption will not be taken for granted, for analysts may or may not be absent during that time. In psychic reality analysts may be vividly present. Indeed, it is likely that analysands will continue to feel their analysts' presence during the ostensible separation and may even continue the analytic dialogue. This continued presence and dialogue may be represented as, for example, benevolently protective or savagely persecutory. And for defensive reasons these representations may wax or wane. Even though this sense of continued contact may be repressed, its derivatives will often be recognizable and interpretable by those analysts who can oscillate freely between psychic elaboration of "actual" events and psychically real negations of these events.

The issue is the same with presence as with absence. For example, an analysand may complain about lack of physical contact with the analyst, a lack that is "actually" the case and should be taken up at some point, and yet psychically the analysand may experience being held, contained, stroked, penetrated, or beaten in the absence of any "actual" physical contact. A "good hour" may be experienced as a good feed, a good spanking, or good sex. Insight may be experienced as gaining a penis of one's own or being penetrated by the penis of the analyst; if so, the experiencing of insight may be strenuously resisted or ecstatically asserted.

It is my impression that any imbalance in an analyst's mode of listening is more likely to be based on his or her neglecting the psychic reality of analytic presence and absence and overestimating the actuality of presence and absence, as well as of abstinence, verbal dialogue, or insight. Understandably, then, such imbalance often results in analyses that seem to be stalled, unnecessarily tumultuous, un-understandably passionate, simply tedious, or discouragingly intellectualized.

In conclusion, although it is by no means the only significant aspect of analytic work, analysts' handling of representations of other people shows the extent to which they are conducting the analysis in the oscillating but consistently analytic way I have described. It shows the extent to which analysts believe in the centrality of psychic reality while yet giving their due to developmental influences and unconsciously carried on communication and reality testing.

CHAPTER 14

Resistance: The Wrong Story?

I. "THE RESISTANCE" AND FREUD'S COUNTERTRANSFERENCE

The extent to which we value Freud's creation of psychoanalysis should be measured not by the tributes we pay to his genius—there has been no dearth of those—but by our entering into the very debate over his ideas that he himself frequently initiated within his writings. He did so in order to think through his ideas and then go on either to revise them and build further on them or reject them. The idea with which I am concerned here is "the resistance." I focus particularly on the narrative of resistance that Freud developed in his papers on technique (1910–1915). In that context, I present a recommended version of a modern technical approach to resistance wherein the analysis of countertransference replaces "the resistance" as a central factor in the analytic process.

Long before Freud wrote these papers on technique, as early as the "Studies on Hysteria" (Breuer and Freud, 1895), he had already constructed his essential narrative of defense: defense against psychic pain and defense in the service of an ego protecting its unity; and he had begun to dwell particularly on the ego's defense of repression. Yet, from the beginning of his psychoanalytic writing, he had also emphasized resistance as an independent force. By "resistance" he intended to convey the sense he shared with the patient that both of them were struggling against a negative force. To begin with, he considered it a force that stood in the way of remembering painful or traumatic memories. Freud's letters suggest that he encountered what

219

he took to be the same negative force in his own early efforts at self-analysis.

As time went on, Freud presented this force as the cause of blocking of associations. More than the patient's conscious withholding, he emphasized in this regard the effects of the unconscious operations of repression. Because the resistance seemed to operate mostly unconsciously, much of the therapeutic struggle seemed to be against an invisible, often unfathomable force of great influence. In the main the patient experienced that influence passively; Freud inferred its presence from its limiting effects on the therapeutic process as well as the conscious effort it took to do the work of analysis. It was effortful to "overcome" it: Such was how Freud termed it repeatedly both before and in the papers on technique. He did, however, insist that the patient's passive subjective experience should not be allowed to obscure the insight that the patient was actively, albeit unconsciously, resisting. I believe that Freud's attraction to militaristic metaphors—weapons, slayings, battles, and so forth—was intensified by this sense of the analyst's waging a campaign against a devious, hostile, and relentlessly active force.

In his preanalytic clinical work, Freud had used hypnosis to gain access to disturbing memories. Soon, however, in a great leap forward, he realized that hypnosis merely bypassed the resistance and so ignored an essential player in the neurosis. He concluded that it was now essential to overcome the resistance rather than try to evade it. To this end, he began to rely on a combination of reassurance, didactic explanation of psychoanalytic principles and findings, exhortation, and physical pressure. His interest grew in the signs of resistance and, as time went on, in specific motives somehow connected to it; however, neither at first nor subsequently did he ever question the need to assume the presence in the therapy of that basic oppositional force. Nor did he abandon his technical emphasis on psychological pressure, reassurance, explanation, and other inducements to give up resistances against remembering; only physical pressure was abandoned. In the end, he accorded resistance equal place with transference when he stated that the analysis of both features defines psychoanalysis as a distinct method of therapy and investigation. Mainstream Freudian analysts have held to this account up to the present; over the years, much valuable experience has been facilitated and organized in its terms.

Notwithstanding Freud's productive start and latter-day developments, it is my purpose here to question the taken-for-granted need for the idea of resistance and the use that is made of it. I argue that the idea of resistance is diffuse and superfluous, too focused on relatively manifest content, and too dependent on theoretical propositions about the therapeutic process that no longer dominate sound Freudian analytic practice. Consequently, I consider the idea of resistance to be technically confusing. My second chief purpose is to suggest that, to a significant extent though not entirely, Freud's emphasis on resistance indicates that he had drifted into a generalized adversarial countertransference.

These two purposes are rather large to be served even in an extended chapter. Ideally, they should have the support of many citations of Freud's formulations. Nevertheless, I believe that I can make a case for my two claims without that support, even if only in broad outline.

UNINTEGRATED ASPECTS OF FREUD'S APPROACH

The first thing to emphasize in my critique is that, upon close reading of Freud's papers on technique, we can discern some retention of his preanalytic and early analytic technical attitudes and methods. In addition to his frequent references to "overcoming" the resistance, he writes of "clearing away" preliminary resistances as if they are difficult underbrush slowing down an expedition. Similarly, he recommends that the best response to expressions of distrust is to urge the patient simply to put that feeling aside and comply with the fundamental rule of free association and, further, to explain to the patient that distrust is merely a symptom, as trust is unnecessary to the analysis. Thus, he assumes that the patient can and should work analytically *in spite of* the resistance. In the same spirit, we find Freud writing of "working through" the resistance; here he means not the analytically sophisticated idea of working through, but rather merely the analysand's continuing to work *in spite of* both the feeling and the indirect evidence of noteworthy reluctance to do so. That is, I believe that he simply means "Do it anyway!" and not "How are we to understand your reluctance?"

To be complete, however, I should note that on the very same page where Freud mentions "working through" in this pressuring sense, he does begin to speak of "the working through of the resistances" (1914a, p. 155). We may take this small but significant revision of wording to be the beginning of his transition to the modern understanding of the idea. Nevertheless, I will venture to say that in these technical papers he had not yet arrived securely at that modern understanding. And I believe he never did. His attitude continued to favor pressing on *against* resistance and *in spite of it;* thereby he retained unanalytic impurities in his new analytic method.

Technically, this mixed analytic and preanalytic aspect of Freud's narrative is not just confusing, but superfluous. As I said, Freud already had in place his basic narrative of defense and a well-developed clinical idea of repression. His works on dreams, parapraxes, and jokes, written prior to these technical papers, show this to be so; even his earlier case reports show it. He could have made do quite adequately with the following schema: In the therapy, analyst and analysand are obliged to identify, analyze, and work through the repressive defense maintained by the analysand's ego. Freud could have taken this step even though he had not yet developed the later, far more sophisticated and balanced position implied by his 1923 (1923a) and 1926 theory of the ego with its motives and mechanisms of defense. But he was, I infer, too much in the grip of his own conscious subjective experience in doing clinical analysis: He felt that his way was being blocked by a powerful counterforce.

What can be surmised about this subjective experience? We may infer from his narrative that Freud saw his patients as failing to collaborate adequately in the treatment process. Specifically, they did not consistently associate freely in the manner he required of them, and their remembering remained spotty at best. As we know, Freud was banking very heavily on the method of free association to gain access to the pathogenic memories that he viewed as the analytically crucial content of the repressed. He believed that he could not reach his goal without breaking through the barrier represented by the infantile amnesia. He reasoned that the more he could do away with that amnesia, the more convincingly could he show his patients the disturbing memories organized around the conflictual infantile sexuality that unconsciously was dominating their current lives. The crucial insights concerned conflictual sexuality that was dominating their lives to the extent of necessitating the formation of their symptoms and symptom-like character traits. Freud believed that not only would those insights into their own histories, mental makeups, and current difficulties have a curative influence, they would also lead analysands deeper into their minds and thereby lead him to buried treasures of evidence to support and extend his theories of psychosexual development, neurosis, dreams, and the organization of the psychic apparatus. More than developing insights for his patients, he wanted to impress those insights on the world: the world he experienced as persecutory, keeping him under constant hostile surveillance. Here there was a basis for the significant generalized countertransference that I mentioned earlier.

I believe there is a discrepancy between Freud's ostensible thera-peutic aims and his attitude toward his manifestly and implicitly unco-operative patients. In his papers on technique, his attitude toward his patients is not altogether impartial. Heavily invested in his own goals, he is defining clinical phenomena too much from his point of view. He writes as if he does not fully grasp or value his theory of repression in the service of the ego.

FREUD'S CONCEPTION OF ANALYZING THE RESISTANCE

But how, then, might we reconcile this reading with Freud's also going on to emphasize in these same papers the idea of "analyzing the resistance"? With this emphasis, he seems to be transcending the rela-tive one-sidedness I have just proposed. To address this question, we must picture for a moment additional aspects of Freud's situation. It can be said with some justification that, in a way, the early teens of the century, when he wrote these technical papers, were also Freud's early teens as a clinical analyst. Relatively speaking, and notwithstanding the abundant clinical wisdom spread through these pages, it is still the peak time of Freud the Conquistador bravely invading a rich new world and tolerating opposition poorly. In this youthful role, he is not yet ready to be all that impartial; what he is ready to do is to attribute his own difficulties of understanding as well as the unevenness of his results to resistance being put up by the patient. In this respect, Freud's posture is not so different from one that today's analysts some-times adopt, even when they are no longer analytic teenagers and have so much more intellectual sophistication about resistance. Analysts must still count on being constantly tempted to infer resis-tance when they do not yet understand what is being expressed or how to respond and when they are feeling disappointed in their results and frustrated by their patients.

Returning now to Freud's conclusion that it would be important to develop the idea of "analyzing the resistance," it must be acknowl-edged, first, that on the face of it, his emphasis on this technical prin-ciple sounds thoroughly and systematically analytic. I suggest, however, that it suffers from two major limitations. First of all, it seems to me that far too often what Freud means by this technical precept is limited to showing the analysands *that* they are resisting; for example, showing them that their passionate demands for the analyst's love serve the same purpose of blocking the uncovering of the repressed as their simply withholding associations or "failing" to associate or casually pooh-poohing interpretations. All such events and postures serve the resistance. Just this much *is* insight of a sort, provided that it can even be gotten across to the analysand convincingly. Even then, common experience has shown that it is insight that is very limited in scope, usually without great influence, and unstable in that it rests on a still-unanalyzed base of transference and unconscious defensive measures. Often it turns out that in that very insight there is much superficial acquiescence to the authority of the analyst as a transference figure. Freud was familiar with the phenomenon of veiled submission to his analytic authority; nevertheless, that submission seems to have had its appeal to him in his role as Conquistador. He referred to it favorably as "compliance" with his method.

The second limitation on Freud's conception of analyzing the resistance may be found in the inconsistent way that he deals with the dynamics of resistance. For one thing, he refers to those dynamics variously as the motives of resistance, the motives that stimulate the resistance into action or reinforce it, and the motives that the resistance puts to use for its own purposes. He also asserts that, like all other unconscious motives or wishes, the unconscious motives implicated in resistance have their own reasons to resist their becoming conscious; here he is referring to what he had postulated in earlier writings as the pull of the repressed, the so-called pull from below. Thus in this respect he is introducing yet another force—not a defensive one—into a narrative of resistance organized around repression. Additionally, he indicates awareness of the motives of secondary gain, in which connection he is bringing in an ego-based aspect of pleasure-seeking and thereby further compounding his ideas of repressive resistance. In support of Freud's variety of formulations, we could call on the idea of overdetermination or a view of resistance as a compromise formation, but I do not believe that Freud's writings support this rationalization of his conceptual diffuseness. "The resistance" retains its status as an elemental force and featured player throughout his writings.

More important than this diffuseness, however, is Freud's conceptual poaching on the territory of transference—which he did even before the technical papers. For example, in his study of Little Hans, he wrote that once he had enlightened Hans about his hostile and jealous feelings toward his father, he had cleared away Hans's most powerful resistance. Not his transference: his resistance! The background of this formulation is this: Among the motives implicated in men's resistance are, as Freud put it, fear and defiance of paternal authority and disbelief in it. Here transference and resistance lose their separate identities.

Then, in the course of writing these technical papers, Freud goes on to deepen his grasp of the erotic transference and the negative transference, and he begins to conceive of them largely as intensifying resistance: They are, he says, "accessory motives" that patients use to rationalize resistance. As such they protect patients by serving as warnings against the dangers of excess in emotion and its expression. In other places, Freud similarly suggests that these transferences are largely the work of the resistance; for example, they constitute destructive assaults on the analytic compact itself.

I believe that Freud had a sense of these new conceptual difficulties because he began to use that implicitly hyphenated concept "transference resistance." In my view, however, transference resistance is one of those bridge terms that, while perhaps useful as a very casual technical shorthand, cannot be explanatory in that it merely gives an awkward name to the conceptual problem and does nothing to solve it. Already then, I think, Freud could have subsumed all these phenomena, including even some core aspects of the erotic transference, under the negative transference—as analysts are likely to do today. He could also have included the technical challenge encountered and the effort required in dealing with these transferences among numerous other understandable issues in analytic work. This precisely is what he did when he took up transference and acting out: He continued to elucidate them brilliantly as he forged ahead. Not so for the resistance and the transference resistance, and the result was notable narrative unevenness in the quality of his technical papers.

FREUD'S NEGATIVE COUNTERTRANSFERENCE

I have been trying to show that in Freud's pioneering texts on the analysis of the dynamics of resistance, he introduced unclarity along with clarity. While the problem was not so important during the creative spells of genius, it is important for those of us who now constantly look at our patients through the eyes of this genius. I have just described the unclarity. On the side of clarity, I would say that, when taken together, these loosely organized motives and relationships have helped analysts recognize a set of interpretive possibilities by means of which they have often been able to reduce the so-called force of resistance and thus, in Freud's terms, help "overcome" it. The narrative is serviceable even if fundamentally flawed.

It is, however, not enough just to recognize this unevenness of quality. We must, I believe, go on to ask the following questions: Why did

Freud need to present resistance as an *independent* powerful force? Why was he so ready to take the common subjective experience of analyst and patient that analytic work is effortful as a crucial datum in and of itself? What can account for his failing to bring to bear his own understanding of the limited significance of manifest content, for, relatively speaking, the effortfulness in question lies in or close to the realm of manifest content: conscious or preconscious subjective experience that both indicates and obscures unconscious conflict?

We can say Freud was overresponsive to manifest content even after we take into account his recognition that the resistance also operates unconsciously and therefore requires its own interpretation before it can be, as he said, uncovered; there is, he said, resistance to the uncovering of resistances. Our attribution is warranted because frequently he describes resistance as phenomenon, not as theory or inference; for him, it is repression that is theory. It is also warranted because, in his view, resistance merely covers over the content he deems most important, that is, the repressed infantile sexuality. Functionally and descriptively, therefore, Freud's evidence of the resistance can be located as falling within or close to the realm of manifest content.

There is no denying that it takes effort to be alert to the myriad forms of transference and defensiveness, to think through ways and times to take them up, and, at the same time, to keep a firm grip on one's countertransference tendencies. Freud knew this, and, in broad outline, he taught us that this is so. Why then was he not ready to take this step: to subsume all these dynamic factors under the conflictual positive and negative transferences and the defensive operations of the ego. It was ground he had already prepared. Had he taken that step, he would have concluded that it is the analysis of both transference and the defensive ego that distinguishes psychoanalysis from other therapies. He would have seen the inadequacy and analytic inappropriateness of emphasizing so strongly uncovering "resistances" and exhorting the patient to fight them.

We come now to my proposed answer to my question about why Freud needed and remained stuck on the concept "the resistance" and his ideas about handling it: From the beginning of his creative labors, Freud remained under the influence of some negative countertransference. I suggest that because Freud felt he was in some sort of argument, he believed he had to introduce an adversarial orientation into his clinical and theoretical narratives. This proposed answer is consistent with the work of those authors who already have examined Freud's difficulties in his work with Dora: Finally alert to her adversarial transference resistance, as he would have called it later on, he still gave no evidence that he recognized the role of his complex countertransference in his conduct of the treatment and its outcome.

A MODERN ANALYTIC APPROACH TO RESISTANCE

To bring home my points about the limitations of Freud's attempts to work out what it means to analyze resistance and how countertransference may have entered into these attempts, I present next a brief, generalized sketch of what I consider a more adequate and less countertransferential modern analytic approach to the phenomena in question. In so doing, I also take a closer look at the way in which the diffuse, blurred, and superfluous aspects of Freud's narrative of resistance may facilitate and help rationalize countertransference in analytic work.

I believe that, in the most appropriate analytic approach, we as analysts hardly give any weight to the idea of resistance. Instead, we think in the general terms of transference and defensive operations. Specifically, we think in terms of enactments within the analytic relationship that are about the analytic relationship itself. These enactments can be taken as unconsciously devised communications; they communicate the fantasies that dominate the analysand's experience, unconscious as well as conscious, of the conduct of both parties to the analytic relationship. That experience and that conduct may concern every variety of self and object representation: loving, hating, suspicious, omnipotent, depressed, merged, lonely, sexually excited or frigid or impotent, sadistic, masochistic, and on and on. Analysts approach them as concrete manifestations of unconsciously elaborated transference fantasies.

On this view, we would take the withholding of associations that Freud emphasized so much not as a sign of resistance, as opposition that the analysand must acknowledge and overcome, but, for example, as an implied provocative move in the transference, perhaps a seductive move that enacts a sadomasochistic transference fantasy, or perhaps as an oblique reference to keeping a guilty secret in a transference enactment of guilty secrets from childhood. Analysts might adopt similar interpretive orientations to the analysand's attempt to be disarming by good behavior, or attempting to create distance by making direct attacks on the analyst's empathy, or trying to establish omnipotence by turning the tools of analysis against it or by doing "analysis" without help from the analyst.

Analysts view these and other such phenomena as communications that the patient must make repetitively and in many different guises. Analysts are always weighing the question of whether such enactments as being good, withholding, amorous, superficial, or in control of the analysis are now playing major parts in the analysand's life that it would be well to explore. Thus, far from its being dealt with as if it were an alternative to analysis, each line of action will be approached as a telling and a showing that might pertain, for example, to symbolic gaseousness or constipation, using a posture of innocence to disguise a guilty conscience, initiating a seduction, throwing out a hint that one possesses a stolen or a hidden penis, flaunting a flashy manic denial of one's own destructiveness, or parading cleanliness as a form of analytic godliness.

In every case, the clinical question about "the resistance" remains: How are we to understand the manifest or implied reluctance? The goal of understanding is a fixed constituent of the modern analytic attitude. As always, analysts continue to search for what is unconsciously conflictual, that is, for what has mixed defensive, gratifying, and self-punitive elements. And as always, there is no guarantee that analytic answers will be found to this question or that the analytic relationship will ever again change. But that uncertainty, too, and even that occasional total stasis will be made part of the subject matter of the analysis; instead of being seen as obstacles to be removed, they will be occasions for inquiry. In this respect, we do today as Freud did when, not long after he wrote his papers on technique, he reflected on the negative therapeutic reaction: Clinically, he saw that reaction as further analytic material bearing on the transference, he understood it as an expression of unconscious guilt, and he went on to install it in the foundation of his structural theory—that narrative in which the superego figures so majestically. Even then, however, he maintained his fixation on the idea of resistance, for, a few years later, he went on to name a new kind of resistance: superego resistance.

I do not present this formulation of a modern approach to analyzing resistance as original or singular. Although it appears in different analytic contexts, is expressed in significantly different languages, and is referred to with noteworthy variations in explanations and emphasis, this approach may be discerned in modern Kleinian object relations theory, Kohutian self psychology, and Freudian character analysis. It is also found in certain post-ego-psychological conceptual revisions such as I have been presenting in connection with what I have called the affirmative analytic attitude, action language, and a narrational and dialogic view of analysis (1976, 1978, 1981, 1983).

Fundamentally, each of these developments rejects the idea of an independent adversarial force that accompanies the analysis "step by step," as Freud said; and they all do so without denying that aggression, along with desire, self-protectiveness, and self-punitiveness, not only pervades every analysis but is its life-blood and is therefore one of its principal subject matters. And not one of these theories relies on the militaristic metaphors and storylines that Freud favored when describing the analytic relationship.

NEGATIVE COUNTERTRANSFERENCE: HELP AND HINDRANCE

In these alternative and affirmative approaches, when analysts begin to feel that they are engaged in an argument or a power struggle, they are prepared to realize that they have begun to shift out of the analytic attitude. Often they may understand that shift as a sign that they have been successfully manipulated into a countertransference that fits into the patient's transference fantasy. At that point they realize that some self-analysis of countertransference is required, not only to restabilize the analytic attitude but also to illuminate the analysand's current emotional status and aims. Under ordinary working conditions—that is, when analysts are not suffering severe countertransference for neurotic reasons—they will understand that the analysand is unconsciously enacting conflict or distress in the here and now of the analysis. The patient is involving the analyst in that conflict by stirring up adversarial attitudes and perhaps even a limited and discouraging view of the patient as uncooperative and in need of prodding and various blandishments to "get on with it."

By working in this way, contemporary analysts show that they value early stages of countertransference, seeing them as essential elements in the network of communication that evolves during every ongoing analysis. They do not automatically adopt the traditional but mistaken adversarial stance toward signs of countertransference; instead, they do as they do with signs of the so-called resistance: They take an analytic interest in them. Consequently, as well as asking the question How can I understand the patient's reluctance? today's analysts are likely to go on to question their own feeling that, at some moment, a struggle against resistance is taking place or that any kind of interpersonal struggle exists. By questioning themselves, analysts show their awareness that they may be beginning to play an assigned role in their patients' fantasies.

Carrying that inquiry further, they will search for ways in which they may be contributing to the stimulation of the patients' enactments by their own mode of construing and responding to the messages being conveyed from the couch. Many of these messages are sent in the form of enactments rather than words, and they are responded to in kind—by analysts' shifts in attention or morale, by flux in tone of voice and tempo of response, by one-sided interpretation, and so on. As we know, and as Gill (1982) among others has been insisting, that aspect of the analytic dialogue is all too easy to miss or misconstrue. I would, however, add a note of caution here: Often that here-and-now aspect of transference-countertransference interaction is fraught with ambiguity when it is noted, so that it is easier to raise questions about it than to answer them decisively and promptly. Still, analysts may clarify current problems in the analysis merely by raising such questions to themselves or on occasion with the analysand. I believe that analysts' ever-increasing alertness to and curiosity about early and implied signs of countertransference are becoming most important parts of the analytic dialogue. And so we may draw another important conclusion: *In place of the analysis of resistance, we may install the analysis of countertransference alongside the analysis of transference and defensive operations as one of the three emphases that define a therapy as psychoanalytic.* In this respect, analytic terminology has lagged behind practice.

DISCUSSION

When listening to an analysand, analysts are constantly ready to raise questions, as well as in time to suggest some answers, concerning what the analysand means by depression, anxiety, love, hate, abuse, guilt, desire, frustration, gratification, dependency, frankness, lateness, cleanliness, pride, truthfulness, and so forth. In this chapter I have been extending this methodological principle to the language of Freud's narrative of the analytic process, specifically to his use of "the resistance" and of other words, many of them militaristic, that he used in relation to that term. Reading Freud as I would listen to a patient— legitimately, I think—I have concluded that this language indicates a significant involvement of generalized negative countertransference on Freud's part.

It is not my intention to treat the word *resistance* as the culprit in analysis and to propose that it be eliminated. I recognize the usefulness of "resistance" for descriptive purposes, and I recognize, too, that the word is so well established in the clinical lexicon that it is not likely to be deleted. My claim here is different; it is that "resistance" is a perilous word to use emphatically and in an explanatory fashion, as when it is said that what distinguishes psychoanalysis from other therapies is its analysis of the resistance as well as the transference, and when it is said that resistance is the dynamic cause of a clinical phenomenon. This emphatic use distracts our attention from intrapsychic conflict and compromise involving defensive and self-punitive operations; it also distracts us from the analysis of countertransferences. Moreover, judging by how "resistance" is used, it seems destined to take on a strong interpersonal as well as a strong negative connotation. Neither fits a depth-analytic approach and both help rationalize negative countertransference positions that reduce empathic concentration on the patient's compromised strivings toward both psychic equilibrium and psychic change.

We might attempt to account for Freud's conceptual difficulties with "the resistance" by noting that he was in the throes of creative activity. Yet this suggestion establishes a questionable split between the throes of creativity and transference. It seems to me more consistently analytic to affirm that, in the heightened and fluid emotional states characteristic of creative work, it is *more* likely, not less likely, that strong transferential processes will be stimulated. I believe that when Freud advised against doing research on current treatment cases, he was doing so for the same reason, though it would be disruptive countertransference and not transference that would be the danger then. And when Ernst Kris (1952) discussed creative work from an ego-psychological point of view, he emphasized the regressive (and therefore inevitably heightened transferential) aspects of its inspirational phases. I would add that splitting Freud's creativity and countertransferences can only foster those submissive, idealizing attitudes toward Freud that have always interfered with the development of psychoanalysis.

My accepting the broad use of the idea of countertransference might be questioned. It might be claimed that as my usage fails to recognize the importance ego psychology accords to external reality, reality testing, adaptation, and ego autonomy, it signals a retreat to pre-ego-psychological reductive thinking. To this challenge I would reply that these ego-psychological factors have always been assumed and established within the framework of the analytic enterprise; clearly, they were assumed by Freud, Abraham, and others in their pre-ego-psychological days (see also Section II, below). These factors come into question only when they prove to be so pervaded by conflict and compromise formation that their reduction or impairment may be taken as equivalent to enactments that require interpretation (for example, lack of comprehension as a refusal to be fed or penetrated).

Consider, for example, the autonomy of ego functions. It should be remembered, first of all, that autonomy is *relative* autonomy; that is, it is never closed off to neurotic or regressive complications. We analysts regularly encounter, in work with relatively intact neurotics, striking instances of conflict-laden flux of reality testing and adaptation. Consequently, we have learned to be conservative in making unexamined assumptions about conflict-free therapeutic alliances and "unobjectionable positive transferences" (M. Stein, 1981). It is an important part of our analytic attitude to take nothing for granted in this realm as in all others. The issue of autonomy goes beyond the disruptive invasion of ego functions by conflict. Analysts should not split off countertransference from acceptably accurate reality testing or soundly approved moral values; here the assumption of autonomous functioning does not preclude a more complex analysis. "Reality" is known to be a good defense. It is also known that analysts who appear to be equally well adapted may still see the so-called same situation differently though not unrealistically; and it is expected that analytic inquiry could show that some significant elements of countertransference are contributing to these differences. Thus, in the clinical situation, even when it is recognized that the patient has correctly perceived a trait of the analyst's, even a countertransference manifestation, as a rule it is still best to keep the focus on the transference-significance of this piece of good reality testing. The timing, emphasis, mode of expression, and selectivity of whatever the analysand seems to have perceived correctly: All may signal significant transference and unconscious conflict. Truth, transference and countertransference are not mutually exclusive.

Finally, more should be said on the topic of enactment. Earlier in this chapter I indicated that enactment is central to my conception of the so-called analysis of resistance. I want now to add that I see enactment as a concept that can free analysts and, ultimately, analysands from the tyranny of the spoken word, specifically, from the conventional role of the spoken word as merely a conveyor of content and from verbalization as the only means of narration. The analytic dialogue and the analytic storyline are not developed solely by means of the verbal transmission of cognitive and emotional experience accompanied by familiar, semantically clear expressive movements. Under "enactment" we may include communication through the timing and manner of saying things and not saying things both within the analytic session and outside it; the use or nonuse made of interpretations; lateness, absence, symptomatic regressions and flights into health; and so forth. Enactment is a concept related to acting in, though it has the advantage of lacking the pejorative implication that acting in, like acting out, tends to take on—a mistaken implication in both cases but common enough for us to consider in this discussion.

Once freed from the tyranny of the spoken word and consistently thinking in terms of enactment, we can view the analysand as constantly working, not resisting work; further, we remember that the analysand is working in the only way possible, that is, in his or her own way, and we are prepared to recognize that, in part, the analysand is even hoping to be recognized as a co-worker, however ambivalent he or she may be about this collaboration out of fear, hatred, envy, despair, suspicion, or grandiosity. Seeing things this way neither guarantees nor precludes further progress in the analysis, but it is an affirmative way to take into account the details of the analytic process. That affirmative way sustains the analytic attitude against the hazards of disruptive countertransference. It also contributes to the flexible and tactful framing of analytic interpretations, the kind of interpretations that have the best chance of being heard as such by the analysand.

We have come far from Freud's approving reference to "compliance" with the psychoanalyst's instructions and far from his antagonistic narrative of resistance, with its unself-critical militaristic metaphors. In this respect as in many others, analysts have carried forward Freud's work of genius; continuing in the spirit of his labors, they have revised, extended, and enriched his technical as well as theoretical narratives.

II. A CLINICAL CRITIQUE OF THE CONCEPT OF RESISTANCE

Here I extend my critique of the inclusion of resistance (as against defense and countertransference) in any formal definition of analysis, by presenting a series of clinical examples in which apparently resistive phenomena, once they were approached as further contributions to the analysis, yielded up a rich store of memory, affect, and conflict. I present these examples after some further comments on Freud's legacy and his technical discussions as a model for practice.

That Freud greatly valued the concept of "the resistance" he showed almost from the very beginning of his creative labors by being so preoccupied with the many problems of theory and technique he could include within its boundaries. He had already relied heavily on it in the "Studies in Hysteria" (1895), and in his great paper on transference (1912b), some seventeen years later, he spent much time on "the resistance." To understand this emphasis, we must imagine how important it was to him during those years to have developed the idea that, unconsciously, people seem to fight tooth and nail against the treatment and the very recovery for the sake of which they have come to the analyst in the first place. Gradually, Freud came to understand that it was necessary to analyze "the resistance" rather than just fight against it or to try to get around it. As I argued in the first part of this chapter, however, he never clarified and explored fully the idea of analyzing "the resistance," and he never recognized that "the resistance" is an optional concept rather than a necessary one; that is, it is only one way to describe some subtle as well as dramatic, superficially obstructive phenomena in the analytic process.

Freud prepared the ground for a modern understanding of analyzing resistance in his 1926 monograph, "Inhibitions, Symptoms and Anxiety." There he set down the crucial series of infantile danger situations. In psychic reality, these situations are carried forward unconsciously into the present. They require all of us always to rely on defensive activity. In that way, analysands carry into the psychoanalytic situation much of the motivation for "the resistance." After 1926, therefore, to speak of analyzing "the resistance" could only mean to explore the expression in the present of all the wishes and fears of early childhood and the means of coping and mastering that were developed over the years of the patient's life and have continued to be psychically real. On this understanding, we think of trying to use interpretation to reduce the anxiety, guilt, and shame that necessitate defensive activity and culminate in conduct that manifestly seems to be simply oppositional ("the resistance"). The analytic emphasis is on changing psychic conditions, not on removing anything and certainly not on fighting against it.

But if this is so, is it not the same understanding and the same practice that analysts engage in when they undertake the entire task of clinical analysis? Is it not also what they mean, or much of what they mean, when they speak of analyzing transference, or analyzing repetition, acting out, or the compromise formations that express unconscious conflict in general? If, in modern practice, "analyzing the resistance" seems to refer to everything in the analysis, then it loses its linguistic identity; it is different from nothing, so that, on linguistic grounds alone, the term can no longer be considered useful. Certainly, by the standards of ordinary common sense, patients do do things that manifestly seem to interfere with what analysts regard as the progress of the analysis. Yet it can now be argued that "the resistance" is no longer the best way to think about that conduct. There seems to be a contradiction between analysts' practices and the technical terms they use. As our next step, therefore, we must go on to ask how it is that "resistance" has continued to be an unquestioned ego-psychological Freudian term in psychoanalytic discourse.

I think there are many reasons for this continuing emphasis. One reason, but not the most important one, is analysts' idealizing submission to the authority of Sigmund Freud's eloquent way of writing. Another reason is that analysts have organized much experience, expertise, teaching, writing, and professional identification around "the resistance," just as they have around other traditional major terms, such as "the transference." A third reason I developed in the first part of this chapter: "the resistance" as the expression of a negative countertransference. Here analysts misunderstand as opposition the fact that analysands seem to be not cooperating in the analysis *in the way that analysts would wish or have expected or are demanding;* analysts wrongly think that analysands are following a course that in conventional terms is merely rebellious, limiting, unnecessarily puzzling, unresponsive, superficial, or irrelevant.

In the context of this third reason, I suggest that the problem may lie with the analysts in many instances, specifically in their not yet understanding what analysands are communicating by acting in this way. Perhaps analysts are witnessing old, unconscious, perseverative attempts at escaping or re-creating infantile danger situations. In that case, a patient, feeling endangered, thinks that this is the only safe way to act at this time. Alternatively, the analysand may be unconsciously enacting old patterns of family relations that are based on real and imagined, physical and emotional experiences with self and others, and the patient may even be trying to remember and communicate these very patterns to the analyst. Or perhaps it is a vicious circle in which an analyst's countertransference leads to one misunderstanding that results in more misunderstandings and finally brings about what seems to be a stalemated power struggle, in which case the analysand is protesting against the analyst's misunderstanding and the analyst's mistaken demands for a certain kind of behavior. These alternatives are not mutually exclusive, and other issues, too numerous to be mentioned, might also be involved in the disturbing and puzzling behavior of the analysand—or is it of the analyst?

CLINICAL EXAMPLES

As I said, if we were to approach the following clinical examples in the traditional manner, we would think of them as illustrating the workings of "the resistance," that force making for interference in the work of analysis. My intention, however, is to use these examples to bring out enough of the complexity and richness of the analysis to throw into serious question the usefulness of the idea of "the resistance." My examples, which are drawn from my own work and from that of some supervisees, vary both in how strong "the resistance" appears to be and in the form it takes. I have avoided extreme examples that would require long case studies to fit usefully into this discussion. Furthermore, as so much therapeutic work deals with less-than-extreme phenomena, it should be more useful to work the middle ground; as a rule, the extremes do not make the technical and conceptual issues clearer.

A Sluggish, Silent Man

Early in the analysis of a young man, there is a session in which the patient's thoughts seem to be unusually wandering. The analyst says nothing in response. The next day there comes a similar session in which his speech and manner are also so sluggish as to give the feeling of slow motion. Finally, after having remained silent for some time, the analyst comments that he does seem to feel sluggish today. He replies that he may be slowing things down. It is then suggested to him that, if so, he might be feeling threatened by something that he is afraid might come to mind unless he is careful. He tells then that, today, in a way that was unusual for him, he had briefly thought of skipping his analytic session, and he goes on to ask if being absent is a way to slow things down. In reply he is told that that is one of many things people do when they are worried about their sessions, so that the question to consider is what it is that he now fears. The analyst does not challenge his show of naïveté. The session ends here.

The next day he slowly brings out his being angry at the analyst. He knows in his head, he says, that the analyst was not criticizing him the day before, but he felt criticized anyway. It felt like his father's criticism: Usually his father would just fly into a rage, but sometimes he would just make one remark and fall silent and at times remain silent for days. The analyst then says that although his own having been silent as well as his remarking on his patient's sluggishness had made him angry, he had not said so at the time. (The technical point here is to focus first on his anxiety about being forthcoming in his sessions.) He says then that he realized he was angry only after the end of the session. To this it is replied that he must have been afraid even to be aware of it during the session, that he had dulled his awareness of himself just as he had dulled himself in response to his father. (That he had learned to dull himself as a boy he had related in earlier sessions.)

Next he tells about the violence of his father's rages and his own frightened reactive policy of make-no-waves, that is, of remaining quiet. The analyst says, "You kept your mouth shut but your resentments piled up with him, as they have with me." This leads him to tell about his having changed at puberty from an A+ student to one who failed his school courses and barely got by. His mind just would not work. The analyst comments then that he was trying to kill his mind in the same way he had just done here. "Yes," he says, "I just couldn't think. I also used to worry about my mother at that time, because he punished her when I disappointed him. And being in school, I was not at home to make peace between them." At this point, it is mentioned that he had told in the past that, at puberty, he had been sent to a certain private day school much against his will and only because his angry father demanded it. He spontaneously continues that thought, saying that there was rebellion in his attitude and that at that time he could see that form of rebelliousness in lots of the boys. "Hoping to flunk out, possibly," it is suggested, and he agrees, but then mentions again how preoccupied he had been with his father's verbal attacks on his mother.

This example could be considered simply as resistance, in fact, a double resistance: first the resistance implied in his wandering and dulled thinking, and subsequently his mental sluggishness based on unexpressed resentment and rebelliousness over what he took to be a critical demand. I remind you here that Freud cited fear and defiance of paternal authority as a dynamic of men's resistance—perhaps even *the* chief dynamic of their resistance—but I would say that much more than that problem with authority emerged in these sessions, and it emerged fairly rapidly. There were the issues of his use of silence and of his attack on his own mind as part of making no waves with the analyst, which was itself part of his transference from the dreaded father, a man who had often fallen into threatening silence. Both of these factors touch on the patient's unconscious identification with his violent father and his associated fear of his own violence. There was unconscious violence in his negative transference. These two factors—silence and mind-destructiveness—also fall under the heading of transference, which we must regard as a valuable contribution to the work of interpretation and reconstruction. Only superficially does it look like interference.

Additionally, the patient referred to what might have been an early school phobia centering on anxiety over his mother's safety while he was away from her. That phobia probably would have been based in part on sadistic primal scene fantasies, and his mentioning it now prepares the way for suitable transference interpretation of primal scene material and perhaps a need to protect the analyst, too.

Taking all of these references and plausible conjectures together, we might say that this analysand's wandering, sluggishness, dullness, and silence spoke volumes about his inner struggle to control his own turbulence and violence. Would any further understanding have been gained by labeling all this the analysis of resistance? I think not. Instead, I believe that using that term would have indicated some impatience and blindness on the analyst's part that could only be explained in terms of disruptive countertransference. And he would have been thickening the analytic plot with superfluous ingredients.

A Woman Tells a Disturbing Sexual Dream

This patient is a middle-aged woman from the academic world. In the session preceding the one I concentrate on, she had reported a two-part dream: In the first part she was in the analytic office naked; in the second, she knew that she had told the analyst something dishonestly but she did not know what it was. She then said she had found it very difficult to tell the dream because it suggested to her that she was having sexual thoughts about the analytic relationship. Her associations had then turned to her having a cold and how, over the preceding weekend, her mother, whom she was visiting, characteristically had made a great fuss about it. She also associated to the fact that she had been feeling more sexual interest in men lately. Because she had brought this up near the close of the preceding session, the analyst had limited himself to saying that her thoughts suggested that she was not clear whether she was feeling more sexual interest in him than she had before or was now wanting some mothering from him; it was also unclear why she would not want to talk about these topics.

The patient enters the next session with a smile. She says she is smiling because she had not been sitting in the waiting room as far from the door to the consulting room as she usually did, and she does not want the analyst to think therefore that she is overjoyed to see him again. Next, she thinks again of the two-part dream she had told the day before. She had thought a lot about it since yesterday's session, but now she does not want to reveal those thoughts because it is really for her analyst and not for her to interpret her dreams. She goes on to report that, although over the weekend she had wanted to get away from her mother's fussing over her, she is not concerned about wanting mothering from the analyst; rather, what she does worry about is that it would trouble him to be put in that position. She then says that in her relationships with men, being taken care of, being held, being close is more important to her than sex, and she thinks that this kind of feeling is true of women in general.

At this point the analyst comments that she is afraid he might take her interest in getting closer as an expression of sexual interest, and he reminds her of an insight that they had worked on in earlier sessions, specifically, that she picked men to get involved with whose character helped her avoid and deny the uncomfortable issue of sex. In response to his comment, she thinks of a female colleague in relation to whom, as in relation to her mother, she herself is supposed to be the sick, weak, needful one and in this way to help her colleague feel strong. This set of rules reassures her colleague that she is not a cold person. The patient goes on to say that her mother had been sickly as a child and had gone through some of the same experiences that she was now forcing on her daughter, the patient. She then wonders if she might be exaggerating her present illness, her cold. The analyst says that if that is the case, it would show her wish to make sure of his interest and concern. With some shame, she responds with the thought that if he had grown up under her circumstances, he would act as she does now. Clearly, she is feeling defensive at this point.

The analyst then offers a broader interpretive comment. He says that it must be a burden as well as a threat to her to appear to be well, as in showing her pleasure on seeing him again or offering interpretations of her own. To this she replies that in fact she is pleased that she is now so much more secure with him that she can feel good about coming in to see him, and she remarks on how different she used to be; nevertheless, she remains concerned that she has to be ill in order for the analyst to be warm and concerned about her. At this point, he adds that she is also afraid that he will misunderstand her showing any good feelings and closeness to be a sexual act. Throughout this exchange over her anxiety about being well and closer, she has been coughing a lot, as if her cold has gotten worse, but she leaves the session looking far more composed than she had when she entered, smiling comfortably but still guarded in manner. The analyst had not commented on her need both to bolster him and to protect him against her feelings, as that factor was not clear to him at the time.

I believe that in these two sessions this analysand was communicating her fear of getting well and being emotionally closer at the same time as she was showing that she was experiencing just those changes taking place in her. She had had to emphasize the negatives, such as shame, dishonesty, illness, and inability. For her, the danger was that the favorable changes would either chill the analytic relationship or overheat it, and they would bring about one or the other result because of the way the analyst would be affected both as a mother-figure and as a man. Thus, she had to disown parts of her self: her enthusiasm, her excitement, her gratitude, her wish to show herself and move closer freely, both emotionally and intellectually. Also, she would be dangerous.

To label her doing all this a manifestation of resistance would, it seems to me, miss the point badly. The analytic way to begin to think about it would be to frame these questions: What was she enacting in the transference that expressed her wishes, her anxiety, the nature of her danger situation, and her defensive strategies? What was her conflict? In one respect, the one taken up, it was the conflict between showing herself in a very alive way and hiding herself in illness, inhibition, and distance. In another respect, she was in conflict over trust. Could she trust the analyst to understand her, to understand not just her wishes but her fears and self-protectiveness as well, so that he would neither fuss over her excessively nor retreat from the possibility of sexual excitement in the new, more open encounter or else respond to it too strongly? Additionally, her manifest conflictedness, signaled by her increased coughing, was itself a bid for his analytic care of her in the role of patient, which is to say, his fussing over her by making interpretations and his having nothing to fear from her.

At the same time I would infer that her bringing this rich material is also a sign of her continuing to get well: better able to hear analytic interpretations primarily as such rather than in the terms of the restrictive maternal transference, though now also as worrisome indications of the analyst's being analytically/sexually aroused in response to her progress toward experiencing herself as a whole woman. In other words, I infer that, for her, moving forward has both sublimated and directly heterosexual implications, while moving backward or staying in the same place has implications of invalidism and oral subjugation mixed with omnipotent control. In this session, she has been enacting an unconscious conflict over which direction to move in and on which developmental level.

Therefore, it could not have been correct or helpful to think that she was resisting by forgetting part of her dream, by alluding to dishonesty, by withholding her own interpretations, and by clinging to the role of the damaged, anxious, and presexual patient. It was more to the point to think that she was both telling and showing where she was psychically at that moment in the analysis; in that way, she was contributing to the further progress of the work.

Delaying Acting on Insights

The patient is a young nursery school teacher, the divorced mother of several children. In recent weeks, one of the themes that was being followed was her avoidance of coming to her session in the short skirts and tank tops she might otherwise wear in hot and "sweaty" weather. Analytically, this avoidance had been related to her fear of sexual encounters with men. She has also been endlessly not acting on her wish to seek out situations in which she might meet suitable men. In the preceding session the analyst had remarked on her holding back from acting on the many insightful discussions they had had of all these problems, and he had proposed that they should give that delay of action some thought.

In the current session she soon brings up the idea that it is not helpful to patients to push them into actions they are not ready to take. The analyst replies that it seems she had understood his comment and question as a demand for action and that she now feels she is in a fight. She says that that is her feeling even though she understands rationally that he had not been making a demand for action. Then she remarks that she had noticed herself smiling when she thought that she was delaying taking action. Thinking about her smile now, she thinks of the derisive smile of a woman she met recently, and she says, "I don't like that thought; it's not quite it; I think now of play in connection with that smile."

At this point, inferring that open fighting is stating the theme of the moment in too strong terms, the analyst takes her cue and suggests that, by not making active use of the analytic work, she may be expressing her resentment through teasing him or keeping him dangling. She then mentions—or confesses—that she had bought an attractive, sexy dress during a recent shopping trip and was proud of it. He notes aloud that, in an earlier account, she had not mentioned the sexy dress. She then tells him once again that she becomes tense and anxious whenever a man becomes physically or emotionally demonstrative. He wonders aloud if she had been afraid that she might follow through sexually were she to make herself attractive and act flirtatiously. She agrees with that surmise and then notes an image that has come into her mind of her youthful, vain, attractive, competitive mother, and she goes on to think of how much her mother has always boasted of her own many conquests of men.

After critiquing her mother's vanity, she returns to her fear of sex.

She wonders why she is afraid, because, as she thinks about it now, it seems as if it would be soft and warm. She thinks that she has had a similar feeling whenever she reads anything in the popular press touching on psychology. She reminds herself then of an earlier discussion of her fearing to "take in" that reading and enjoy it because it felt too close and too sexual. She thinks next of sexual intercourse and how after its completion the man would withdraw and leave her feeling "empty." The analyst suggests that she fears she cannot keep that pleasurable experience alive, that somehow she will kill it and end up feeling empty. And would that not, he goes on to wonder, imply that she would feel guilty about the pleasure and gratification? That kind of guilt had, in fact, come up repeatedly during the analysis; typically, whatever first felt good within her somehow soon turned bad and became a reason to reproach herself. At this point, she spontaneously remembers that interpretive work, and she says she can see that she could or would do something bad to her good experience of sex. She concluded the session speaking of her negative perceptions of her sexual anatomy.

In this example, rather than taking as resistance her delays of action and her criticism of the analyst's calling attention to it, he took it as an opening to begin to explore, first, her aggression toward him, then her attacks on her own pleasures in sex as well as elsewhere, and then the guilt feelings that both stimulated these attacks and were increased by them. In the process there emerged new hints of her identification with her much-feared and vain mother and its entry into the analytic relationship in the form of subtly and derisively controlling the analyst. He did not take up this theme of identification now and in this context, even though it had already been touched on in other contexts, as it did not seem to be the appropriate time to do so. Nor did he refer directly to the many transference implications, having found it helpful to proceed a bit slowly with this woman. Overall, however, they were jointly busy clarifying how she was enacting significant parts of her basic transference. They were treating her associations as significant contributions to the analysis rather than as interferences with it. Far from being antagonists, they were collaborators.

Reluctance to Come to Sessions and Free-Associate

My last and longest example centers on the early phase of the analysis of a woman who, after having worked at relatively low-level clerical jobs, had obtained advanced business training and had been working her way up in a high-powered headhunter organization. Recently she had been assigned to a new and lucrative post there. A red-haired woman whose very good looks attracted men to her, the patient was already forty years old and recently separated from her husband. She began treatment feeling depressed over the breakup of her marriage to Ted.

By her account, she was the daughter of a hypercritical mother and a weak, unresponsive father. She seemed to have incorporated and elaborated a severe internal critic, in large part to master her mother's attacks on her. Her characteristically low self-esteem had fallen even lower subsequent to the breakup of her marriage. During her early oedipal years, she had been approached sexually on several occasions by an uncle. She remembered from those occasions her pleasure in his attentions, her fear, and her keeping it all secret.

My partial account of two consecutive analytic sessions would, I think, fit easily into any traditional writing or teaching about resistance in analysis. In these sessions, there were taken up or at least mentioned or mentioned again the following themes: difficulty in free associating, defensively making order, feeling emotionally frozen or dead, and playing a role in order to cover up her true self.

The analysand begins by saying that once again she felt reluctant to come. She does not know why, particularly because, as she thinks about it, the treatment has been helpful to her so far. Gradually she begins to indicate that she felt criticized. The analyst asks, "How come?" and she explains, "Because I am angry at myself because I'm still in the same place about Ted." He asks how she connects this to him. She answers that, in the previous session, he had said that she continued to use her preoccupation with Ted to ward off other thoughts and feelings. She was referring to his having said that he thought she felt very uneasy without a specific topic to focus on, as if threatened by the prospect simply of saying whatever came to mind, regardless of what it might be, and so had been dwelling somewhat repetitively on Ted, and he thought it important to understand what she feared. Now he says that having taken that comment as a criticism, her feelings had been hurt, but that both then and now, instead of being openly angry at him, she had on her own mentioned only her anger at herself. She sees that this is so and then recalls a three-part dream of the night before.

First, there was something about a freezer in the basement that had a door that would not close. Second, some children were climbing up the side of a house in which she had lived as a child; they were pulling up the blind on the window of the room her sexually abusive uncle had occupied when he lived with them. She was watching all of this from a house across the street. There was a woman lying on the bed in this now-exposed room; she looked like one of her sisters-in-law. The analysand hastened to emphasize that this woman was dressed, as if to make it clear that the dream was not about sexual peeping or exposure; the boys, she said, were just being naughty. The third part of the dream showed a row of cars double-parked; she and someone else were picking up the cars and putting them in a row inside the parking line.

The analyst asks for associations to this third dream segment. She says that in the dream she felt pleasure in making things orderly and then has nothing more to say. He then mentions pulling up the blind, and she adds that in the dream she thought her mother had come and straightened things out with the boys, and again trails off into silence. He mentions next the freezer with the door that would not close. First, she thinks that the things in the freezer would thaw out. Then she associates to how she has always used food to fill up her loneliness. She explains that her development has been filled with loneliness. Sometimes, however, when she was alone, she used to play with plastic puppets and would get very involved and very creative and her bad feelings would go away. As she talks about her chronically lonely feelings, tears run down her cheeks—a not unusual occurrence—and she takes some tissues from the box of large-size Kleenex beside the couch and wipes her eyes. She says that the thoughts and feelings that come up are disturbing to her.

The analyst then interprets that he thinks her reluctance to come to her sessions is connected to her having recently reported that she was experiencing some freeing up of her feelings. He comments that, on the one hand, that freedom seems to have an upside in reducing her loneliness and letting her feel closer to her creativity, but that, on the other hand, there is the downside of its being painful for her and making her afraid of her associations because of what they might lead to if she continues thawing out. Then, for the first time in the analysis, she acknowledges, "There is something frozen in me, even dead." In earlier sessions, she had only emphasized her need to feel loved, implying that she was full of warm feelings but had no one to share them with. The analyst ends the session at this point, and she leaves with a winning smile and, unusual for her, with a comment on the way to the door: She says, "I like your big Kleenexes."

The following session included further work on the dream. After first thinking she was going too fast at work and in her social life, and then mentioning her having deferred asking her mother questions about her childhood, as she had volunteered to do in an earlier session, she complains that her thoughts are all in a jumble and expresses her need for order. At this point the analyst says that what she has been bringing out also applies to problems she has been having associating during the sessions. Specifically, she feels a need to line up her associations in a row, as she can once she has a topic to talk about. The problem for her is to go freely with her associations, which seem so jumbled to her; they are a problem even though she understands, from what has been seen before, that the jumbled ones can be at least as useful as those involved in developing a topic.

Soon she is dwelling on needless worries and self-consciousness about her physical attractiveness, from the time she was an adolescent up to the present—needless because she is much admired and envied. The analyst comments on the implication that she is self-conscious about her being exposed and observed on the couch (the blinds being up in the dream), but that she does feel dead or frozen even as she reassures herself that she is attractive, and he suggests that there is a link between being "jumbled" and being sexually aroused. To this she responds, "No . . . well . . . yes, that's true, but I have found ways to excite myself in sex by having fantasies that I'm somebody else. I've done that for some years. I know that if I were thinking about myself, I would be unloved and rejected." She then says that her fantasies concern a woman being raped, degraded, and put on exhibition. She protests that she has been looking only for recognition and love, but the men in her life always put pressure on her to be sexually active: "They didn't force me exactly, but they manipulated me to engage in acts that required me to open myself up and be exposed and with nothing being returned. It was ultimate degradation."

It is time now to end the session, and the analyst chooses to comment on her anxiety, saying that all of this must color her experience of the way the analysis is set up; it could be contributing to her reluctance to come and to her not knowing what to talk about. It feels safer and terribly important just to talk *about* things and not to leave herself free to bring up these painful thoughts, feelings, and memories, and all the concerns that right now could refer to her and him.

In these two sessions, I would say, they were continuing the analysand's induction into analysis by clarifying her initial difficulties in coping with the analytic situation. She was experiencing the analysis in terms of her infantile and later childhood danger situations, including sexual pressures inflicted on her, as well as a persecutory mother, and that she was dealing with the analysis in the characteristic ways she had developed in earlier years. These ways included the incorporation of a hypercritical, degrading, controlling maternal figure, which now, through projective identification, she was beginning to locate in the analyst. Consequently, when he tried to help her reflect on her difficulties in the sessions, she could only hear him criticizing her for being a resistant patient, and she reacted with depression as a defensive cover for anger and with avoidance—her reluctance to come to the sessions. In effect, then, it was she who was introducing the idea of resistance, not he. Resistance was her way to understand her transference and her projective rendering of the analyst as a persecutory, withholding, and certainly unempathic figure.

Why did he not point out that, as her analyst, he was the voyeuristic, seductive, sexual abuser whom, on the one hand, she feared, resented, and desired to attract or be popular with by exposing herself and, on the other hand, wanted to keep composed and in line? Because they were in a very early stage of the work and she felt she was rushing and also under pressure; because she was very anxious and might easily hear him as making a sexual approach and be unprepared to cope with that; because at this point there was no way he could discriminate sexual "acting" from genuinely sexual content; because of the sadomasochistic and narcissistic loading of her sexual allusions; because it was the very end of the session, a time when he believed it best not to send the patient packing, as it were, after delivering disturbing interpretations; and because he had not yet put together consciously all the connections and implications that I am noting here. Consequently, he contented himself with pointing her toward the here and now in his concluding comment: It could refer to her and him. I regard this decision as contestable; it might have added to her difficulties. But I am presenting this example not to illustrate fine technique; rather, I am trying to show how much complex allusion to, and enactment of, here-and-now transference and defense there can be in attitudes and behavior that, traditionally, could be subsumed under "the resistance."

CONCLUDING COMMENT: WHOSE IDEA IS "RESISTANCE"?

In closing, I should like to supplement what I said earlier about the way in which "the resistance" has remained an unquestioned entry in our psychoanalytic lexicon. In addition to tradition and other such factors, and in addition also to its usefulness as a sign of negative countertransference based on lack of understanding, emphasis on "the resistance" may indicate that the analyst is being controlled by introjection of the patient's transference. Specifically, that emphasis may show that, through projective identification, the guilty patient is portraying the analyst as an unempathic, critical, ungrateful figure whose interventions are simply accusations of badness and noncompliance; in other words, the patient is saying or implying that it is the analyst who is accusing the patient of resisting. In this way, the analyst is to bear the burden of the patient's own self-criticisms and guilt feelings. In such situations the analysand's unconscious guilty transference might stimulate in the analyst some complementary hostile countertransference. In an effort at mastery, the analyst then might develop the conviction that there really is an essence "out there" and "in" the analysand, an essence that deserves to be called "the resistance" and requires to be analyzed as such, neutrally and at length.

I am suggesting, however, that it is more plausible to view this attribution of resistance as a mistake that takes the outward form of responding to manifest content as if it were depth material. In this one aspect, it is a mistake based on an induced disruptive countertransference. The analyst is not detecting another kind of force in the patient, a force, moreover, the analysis of which is on a par with the analysis of transference as a chief identifying feature of true analysis; rather, the analyst is playing an assigned part in the patient's projective enactment of transference. It is the kind of mistake that on the surface seems to be very analytic, while, in effect, it shows that the analytic work has been thrown off course. It might be said that the analyst has begun telling the wrong story about the analytic dialogue.

CHAPTER 15

Problems of Training Analysis

IT has been argued by Harold Bloom (1973), the noted literary theorist, that strong poets are bound to feel they have arrived on the scene of creative writing belatedly. Acutely aware of the great works already written by others, they have the sense that they are barging into the company of the true masters, those who have already laid out and explored the major poetic possibilities. Surrounded by all these exemplary figures and works, strong poets must suffer "the anxiety of influence." Consequently, while drawing strength from their predecessors, they must also struggle against these figures in order to find their own poetic voices and be bold enough to let them be heard. There is, Bloom emphasizes, a disturbing patricidal undercurrent in this struggle. The poet is yet another Oedipus.

I cite this conflict-centered account of creativity in a chapter on training analysis because it describes well the experience of becoming the kind of analyst who can work within the analytic tradition and yet come to do so in his or her own voice—in other words, become a strong analyst. There is a definite parallel between, on the one hand, the poet's struggle and, on the other, the analytic candidate's anxiety of influence vis-à-vis the training analyst, supervisors, other teachers, Freud, and the entire analytic tradition as embodied in the pantheon of great analysts. Ernst Kris, no slouch himself as a creative analyst, was so self-conscious and self-effacing in this regard—in Bloom's terms, so oedipally frightened, so engaged in shrinking back from any suggestion of parricide—that somewhere he described everything written by analysts subsequent to Freud as not much more than footnotes to the master's writings.

Psychoanalytic belatedness is not, however, just a matter of recognizing the genius of Freud's pioneering efforts and the contributions made by all those other analytic figures whom we have encountered personally or through reading and who have exerted a powerful formative effect on our own analytic development. Much of this sense of belatedness can be traced to transferences. We may say that the oedipal child has arrived belatedly on the scene of parental sexuality and procreativity. And we may add that the preoedipal child is a Johnny-come-lately or a Joanie-come-lately on the scene of nurturance and power, in all their threatening as well as reassuring aspects. This early experience of belatedness leaves all of us feeling forever that, after all is said and done, we have remained the kids of our parents and secondarily of our mentors and the authors we read during our training. Our most strenuous efforts to defend against this feeling through forgetfulness, relentless competitiveness, or grandiose fantasy can never quash it completely.

Each training analysis should take account of this mix of personal and professional belatedness. It should not, however, crassly reduce the professional purely to the personal. We do after all live in intellectual and social histories, too, however personalized our view of our place in these histories may be. It was of this consideration that Kris, who was an art historian to begin with, was so keenly aware. We do not make up our own ideas completely; nor do we invent our own practices. No one does and no one ever has, neither in art nor in psychoanalysis. But I am not sure that training analyses always include this complex taking account of the anxiety of professional influence; here I have in mind the facts that, in our field, fitting in is usually rewarded more richly than originality, fifty-year-old colleagues continue to be called young analysts, and many analysts suffer a malaise that renders them all too eager for someone else to inject novelty and explosive controversy into the arenas of theory and technique. Most likely, the anxiety of influence will be taken up in analysis in its personal aspects, such as the influence of dominant identifications.

There is, of course, much more to work through in a training analysis than professional belatedness and its associated anxiety of influence, and I shall soon come to some of the other requirements. At this point, however, there is more introductory work to be done. First of all, a brief note on my own sense of belatedness in writing on training analysis: A number of excellent papers have already been written on training analysis, and they have been chewed over in other excellent papers, so that taken all together, the analytic literature seems to have pretty much covered the ground. To appreciate this state of affairs, we have only to consult the reviews and presentations included in recent monographs on training analysis published by the International Psychoanalytical Association (1985, 1986). Perhaps, though, in joining the conversation, I may develop some of the important points more fully, vividly, or consequentially than has been done up to now. Also, I feel obliged to try to counterbalance some well-established positions that I consider problematic.

A second introductory note: To take training analysis as a topic is to plunge into the thick of every major psychoanalytic controversy—the clinical, the theoretical, the pedagogical, the ideological, and the political. And it is to thereby plunge into the metacontroversy over whether these five controversies are distinct or are so intertwined as to be inseparable, or are so much the same thing fundamentally that they add up only to one topic being approached in different ways. For example, in certain respects theory is a political matter; so is the selection of some training analysts and the selection and progression of some candidates. Phyllis Greenacre's (1966) well-known discussion of how certain candidates get to be "convoyed" through training implies the important role that analytic power politics may play in analytic education. To Greenacre's point, I add that convoying is often done by others out of respect for, if not fear of and to curry favor with, powerful figures in the field.

Further by way of introduction: A writer on this topic also plunges into the thick of the transference residues and transference crises of those readers who are analysts and analytic candidates. Their "reader response" cannot help but express strong feelings about their own analyses. More than other readers, they have axes to grind or wield and illusions to sustain. Accordingly, a certain amount of unfinished analytic business must be expected to color every reader's grasp of the argument. In fact, such unfinished business must have already colored this argument, though it is not for me to decide how that is the case.

Some notes on methodology: Because any one analyst cannot have treated many analytic candidates, and because each training analysis, if it is reasonably thorough and well conducted, is likely to have many unique features as well as some that remain ambiguous, it can be argued that no training analyst is in a position to come to general conclusions about training analysis. But this cautionary consideration does not lead to the conclusion that we should simply keep our mouths shut. In this respect, four sets of considerations should be taken into account. First, while no one analyst concludes a huge number of ordinary clinical analyses to the complete satisfaction of both parties involved during his or her entire career, that fact has not prevented many analysts from writing valuable papers and books on every conceivable analytic topic and at every point in their careers. Second, any one analysis provides so many repetitions and multilayered variations of the themes and problems that come to be central to it that it proves to be a gold mine of data once it has been subjected to circumspect, insightful, and systematic processing. In psychoanalysis, valuable conclusions are reached in ways that do not and cannot conform to traditional experimental models. Third, published papers and symposia as well as informal discussions among colleagues have already led to consensus on many points concerning training analysis.

The fourth and final methodological note concerns the reality that each school of analytic thought provides a good deal of standardized theory to guide analysts in preparing their interpretive expectations and storylines. These expectations and storylines help them establish their sense of what makes sense and how to make sense. The reality is, then, that analysts never do start their work with individual analysands from scratch; instead, and fortunately for everyone concerned, the analysts' degrees of freedom are limited, much of the way toward their clinical conclusions having already been paved for them. Consequently, clinical experience, including experience doing training analysis, can never be and need never be viewed as a powerfully forbidding independent variable. Also to be taken into account is the fact that training analysts do have to conduct their first, second, and third training analyses, and who is to say that these analyses are any less effective than those conducted by other, often much older training analysts?

On the basis of these four methodological notes, I do not regard it as presumptuous to address the fundamental, fascinating, and problematic topic of training analysis. I attempt to join the conversation by reviewing the circumstances in which training analyses are conducted and spelling out the influences those circumstances may exert on the analysand's transferences and the analyst's countertransferences, matters of common concern in analytic institutes.

THE INFLUENCE OF CIRCUMSTANCE

Training analyses cannot afford to neglect the extent to which they are significantly influenced by the complex interaction of intellectual, professional, and personal circumstances. These interactions consti-

tute the context of training analysis. I assume a context of circumstance that obtains widely, though not universally, in analytic institutes.
On the one hand, therefore, my remarks do not apply in equal force
to all aspects of all training setups; on the other, they still apply to the
average expectable training analysis.

What constitutes the fateful context of circumstance in which training analyses are conducted? The training analysis goes on during most
or all of the candidate's training. The training takes place under the
auspices of an institute. It is required that the training analyst be a
carefully selected member of the faculty of that institute. Further, he
or she does not submit reports to the institute on the candidate's
problems and progress, does not participate in decisions affecting the
candidate's progress, and avoids administrative and pedagogical discussions that might include news about the candidate's behavior and
standing. By these means the training analyst and the institute attempt
scrupulously not only to observe the rules of confidentiality but also to
protect the analytic relationship against the intrusion of third-party
observations and influences. They see that intrusion as obstructive
and diverting. These, at any rate, are the ideals.

But even when the training analysis is conducted under conditions
that approach the ideal, it is bound to encounter more than a few
potentially disruptive circumstances. To begin with, there is the fact
that the training analysis is required of the candidate rather than its
being voluntarily elected by him or her. Moreover, everyone concerned expects the training analysis to play a major part in the candidate's attainment of professional competence, security, and identity
within one school of analytic thought. These facts alone tend to aug-
ment—not create—the candidate's idealizations, negative therapeutic
reactions, defensive identifications, and rebellious holding the analyst
at bay. In other respects, the analysis will be regarded as an imposition; another course requirement; a chance to show that one is a
good, compliant boy or girl; an enforced infantilization, castration, or
brainwashing; an opportunity to defeat the oedipal parent; or, most
likely, some combination or layered arrangement of these views. On
this account, it may be said that because training analysis is institutionalized, it is even more problematic than the ordinary clinical analysis.

Adding to these problems are those that arise from the opportunities available to both candidate and analyst to observe one another
and on occasion to interact outside the consulting room. And then
there is the gossip about the analyst that is often imparted to the candidate by fellow candidates, colleagues, and friends: Ostensibly a
friendly gesture made to a manifestly passive recipient, this gossip is

most usefully understood analytically as an intrusive, controlling, voyeuristically seductive and hostile piece of acting out by all concerned. The analysand may be expected to use both the inevitable observations of the analysts in public and the gossipy information to rationalize transference fantasies and thereby make them all the more difficult to analyze. Here, as elsewhere, "reality" is being used in the transference defensively, seductively, and aggressively.

Additionally, in many instances publications and presentations by the training analyst are easily accessible. These, too, may be used by the candidate in a voyeuristically seductive and hostile manner and used, as well, as an intellectualized bulwark against frightening transference fantasies and reconstructed traumatic experiences. Of course, all of this "information" can also be used for some worthwhile reality testing (for example, the analyst's own life also contains problems), but that use never excludes problematic uses of whatever "knowledge" comes the analysand's way.

Into this part of the picture there also enters the relative status of the training analyst in the institute and in the world of analysis at large. Here there is not only much readily available and not easily avoidable information, but, as analysts hear from the couch, a good deal of misinformation as well. Among themselves, candidates often tend to compare the prominence and analytic conduct of their analysts, the lengths of their analyses, the intensity of their own joys and of their suffering during vacations and other periods of experiencing liberation and deprivation, their transferential loves and hates, and so forth. And often, as the training analyst hears all this and also remembers it from his or her own days as a candidate, it sounds as if the candidates are comparing fullness of breasts, lengths of penises, personal passion and lovability, grades on moral report cards, parental failures, nobility of suffering, and grace under pressure. The language, the metaphors, the attitudes seem loaded with infantile meaning. All of which is potential analytic material, to be sure, and so to be looked into empathically and carefully. But these contacts, revelations, distortions, and sometimes fabrications, which typically continue after termination of training analysis, are also bound to limit to some extent the type and degree of resolution of transference conflicts and defensive strategies. On this account, the end result may differ significantly from what is observed often enough in nontraining cases. These limiting circumstances cannot be ignored.

Training analysts, too, are subject to a variety of circumstances that act as pressures and temptations. For example, just about everyone at the institute seems to be looking over their shoulders and deciding how good they are. These observers may base their estimates of quality, often recklessly, on how insightful, responsible, clinically effective, or just plain attractive an analyst's candidates are or seem to be. They may also base these estimates on how long each training analyst's analyses last on the average, how warm each seems to be in public, and how highly rated as a teacher, a discussant, or analytic writer. Thus, training analysts swim in the same fishbowl as their candidates. Not only that, but like their candidates they are on display before an audience ever ready to make personal interpretations as well as professional judgments that can affect the training analyst's morale, general reputation, livelihood, and on occasion even friendships.

For present purposes, I need not go on enumerating circumstances that exert significant influences on the analytic relationship and process. I have been leading up to making a few main points about the understanding and handling of these circumstances, points I have already implied in my remarks on institute gossip and some other matters. My leading point in connection with influential circumstances is this: Everything in the analysis depends on the extent to which the training analyst keeps in focus the importance of developing psychoanalytic interpretations of what is brought up about these influential circumstances, and also of when and how it is brought up. It is generally agreed that it does not advance analysis simply or primarily to confirm or disconfirm claims to knowledge or to ignore the nature and force of the influential circumstances themselves. The analyst must develop interpretations of the candidate's unconsciously constructed, infantile perceptions of, wishful fantasies about, and defensive measures against these circumstances. As far as possible, the analyst approaches references to these circumstances as so much more manifest content. These references are material of the same order as the manifest dream. The training analysis depends on the analyst's never taking these circumstances simply or primarily at face value.

I am saying that everything depends on the importance the training analyst accords to that other reality, psychic reality. To put it more sharply, what is crucial is that the analyst understand that "external reality" is not even a psychoanalytic concept: For that reason I have avoided using the term, even though I recognize that words alone cannot be decisive in this respect. To the analyst, what is conventionally called external reality is something that can only be defined and understood *analytically*, that is, only after it has been worked out how the perceiver has processed it on many subjective levels and filtered it through dominant unconscious fantasies that have been organized in varied cognitive modes and in relation to varied psychosexual perspectives (Arlow, 1969a, b; see also chapter 13). What to the analyst is compelling, commonsensical external reality may not have that significance for the candidate, and vice versa. The reality that counts is the one that is developed through analysis. This respect for psychic reality is an essential component of the analytic attitude (Schafer, 1983).

Deferring for the moment consideration of the influence of countertransference, the crucial thing is that the training analyst believe in a relatively unthreatened way that, for the candidate, the training situation cannot fail to lend itself to family drama, fantasy, and reenactment: primal scenes; incestuous seductions, both heterosexual and homosexual; rapes, castrations, impregnations, and abortions; death wishes toward and from parents and siblings; enforced feedings, traumatic weanings, and starvation; constipation, incontinence, and enemas; abrupt abandonment and blissful mergings and reunions; imprisonment, slavery, torture, and rescue. You name it. The analysis of this material should be at the heart of training analysis. Seen in this light, the influential circumstances I have been discussing are not so much disruptive interferences as they are analytic opportunities, akin to those offered by dreams, daydreams, symptoms, and other such, to develop the analysis in depth.

It does help, however, to view this same material in another, darker light, for often it is not easily reachable, and once reached, not easily or fully analyzable. On this point, some analysts would disagree. They seem to believe that, because everything is open to analysis in principle, everything can be elicited and worked through in practice. They believe that if something can be talked about, it can be analyzed in a worked-through fashion. In some of his more heated polemical moments, Merton Gill (1982) seems to be such an analyst. So are all those training analysts who are altogether casual about their analytic incognitos. I am among those who reject this belief and the obtrusive conduct it can lead to. I believe, for example, that difficulties in analysis may become insurmountable when the stimulus of circumstance is unusually strong or prolonged, for then there is, in the analysand's psychic reality, so much seduction, hostility, and deprivation in the analytic relationship and, as a consequence, so much reason to cling to primitive defensive strategies, that even the most patient and clever interpretive work makes no evident headway against a candidate's transference and defensive moves.

A case in point are those situations that involve a candidate's becoming a favored analytic son or daughter or the persecuted victim of someone in analytic power; the candidate's being forced by confrontational tactics to deal with major and painful issues prematurely;

the candidate's being required to modify important career and family plans at critical points in his or her life cycle in order to be able to meet all the demands and pay all the costs of analytic education; and the candidate's being bound by training requirements to stay in analysis beyond the time when the analysis is ready to come to what seems, to analyst and analysand alike, its natural end. Factors such as these may so recapitulate oedipal victories and defeats and other contexts of overstimulation, deprivation, despair, and psychic pain that the candidate cannot be counted on, even with help, to draw and maintain necessary distinctions between the here and now and the there and then. It is generally recognized that excessive and unrelieved countertransference is dangerous to an analysis in large part because it renders unanalyzable many of the basic issues touched on within that analysis and perhaps within any subsequent analysis. I argue that that line of thought applies equally to any other strong and unrelieved stimulating or pressuring set of circumstances surrounding and invading an analysis. Interpretation has its limits.

In addition to overconfidence in the power of interpretation, a second attitude may lead to counterproductive effects on the training analysis. There are candidates who are subject to analysis in which the analyst uses egalitarianism in its most manifest and superficial sense as an argument in favor of a variety of conventionally free and open contacts and interactions, both in and out of the treatment room. In these instances, infantile wishes, fears, and defensive strategies may be so stimulated and seemingly gratified or confirmed in their nature by this analytic forwardness that their deeper aspects become sealed off from interpretation and working through. These candidates will emerge from training not having defined some fundamental, unconsciously maintained fantasies and not having experienced and mastered some essential conflictual issues. Consequently, they will be inadequately prepared to deal with these issues effectively when they arise in the analyses they conduct in their subsequent independent careers. Sometimes this egalitarianism is rationalized as a way of not infantilizing, enslaving, abandoning, or castrating the candidate. Ultimately, however, this way of thinking is nonanalytic or even antianalytic in principle, practice, and consequence, in that it conveys an analytically naïve faith in the power of conventionalized social conduct. That faith latently encourages further repression of infantile desire, fantasy, and conflict and further minimization of psychic reality; also, it often encourages certain forms of dramatic acting out. And countertransferentially, it may manifest some sadistic seductiveness that plays on the candidate's masochistic tendencies at the same time as it sugarcoats them.

THE TRAINING ANALYST'S COUNTERTRANSFERENCES

It is not the candidate alone who is subject to situationally intensified turbulence in psychic reality. Like the candidate's, the training analyst's turbulence, though it is not created by the circumstances of the training situation, may be very much intensified by it. In response to this intensification, the analyst may use defensive strategies and construct conflictual perceptions and fantasies of the same general sort as the candidate does. For instance, the analyst may develop his or her transferences to the figures who make up the institute, including all the candidates and not just the one on the couch; these transferences will then surely enter into or reinforce the training analyst's countertransferences to the candidate of the moment. Analysts have, however, learned to live with these countertransferences—at least, to try to live with them by interpreting their disruptiveness so as to provide information about the analysand: what is being enacted and why and so forth.

At their best, analysts are also alert to their characterological countertransferences, those that Annie Reich (1951) discussed so helpfully in her basic paper on countertransference. Characterological countertransferences originate in the dynamics that led in the first place to a person's having chosen the career of therapist and analyst. These dynamics continue to play a part in the analyst's relations with analysands. To varying degrees, these countertransferences have voyeuristic, reparative, sadomasochistic, paranoid, perfectionistic, and other such features. They can add significantly to the analyst's motivation, stamina, steadfastness, perceptiveness, empathy, range of skill, and personal style of working. But at the same time, in that they are still rooted in their infantile conflictual soil, they can make of every one of these motivations a jungle of confusion and obstruction. Therefore these characterological countertransferences are mixed blessings or, at best, fortunate falls from the grace of neutrality.

Well-analyzed and thoughtful analysts get to know a fair amount about those characterological countertransferences during their own training analyses. They get to know a lot more about them subsequently in the course of doing independent analytic work, provided that they pay open-minded attention not only to what analysands have to say about their experience of being analyzed by them but also to what they themselves experience in doing analysis. Doing analysis is never entirely free from the influence of the dynamics that led to this career choice. No "work ego" is altogether autonomous, nor should we hope for anything different, for in this respect the nuclear dynamics of talent and trouble are the same. As Freud (1937b) noted in

"Analysis Terminable and Interminable," however much our own analysis may help master the seriously deleterious consequences of these nuclear dynamics, the vulnerabilities linger on and with them the defensive measures they have necessitated, albeit in less extreme forms. Much earlier (1913), Freud had emphasized the resistances that are put up by those already working as therapists and dealing with the resistances of their own patients.

As I mentioned, during a training analysis conducted in the stressful and transference-laden circumstances of institutional training, the process can be said to be institutionalized from the first. In the training analyst, the institutional setting may stimulate characterological countertransference continuously. Consequently, in order to stay on top of things, the training analyst must keep on trying to take account of his or her transferences to figures in the local analytic world, all the other analysts in his or her pantheon, and all the protagonists in the theoretical and technical controversies in the field of analysis. Through transference, the institute itself becomes a good but also bad family and home. The training analyst functions in a social system that lends itself to the enactment of every kind of family drama, and its being drama in a fishbowl means that it all takes place at very close quarters and under the pressure of the incestuous, voyeuristic, exhibitionistic, and hostile tendencies and conflicts of all concerned. It might be called analytic theater in the round.

Within that social system, the training analyst will feel that the ranks of the anointed do not include some who are deserving or who are friends who take their exclusion badly, while these same ranks do include others who are thought to be unfit, unlikable, or just too different to be *sympatico*. The system or family will seem to distribute power and recognition unevenly and sometimes capriciously. It will have its share of pretense, pretentiousness, overweaning ambition, factionalism, toadies, and ostracized heretics, mavericks, and incompetents. In these respects and contrary to our hopes and perhaps our illusions, the world of the institute proves to be not all that different from the so-called real world.

In a characterologically based response to all these impressions, involvements, and perhaps disappointments and resulting bitterness, the training analyst may overemphasize some factors in each training case and minimize others. To give one set of examples—one that is especially important for the vitality of our field—I mention that the training analyst may overreact to originality, seeing it simply as dissident acting out of oedipal rebellion and parricide or as incorrigibility based on pathological narcissism or defective ego functioning. That same training analyst will take too readily and too generously to the conforming candidate who makes no waves and so neither adds to the analyst's professional and personal insecurity nor rocks the institutional boat.

A rigidly conforming candidate is defending by remaining consciously blind to the overcharged and often contradictory circumstances in which training takes place. In this regard, the candidate's defending may also amount to being on "good behavior" in order to get through and out of training, much as if he or she were serving a sentence. In this there may be much splitting of transference as well as defensive idealizing of, and surreptitiously identifying with, the analyst; thereby the candidate limits him- or herself to presenting only a "false self" for analysis. Exceptionally difficult to eliminate through analysis are the unconscious fantasies on which this defensive strategy is based. This problem will be all the harder when these fantasies seem to be amply supported by observations of such questionable administrative and clinical practices in the institute as "convoying" or its persecutory opposite. For purposes of the training analysis, it becomes especially important, through appropriate interpretation, to help free the candidate's sense of reality with regard to the practices that prevail in the institute and also to liberate his or her capacity for expressiveness and adaptive action (not to be confused with passive acquiescence) within this system.

There is a notable alternative to quashing originality and perceptiveness while rewarding conformity. In the name of empathy, antiauthoritarianism, and the fostering of creative self-expression, the analyst may be so keen on originality that, out of countertransference, he or she encourages the displacement of every kind of negative transference onto the institute or the field of analysis generally. This evasion is accomplished by not analyzing what it means to the candidate to be using originality as a way of warding off analysis itself, when that is the case. In question here is analysis of the student's ambivalent, envious, and parricidal transferences, for in the guise of independence of mind, the candidate may act out the role of serving as his or her own womb, breast, paternal phallus, and fount of analytic wisdom. This is the role of the one-person tradition, the child prodigy, and, in time, perhaps the crucified savior. Much more than the assertion of talent and originality will have entered into the candidate's conduct.

It is worth emphasizing that this sort of self-generative fantasy of the talented may be analyzed to death or counterproductively fostered by neglectful handling. Of more general significance, however, is the question of how institutionally reinforced characterological countertransferences inevitably color the analyst's responses to manifestations of independence of mind. These high-spirited manifestations, which in the long run can be fostered in the analysand only by effective analytic work, may along the way develop into barriers to further analysis. Their becoming barriers may be due simply to the candidate's defensive use of them, but it may result from the training analyst's countertransferences to content that bears on conformity, individuation, or group belongingness; most likely, it is due to some complex combination of all these factors.

Who is to say that in the end a certain amount of limit-setting on analysis by the analysand should not be tolerated and respected? Do analysts know that much about what in the long run makes for a good-enough analyst or enhances a creative one? Can analysts generalize across all candidates in these respects? Can they even hope to eliminate completely all barriers and blindness? While there is no substitute for sustained analytic attentiveness, the line between attentiveness and hypervigilant and perfectionistic coercion is fuzzy and shifts from one case to the next. Certainly, institutionally reinforced characterological countertransferences can get in the way of tolerating this ambiguity, in that they exert a pressure on the analyst to try to turn out what looks unquestionably like a "finished product."

It has been much discussed whether training analysis should have as its general goal producing a "finished product," that is, a recognizable, acceptable, and safe member of the analytic community that is providing the training. In my view, it goes against the basic conception of psychoanalysis for the analyst to have any such analytic goal. Here I leave aside questions pertaining to the carefulness and correctness of the process by which candidates are selected. Thereafter, however, the best way to turn out a good-enough analyst in each case is simply to do the best clinical analysis we can; the rest should be left up to the candidate and the remainder of the training. In other words, the best way to show concern as an analyst and the best way to discharge our responsibility to the discipline of psychoanalysis to which we have committed ourselves is to reject the unanalytic role of watchdog, enforcer, or cautionary moralist; for in this role the analyst becomes at one and the same time a seducer and a superego figure.

Certainly it would strain analytic credulity to think that the candidate's departing significantly from the analytic community's prevailing orientation and ethics will never come up for analysis in the form of conflictual experience within the transference and erratic action outside it. Even so, successful analysis of this deviationism requires that the training analyst have a flexible conception of what is required for an analyst to have "the right stuff"; otherwise, he or she shows a lack of confidence in analysis itself and in the candidate's future and independent use of the analytic experience.

Contrasts to my position are, however, plentiful. To give only one example: In Edith Weigert's (1955) excellent paper on the problems of training analysis, after wisely and frankly discussing numerous countertransference problems, she ended with what I regard as a thinly veiled countertransferential sermon on the exemplary figure the training analysis should produce. The contrasting position I advocate is neither easy to arrive at nor simple to maintain consistently, but I do recommend it as an ideal. It is, however, an ideal way of working analytically, not some idealized end result.

I believe that all the countertransferential difficulties I have been mentioning have been steadily increasing as a result of the rapid increase in the number and variety of schools of thought on analytic theory and technique. It seems that attitudes toward rigorousness, constraint, tradition, and sometimes even integrity have become both more controversial and more casual among those entering training. And it seems to be true, too, among prospective patients. Consequently, candidates are more likely than ever before to view as so many manifestations of empathic failure, tyrannical rigidity, elitism, and repressiveness the devoted efforts their elders make to maintain the conventional rigorous standards of the past and to do so in the customary way. Today, conventional respect for continuity of ideals and practice is often regarded as uncritical submission to "the establishment" or to "the medical model." Candidates may even minimize or block reading the analytic literature during training. And candidates' increased awareness of countertransference as a discussable issue may be used to question disturbing interpretations of transference.

Thoughtful training analysts, struggling to adapt their old bearings to changing times and mores, need not be less secure analytically on this account, for being provisional rather than certain is consistent with these times. But if they are more insecure, they are more likely to react countertransferentially to the new ambiguities of transference, defense, and acting out, and also to those ambiguities having to do with becoming one's own person as a result of effective analysis.

To these considerations it might be retorted that it has ever been thus; many members of each older generation are disheartened and perhaps offended by what they see as the waywardness of the young. I will, however, venture to mention an alternative view: The rate of change has accelerated in recent years, and traditional modes of quality control have become a problematic of psychoanalysis rather than an ostensible given. I say "ostensible" because I believe that some amount of generation gap in values and practices is inevitable and that, except for the denials and repressions of candidates and the unconvincing official proclamations of unity and stability by the psychoanalytic bureaucracy, nothing has ever been totally "given" in psychoanalysis.

I further believe that the accelerated rate of change in values and practices has increased the countertransference hazards facing training analysts. The undecidability of many technical and interpretive issues has become a more prominent circumstance of analytic work (Schafer, 1985a). For this reason, it has become useful to explore the fantasy meaning to the analysand of the undecidability of important analytic issues. In this connection, countertransference may show itself in the analyst's being either wishy-washy or inflexible or alternating between the two. When the analyst is too indecisive or too quickly comes to traditional conclusions, the candidate will not be initiated adequately into an essential segment of contemporary psychoanalytic work, namely, dealing consistently with qualitative and quantitative ambiguity in clinical, theoretical, and professional matters of great moment. In this area of concern, however, there is not likely to be a general consensus among training analysts and certainly not among candidates.

Before closing, I want to take up one more important aspect of countertransference. Mention of this factor is required by my discussion of heterogeneity in the field of psychoanalysis. It is arguable that increased psychoanalytic tolerance of heterogeneity has resulted in a relative shift of emphasis away from superego analysis and toward pre-superego analysis or analysis of forestages of the superego (for example, introject experiences stemming from early object relations and also disturbances in the formation of self and object constancy). Consequently, the tolerant training analyst, being less prone to the countertransference of overexactingness, a countertransference that can be experienced in a well-defended way by the modern candidate only as accusatory, punitive, and untimely, is not likely to develop a sustained focus on oedipal rebelliousness and oedipal guilt in the transference.

There is, however, an upside to this change. By being more open to the analysand's archaic types and levels of experiencing and functioning, the analyst is less likely to pressure the candidate into presenting an ordinary oedipal self that is in some crucial respect a false self. It will be a false self not because there is nothing oedipal there to analyze, but because too much is then left out of the analysis that pertains

to atemporal, dyadic, intensely physical experiences of being shattered, empty, abandoned, persecuted, depressed, paranoid, anxious,
and traumatically overstimulated. The new openness broadens the
scope of the individual training analysis to include more of the candidate's preoedipal madness. True, this gain in breadth may for its part
be at the cost of adequate superego analysis, and with it, of course, of
oedipal issues and all that is associated with them. I am inclined to
think that this is the price paid for the sensitive aspects of the work of
Kohut (1984) and his followers.

Taking these changes into account, we may go on to specify an
"equidistance" in the analyst's neutrality other than the equidistance
from id, ego, and superego that has been recommended traditionally.
Now we must aim to be equidistant from oedipal and preoedipal
issues. It is not that analysts have neglected to position themselves that
way; rather, it is a matter of emphasizing explicitly another facet of
neutrality.

In some cases it may be inevitable that getting deeply into the preoedipal will slant the emphasis mostly away from the oedipal. In my
view, the language and the narrative organization of the entire analysis
and the corresponding shape of the analytic relationship may not be
able to include full and equal representation of both phases of development. To repeat a point that cannot be overemphasized: Not everything interpretable in principle can be effectively worked through in
practice. Where it seems that a choice must be made, I believe that, as
a rule, it is desirable to go for the more archaic and to entrust beneficial modification and future growth of useful superego functioning to
the analysand's strengthened preoedipal functioning or "ego," which
is, anyway, the foundation for adequate superego functioning. It
should be borne in mind in this connection that, throughout the history of psychoanalysis, many analysts have had to seek second or sometimes third analyses to deal with all that has been left out of a first,
"correct" Freudian analysis biased toward oedipal and superego issues.
But, as with so many other analytic issues, I cannot simply assert that
the criteria for decisions of this type are very clear or easily generaliz-
able across cases. The problem of how to work through important
issues adequately on all levels of development is easier to mention
than to manage with complete confidence.

In these last remarks, I have not wandered as far from countertransference as it might seem. Suppose, now, that the training analysis is
centering on preoedipal issues. Then such concepts as the analyst as a
new object, the holding environment, the depressive position, and the
like seem inevitably to recommend themselves. In practice, the conse-

quence is that all the doors open wider to disruptive experiences and expressions of countertransference, whereupon the training analyst may make poorly rationalized, ad hoc, premature departures from his or her own version of the traditional technical baseline.

Many analysts seem to have decided that they must relate more openly and variously to their analysands than even the most liberal published versions of the tradition seem to allow. They believe that a method that is limited almost totally to interpretation and its judiciously managed preliminaries—listening, questioning, confronting, and clarifying—is inadequately responsive to all the clinical manifestations of early developmental damage, arrest, and tension; rather, it has become something of an obstruction to fundamental analysis (see, for example, Loewald, 1960). Their experience seems to tell them that their analysands do not develop confidence that the analyst is fully and empathically there for them, available for whatever nutriment is required in psychic reality: merging, holding, mutual incorporation, as well as identification. Not through dramatic enactments but through subtle manifestations of presence, analysts can foster that confidence and enable the hampered and overwrought analysand to tolerate, and get to understand analytically, early infantile terror, rage, paranoia, depression, withdrawal, and hypochondriasis. Failing that sort of thoroughness on the part of the analyst, the analysis may become a pseudoanalysis in which the analysand plays the part of a good blind boy or a good blind girl. Consequently, that candidate's future analytic patients may well not get at, or be helped to get beyond, their own preoedipal wastelands. And so on down through the generations.

On the other hand, as I have already indicated, analysts who work with greater presence are exposed to their own increased emotionality and disruptive countertransferences. Then they may too readily and rigidly play the role of good mother or father, or soother and rescuer, and neglect the more traditional, formalized, relatively impersonal approaches to castration anxiety, penis envy, womb and breast envy, sadomasochistic anality, and supergo savagery; instead, these analysts may favor sentimentalized and externalized rapprochements and good cheer. It is, I believe, quite a widespread characterological countertransference to want to improve on one's own parents and to do so as a way of all at once getting revenge on them, making reparation to them, and obtaining vicarious and belated gratification from them. It is not easy for analysts to maintain perspective on this countertransference when working responsively with preoedipal material, and it is here that characterological countertransferences may rule the day.

Controversies that have been going on for a long time in this more tolerant era of psychoanalysis may revolve not around hard evidence but around the pros and cons of radically different characterological countertransferences and the "clinical experience" they have shaped and which is now used as hard evidence. Perhaps that is one main reason why these controversies over technique do not seem to be decidable by theoretical argument, clinical example, and the rhetoric of panel discussions.

I feel that I am closing this discussion of training analysis belatedly, having wandered all over the map in spite of my efforts to maintain the interrelated foci of circumstance and countertransference. And yet I cannot escape the sense that I am closing too soon in that I have scarcely done justice to any of the major issues I have taken up and to alternative points of view. My story of training analysis is not the whole story, but I think it is one that should be told as I have told it.

CHAPTER 16

Psychoanalysis, Pseudoanalysis, and Psychotherapy

I believe the following: What is sometimes presented as Freudian psychoanalysis proves on close examination to have many of the features of eclectic psychotherapy. What is ostensibly psychoanalytic psychotherapy may prove to have many of the features of Freudian psychoanalysis. Some analysts doing psychotherapy get more analysis done, at least with certain patients, than other analysts do in carrying out conventional analyses. And some patients in psychotherapy get more analysis done, at least with certain therapists, than other patients get done in psychoanalysis proper; in this case it may be argued that that therapy deserves to be called psychoanalysis even if it is, to a purist, imprecise and incomplete. After all, how many analyses meet an ideal standard of purity and completeness?

There may be advantages, then, in treating the three therapeutic categories in this chapter's title as therapeutic approaches that differ in degree rather than kind. However, to focus on differences of degree does violate the assumption made by many or most analysts that the three are distinct categories. We encounter here some of the difficulties presented by *narratives of difference*. Typically, these narratives are developed in a manner that is decisive and perhaps even severely judgmental: "That's not analysis at all!" "That's wild analysis!" "It's merely psychotherapy!" and so forth. These narratives of difference are told in official presentations, such as in the "best" journals or the comments of their referees as well as at meetings and in informal shop talk. But they rest on the arbitrary assumption that all analysts would agree in specific instances; it is arbitrary in that actually it is analysts who are criticizing one another's work in just these terms. In the short run, the judgments that usually prevail are those that are voiced by analysts with the most power (by reputation or professional office). Additionally, these arbitrary narratives of difference discourage further thought, and that should be considered their most serious fault. Finally, these strict divisions and judgments seem to suggest that the necessary criteria are already clearly formulated and readily available, when actually, I believe, each judge may, if pressed on this score, encounter difficulty in laying out an adequate and persuasive supporting argument and then, explicitly or implicitly, may resort to the unsatisfactory pronouncement: "I know it when I see it!"—at which point the authoritarian impulse stands naked before us.

In order to approach the three "categories" as headings for stories of difference of degree, we must, it seems to me, begin with a general summary of an ideal standard for clinical psychoanalysis. Only then and in relation to this standard might we take up the others. To proceed in this manner is to develop a position in terms of comparisons rather than self-evident absolutes: "pseudo" as compared to what? and so on. It should not be expected, however, that this comparative approach will eliminate all difficulties with drawing sharp distinctions. We would, for example, still have to ask such questions as these: If wild analysis is a form of pseudoanalysis, how far can we go in making interpretations before being judged "wild" rather than being accepted as intuitive, or creative, or highly individual in style but still sound? Also: If insubstantial analysis is another form of pseudoanalysis, how accepting of a specific patient's limited capacity for change, such as that referred to by Freud (1937b) in "Analysis Terminable and Interminable," should we be before being classified as conducting an insubstantial analysis? Even to begin meditating on these questions will plunge us into some formidable problems in methodology and epistemology. My narratives of difference will venture that far, especially in connection with my contention that the extravagant promotion of short-term dynamic psychotherapy may be a form of pseudoanalysis: venture that far, not so much to attempt to arrive at compelling conclusions as to establish some of the groundwork for genuine and productive debate in this vexing area of clinical judgment.

PSYCHOANALYSIS

My list of general criteria for Freudian psychoanalysis begins with the steady fostering of a free-associative atmosphere. To foster this atmosphere the analyst must maintain a neutral, receptive, and interpretive stance. The analyst's primary focus of interpretation must remain on unconsciously devised defensive operations and enactments of transference and countertransference. Transference enactments are best taken up extensively and not hastily reduced to experiences and fantasies of early life; by "taken up extensively" I refer to full development in the here-and-now relationship, although I do not exclude the analysis of displaced transference enactments so long as these are not being used as substitutes for engagements in the here and now. Interpretation will be guided by the search for conflict and compromise formation under the umbrella of the principle of multiple function. The analyst will use the genetic and developmental approaches of psychoanalysis to strengthen the analysand's interest in a coherent, psychoanalytically meaningful history of her or his conflictual constructions of psychic reality in the past: all, however, as leading into a better grasp of the present. In the process, the analysand will develop more or less intense, complex, primitivized, and repetitive transference reactions to the analyst that will warrant the designation *transference neurosis* so long as it is not seriously contaminated and rigidly reinforced by the analyst's own countertransferences and so remains interpretable as being based on the analysand's self-expressive fantasies.

Analysts recognize that the analytic process is not defined simply by the analyst's interventions, for there are many noninterpretive elements in the analytic situation, such as being listened to attentively, nonjudgmentally, and empathically. Leo Stone (1961) has reviewed many of these noninterpretive factors. The analyst's theory of the therapeutic effects of analysis will, accordingly, take these noninterpretive elements into account. Also to be taken into account are the many noninterpretive elements inherent in interpretive activity itself: implications of attentive and concerned listening; concerns with tact, timing, and dosage; a willingness to participate as well as observe; and a readiness for empathic experience as well as deliberate reflection. All these elements convey a special kind of relatedness that itself may move the therapeutic process forward in ways both visible and, for the time being at least, invisible.

Further, analysts assume that the therapeutic process cannot be defined as analysis just on the basis of what they think, say, do, or intend—that is, by their methods and goals. Neither will they define an analysis just by the procedural arrangements of frequency and use of the couch, length of treatment, emphasis on the fundamental rule, maintenance of a relative incognito and abstinence so-called, and other frequently mentioned desiderata of analytic conduct. Nor will they define analysis just by what the person who has come for help calls it, wishes it to be, or believes it to be. After taking all of these factors into account—which we should—analysts go on to ascribe a crucial role to the kind of participation in the process that the patient is ready to develop: the changes that he or she is prepared to seek, undergo, and understand analytically, and the method she or he is prepared to tolerate and use. As I indicate soon in taking up pseudoanalysis, these questions of readiness apply to the analyst, too, though ordinarily not at all to the same degree as to the suffering but as yet unanalyzed patient.

In turning next to pseudoanalysis and then to psychotherapy, I am adding to the exposition of my general view of psychoanalysis.

PSEUDOANALYSIS: THE WILD AND THE INSUBSTANTIAL

I use the term *pseudoanalysis* to refer to a number of cases that share only one feature: They represent themselves as analysis in form and substance despite their either violating the principles of psychoanalysis in some fundamental way or giving only the appearance of being analysis. In the former group are the varieties of wild analysis; in the latter group, analyses that exist in form but not in active process. Both groups are not so rare as one might wish.

Wild Analysis

Wild analysis as a characterization of interpretive therapy makes sense only within the context of one or another system of psychoanalysis, for what is wild in one system may not seem to be so in another and vice versa (Schafer, 1985a). In this chapter, as my context is my version of contemporary Freudian analysis, I refer to wild analysis without further systematic contextualization (see also Schafer, 1985a).

The characterization *wild analysis* is usually reserved for the making of interpretations that are neither warranted by the material at hand nor invited by the analysand's basic, even if erratic, acceptance and use of the analytic method and the collaboration it calls for. Usually, the charge of wild analysis is made when the analyst rapidly makes deep interpretations of unconscious conflict or hastily engages in reductive reconstructions. In a general way, this kind of work seems to refer to the id so called. In my view, however, the designation *wild* should apply equally to superego- and ego-centered interpretations and reconstructions and also to relatively superficial issues and deep-lying issues. The crucial factor should be that the intervention is unwarranted by the evidence available and inappropriate to the patient's state of preparation for that kind of intervention. Accordingly, I divide wild interpretations into structural types—id, superego, and ego—even though I recognize that in practice none of these types is pure. Rather, I am referring to differences in emphasis and explicitness.

To begin with the most familiar: Wild id analysis is illustrated by hasty, ill-founded, tactless interpretations of kindness as simply a reaction formation against anal sadism, curiosity as primal scene voyeurism, and demandingness as an expression of exaggerated orality or of psychological emptiness. Similarly wild are mechanical interpretations of political radicalism as simply or mainly oedipal revolt, of a woman's feminism as simply or only an expression of penis envy, or a male feminist's beliefs as showing his self-castrating identification with penis-envious women.

Wild superego analysis is exemplified by hasty, ill-founded, inappropriate interpretations of unconscious guilt and need for punishment, of primitive object-related fantasies of damage or retribution (as superego precursors), and of the apparent absence of guilt as being due to defective superego development.

Wild ego analysis may take the form of too quickly and narrowly interpreting intrasystemic conflict, such as that between ambition and humility. It may simplistically make interpretation in terms of past and present interpersonal conflict only. It may accept representations of other people at face value and use them in interpretation, as if the analysand is bound to be a reliable informant. Often it is evident in discussions of ego autonomy, a conflictless sphere of the ego, and sublimation. In my opinion, many discussions of nonconflictual and nontransferential therapeutic alliance also qualify as wild ego analysis.

We must also recognize complex forms of wild analysis, such as early, overly specific, comprehensive, deterministic formulations of psychodynamics. These implicitly omniscient formulations cannot amount to much more than intimidating and indoctrinating the patient and perhaps additionally, irrationally supporting the analyst's confidence that he or she understands and is adequate to the occasion. The material with which analysts work cannot be shown to sup-

port this kind of intervention; it is intervention by formula or preconception, and it rides roughshod over the ambiguous and often
unclearly interrelated phenomena of analysis. It also ignores the evidence that the same material can be interpreted in a number of ways,
depending on one's school of thought and one's predilections within
that school.

A special instance of interpreting wildly and by formula may often
be observed in reports of time-limited dynamic therapy. At their best,
these time-limited therapies do not pretend to be anything more than
a limited form of applied psychoanalysis. Often enough, they can help
reduce acute suffering, eliminate some symptoms, improve impaired
functional efficiency, and make immediate life crises more manageable. In many cases changes of this sort are very helpful to the patient.
But an analyst would have to insist that these therapies cannot provide
an adequately rich account of how these beneficial changes have
come about; nor can these therapies specify convincingly and in depth
what, in each instance, these changes mean to the patient. Only on
the basis of the general and specific methods and theories of psychoanalysis could we even begin to hope to provide that account. Even
then, that account would have to remain tentative because the methods and theories require recognition that time-limited work eventu-
ates in such a limited sample of phenomena that it cannot support
decisive formulations. Even full analyses do not seem to provide data
that are entirely adequate to explain their own effects: Witness disagreements among Freudian analysts on this score.

In narrational terms, the overexcited proponents of time-limited
dynamic therapy have been using the master narratives of psychoanalysis to tell the story of an activity that does not meet the criteria of psychoanalysis that I just mentioned. As a crude analogy, it might be said
that it is like telling a musical comedy as if it were grand opera, or perhaps that it is confusing fast food with a gourmet meal.

Analysts cannot accept the claims of Malan (1979), Davanloo
(1978), and others that their short-term or sector therapies can bring
about the worked-through insights and so-called structural changes
that are distinctively psychoanalytic. However impressively stable and
extensive the changes wrought by these therapies might seem, they
cannot take precedence over the theory and methodology of psychoanalysis. If we accept this theory and methodology, we must assert
that, in their inner makeup, changes wrought by short-term therapies
cannot be the same as psychoanalytic changes; they can only resemble
them superficially. Any other conclusion effectively junks psychoanalysis and its long and complex history. And so we might say that the

ardent proponents of brief therapies are advocating not just wild clinical analysis but wild theoretical analysis: They make too free with theories and their histories and too free with the hard-earned methodology and interpretive resources of psychoanalysis. They lay claim to legitimacy and a respectful hearing on the basis of their seeming to deal adequately with transference and resistance and in this way to be meeting Freud's announced criteria for the conduct of psychoanalysis. However, their claim is fundamentally mistaken in that it does not meet the spirit of Freud's succinct (in my opinion, too succinct) definition of psychoanalysis, the spirit that can be recognized only in the context of *all* of Freud's writings about the psychoanalytic process and the psychoanalytic theory of human mental processes.

In order to remain consistent with the master narratives of psychoanalysis (true to its theory), we would have to speculate that the benefits brought about by time-limited therapy are based on some mixture of the following. Within limits, clarification of problems brings about significant relief and increased adaptability. Faltering defenses are buttressed by intellectualization. Wild analytic interpretation of basic conflict frightens the patient into a flight toward health or into a more obscure form of neurosis. Transferential, possibly masochistic submission to the dominating superego figure of the therapist leads to apparent cure. And so forth. Although speculative, these ideas conform to observations repeatedly made by analysts in the course of conducting the most careful and lengthy analyses. Patients are constantly, though mainly unconsciously, on the lookout for these alternatives to worked-through insight and change, and on the lookout, too, for opportunities to enact their core problems and their transferences rather than come to understand them and modify them.

I have gone into these methodological and epistemological aspects of the claims for time-limited therapy not to dismiss it from consideration, for as I have already asserted, that approach does have its clinical uses and occasions. Rather, I want to indicate that psychoanalysis is to be regarded as more than a specific, empirically focused technique. Psychoanalysis provides a systematic point of view on all clinical practices, even those of behavior therapy, so many of which have been promoted as superior alternatives to psychoanalysis. Whatever its internal variations, psychoanalysis is a well-established tradition, an organized basis for attempting to understand, a way of constructing the world it tells about through application of its master narratives and the story-lines they generate. And it is also a way of reserving judgment on what appear to be phenomena it cannot incorporate. In all these ways psychoanalysis has laid claim to being a basic discipline.

In order to debate clinical matters rationally, instructively, and productively, we must have a systematic point of view. Such a viewpoint is an epistemological necessity. Without it, we can make only obvious or disguised pronouncements based on inadequate or irrelevant observation and personal power, and in the field of psychoanalysis we already have had far too much of these unhealthy practices. Emphasis on dramatized data and personal authority relies for its effectiveness on manipulating the audience's transferences. Freud said that one should never underestimate people's inner irresolution and their craving for authority, that is, their readiness for submissive transference. Analysts are not exempt from this generalization; if anything, the anxiety-arousing aspects of therapeutic work make us vulnerable to these transferential manipulations, thus the advantages of having been treated in depth ourselves. The therapist's transferences aside, however, we should not aspire to eliminate rhetorical persuasiveness from our debates, and we must not pretend to work with altogether unambiguous data. Consequently, it behooves us to develop our narratives as systematically and persuasively as possible. In this way, we can orient our audience both to the goals we are using our narratives techniques to reach and to what these goals require us to certify as significant facts, plausible arguments, and noteworthy results.

Once the system is in place, it takes precedence over new, apparently discrepant findings. If Freudian theory changes, it is because in its existing form it cannot meet the challenges raised by some new findings, no matter how much these challenges are redefined in terms of the theory itself. Even then, however, the theoretical changes that are made are designed to *repair* the theory rather than replace it; they bring the theory up to date, so to speak. For example, Freud's (1914b) reconsideration of the phenomenology of psychosis launched his new systematic account of narcissism in which the role of ego instincts began to give way to libidinal contributions to ego development. It was a change that was still recognizably part of the development of Freud's system of psychoanalysis. And in turn, that theoretical change played a part in Freud's (1923a) later revision and further development of ego psychology and his introduction of the structural point of view. Still, the fundamentals remained the same: drives, defenses, conflict, infantile sexuality and amnesia, primary and secondary process, unconscious mental processes, and so forth. Theory continued to take precedence: It shaped the "data" needed to assure the theory's value as well as to broaden, deepen, and articulate it further, and in some cases to help get rid of its unnecessary complications and glaring faults.

Insubstantial Analysis

Analysts are familiar with those would-be analysands who, though they lie on the couch five times a week and talk at length, hardly ever associate freely. Only occasionally do they hear the analyst's interventions as anything but criticism, exploitation, or guidance. And they seldom seem to accept the idea that thoughts, feelings, and behavior can be interpreted neutrally as having crucial, unconsciously conflictual libidinal and aggressive meanings. These are meanings that must be, on the one hand, traced back to the past and, on the other, shown to have entered into every significant, real or imagined interaction with the analyst. Only then will they be *analytic* meanings.

Given that these would-be analysands have the requisite intelligence and mental intactness for analysis, their unresponsiveness to analysis must be understood as a manifestation of a stand-pat strategy that is too powerful to be dealt with analytically. By standing pat, they are indicating that, unconsciously, the analysis and the prospect of personal change constitute too much of a danger situation for them. They are unprepared to tolerate the ambiguity, the open-endedness, and the plain distress of the free-associative atmosphere with both its progressive and its regressive pressures. Analysts say finally of those who take this position unyieldingly that they are unanalyzable.

Often it is these would-be analysands who break off the analysis; sometimes the analyst must do so. Sometimes, however, the analyst maintains the analytic format, correctly or incorrectly, in the belief that it gives much-needed support to a fragile personal integration. Such instances are likely to be static, insubstantial, pseudoanalytic relationships that may continue for many, many years. On the one hand, this static nature may be a manifestation of an unanalyzable, ambivalent, dependent transference, or perhaps of sugar-coated, exploitative, sadomasochistic collusions into which the analyst has entered. On the other hand, however, it may be a manifestation of the analyst's judiciously arrived-at understanding of the would-be analysand's primitive needs for support through frequent contact in an analytic format. Thus it is not easy to distinguish competent from incompetent procedure, though it is all too easy for third parties to become hypercritical despite their inadequate evidential base.

Other would-be analysands' unresponsiveness takes a form that is not blatant. Manifestly accommodating themselves to the analyst's need to go on as if doing analysis, they play at the part of analysand. Latently, however, their appearing to fall in with the analyst's interventions gets to be recognized as a means of warding the analyst off:

Ready compliance is usually an unconvincing response to the analyst's interventions.

The danger of successful analytic pretense becomes particularly great when the analyst departs from the reserved Freudian model and becomes overactive and personally obtrusive. I am referring to those analysts who insistently confront, clarify, and interpret, no matter what is considered: the transference, defensiveness, the patient's current life outside the analysis, the infantile past, or some combination of these. The overactive analyst believes that sooner or later this inevitably obtrusive way of working must be effective. There are many reasons why an analyst may hold this belief in the ultimate triumph of interpretation, among them narcissistic strivings for omnipotent mastery, guilty emphases on reparation, and intolerance of feelings of boredom or helplessness. Analysts with these problems may then rationalize overactivity on the basis of some sort of questionable theoretical and technical dogmatism, such as the centrality of early infantile experience and the patient's need for contact or "holding." It does not help these analysts make a strong case when they point out that the verbal content of their interventions seems to be of a conventional analytic sort and seems to be corroborated by the analysand's responses. A one-sided attempt at analysis does not qualify as a Freudian analytic dialogue. It is correctly regarded as a miscarriage of analysis, what I call one kind of pseudoanalysis.

Many or most analyses, of course, include periods that give the appearance of pseudoanalysis; these are periods during which the analysand implicitly draws a line on further insight and change or the analyst falls behind the analysand's progress. However, so long as they are no more than intermittent periods of analysis, they do not justify the designation "pseudoanalysis" or "insubstantial." But not all pseudoanalysis is ascribable to the analysand's analytic limitations. All too often it is the ill-equipped analyst who promotes pseudoanalysis by dealing inadequately with transference and its allied defensive measures. It may be that this analyst's emotional limitations require him or her to work at too great a distance from the emotional immediacy of the here-and-now transference relationship and situation. In these instances, the analytic pair will collude unconsciously to maintain the appearance that they are engaged in analysis.

Fuller discussions of the part played by analysands in developing insubstantial analysis can be found in the extensive literature on resistance; the part played by analysts, in the extensive literature on disruptive countertransference. Here I intend only to begin drawing the contrast between psychoanalysis and pseudoanalysis and to suggest that it is a topic that deserves careful reflection and investigation.

Before turning to psychotherapy as the third major designation, it would be well to juxtapose insubstantial and wild analysis, the subvarieties of pseudoanalysis. In many instances, insubstantial analysis may not be all that different from wild analysis. What the two may share is a disregard of the analysand's defensive operations. This disregard may be most evident in those instances when the analyst is busily interpreting or knowingly attempting to "break through" or defeat "resistance." It may still be the case that the patient is warding off these interpretations, too, doing so perhaps by superficial accommodation that the analyst fails to recognize. The analyst is being wild in that he or she is interpreting *at* an unprepared patient and not talking *to* a truly collaborative one. The problem may persist even after the analyst recognizes that the patients is only being accommodating and interprets *that* to the patient. As I said, these would-be analysands may have to hear almost everything in a fixed way, including these new interpretations of defensiveness, and thereby remain able to block dreaded insight and basic change.

As Freud (1910a) emphasized in his discussion of wild analysis and in many other places as well, someone may know something intellectually and yet not know it in the transforming way that is characteristic of analytic insight. Interpreting *at* an unprepared patient conveys analytic content that is dead and, most likely, deadening. Freud was saying that interpretation cannot do anything and everything. That this is so amounts to one more important reason why analysis is to be thought of as a matter of degree: The analyst always and necessarily finds out how far and in which ways each analysand will be able to use the best of interpretations (see Freud, 1937b).

PSYCHOTHERAPY

There seems to be no limit on the ways in which psychotherapy can be practiced. Even psychoanalytic psychotherapy—our present concern—comes in many flavors. We encounter in this respect a formidable obstacle to discussing psychoanalytic psychotherapy in relation to psychoanalysis. With so much variation, it makes no sense to set up a hypothetical or ideal norm. Such a norm can still be set up for Freudian analysis, as I have done earlier in this chapter, despite the variations in that sphere of practice.

As I indicated earlier, nothing necessarily stops the psychotherapist from working analytically and well. By this I mean that the psychotherapist can maintain a neutral, consistent, but unpressuring focus on transference and countertransference and defensive measures, both in the here and now and in relation to their origins and transformations over the course of a lifetime. And nothing necessarily and totally prevents the patient in this context from associating relatively freely; working on dreams, daydreams, transferences, and defenses; developing some elements of a transference neurosis; and developing some important insights on the basis of limited change and then changing further and perhaps profoundly. On this basis, and provided that they are not time-limited, the therapist and patient may get a good deal of analytic work done even when they meet twice a week and face-to-face. This effect is more likely to be achieved when the patient is someone who could be in analysis were it not for life circumstances that preclude that arrangement.

Such an effect is far less likely to be achieved when the patient will accept only a more structured and limited format despite the fact that life circumstances do not preclude a conventional Freudian analysis and despite the therapist's best efforts to resolve the difficulty through interpretation. In this instance, the patient's unyielding decision to limit the work, sometimes just by refusing to use the couch, is most likely to signify quite desperate defensiveness, possibly involving significant paranoid tendencies. In any case it will be based on anxiety, guilt, fragility, or rigidity, and most likely also based on environmentally supported patterns of gratification and protection that the patient wishes to keep hidden from the therapist's scrutiny. No one can say with confidence that such patients are ill-advised to set these limits on the therapy.

Now, suppose we take into account all the factors I have mentioned. Suppose that analysis is always a matter of degree, that much of what passes for analysis is pseudoanalysis, that some psychotherapy is very like analysis proper, and so forth: Why not just call any psychoanalytic psychotherapy *psychoanalysis*? Recognizing that psychoanalyses themselves vary in effectiveness, where could we draw the line between them and comparable psychotherapies? I believe that there are two major reasons for retaining the distinction between psychoanalysis and psychotherapy, even though many cases seem to fall in an ill-defined intermediate area.

First, the aggregate of Freudian theories requires that some such distinction be drawn. If most or all of the traditional conditions of psychoanalysis are not being met, it is unlikely that the therapy will achieve the altered and facilitative mode of functioning required of both participants. This altered mode of functioning has been described in various ways. One way of putting it is that the participants cannot achieve enough of the required, sustained shift toward a more dreamlike or primary process mode of functioning. At best, they will only sample this mode; at worst, they will simulate it by dint of much intellectualization and more or less wild analysis. Only to a limited degree will the analyst be able to establish a fluidly receptive and responsive mode of participation in which listening predominates. As for the patient, he or she will not have the frequent and regular opportunity, the safety, and the situational pressure that promote shifts toward those more primitive forms of self-expression that provide access to unconsciously persisting, infantile, conflictual material. Then the phenomena and the results of the process cannot be quite the same, and the problems of interpretation and working through cannot be identical. And if the same is true of some analyses, then it would be better to recognize a border zone or gray area between the two approaches than to collapse the distinction entirely. Better for what or for whom? Better for analysts who should be paying attention to the degrees of analysis achieved in their psychoanalyses proper, and on that basis better for all their current and future patients.

In this perspective, psychoanalytic psychotherapy might be characterized as another form of limited or incomplete analysis. It is limited or incomplete not just in the sense that, with respect to a hypothetical ideal, every analysis is, but because the design of the therapy must lead to different expectations of the process. I do not question that psychoanalytic therapy can be enormously helpful. What must be recognized is that any combination of reduced frequency and continuity; face-to-face work; the therapist's more active, discussionlike participation; and other departures from the traditional psychoanalytic format militate against the process being the same as traditional analysis.

From this point of view, I am critical of certain psychoanalytic psychotherapists for being overambitious. Out of too much therapeutic zeal and inadequate appreciation of the rationale of the psychoanalytic method, these psychotherapists decide—recklessly, I would say—to get as much conventional analytic work done as possible. I say "reckless" in that they do not take seriously the constraints imposed by departures from the traditional psychoanalytic format and its rationale. Instead, they freely and hurriedly make ostensibly analytic interpretations on the basis of whatever cues come up. Frequently they engage in interpretation of manifest dream or fantasy content, of incidental expressions of attitude by word or deed, of unprocessed reports of life historical experience, and of other such material. In these respects, they are behaving in the same way as the practitioner of wild time-limited therapy.

A more subtle but equally problematic form of wildness may be practiced by the psychotherapist who, on the basis of a diagnostic appraisal of severe ego weakness, recommends a face-to-face therapy rather than a psychoanalysis, and from then on presents the patient with an extremely reserved, noninterventionistic, pseudoanalytic posture. In so doing, this therapist may leave the patient to flounder unproductively and often quite painfully and self-destructively. It is as if this therapist (usually male, in my experience) has decided that he at least will behave "analytically" even though the patient cannot, reasoning that it is better for at least one of them to proceed "correctly" than for neither of them to do so. I would call this conduct wild in that it adopts an inappropriate analytic approach to a patient who cannot be prepared for it.

Decisions are not always easy to make in this respect. Certain psychotherapy patients seem to do best if they are left pretty much on their own. These patients tend to get paranoid or depressed if, as they experience it, they are invaded and demeaned by conventional therapeutic interventions.

Many instances of psychotherapy meet few, if any, of the criteria for psychoanalysis. In these cases, we should not even speak of psychoanalytic psychotherapy. An example is when the therapist deliberately and manifestly meets needs, such as those for advice, reassurance, relief of ignorance; introduces personalized comments; and explicitly accepts severe limits on exploration and disclosure. It is also the case when the patient cannot enter into the free-associative atmosphere and when the patient's conception of the entire process thoroughly excludes exploration and interpretation of psychic reality. If analysts are providing this form of therapy, they will still be guided by psychoanalytic considerations so far as possible; in such cases it follows only that the analysts practice supportive therapy, not that it is psychoanalytic therapy.

There is a second reason to maintain the distinction between analysis proper and psychoanalytic therapy. This reason concerns training and professional standards. If the distinction is abandoned, what is to stop someone who has undergone a limited form of psychoanalytic therapy from claiming to have been analyzed and to have met the requirements for analyzing others, often then using the couch, free association, and frequent sessions in the attempt? Those who deny the distinction would perhaps say, "What does it matter, as long as he or she has had an analytic experience?" Again, the Freudian analyst would be required to fall back on the aggregate of Freudian theories and say that, in all likelihood, the therapist is not optimally prepared to conduct full-scale analyses in the modern manner.

CONCLUDING REMARKS

In conclusion, I emphasize that the fundamental factor determining what is to be called analysis, pseudoanalysis, and psychoanalytic psychotherapy is the analyst's understanding: specifically, his or her understanding of the kind of dialogue that is being carried on in the consulting room and his or her understanding of the mutative effects and the limits of this dialogue. Often, perhaps typically, this understanding develops only over the course of the work. That this is so is entirely consistent with the set of general and specific theories of psychoanalysis, for psychoanalysis is the basic discipline of finding out in depth. Among other things, it is a way of finding out in each individual case what can be found out, what is being found out, what is beyond understanding and influence, and what, after all is said and done, must remain undecidable.

Not that "finding out" is merely a matter of common sense; rather, it is primarily a matter of adhering more or less systematically to the master narratives we subscribe to, as we show by following the storylines laid down by these master narratives. In practice, the tension is always between finding out in the empirical sense and looking for the factors that fit our narrative expertise; that is, between on the one hand uncovering, discovering, and recovering, and on the other hand constructing the interpretations that are appropriate to our methods and narrative preparedness.

CHAPTER 17

Narrating Psychotherapy

I. TALKING TO PATIENTS

Talking to patients is a resource that, in my observation, psychoanalytically oriented psychotherapists neither draw on as often nor employ as masterfully as they should. Of the many reasons for this limitation, I emphasize only one now—the psychotherapists have uncritically fashioned their therapeutic activity in terms of the so-called psychoanalytic model. According to this model, psychoanalysts limit themselves to making interpretations; otherwise, they remain as nondirective as possible. They neither instruct nor speak personally because they believe that instructing their patients will intensify their resistances by encouraging them to intellectualize and, further, that speaking personally or emotionally will contaminate the analysis of the transference. Those who rely on this model reveal an inexact understanding of the subtle and complex rhythms in a psychoanalyst's work: nondirectiveness and active curiosity, laissez-faire and forcefulness, neutrality and emotionality.

Yet even from this corrected model we might safely draw only one guideline: Psychotherapists will usually facilitate exploration mostly by listening thoughtfully and intervening mainly when they can impartially point out and perhaps interpret those expressions of major conflict that become clear in the conscious and preconscious communications they receive. Although I do not question the value of this guideline, I do want to stress that by honoring in this way the artificial and inappropriate psychoanalytic model, psychotherapists have not systematically considered the resource of talking to patients and, therefore, have not yet understood, tested, and mastered this technique.

In the following account of psychotherapeutic work, I describe and explain two major aspects of talking to patients: talking pedagogically and talking personally. Both are aimed at facilitating investigation and refining understanding. They are not, in my opinion, universally applicable. As I have found them especially useful when doing time-limited therapies, I refer mainly to those therapies, although I believe that my suggestions apply more broadly than that.

TALKING TO PATIENTS PEDAGOGICALLY

Psychotherapists never start from the beginning with any patient. They already know a great deal about all patients prior to acquiring any factual information about each one. They know a lot about the psychological development and existence of human beings of both sexes. Even in an opening statement the therapist could—though rarely would—impart to a patient all sorts of things about her or him. Yet therapists would not on that account necessarily be offering gratuitous remarks; that is, universals that, because they fit everybody, communicate nothing, however much they might impress the recipient.

For one thing, few people will know as much as psychotherapists do about these "universal" factors and their interrelationships; in this matter, most patients are as amateurs to professionals. Second, when patients are working within the realm of their greatest conflicts, they are hardly likely to maintain intact and consciously available the knowledge they do have; they cannot be expected to keep their trials and tribulations consistently in perspective. Third, we must grant that the fact that something is believed to be universal does not render it insignificant; for example, it is universal, relevant, and significant that all people need oxygen to live and that all adults were once children, and it may be very much to the point to emphasize these propositions in certain therapeutic or other contexts. And, finally, we know that, to the extent that they are neurotic, patients are locked into static existential positions as a result of their having closed off large portions of their world of subjective experience. On this account they are always decidedly ambivalent about reducing their emotional hardships; they see that change as requiring them to modify their valuations and their categories of understanding and to resume, after so long a time, the personal development they have viewed as so dangerous. The business of psychotherapists is to help patients understand and master their chronic fears of pleasure, change, and development, and their preferred ways of coping with these fears, in order to live in subjective and objective worlds more open but not as unstable than those they have settled for. Incidentally, these few points about knowledge and change convey some of the insights available to psychotherapists before beginning therapy with any patient.

Psychotherapeutic knowledge of the patient is both general and specific. *General* knowledge includes:

1. The *complexity* of human problems: the place in these problems of "mixed feelings" and multiple perspectives, especially with respect to the psychotherapy itself.

2. The *continuity* of these problems: the idea that one repeats them throughout one's life, including in psychotherapy, however consciously painful they may be.

3. Their *coherence:* the usual relationships among problematic situations, experiences, and actions that the patient is likely to isolate from each other in her thinking.

4. The *significance of fantasies,* both fearful and wishful, mostly unconscious in their archaic and most threatening aspects, and usually sexual or aggressive, or both, and simultaneously self-directed and other-directed.

5. The *significance of defense,* especially patients' readiness to overestimate the extent to which independent conscious reasoning about their major psychological problems can be consistently objective and influential.

Specific pretherapeutic knowledge includes the various problematic modes of responding emotionally that are regularly associated with certain types of events or certain periods of life. On the basis of this knowledge, psychotherapists are able to say a good deal about any past or present absence or extremeness of these modes of action or reaction. In those common instances, they are far from being limited to puzzlement and the asking of questions. Therapists have knowledge of: various forms of desire, frustration, fear, aspiration, and rage that occur regularly during specific phases and typical circumstances of development; the pervasive importance of self-esteem, anxiety, and guilt; inescapable fears of loss and the prevalence of strangulated grief; and the many developmental conflicts surrounding the questions of masculine versus feminine, passive versus active, and success versus failure—whatever these words are understood to mean in specific cases and whatever the master psychoanalytic narratives they employ in their work.

I cannot overemphasize that in doing brief exploratory psychotherapy, therapists are working at a decided disadvantage—as are the patients—because on the one hand the patients are usually relatively unprepared for psychotherapy, while on the other hand only a short time and a limited number of visits are available in which to achieve any insight and consolidate any change. It is important that psychotherapists not be pressured by these facts into acting hurriedly—such as engaging in wild analysis to "get results." Nevertheless, it may be argued that under the circumstances, and *always following the narrative leads patients provide,* therapists can offer their patients some helpful instruction in the work to be done. By offering instruction, I do not mean delivering an orientation lecture; nor do I mean producing a set of demonstrations. Rather, I mean leading patients to appreciate those vantage points most likely to be useful in considering the problems they present. Their "instruction" can extend a patient's sense of relevance, grasp of the kinds of questions that must be asked about personal problems, and access to the kinds of information it will take to answer these questions productively.

Let me put it another way: Must patients in brief psychotherapy discover for themselves everything about the conduct of their own treatments? Must they shape every aspect of the work? Will their own sense of autonomy and their own conflict-revealing way of shaping the treatment still not have adequate scope even after their psychotherapists have offered their pedagogic efforts? I am confident that their problems will emerge with some clarity, especially in the form of engaging in defensive operations and enacting transference, so long as psychotherapists remain genuinely receptive to these responses. We may also expect that patients will feel no disrespect in these pedagogic efforts beyond what they would inevitably feel in connection with any of their therapists' actions, such as silences, questions, and authoritative pronouncements.

Consider, too, that effective exploration requires a framework of security based on both a working relationship with a nonjudgmental psychotherapist and some grasp of the nature of the work to be done. The patient never feels more alone than at the beginning of psychotherapy and is never more in need of some kind of bridge to the therapist in order to stop perseveratively defending against the dangers of self-exploration in the presence of an enigmatic stranger. The psychotherapist's imparting some general and specific knowledge about the patient, sharing some insights, and doing so in a way that can be genuinely empathic: These are means of both educating the patient and securing his or her position within the therapy.

Consequently, these efforts may help launch a brief psychotherapy auspiciously. It may be only on this basis that patients who initially are shy, guarded, doubt-ridden, or otherwise "shut in" or "bogged down" will be able to begin the work productively.

Each of these insights is an introduction to understanding rather than a well-developed understanding. Before it can be very useful, it will have to be detailed and qualified in terms of subjective experience and overt behavior, both in the past and in the present.

A representative list of these insights: "It's frustrating to be always looking after a lot of younger brothers and sisters." "A defeat like that is bound to be depressing." "A girl can't be indifferent to her parents' getting divorced." "It's the kind of guilt that you'd never want to admit to yourself." "People often find it disturbing to get sexually excited beyond a certain point and so they deny that they are excited at all—even to themselves." "You couldn't have always despised your father." "If you got that depressed over it, you could have been quite angry but unable to face that fact." "There's probably some connection between your guardedness with me and your general mistrust of people." "Your mother sounds like the kind of woman who would burden her children with the feeling that they have to protect her mental stability or else feel terribly guilty." "Your beginning to menstruate must have been filled with meaning for you."

In one way, statements of this sort say a good deal. They may even be so threatening to the patient that, in particular cases, psychotherapists will be well advised to refrain from speaking out in this manner, at least for a long time. And yet they may still be characterized as introductory, for the psychotherapist is not saying flatly that they apply to the patient or, insofar as they do, just *how* they apply in his or her case—how intensely, predominantly, conflictually, consciously, or consequentially, with respect to specific situations. In our role as psychotherapist, we think about such things while listening; in saying them aloud, we are literally thinking aloud. And yet thinking aloud is not the same as presciently saying "You are thus and so"; "This means thus and so"; "The important connection is this one"; "The crucial context in your past is that one."

At this point, the following question might be raised: What happens when a patient—say, a female—says that this imparted information does not apply to her? In other words, what if she will not be instructed? The answer, simply, is that the therapist—say, another female—stands her ground, the ground she truly believes she knows on the basis of her training, experience, general understanding, and, most important, her immediate self-awareness. If nothing else, she does know what she thinks, even if it is only that she is confused and does not know what to think. In standing her ground, she does not, of course, twist her patient's arm for a confession. But in some useful way she might say that she finds the patient's disclaimer surprising, and she might surmise that perhaps the patient has some need to deny to the therapist and even to herself that she feels a certain way or has a certain expectation or aspiration. Alternatively, the therapist might say there must be some other factors peculiar to the patient's situation that would help account for her being different in this respect. Or she might say a number of other things to continue the dialogue, or she might just wait silently while the patient continues to resonate to her initial remarks. No matter whether the patient agrees, disagrees, elaborates, disgresses, or flounders in uncertainty, it is likely that her reaction can be construed in a way that further defines the best questions and answers for this treatment. And it is always possible that the patient will go on to bring out another, perhaps altogether unsuspected factor that becomes the one to work on. This factor will be a welcome correction of the psychotherapist's surmise. I must emphasize in this connection that there is all the difference in the world between thinking aloud and being a know-it-all. Actually, the know-it-all's insecurity, vanity, and impatience will preclude the development of any sustained and deeply felt therapeutic dialogue. As in so many other connections, a respectful, collaborative attitude makes many difficult things possible.

In effect, I am describing one version of an approach recommended by Anna Freud (1936) in a discussion of child analysis. She suggested that the child analyst, not having the free associations of adult analysts to work with, looks for the distortion or absence of the expected affective responses as equivalent material on which to base his or her interpretations. The brief psychotherapist must adapt to a similar limitation in a similar way.

I have mentioned that taking this approach entails risks. The chief risk, of course, is that of encouraging patients to intellectualize. Additionally, therapists have to worry about stimulating a general intensification of the frightened patients' defensiveness through forewarning them of what is yet to come as well as seeming to demand tacitly that it *must* come if the patients are to prove themselves "good patients." Further, there is the risk of the therapists' imposing their thoughts on the patients or blocking or muddying the spontaneous development of their material. We must also consider a seduction to collaboration, a seduction that may erotize the work and obscure the patients' hostile reactions to it. And then there is the risk of intensifying the patients' idealizations of the psychotherapist as omniscient. All these risks endanger the prospects of the patient's understanding and later acting on what often proves to be indicated—the need for a more intensive and extended psychotherapy.

Earlier I mentioned that thinking aloud serves both as a supportive personal bridge and an illuminating pedagogic introduction or guide to exploratory psychotherapy. But there are other sides to thinking aloud that may advance the therapeutic work. For example, it conveys an unambiguous offer to share the work of exploration, and it establishes a suitably provisional or tentative mood for the therapy. Far from being consigned to the role of a passive object by psychotherapists eliciting information from them and then directing statements at them, patients are invited to join the therapist in discovering and framing the statements that might make a therapeutic difference to them. In this there is something that counteracts or exposes defensive passivity, ingratiating compliance, and extravagant idealization; there is also something in it that tends to make future, more ambitious therapeutic efforts increasingly understandable and acceptable to them.

And, with regard to seduction, I would ask whether it is more than the limited seduction Freud (1913, especially pp. 139–141) recommended when he advised building a positive working transference before attempting very much in the way of definite interpretation. Although it is true that a psychoanalysis, unlike a brief therapy, provides the time and opportunity to analyze the erotic overtones of this seduction, I do not think that psychoanalysts usually spend much time on this part of the work; it is so much more urgent, fruitful, and time-consuming to attempt to analyze the inevitable and basic infantile erotic transference and the defenses against it, factors that remain influential up to the very end of the psychoanalysis. Consequently, we should be careful not to exaggerate the risk to brief psychotherapy of a patient's reacting, probably unconsciously, with some erotic excitement to the invitation to therapeutic collaboration.

In offering these introductory insights, psychotherapists manifest both their expertise and their ignorance. They need not touch their fingertips, gaze at the ceiling, and ostentatiously muse aloud, seminar-style. They should not gun down their patients psychologically with rapid-fire, decisive interpretations; the offers they make should be offers than can be refused. As a rule they will avoid extended clarifications of their and the patient's roles in the therapy; instead, they will mainly wait for the anxious questions and disrupted communication that will give them a chance to demonstrate in action, through their steadfastness and curiosity and preliminary understanding, what it is to work with a psychotherapist and how the roles of the participants are as much the preoccupation of therapy as they are its framework. And, finally, they will not engage in those hasty, indiscriminate, presumptuous, "soupy," and frightened attempts to be empathic that some psychotherapists, especially novices, make with the hope of achieving quick, forceful, and comfortable therapeutic relationships. A solid therapeutic relationship is hard to develop and is arrived at in unanticipated ways; its goodwill can never be altogether counted on. It certainly cannot be described as the psychotherapist's being steadily and comfortably at one with the patient; tensions and lapses of contact are bound to occur. I return briefly to the topic of empathy in the next section.

The point of emphasis in any psychotherapy is the importance of patients' developing some skill in conducting their own continuing investigations of their lives and, through learning and identification, doing so with a constructive, self-supportive attitude. Certainly patients will almost always intellectualize and idealize to some extent, and probably they will be stimulated to intellectualize and idealize even more by the psychotherapist's utilizing pedagogic moves. But if therapists are not extremely interested in intellectualization or being idealized, and if their instructive comments make exploration more possible and thus more secure and informed, then their instructive efforts will promote change through understanding at least as much as they will create barriers to it. Probably more. The conduct of therapy, it must be borne in mind, is always a matter of weighing one thing against another and making complex, not altogether certain, choices. Claiming to know the one way that is the right way and the one interpretation that is *the* interpretation has no place in sophisticated and responsible work. There is too much we do not yet understand.

TALKING TO PATIENTS PERSONALLY

In many psychotherapies, therapists do not make enough use of speaking personally to the patient. Although it is easy to say that the type and degree of the therapist's "self-expressiveness" has to be suited to each patient's needs and tolerance, we do not know very much about making these estimates and adjustments. For too long we have been content automatically to use a fundamentally *impersonal* diction: It seems so safe and effective, so tried-and-true. But working *only* in that way no longer seems adequate to the variety of situations we encounter or arrange. Certainly being compelled to work in that way should be a cause for concern.

Next, taking as our model now a male therapist working with a male patient, we may ask, "What is the difference between the psychotherapist's saying to his patient 'You are not making yourself clear' and 'I don't understand you'?" There is no doubt more than one difference, but the one I want to emphasize is that the first intervention sets the therapist apart from and above the patient as his judge, however benign. Speaking thus from on high, he brackets himself off from a true interaction. It hardly captures the difference to which I am referring to think of it, in Phyllis Greenacre's phrase, as a "tilted relationship" (1954, p. 674). In this connection Harry Stack Sullivan's (1940) preferred response to a psychotic patient's disclosure of a hallucination might be recalled: "I don't see it" rather than "It isn't there." Sullivan viewed speaking personally as the therapeutic response of choice. I believe that therapists should speak personally in some measure in all psychotherapy. Such behavior supports every patient's speaking of and for himself while at the same time it clarifies that there are difficulties in the way of his doing so. The fact that the therapist freely makes certain personal declarations enables both therapist and patient to engage each other beneficially in the task.

The same difference in interaction obtains between the psychotherapist's saying "You must have felt awful" and simply saying "How awful!" A therapist could not have uttered the first response genuinely without having previously or simultaneously responded in the "how awful" way. Why, then, should the therapist bracket him- or herself off by referring only to how the patient "must have" felt? This customary form of empathizing is inherently uncertain, overcautious, or condescending, and its effect is to create undesirable distance in the therapeutic relationship. Therapists detach themselves even more questionably when they simply ask "How did you feel?" upon hearing one of the terrible things therapists so often hear from their patients—or one of the thrilling things they sometimes hear. It does not explain the bracketing-off response to point out that horror stories and thrilling stories are often told manipulatively, for example, as plainly erotic or masochistic seductions or subtle attacks on the therapist. If it is clear that they are being told in such a way, psychotherapists can say so (if they decide to say anything at that point); if it is not clear enough, they will have time to get to it, perhaps in not more than a few minutes. They do not compromise their position by responding simply and directly to these grim or gratifying accounts, and there is no sound basis for their losing their poise upon discovering that they have been "had." Why should they? Indeed, how have they been "had"? Were they so thrilled with their previous empathic response? Were they unusually overidentified with the patient? Were they falling back on the same defenses as the patient? Do they pride themselves on being absolutely unmanipulable or unfailingly correct? If any of these, all the correct therapeutic diction in the world will not save the therapy.

It is true, however, that when speaking freely in the way I mean, psychotherapists tend to experience the situation more emotionally than when speaking otherwise. At one time or another, they must expect to experience more "choking up," giddiness, irritability, anxiety, and other emotional responses than they are used to or secure with. This significant, unsettling, enriching, and perplexing complication of therapists' expressiveness deserves an extended discussion in its own right. Obviously, psychotherapists will be better able to keep their balance while interacting emotionally in this endeavor if they have had, or are having, the benefit of a personal psychoanalysis and some well-supervised professional experience.

Here are a few more illustrative contrasts: "I am wondering what that could be about" as against persistently remaining thoughtfully silent. "Congratulations!" as against "You must be very proud of yourself." "I don't feel at ease somehow and I have a hunch you are trying to get me to feel that way" as against "You are trying to make me ill at ease." "That's a helluva way to live" as against "Your life does not seem very satisfying or easy." And "I'm not surprised" as against "That might have been expected."

The statements I favor are those whereby psychotherapists speak directly to the patients. They are not telling the patients everything, of course (I know there are psychotherapists now who would challenge my "of course"); actually they are telling patients very little. They are simply saying what they might ordinarily say on the kind of occasion to which they are responding. They are speaking in ordinary good faith. Any sophisticated observer would wonder at a therapist's *not* responding in that way, at least silently or privately. After all, the expectations of response that apply to the patient, which I mentioned earlier, ought to apply in some measure to the psychotherapist as well. What I want to emphasize is that it may help the treatment considerably if psychotherapists respond aloud or publicly, that is, directly to patients. Their doing so may be all at once supportive, enlightening, and highly evocative. And by enhancing the exploratory dialogue through not placing brackets like armor around themselves, they do not preclude their monitoring the effects on them of making these approaches to intimacy and going on to regulate them if necessary. They are not in an either/or situation in this regard.

As there are many kinds of people practicing psychotherapy, there are many ways of speaking personally as well as pedagogically. I am not prescribing a specific style or language.

To say that the self-expressive remarks are introductory and incomplete is not to damn them. For example, "I am wondering about that" is basically quite noncommital and undeveloped; it must be said in a certain way to be engaging and open-ended. Essentially, the remarks I recommend differ from the others in not having been "professionalized." They have not had their evocativeness needlessly sacrificed. In speaking for and of themselves, psychotherapists establish personal presence—that quality that seems to grease the wheels of all therapies. And their being sensitively and informedly selective in what they say does not compromise the authenticity of their remarks—only the pretense of total frankness could do that.

It need not be argued here that psychotherapists may and do communicate nonverbally all the time. Their attitudes toward patients and the current material may be suggested, if not fully revealed, by tone, timing, attentiveness, mood, and so forth. Thus, a smile, a frown, a quizzical look, and the like may do some of the recommended work of personal expression in the service of investigation. But the risk of being misunderstood by a patient, which is anyway a continuous one, is increased in proportion to a therapist's reliance on nonverbal communication. Nonverbal communication is inherently more primitive, ambiguous, and fluid than words in sentences, which organize and establish a more definite record. Heavy reliance on nonverbal communication is also a way of being emotionally evasive, for, as we all know from our personal lives, we can hardly exaggerate the emotionally evocative potential of the spoken word and the dread that restricts our saying some of the things dearest to us or otherwise important to the conduct of our lives. Here again the psychotherapist is not in an either/or situation.

The idea that there is some one naturally spontaneous way of conducting oneself in any relationship is psychologically indefensible. Indeed, according to my observations, most of those psychotherapists who allegedly talk "naturally" to their patients and who might think my recommendations altogether unnecessary do not do so in the optional, selective, and investigatory sense I have suggested. Rather, they do it routinely, that is, most or all of the time with most or all of their patients. They are, in fact, relying on what I call force of personality—an eclectic mixture of interpretation, warmth, guidance, reassurance, firmness, exhortation, and other deliberate or unwitting manipulations of transference potentials. Usually they seem to be doing so in order to bring about corrective emotional experiences within the therapeutic relationship, and, if so, they tend to rationalize their actions by making the questionable assumption that the patient will transpose this experience to the rest of his or her life in a stable and satisfying way. In some instances this strategy seems to gratify the therapists' needs for excitement and activity, to allow them to engage in the vanities of the "wise man" or "guru," or simply to avoid the tensions of sustained exploratory discipline and its frustrations. It cannot be denied that this stereotyped, basically controlling, and repression-reinforcing conduct often leads to their patients' experiencing symptomatic relief. So many things do! But what it cannot lead to is the kind of insight and change that may be generated by a genuinely exploratory psychotherapy.

II. THE TERMINATION OF BRIEF THERAPY

Supervisors of brief analytic therapies cannot fail to notice how often, during the termination phase, all the gains that have been made earlier are seriously threatened, compromised, or lost. But as these developments do not invariably and automatically forecast the outcome, they cannot be written off as due merely to the superficiality of the therapy, the illusion of improvement based merely on intensified defense and transference gratifications, and the inevitable power of infantile unconscious conflict. We do, of course, expect these undoubtedly powerful limiting and regressive influences to be operative during any therapy, including psychoanalysis, and we do expect them to be difficult to define precisely and fully, and especially difficult to modify for the better in brief therapy. But merely to acknowledge these points and then suspend further inquiry and reflection is to do injustice to patients and therapists alike.

Recognizing that there are various ways of practicing brief analytic therapy, I limit myself here to the way I have practiced it and taught it. After describing that way briefly, I discuss the kind of changes it seems to bring about, the crisis that frequently develops around termination, and the problems of the therapist in dealing with this crisis. Then I return to closer examination of the changes that seem to occur, and I conclude with some remarks on the problems of validating the claims made for brief analytic therapy. It may well be that I am merely covering ground that is well known; my experience, however, is that what should be well known often is not, even in the best training centers, and that, even if it is well known, there are always further important points to be explored, clarified, or debated. My narration may make its own contribution.

BRIEF ANALYTIC THERAPY

By brief analytic therapy, I mean therapy in which the patient is seen individually, once a week, for about fifty minutes, in face-to-face verbal interchange that is focused on the patient's difficulties in his or her life in general and in the therapy in particular; and I mean therapy that continues for some months, perhaps for as long as a year. Such therapy is more or less clearly time-limited, as is often the case in clinics and other institutional settings and also in private work due to limited funds or motivation or rapid increase of defensiveness once some relief is experienced and the prospect of deeper involvement looms (Ernst Prelinger, personal communication).

In this therapy the therapist—say, a woman—tries to establish as much of an exploratory or investigative atmosphere and discipline as possible. She is particularly alert to signs that the patient is having emotional difficulty in the therapeutic relationship. I mean especially difficulty of the sort that entails anxiety, guilt, or shame and the evident withholding, circumventing, or dissimulating of certain experiences on account of these relational difficulties. In other words, the therapist pays special attention to manifestations of conflict, defense, and transference. Mainly she indicates this attentiveness in the form of noting aloud and perhaps raising questions about these manifestations. In this regard, sexual and hostile feelings and dependent feelings are touched on or alluded to or named directly, along with anxiety, guilt, and shame. The pace, directness, and persistence of these interventions are regulated by considerations of tact, anxiety tolerance, the patient's reaction (as it can be reasonably surmised) to these interventions, and other considerations familiar from classical psychoanalytic technique.

Often the approach is indirect, following displacements and other detours. There is no hurry to explain anything, either in terms of current life issues or in terms of genetic antecedents, as what matters most is the drawing out of unarticulated, undeveloped phenomena and especially the difficulties in the way of that articulation and communication. The patient—say, a man—is helped to describe what his life is like for him—especially along the lines made familiar by psychoanalysis, as mentioned above. Elaborate or far-reaching interpretations usually are not be attempted. A kind of psychoanalytically informed phenomenology is developed. When the patient raises practical questions, such as requests or demands for advice or intervention in his outside life or even in his conduct in the sessions, the therapist generally encourages reflection on the nature, implications, and background of, or reasons for, the request or the dilemma to which they pertain, or reflection on the feelings that accompany those requests and demands, or the feelings of the therapist they seem designed to stir up or play upon. But in so doing, she remains flexible and does not attempt to play out in full the "incognito" of the clinical psychoanalyst, itself often exaggerated both within and outside the field of psychoanalysis.

Ordinarily, psychotherapy of this sort requires a patient who is reasonably intelligent, capable of some reflectiveness, able to verbalize, and not acutely psychotic or agitatedly near the edge of psychosis or in an extreme life crisis in which family, community, or legal figures are active. In other words, it requires a patient who ideally should be—or at least could be—in analysis but who, for whatever reason, will not or cannot undertake analysis. Typically, such patients complain of inability to work or enjoy work, uncertainty or moderate despair about their course in life, neurotic symptoms, attacks of anxiety or moderate depression, or unsatisfactory relationships with parents, peers, members of the opposite sex, children, teachers, or supervisors at work. They are people with acute psychological problems who knowingly have come for psychological therapy, although, on account of their defensiveness, they are not always equally clear about that or equally cooperative in those terms. Some borderline psychotic patients can be worked with in the way described, though often with a different mode of developing understanding—a mode I cannot elaborate on here.

CHANGES DURING EFFECTIVE THERAPY

Now, what typically happens as an effective therapy of this sort goes along? The following is a composite picture; there is considerable individual variation. What is most clear is that the patient develops a more definite and more comprehensive idea of the scope, multiplicity, and complexity of his problems. He discovers symptoms and inhibitions he never acknowledged consciously, as well as attitudes and feelings of all sorts—dread, remorse, resignation, mistrust, overweening pride, and also hopeful, tender, sentimental, compassionate, adoring, and loyal sentiments that he formerly would have blushed too much or wept too much to acknowledge. In one sense, he comes to realize more fully the extent of his illness. But, in another, he realizes the extent of his human existence, with its suffering and its possibilities, both enlarged in his subjective experience and objective view. Most of all, and especially through his examination of his problems in the therapeutic relationship, he may begin to realize something of the extent of his active participation in bringing about the difficulties that to begin with he experienced passively, such as his social isolation, his alienation from his family, his failures in sex, his poor performance at work, his dismal outlook itself. In this way, he discovers the centrality of personal conflict in his existence.

It is impressive that, as these changes take place in the patient's conception of himself, often by dint of and with the accompaniment of much suffering, he begins to feel better and to function better. His symptoms diminish in scope and persistence; his mood improves; his social and sexual relationships are enhanced. It seems that it can be a gain just to be able to recognize one's neurotic misery.

A skeptical observer of psychotherapy might easily challenge that all these changes can take place when no exploratory work of the sort I described has been undertaken or on account of factors other than the exploration itself. I do not think this challenge succeeds, however; while people do certainly get to feel and function better in response to all kinds of interventions or noninterventions, including simply being on a waiting list for therapy, the terms in which they are better and in which they view their being better and the context in which they are better vary considerably. The enlarged appreciation of activity in apparent passivity, for example, or the coexistence of enhanced suffering and doubt *and* pleasurable and effective living—all accompanied by an increased sense of meaningful conflict—is not typical, in my view, of the other types of improvement.

The test of these changes comes as termination approaches, for, as I mentioned, it then appears as if all were built on sand. Then, with the patient apparently as depressed, morose, provocative, or helplessly symptom-ridden as when the work started, the therapist may well wonder whether the patient's enlarged and active view of his life was worth anything. Much escapes understanding at this point, and where understanding fails, resentment flourishes. The therapist may then justify her negative countertransference as appropriate to the passive aggression of the patient or to his masochism or negative therapeutic reaction. She may blame the superficiality of the therapy. She may develop inclinations to extend the therapy; clearly, she rationalizes, it is too early to stop; a few more sessions beyond the cutoff date should turn the trick. Or she may determine that now, finally, she must replace or at least greatly modify her neutral investigative approach with a display of personal feeling; that will save the day . . . she hopes. Here are all the signs of a relationship and a job in crisis; some serious sorting out of issues and assumptions is necessary in order to avoid the kind of cruelty in failure that marks the course of such crises and their attempted resolution.

THE THERAPIST'S POSITION AT TERMINATION

The therapist is observing a regression, of course. It is very similar to the regressions repeatedly observed by the classical analyst in ongoing, effective analyses, and as such it is by no means a cause for despair. Like everything else in treatment, rightly construed, the regression teaches something about the current difficulties of the patient and their history. It helps matters considerably if the therapist does not falter at this point but continues the work of investigation. Among other things, at least in her own thinking, she must keep track, as best she can, of the various oral, anal, and phallic meanings that the patient attributes to termination (for example, being weaned abruptly, being put down in disgust or pushed away in horror for being too "instinctual" or "animal"), together with the defenses against recognizing these meanings and the feelings associated with them. In order for this to occur, however, the therapist's own narcissistic investment in therapeutic results must be of a certain sort and not go beyond a certain point in intensity. Above all, she must realize that her ideal should be to do the best she can and not necessarily to get "results." I shall discuss this further later.

But more than a narcissistic demand for "cure" is at issue here. It is during termination that all the unspoken promises, expectations, transferences, and defenses on the part of both persons in the therapeutic relationship may come to light: all their fundamental assumptions about illness and human existence, and about the role and duty and merit of therapists as well as their satisfaction and pride in their work; and all the collusions by which issues were skirted during the therapy. All are asserted in such various and devious ways that patient and therapist can easily be bewildered and disheartened. The objective assessment of change, of the course of the work and of its reasonable prospects, then suffers considerably.

Among the problems that emerge is that of facing the limitations of what therapy can do. These limitations concern the therapist in quite a powerful personal way. Through them she must recognize that her effectiveness as a healer is quite limited, which means that important narcissistic ideas about herself and ideals for herself are seen to be forcefully contradicted by experience. The roots of these ideas and ideals lie in infantile fantasies of omnipotence, which no one ever renounces completely. Most likely these ideas and ideals played an important part in her having chosen to become a therapist. These ideas and ideals concern valuing activity greatly over passivity (at least with regard to other people's problems!) and, in the extreme, "choosing" to be omnipotent rather than helpless, a savior rather than a destructive force, and/or a breast of infinite capacity rather than a ravenously hungry parasite. On this account, the terminating patient, who is still saddled with problems—and perhaps, through regression, with apparently accentuated problems—and who quite likely is expressing dissatisfaction with the therapist, is bound to become very much of a disappointment and threat to her. This problem is often increased by the patient's increased recognition of the extent and complexity of his problems, which seems also to be, as I mentioned, one of the beneficial achievements of the brief psychotherapy.

Because it is too complex to go into here, I only mention in passing the additional problem introduced by the therapist's reluctance to give up her relations with patients she has gotten to know and to be able to feel with and for. One of the best protections against disruptive countertransference responses to the terminating patient is a reasonable and stable sense of one's own goodness. I mean "goodness" in two senses. The first sense is goodness as a therapist in terms of having offered something good, having made a sincere effort, and having achieved some results (if that is the case) under very disadvantageous conditions—and brief psychotherapy *is* work under disadvantageous conditions. The other sense of goodness is the archaic or infantile sense that, on the whole, one is a worthwhile, benign person, whatever one's faults and limitations. Here I am in a way adapting Edith Jacobson's (1964) point about the "good but also bad mother" who constitutes the necessary constant object representation the child must achieve for his or her satisfactory development. I am also speaking of the fact that the child and, later, the therapist herself is a "good though also bad person." If the therapist's self-confidence is lacking or easily undermined in this regard, the vicissitudes of termination are bound to get to her and she is likely to intensify the crisis of termination rather than turn it to advantage.

It is in this context that all the unspoken understandings, mutual transferences, and collusions that I mentioned earlier are relevant, for they are all temporary expedients that the therapist adopted to protect her narcissistic vulnerability. For, contrary to what she may have suggested or declared, the therapist is not, cannot be, and should not try to be endlessly and totally dedicated to the ultimate welfare of particular patients. Nor is she able to effect any and all desirable changes that she may have vaguely promised, or always to feel and act with equal understanding, acceptance, and benevolence toward her patients.

The therapist requires a corresponding view of patients as "good though also bad." During crises, such as the one at termination, it is the "good," at least in the sense of hoping to become more of a person, that is so easily lost sight of by patients and therapists. And it is here where a foundation of patience and steadiness is required.

I mentioned earlier that among the possibly disruptive factors at termination are certain assumptions about illness and human existence. Many therapists, and in my view many analysts, too, do not like to face the prospect—I would call it the fact—that irrationally based or neurotic problems are not entirely eradicable by the best of therapies; that there is more to it than, as Freud put it, freeing people from neurotic miseries so that they can deal more effectively with the inescapable objective miseries of existence; that, in other words, what we call illness and what we call human existence are not sharply and clearly separable, except in textbook definitions. There is no doubt that many people can be helped by therapy to assume more stable, effective, and satisfying positions, and certainly less anguished positions. However, there is no evidence that all infantile neurotic problems are totally and finally resolvable; certainly they are not resolvable through brief therapy.

All of this has disturbing implications for therapists, for, in terminating with their—at best—partially improved patients, they must face again the prospect that their own lives are only partially improvable. Especially in the United States, I think, with its traditionally unbounded melioristic enthusiasm and expectations, this is a difficult prospect to deal with. Progress is almost a state religion. Psychotherapists must resist such naïve enthusiasm, in order to maintain the proper *scale* as well as perspective. These are essential to good work, especially during the doubt-ridden crises of termination. Perhaps, above all, psychotherapists must believe in the great difficulties in the way of significant changes and in the great value to their patients of their symptoms and other problems, however much the patients may consciously wish to be rid of them. These difficulties and the value of symptoms are among the great lessons taught by psychoanalysis.

I cannot prevent the various exaggerations and misunderstandings to which these brief remarks on a very complex and emotionally arousing subject are vulnerable, but I can go on to discuss two very important, though limited, accomplishments that not infrequently are observed in brief psychoanalytic psychotherapy. A clear conception of these changes and their value can be a powerful support against the doubts and disappointments that can fill the air during termination. Affirmations are, after all, still in order.

FURTHER REMARKS ON CHANGES DURING BRIEF THERAPY

I have already mentioned two of the changes that may occur during brief therapy: (1) the patients' recognition of the extensive and complex nature of the problems with which they are dealing; and (2) their recognition of the activity on their part that has contributed to bringing about and continues to support the existence of these problems. And I have pointed out that these changes, though burdensome and painful in some ways, seem to have a liberating and strengthening effect. I particularly emphasize the extent to which these gains depend on consistent attention having been paid during the therapy to the discomforts and disruptions of rapport and collaboration with the therapist—that is to say, to the anxieties, dishonesties, evasions, flights, and manipulations in which the patient has engaged in response to the anxieties of the therapy situation. In principle, these anxieties must be those at the core of his disorder or at least offshoots of them. These discomforts and disruptions are heightened by irregularities in the schedule of appointments, such as absences, holidays, lateness, and interruptions, and by the relative briefness of the therapy itself. They are reinforced by the therapist's role, which is, on the one hand, relatively unstructuring so far as specific topics are concerned and, on the other hand, relatively leading with regard to the focus on the phenomenology of experience, the so-called internality of the patient's existence, and especially the implications of "inner" conflict of purpose, goal, or value in what appear initially to be simply problems with a past or present unaccommodating surrounding world.

The patient is made uncomfortable by the therapist's role and the procedure it defines because they threaten his or her accustomed modes of defense and adjustment. But what *is* the procedure that is defined? In one crucial respect this procedure is an invitation and a pressure for patients to become more fully acquainted with themselves and to achieve and experience the discovery of themselves in the medium of communicating with another person. It is precisely this discovery in a medium of benign relationship that all patients, in their own ways and for their own reasons, have grown to feel hopeless about. They anticipate that the discovery will be unbearable and the disclosure of it either intolerable in itself or intolerable as the certain cause of a forthcoming traumatic response by the other person, the therapist. This hopelessness is at the core of a radical discontinuity or fragmentation of patients' knowledge about and tolerance of themselves. They have blinded themselves to themselves; they have lied to themselves about themselves; and, to maintain these blind spots and lies, they have given up both major achievements of their past lives and major possibilities in their current and future lives. They have a stake in seeing their lives as incomprehensible or chaotic, however dismaying that may be.

But now, in the therapy, with the support of the benevolent but tough-minded curiosity of the therapist, and in order to pacify the therapist and to be loved by him or her in the transference, patients begin to explore, organize, and express, whereas before they had felt it was hopeless to begin anything along that line. They *discover*—often actually rediscover—and they *connect* and *express* fear, hate, shame, desire, sentimentality, pride, aspirations, and longings. They see that these emotions do matter to them, that they are endurable, and that their difficulty with the emotions and their way of dealing with that difficulty are understandable, manageable, and revisable. At least they make a beginning in that direction. And to some extent patients see that, rather than being unique to the therapy situation, these tendencies and difficulties are virtually a distillate of chronic problems in major relationships of their lives. I cannot overemphasize that the core problems in question are not fully defined and certainly not resolved. Often patients only glimpse the problems and possible solutions. Nevertheless, something new and vital has been added: the possibility of doing something about the problems that have begun to be defined in a new and more organized and hopeful way. The redefinition itself makes activity and hope more acceptable to patients.

Thus, the hopelessness is qualified, tempered, even questioned as a premise. With that, patients can envisage the possibility of becoming more whole and understandable beings. And while at best it is only a beginning, it is a beginning that seems to make a big difference in a patient's view of the situation. Here, a little seems to go a long way, especially if the patient is still young. Though it is correct, it does not go far enough simply to say that we are observing a "realignment of defenses."* And it is not just that patients see that they have been active in bringing on their own misery, whereas they thought they had been merely passive. They see, too, that they can also be active in another way that alters their past, present, and future, all at once.

This reference to altering the past serves as transition to the second of the two additional accomplishments I said were possible through brief therapy. I should also mention transitionally another remark I made earlier: that patients' radical discontinuity and fragmentation of their knowledge about, and tolerance of, themselves may be reduced as their hopelessness is reduced. That discontinuity or fragmentation is essentially cross-sectional. The point I am leading up to is the reduction of a longitudinal or historical radical discontinuity or fragmentation. What is at stake is interrupted personal development due to the patient's having resorted to massive repression, denial, or other defense in earlier times, in order to deal with intolerable life situations. Such life situations may include the death or psychotic breakdown of a parent or sibling, severe injury or protracted illness, parental conflict and divorce, the birth of a sibling, or cruelly dishonest, exploitative, or seductive parental behavior in relation to the future patient. It is not unusual for therapy to establish that, in connection with such disruptions of life, a major relationship that was filled with feeling—good feeling as well as bad—was ostensibly broken off on the initiative of one or the other or both persons involved, and that there followed an attempt by the future patient at thoroughgoing repudiation, repression, or isolation of all that had gone before. In that predicament, a patient then rewrites his or her history: for example, "I *never* loved him," or "If I did love him, I was *deceived* and *shouldn't have,* and in any case I *don't* any more," or "It wasn't *really* love." Therapists, who are familiar with these disillusionments and disclaimers, know that they do not really work: The anguished love persists, the denied emotion is all the more threatening and painful because it is not faced and lived through, and it is all the more costly to the personality as a whole because the defense invariably necessitates a breakdown in the patient's sense of historical continuity and authenticity and restricts the kind of relationships and feelings that are tolerable from then on. Typically, this restriction means consciously avoiding relationships and feelings that are reminiscent of the repudiated ones, while unconsciously repeating endlessly the worst aspects of those very relationships and feelings.

I am thinking, for example, of several young women who had "irre-

---

*Mentioned by Anna Freud at a staff conference.

vocably" broken with their fathers, to whom they had once felt very close. In one case, the father had been seductive and exploitative; in another, cruelly depressive; and in a third, sadistically overcontrolling and paranoid. These women were now caught up in one or a series of quite unsatisfactory relationships with men who were, in fact, not unlike their fathers. As a therapist, I could not question that these three women had been much abused in one form or another. But I also could not help seeing how tied they were to these fathers and how hampered in their relationships to other men and to themselves as individuals, by their continuing repudiation of tender, admiring, hopeful, and sentimental feelings for them. Of course, ambivalence at such close quarters and of such intensity is terrible, and people just do not bear it well. During therapy in these and similar cases, it is sometimes possible to bring about some reexperiencing of the continuing positive feelings for father, mother, sibling, or self by paying particular attention to the warding-off positive feelings toward the therapist that arise in the therapy hours, especially at times of crisis, separation, and, most of all, termination.

I say "most of all, termination" because the potential for virtually every significant human emotion resides in the termination situation—assuming, of course, that the patient has formed some felt relationship with the therapist, with its inevitable transference components. The ideal termination would explore all these emotions—for example, feelings of deprivation and longing, guilt and unworthiness, gratitude and envy, triumph and defeat, love and betrayal, disappointment and elation, rage and grief—from all levels of psychosexual and ego development, insofar as they are accessible and significant. But it can be useful, within the narrow limits of brief psychotherapy, to explore one or two of them, and then only in a limited way. These feelings are or should be the ones that are most recognizable at the time, for in all likelihood they are emotions that patients can best tolerate dealing with at that time. They are not the root problems, there to be dealt with directly, though most likely they are offshoots of them.

And so therapists have an excellent opportunity to demonstrate that patients are understanding the termination in the terms of key conflicts that have been identified during the therapy; are actively and arbitrarily setting that interpretation on it; are fragmenting themselves cross-sectionally and longitudinally in so doing, just as (according to the therapy up to that point) they have done at critical junctures in the past; and thereby are again reducing the possibilities of their very being. Then gratitude, love, regrets, and sober appraisal of continuing problems are more likely to be mingled in patients' communications and are likely to be experienced and conveyed more directly than it might have seemed they could ever be when therapy began. This change may not come when expected, and it may not last more than a few moments. But, however confused and conflictual it may be and however oblique and brief, this change during termination demonstrates the effectiveness of the therapeutic work.

Often patients are able to begin to appreciate the value of long-range, perhaps more intensive therapy or psychoanalysis. They may, however, need the skillful guidance and support of the therapist before they can face and act upon their further therapeutic needs. And if they do so, then, as I mentioned in chapter 1, all this ground will be worked over in much finer detail and greater depth, quite frequently with invaluable benefit for the patients.

VALIDATION

I said earlier that I would finally discuss the problem of validation of the claims made for brief therapy. I shall not dwell on this point, for I do not know what would constitute validation other than the event itself—that is, the experience of therapy and its termination. The issue is one of historical understanding rather than reliance on any behavioral science test. If we put together the available observations and accounts of past history, plus the gist of interventions during therapy and responses to them, plus some common sense and clinical generalizations, we have a narrative understanding of what the therapy has been like for the patient and what has changed; we are guided and satisfied by criteria of intelligibility, cohesiveness, and economy of exposition along certain storylines. We also know that a life crisis has been traversed or reduced with less damage and perhaps more gain than might well have been the case without therapy, given the presenting picture. This is historical understanding.

By *validation* it might be meant proving that the therapy *always* gets results or the *same* results. As no such claim has been made, no such proof need be developed. Rather, what is claimed is that certain people more or less make certain types of gains or undergo certain types of limited change in response to this therapy.

Validation may be used in the sense of providing an answer to the question of how lasting are any of the changes or benefits that are attributed to this therapy. I think that *in principle* that question is unanswerable, for it would require another course of therapy to elicit the data necessary to answer it. How else, for example, could we ascertain that a benign identification with the "lost" therapist not only took place at termination but survived for so many months or years? And there cannot be another course of the same therapy, just as we cannot step into the same river twice, because history is irreversible; the same patient is not there to treat twice, nor is the same therapist there twice, though two people answering to the same names as before might be there. The "same" data are not available. And certainly life circumstances do not persist psychologically in exactly the same way, even if they seem the same to an outside observer. It will be a question of another story to tell. Questionnaires and interviews cannot do this job.

Or *validation* might mean proving that the changes that have occurred can justifiably be attributed to the therapy or, more ambitiously, to particular aspects of the therapy, such as the relationship, the interpretations, or even, in the extreme of ambitiousness, to *an* interpretation. Again, I think that *in principle* that question is unanswerable by the methods of behavioral science, for, rightly understood, the question itself is one of historical understanding. Good historians who share certain assumptions about method and conceptualization can agree on matters of historical understanding; so can good clinicians *in their context* and for quite similar reasons, as I have argued in chapters 9 to 12 particularly. It is that kind of truth we are dealing with. Ultimately, it is the truth of psychoanalysis, which, from the time of Freud's work on, has usually been misconstrued as that of an actual or potential behavioral science.

CHAPTER 18

Analytic Love

AMONG the writers of note in the recent history of psychoanalysis, few have a narrative voice that is immediately felt to be distinctive. Hans Loewald is one of these. Winnicott, Erikson, and Kohut are others. Because Loewald's is a distinctive voice, it does not allow us to pick over his utterances casually or to center on just one of them, thereby to elude the man himself. His voice resists appropriation through reductive synopsis and definition. Although it is consistently meditative and modest, it does what any distinctive voice does: It insists on speaking through us. As we continue to listen, it engages us in the process that Loewald has returned to again and again—the process of internalization: And, as a direct developmental consequence of internalization, it engages us in the unending process of emancipation from internalized authority.

In his now-classic paper, "On the Therapeutic Action of Psycho-Analysis" (1960), Loewald proposed that, in the course of analysis and as the more regressive transferences are analyzed and diminished, the analyst emerges as a new object for the analysand. In one way, this narrative turn is not difficult to grasp and accept, especially not these days, some thirty years and several analytic generations after Loewald ventured to publish it. We would be inclined to follow the storyline that when analysis is effective, it frees the analysand to develop toward levels of integration higher than those reached so far. This development occurs in the field of the analytic relationship. The primary and

forever influential precursor of the analytic field is the field of the
mother-infant relationship, the field in which development necessarily
and fatefully originates. In both fields, first the mother and later the
analyst represent a higher level of being, relating, and mutual definition of selves; they hold out their higher level and create a tension relative to more primitive levels, thereby giving direction and focus to
the developmental strivings of the child and, later, the patient. We
might say that they make of these relationships growth fields.
Consequently, in growing as never before, the analysand enters into
modes of relationship with another person—the analyst—that he or
she has not yet attempted, maintained, or integrated. A new kind of
relatedness is now felt to be not only possible but necessary, safe, and
gratifying. On this understanding, then, we would enter into
Loewald's narrative and agree that a new kind of significant object has
come into existence, and that, along with that object, there has come
a new self which in significant measure reflects that object's perceptions.

The analyst is a new object also in the special pattern of interests,
capacities, functions, ideas, and emotional experiences that he or she
offers to assist this growth process. Included here are the analyst's
readiness to engage in partial regressions to the analysand's response
level, when and where indicated, in order to help free up, through
understanding, empathy, and interpretation, the analysand's growth
potential. Here Loewald continued to draw parallels to (not advocate
literal copies of or replacements for) the infant's mother. And in this
connection especially, we get a clear view of Loewald's consistent and
brilliant inclusion in his narrative of the preoedipal phases of development.

Looked at historically, these were bold narratives to put forward to
the ultra-conservative Freudian audience that prevailed around 1960.
Contained in the storyline of the analyst as a new object were a number of significant modifications of the then-received Freudian theory
of psychological development and neurotic psychopathology. Loewald
was putting forth a master narrative of development in an interpersonal and experiential field: In this field drives, for example, are to be
regarded as products of differentiation rather than primary forces
that seek out objects to discharge themselves on or through. In contrast, conservative theory holds that drives bring into being relationships where, to begin with, none have existed. Loewald's precursors
and contemporaries in this connection include Sullivan, Fairbairn,
Erikson, Winnicott, Kardiner, and Heinz Hartmann (in his work on
adaptation specifically). In Loewald's narratives, drives are no longer

where we begin; they are something between a mode of experience and a developmental achievement, though they retain their propulsive role. Simultaneously, Freud's reflex-arc model of drive stimulation and discharge is thrown into question, and human beings, or the selves of human beings, emerge as social and interactive from the first. Additionally, the analytic patient is now to be viewed primarily from the vantage point of arrested development (arrested both in the interpersonal sense and the experiential sense). In a departure from Freud, the patient's ego is no longer to be regarded as a developed ego with focal areas of fixation and regression. It is only within this radically revised context that we can fully appreciate Loewald's narrative of the analyst emerging as a new object for the analysand. The easily accepted, commonsense view of a new object (for example, "finally a kind-hearted mothering person") does not do justice to Loewald's contributions.

It was in this context that Loewald went on to refer to analytic love, that is, the analyst's love for the patient. Loewald did not seem to mean heightened disruptive countertransference in the usual sense, although as he made plain in his discussion of transference, he would be the first to say that this love includes transference in relation to the patient; it includes transference in the same way that every relationship presupposes or requires transference. (Recall here Freud's [1915c] similar discussion of transference love.) Nor does it seem that he would rule out some heightening of countertransference in connection with the analyst's facilitative, technically less constrained, empathic regressions and identifications with the analysand, especially when working in the context of preoedipal issues. I believe, however, that Loewald was aiming at something more than these factors when he referred to analytic love. He approached his goal when he wrote, for example, of holding in trust the ego core or potential self of the analysand through all the trials of analysis; he approached it when he referred to the analyst's seeing the patient as more than he or she can yet conceive and thereby taking on the responsibility of safeguarding a future for that person. And he expressed his meaning in full force when he wrote the following distinctive passage:

> Scientific detachment in its genuine form, far from excluding love, is based on it. In our work it can truly be said that in our best moments of dispassionate and objective analysis, we love our object, the patient, more than at any other time and are compassionate with his whole being.
> In our field scientific spirit and care for the object flow from the

same source. It is impossible to love the truth of psychic reality, to be moved by this love as Freud was in his lifework, and not to love and care for the object whose truth we want to discover. All great scientists are moved by this passion. Our object, being what it is, is the other in ourselves and oneself in the other. To discover truth about the patient is always discovering it with him and for him as well as for ourselves and about ourselves. And it is discovering truth between each other, as the truth of human beings in their interrelatedness. (1970, pp. 297–298)

To develop further the sense of Loewald's references to analytic love, it will help to turn to a poet, specifically Rilke writing about Cézanne. In a letter to his wife, Rilke is describing his efforts to comprehend the artist Cézanne at work. Cézanne's work has just burst on his consciousness in a way that makes him feel, as he says, "I must change my life."

Here now is Rilke, in a translation by Joel Agee:

We also notice, a little more clearly each time, how necessary it was to go beyond love, too; it's natural, after all, to love each of these things as one makes it: but if one shows this, one makes it less well; one *judges* it instead of *saying* it. One ceases to be impartial; and the very best— love—stays outside the work, does not enter it, is left aside, untranslated; that's how the painting of sentiments came about. . . . They'd paint: I love this here; instead of painting: here it is. In which case everyone must see for himself whether or not I loved it. This is not shown at all, and some would even insist that love has nothing to do with it. It's that thoroughly exhausted in the action of making, there is no residue. It may be that this emptying out of love in anonymous work, which produces such pure things, was never achieved as completely as in the work of this old man. (1907, pp. 50–51)

I suppose that in this passage Rilke was writing about his own artistic aspirations as well as Cézanne's way of working. I further suppose that Rilke was also doing a piece of creative writing of his own about love as well as artistic creativity. I mention these suppositions to indicate my belief that there is no one right way of delivering Loewald's meaning or anyone else's meaning, though there are some ways that can serve much better than others.

Taken together, these two narratives of love in work—Loewald's and Rilke's—may serve as model renderings of an essential component of the engaged analyst at his or her best.

REFERENCES

Arlow, J. 1969a. Unconscious fantasy and disturbances of conscious experience. *Psychoanalytic Quarterly* 38:1–27.

———. 1969b. Fantasy, memory, and reality testing. *Psychoanalytic Quarterly* 38:28–51.

Bibring, G. L.; Dwyer, T. F.; Huntington, D. S.; and Valenstein, A. F. 1961. A study of the psychological processes in pregnancy and of the earliest mother-child relationship. *The Psychoanalytic Study of the Child* 16:9–72. New York: International Universities Press.

Bloom, H. 1973. *The anxiety of influence: A theory of poetry.* New York: Oxford University Press.

Brenner, C. 1981. Defense and defense mechanism. *Psychoanalytic Quarterly* 50:557–569.

Breuer, J., and Freud, S. 1895. Studies on hysteria. *Standard Edition* 2:1–309. London: Hogarth Press, 1957.

Brierley, M. 1951. *Trends in psychoanalysis.* London: Hogarth Press.

Culler, J. 1975. *Structural poetics: Structuralism, linguistics, and the study of literature.* Ithaca, NY: Cornell University Press.

Davenloo, H. 1978. *Basic principles and techniques in short-term dynamic therapy.* New York: Spectrum.

Erikson, E. 1950. *Childhood and society.* New York: Norton.

———. 1956. The problem of ego identity. *Journal of the American Psychoanalytic Association* 4:56–121.

Fenichel, O. 1941. *Problems of psychoanalytic technique.* New York: Psychoanalytic Quarterly.

Fish, S. 1980. *Is there a text in this class? The authority of interpretive communities.* Cambridge: Harvard University Press.

Freud, A. 1936. *The ego and the mechanisms of defense.* New York: International Universities Press, 1946.

Freud, S. 1895. Studies in hysteria. *Standard Edition* 2. London: Hogarth Press, 1955.

————. 1899. Screen memories. *Standard Edition* 3:299–322. London: Hogarth Press, 1962.

————. 1900. The interpretation of dreams. *Standard Edition* 4 and 5. London: Hogarth Press, 1953.

————. 1905a. Fragment of an analysis of a case of hysteria. *Standard Edition* 7:3–122. London: Hogarth Press, 1953.

————. 1905b. Three essays on the theory of sexuality. *Standard Edition* 7:125–243. London: Hogarth Press, 1953.

————. 1908a. Creative writers and day-dreaming. *Standard Edition* 9:141–153. London: Hogarth Press, 1959.

————. 1908b. On the sexual theories of children. *Standard Edition* 9:205–226. London: Hogarth Press, 1959.

————. 1910a. Wild psycho-analysis. *Standard Edition* 11:219–227. London: Hogarth Press, 1957.

————. 1910b. A special type of choice of object made by men (Contributions to the psychology of love I). *Standard Edition* 11:163–176. London: Hogarth Press, 1957.

————. 1911a. The handling of dream-interpretation in psycho-analysis. *Standard Edition* 12:89–96. London: Hogarth Press, 1958.

————.1911b. Formulations on the two principles of mental functioning. *Standard Edition* 12:213–226. London: Hogarth Press, 1958.

————. 1912a. On the universal tendency to debasement in the sphere of love (Contributions to the psychology of love II). *Standard Edition* 11:177–190. London: Hogarth Press, 1957.

————. 1912b. The dynamics of transference. *Standard Edition* 12:97–108. London: Hogarth Press, 1958.

————. 1912c. Recommendations to physicians practising psycho-analysis. *Standard Edition* 12:109–120. London: Hogarth Press, 1958.

————. 1913. On beginning the treatment (Further recommendations on the technique of psycho-analysis I). *Standard Edition* 12:121–144. London: Hogarth Press, 1958.

————. 1914a. Remembering, repeating and working through (Further recommendations on the technique of psycho-analysis II). *Standard Edition* 12:147–156. London: Hogarth Press, 1958.

―――. 1914b. On narcissism: An introduction. *Standard Edition* 14:73–102. London: Hogarth Press, 1957.

―――. 1915a. The unconscious. *Standard Edition* 14:159–215. London: Hogarth Press, 1957.

―――. 1915b. Instincts and their vicissitudes. *Standard Edition* 14:109–140. London: Hogarth Press, 1957.

―――. 1915c. Observations on transference-love (Further recommendations on the technique of psycho-analysis III). *Standard Edition* 12:159–171. London: Hogarth Press, 1958.

―――. 1915d. Thoughts for the times on war and death. *Standard Edition* 14:274–300. London: Hogarth Press, 1957.

―――. 1916. Some character types met with in psycho-analytic work. *Standard Edition* 14:309–333. London: Hogarth Press, 1957.

―――.1918. The taboo of virginity (Contributions to the psychology of love III). *Standard Edition* 11:191–208. London: Hogarth Press, 1957.

―――. 1919. A child is being beaten. *Standard Edition* 17:175–204. London: Hogarth Press, 1955.

―――. 1920a. Beyond the pleasure principle. *Standard Edition* 18:1–64. London: Hogarth Press, 1955.

―――. 1920b. The psychogenesis of a case of homosexuality in a woman. *Standard Edition* 18:140–172. London: Hogarth Press, 1955.

―――. 1921. Group psychology and the analysis of the ego. *Standard Edition* 18:67–143. London: Hogarth Press, 1955.

―――. 1923a. The ego and the id. *Standard Edition* 19:3–66. London: Hogarth Press, 1961.

―――. 1923b. The infantile genital organization. *Standard Edition* 19:140–145. London: Hogarth Press, 1961.

―――. 1925. Some psychical consequences of the anatomical distinction between the sexes. *Standard Edition* 19:243–258. London: Hogarth Press, 1961.

―――. 1926. Inhibitions, symptoms and anxiety. *Standard Edition* 20:77–174. London: Hogarth Press, 1959.

―――. 1930. Civilization and its discontents. *Standard Edition* 21:59–145. London: Hogarth Press, 1961.

―――. 1931. Female sexuality. *Standard Edition* 21:223–243. London: Hogarth Press, 1961.

―――. 1933. New introductory lectures on psycho-analysis. *Standard Edition* 22:3–182. London: Hogarth Press, 1964.

―――. 1937a. Constructions in analysis. *Standard Edition* 23:255–270. London: Hogarth Press, 1964.

————. 1937b. Analysis terminable and interminable. *Standard Edition* 23:211–253. London: Hogarth Press, 1964.

————. 1940. An outline of psycho-analysis. *Standard Edition* 23:141–207. London: Hogarth Press, 1964.

Gill, M. M. 1976. Metapsychology is not psychology. In *Psychology versus metapsychology: Psychoanalytic essays in memory of George S. Klein,* ed. M. M. Gill and P. S. Holzman, 71–105. *Psychological Issues* Monograph 36. New York: International Universities Press.

————. 1982. *The analysis of transference. Psychological Issues* Monograph 53, vol. 1. New York: International Universities Press.

Glover, E. 1931. The therapeutic effect of inexact interpretation: A contribution to the theory of suggestion. In *The technique of psychoanalysis,* by E. Glover, 353–366. New York: International Universities Press, 1955.

Greenacre, P. 1954. The role of transference: Practical considerations in relation to psychoanalytic therapy. *Journal of the American Psychoanalytic Association* 2:671–684.

————. 1966. Problems of training analysis. *Psychoanaltic Quarterly.* 35:540–567.

Greenberg, J. R., and Mitchell, S. A. 1983. *Object relations in psychoanalytic theory.* Cambridge: Harvard University Press.

Greenson, R. 1954. The struggle against identification. *Journal of the American Psychoanalytic Association* 2:200–217.

Grossman, W. I. 1967. Reflections on the relationships of introspection and psychoanalysis. *International Journal of Psycho-Analysis* 48:16–31.

————. 1982. The self as fantasy: Fantasy as theory. *Journal of the American Psychoanalytic Association* 30:919–938.

Grossman, W. I., and Simon, B. 1969. Anthropomorphism, meaning, and causality in psychoanalytic theory. *The Psychoanalytic Study of the Child* 24:78–114. New York: International Universities Press.

Hartmann, H. 1953. *Ego psychology and the problem of adaptation.* New York: International Universities Press.

————. 1956. Notes on the reality principle. *The Psychoanalytic Study of the Child* 11:31–53. New York: International Universities Press.

————. 1960. *Psychoanalysis and moral values.* New York: International Universities Press.

————. 1964. *Essays on ego psychology: Selected problems in psychoanalytic theory.* New York: International Universities Press.

Horney, K. 1924. On the genesis of the castration-complex in women. *International Journal of Psycho-Analysis* 5:50–65.

————. 1926. The flight from womanhood: The masculinity complex in women as viewed by men and by women. *International Journal of Psycho-Analysis* 7:324–339.

———. 1932. The dread of women. *International Journal of Psycho-Analysis* 13:348–361.

———. 1933. The denial of the vagina. *International Journal of Psycho-Analysis* 14:57–70.

International Psychoanalytic Association. 1985. *Changes in analysts and their training*, ed. R. S. Wallerstein. Monograph Series 4.

———. 1986. *The termination of training analysis: Process, expectations, achievements*, ed. A. M. Cooper. Monograph Series 5.

Jacobson, E. 1964. *The self and the object world*. New York: International Universities Press.

Joseph, B. 1989. *Psychic equilibrium and psychic change: Selected papers of Betty Joseph*, ed. E. B. Spillius and M. Feldman. London: Tavistock/Routledge.

Kernberg, O. 1975. *Borderline conditions and pathological narcissism*. New York: Jason Aronson.

———. 1982. Self, ego, affects, and drives. *Journal of the American Psychoanalytic Association* 30:893–918.

Klein, G. S. 1975. *Psychoanalytic theory: An exploration of essentials*. New York: International Universities Press.

Klein, M. 1964. *Contributions to psycho-analysis*. New York: McGraw-Hill.

Kohut, H. 1971. *The analysis of the self: A systematic approach to the psychoanalytic treatment of narcissistic personality disorders*. New York: International Universities Press.

———. 1977. *The restoration of the self*. New York: International Universities Press.

———. 1984. *How does analysis cure?* Chicago: University of Chicago Press.

Kris, E. 1952. *Psychoanalytic explorations in art*. New York: International Universities Press.

———. 1956a. On some vicissitudes of insight in psychoanalysis. In *Selected papers of Ernst Kris*, 252–271. New Haven: Yale University Press.

———. 1956b. The recovery of childhood memories in psychoanalysis. In *Selected papers of Ernst Kris*, 301–340. New Haven: Yale University Press.

———. 1975. *The selected papers of Ernst Kris*. New Haven: Yale University Press.

Lakoff, G., and Johnson, M. 1980. *Metaphors we live by*. Chicago: University of Chicago Press.

Loewald, H. 1960. On the therapeutic action of psycho-analysis.

International Journal of Psycho-Analysis 41:16–33. Reprinted in *Papers on psychoanalysis,* by H. W. Loewald, 221–256. New Haven: Yale University Press, 1980.

————. 1970. Psychoanalytic theory and psychoanalytic process. In *Papers on psychaoanalysis,* by H. W. Loewald, 277–301. New Haven: Yale University Press, 1980.

————. 1972. Freud's conception of the negative therapeutic reaction, with comments on instinct theory. *Journal of the American Psychoanalytic Association* 20:235–245. Reprinted in *Papers on psychoanalysis,* by H. W Loewald, 315–325. New Haven: Yale University Press, 1980.

Loewenstein, R. L. 1957. A contribution to the theory of masochism. *Journal of the American Psychoanalytic Association* 5:197–234.

Macmurray, J. 1957. *The self as agent.* London: Faber & Faber.

Malan, D. H. 1979. *Individual psychotherapy and the science of psychoanalysis.* London: Butterworth.

Orwell, G. 1949. *1984.* New York: Harcourt, Brace.

Rado, S. 1956. *The psychoanalysis of behavior.* Vol. I of *Collected papers 1922–1956.* New York: Grune & Stratton.

Rapaport, D. 1967. *The collected papers of David Rapaport,* ed. M. M. Gill. New York: Basic Books.

Reich, A. 1951. On countertransference. *International Journal of Psycho-Analysis* 41:16–33.

————. 1953. Narcissistic object choice in women. *Journal of the American Psychoanalytic Association* 1:22–44.

————. 1954. Early identifications as archaic elements in the superego. *Journal of the American Psychoanalytic Association* 2:218–238.

————. 1960. Pathological forms of self-esteem regulation. *The Psychoanalytic Study of the Child* 15:215–232. New York: International Universities Press.

Reich, W. 1933. *Character analysis.* New York: Touchstone Books, 1974.

Reik, T. 1941. *Masochism in modern man.* New York: Farrar & Rinehart.

Ricoeur, P. 1977. The question of proof in psychoanalysis. *Journal of the American Psychoanalytic Association* 25:835–872.

Rilke, R. M. 1907. *Letters on Cézanne,* ed. C. Rilke, trans. J. Agee. New York: Fromm International Publications, 1985.

Sandler, J., with Freud, A. 1984. Discussions in the Hampstead Clinic of A. Freud, *The ego and the mechanisms of defense. Journal of the American Psychoanalytic Association* 31 Supplement:19–146.

Sandler, J.; Holder, A.; and Meers, D. 1963. The ego ideal and the ideal self. *The Psychoanalytic Study of the Child* 18:139–158. New York: International Universities Press.

Schafer, R. 1960. The loving and beloved superego in Freud's structural theory. *The Psychoanalytic Study of the Child* 15:163–188. New York: International Universities Press.

————. 1964. The clinical analysis of affects. *Journal of the American Psychoanalytic Association* 12:275–299.

————. 1967. Ideals, the ego ideal, and the ideal self. In *Motives and thought: Psychoanalytic essays in memory of David Rapaport,* ed. R. R. Holt, 129–174. *Psychological Issues* Monograph 18/19. New York: International Universities Press.

————. 1968a. On the theoretical and technical conceptualization of activity and passivity. *Psychoanalytic Quarterly* 37:173–198.

————. 1968b. *Aspects of internalization.* New York: International Universities Press.

————. 1968c. The mechanisms of defense. *International Journal of Psycho-Analysis* 49:49–62.

————. 1970a. The psychoanalytic vision of reality. *International Journal of Psycho-Analysis* 51:279–297. Reprinted in *A new language for psychoanalysis,* by R. Schafer, 22–56. New Haven: Yale University Press, 1976.

————. 1970b. An overview of Heinz Hartmann's contributions to psycho-analysis. *International Journal of Psycho-Analysis* 51:425–446. Reprinted in *A new language for psychoanalysis,* by R. Schafer, 57–101. New Haven: Yale University Press, 1976.

————. 1972. Internalization: Process or fantasy? *The Psychoanalytic Study of the Child* 27:411–438. New York: International Universities Press. Reprinted in *A new language for psychoanalysis,* by R. Schafer, 155–178. New Haven: Yale University Press, 1976.

————. 1973a. Action: Its place in psychoanalytic interpretation and theory. *The Annual of Psychoanalysis* 1:159–196.

————. 1973b. The idea of resistance. *International Journal of Analysis.* 54:259–285. Reprinted in *A new language for psychoanalysis,* by R. Schafer, 212–263. New Haven: Yale University Press, 1976.

————. 1974. Problems in Freud's psychology of women. *Journal of the American Psychoanalytic Association.* 22:459–485.

————. 1976. *A new language for psychoanalysis.* New Haven: Yale University Press.

————. 1978. *Language and insight: The Sigmund Freud memorial lectures, University College London, 1975–1976.* New Haven: Yale University Press.

————. 1981. *Narrative actions in psychoanalysis. Heinz Werner lecture series 14.* Worcester, MA: Clark University Press.

————. 1982. The imprisoned analysand. In *The analytic attitude,* by R. Schafer, 257–280. New York: Basic Books, 1983.

————. 1983. *The analytic attitude.* New York: Basic Books.

————. 1985a. Wild analysis. *Journal of the American Psychoanalytic Association.* 33:275–300.

————. 1985b. The interpretation of psychic reality, developmental influences, and unconscious communication. *Journal of the American Psychoanalytic Association* 33:537–554.

————. 1988. Discussion: Panel presentations on psychic structure. *Journal of the American Psychoanalytic Association* 36 Supplement:295–314.

Segal, H. 1964. *Introduction to the work of Melanie Klein.* New York: Basic Books.

Smith, B. H. 1980. Narrative versions, narrative theories. *Critical Inquiry* 7(2):213–236.

Spence, D. 1982. *Narrative truth and historical truth: Meaning and interpretation in psychoanalysis.* New York: Norton.

Stein, M. 1981. The unobjectionable part of the transference. *Journal of the American Psychoanalytic Association* 29:869–892.

Stone, L. 1961. Notes on the noninterpretive elements in the psychoanalytic situation. *Journal of the American Psychoanalytic Association* 29:89–118.

Sullivan, H. S. 1940. *Conceptions of modern psychiatry.* New York: Norton.

Thalberg, I. 1977. Freud's anatomies of the self. In *Philosophers on Freud: New evaluations,* ed. R. Wolheim, 147–171. New York: Jason Aronson.

Waelder, R. 1930. The principle of multiple function. *Psychoanalytic Quarterly* 15:45–62, 1936.

Weigert, E. 1955. Special problems in connection with termination of training analysis. *Journal of the American Psychoanalytic Association* 3:630–640. Reprinted in *The courage to love: Selected papers of Edith Weigert, M.D.,* 264–275. New Haven: Yale University Press, 1970.

Werner, H., and Kaplan, B. 1963. *Symbol formation* New York: John Wiley.

Wilbern, D. 1979. Freud and the inter-penetration of dreams. *Diacritics* 9:98–110.

Winnicott, D. W. 1958. *Collected papers: Through paediatrics to psychoanalysis.* New York: Basic Books.

Wood, E., and Wood, C. D. 1984. Tearfulness: A psychoanalytic interpretation. *Journal of the American Psychoanalytic Association* 32:117–136.

Woolf, V. 1924. *A room of one's own.* New York: Harcourt, Brace.

CREDITS

INDEX

Action language, xiv; descriptions of
actions, 45–46
Active, use of word, 76–80
Adolescents, 201
Agee, Joel, 308
Agency, disclaiming of, 24
Agent, self as, 21–25
Aggression, 128. *See also* Case studies
and other specific topics
Anality, 122–23
Analyst: as co-creator of analytic data,
177–79; female, antisentimental
male and, 126–27; as new object for
the analysand, 305–7; overactive,
275; presence or absence of,
217–18; superficial acquiescence to,
224; theoretical orientation of, 189;
traditional Freudian image of,
179–80. *See also* Analytic relation-
ship; Countertransference;
Interpretation; Training analysis;
Transference; *and other specific topics*
Analytic data, analyst as co-creator of,
177–79
Analytic love, 307–8
Analytic relationship: benevolent self

interest of analysand and, 19–20;
transformational dialogue in,
156–59. *See also* Countertransference; Defense; Resistance;
Transference; *and other specific topics*
Analyze, use of word, 188–89
Anxiety. *See* Clinical examples *and other
specific topics*
Anxiety of influence, training analysis
and, 249
Applied psychoanalysis, 181–86;
patient's talking back and, 174;
child analysis as, 180; clinical psychoanalysis as, 180–81; Snow White,
interpretations of, in, 167–69; as
therapy, 184–85; value of, 185. *See
also* Critical theory
Arlow, J., 31, 255
Autonomy of ego functions, 232

Benevolent self interest, 8, 9, 14–20;
benevolent interest in others and,
14–20; faking of, 14; foundations of,
17–18

ories, 34, 35; self-reflexive dialogue and, 161–62; structural theory of, 24; theoretical changes made by, 273; on transference, 75–76, 224–25, 273, 287; transformational dialogue of, 156–59; translation of, 152; on the unconscious, 113; verification and, 176; on wild analysis, 276; writing of, 151. *See also specific topics*

Freudian analysis: benefits of, 183; Snow White interpreted according to, 167–68

Frigidity: action narrative and, 98–99; displacement and, 82; factors in, 84–88; fantasy during heterosexual activity and, 86; Freud's view, 84; incestuous significance of the sex act and, 84–85; role of partner in, 86–87; perversions and, 85–86; phallocentric narratives of, 87–89; pre-oedipal or pregenital influences and, 85; selective, 84; use of term, 84

Gender: narrative nature of, xvi; morality and, Freud's view of, 61–66, 68. *See also* Freud; Men; Phallocentrism; Sexism; Women

Genetic approach, 210, 214, 217, 218

Genital heterosexuality, 71. *See also* Procreativity

Genitality, 86

Gill, M., 39, 230, 255

Goodness, 17–19; psychotherapist's sense of, 297–98

Greenacre, Phyllis, 250, 289

Greenson, R., 108

Grossman, W. I., 21, 23, 75

Guilt: narrative of, 96; termination and, 7. *See also* Case studies *and other specific topics*

Happenings, xiii

Hartmann, Heinz, 9, 18, 39, 64, 125, 306

Holder, A., 103

Homosexual issues: Freud's view of, 68; impotence and frigidity and, 85

Horney, Karen, 67

Id: defense of ego against, 42; wild analysis of, 270

Idealization of unhappiness, 109–13; case examples of, 109–13; discrimination against women and, 112–13; parental identification and, 111; in women, 112–15

Idealization, 41

Ideal self: identification and, 103; pursuit of failure and, 103, 104, 106, 107; unhappy, 109, 111

Identification, 18–19; ideal self and, 103; idealization of unhappiness and, 111; marriage and child rearing and, 97; and sentimentality, 121–22. *See also* Case studies

Identity formation, negative, 104

Ideological considerations, in search for common ground, 191–92

Impotence: action narrative and, 98–99; displacement and, 82; factors in, 84–88; fantasy during heterosexual activity and, 86; Freud's view of, 83–84; incestuous significance of the sex act and, 84–85; role of partner in, 86–87; perversions and, 85–86; phallocentric narratives of, 87–89; preoedipal or pregenital influences and, 85; psychical, 83; selective, 83–84; use of term, 83; vagina dentata and, 89–91

Incest, 64, 84–85

Individuation, maternal figure and, 91–94

TWENTIETH CENTURY INTERPRETATIONS
OF

A TALE OF TWO CITIES

TWENTIETH CENTURY INTERPRETATIONS

OF

A TALE OF
TWO CITIES

A Collection of Critical Essays

Edited by

CHARLES E. BECKWITH

Prentice-Hall, Inc. *Englewood Cliffs, N. J.*

10 9 8 7 6 5 4 3 2 1

PRENTICE-HALL INTERNATIONAL, INC. (*London*)
PRENTICE-HALL OF AUSTRALIA, PTY. LTD. (*Sydney*)
PRENTICE-HALL OF CANADA, LTD. (*Toronto*)
PRENTICE-HALL OF INDIA PRIVATE LTD. (*New Delhi*)
PRENTICE-HALL OF JAPAN, INC. (*Tokyo*)

Contents

Introduction

by Charles E. Beckwith

"I hope it is the best story I have written," wrote Dickens on finishing *A Tale of Two Cities*; and elsewhere, "Heaven knows I have done my best and believed in it." [1] Such defensiveness reflects the special circumstances that preceded the writing of this book, and the special struggles that they led to. For one thing, he had undertaken a new magazine, *All the Year Round,* with himself as both editor and chief contributor, which he planned in weekly parts and intended to open with an eye-catching flourish. He therefore had to organize the novel in tighter segments than usual, with more frequent spots of crisis and suspense. The restriction was painful to the usually expansive Dickens ("the small parts . . . drive me frantic"); and he also, for similar reasons, had trouble with the beginning. The paradoxical patterning of that now-famous passage— "It was the best of times, it was the worst of times, it was the age of wisdom, it was the age of foolishness"—is probably the most noticeable single instance of the forms and devices he worked out to tighten the economy, and speed the movement of the whole. It also, of course, sets a kind of distance between the reader and the events to follow, a distance of the sort that is always caused by the mixing of realism and rhetoric, and that, in a variety of forms, runs through the whole novel—as for example in the monotonous repetition of the word *Hunger* early in the book, in the footsteps and the thunderstorm around the Manettes' house in Soho, in the knitting and the counting of heads at the climax. The necessity of such mixing derives in part from the subject matter, which constitutes another of the special circumstances that Dickens had to contend with in treating this particular story. The French Revolution, being so full of exciting real events all well known to Dickens's readers, was always in effect pulling against his own invention of character, incident, and plot. To make matters worse, Carlyle's famous history, *The French Revolution,* which was Dickens's chief literary inspiration and set the background of historical event and social criticism which he followed in general, was also known to many of Dickens's readers, and was as

---

[1] Letter to Francois Joseph Régnier, October 15, 1859; letter to Wilkie Collins, October 6, 1859, in *The Letters of Charles Dickens,* ed. Walter Dexter (Bloomsbury: The Nonesuch Press, 1938), III, 125.

full of excitement and suspense as any novel of adventure. Dickens stated in his Introduction that no one could "hope to add anything to the philosophy of Mr. Carlyle's wonderful book," and he might have added that no writer of fiction could hope to improve on it in dramatic movement and pictorial brilliancy.

These were some of the special circumstances that occasioned Dickens's struggles with *A Tale of Two Cities*. There were also matters more personal. He was at the very top of his career when he began it and had achieved worldwide fame as a creator of fanciful characters, elaborate and often mysterious plots, and even more elaborate passages of commentary and description, often comic, but equally often sentimental or grotesque; and from the time of his first novel, *Oliver Twist*, he had been also a bold critic of social evils and a prophet of social dangers. But all these strengths had by now shown their obverse side. Fancy and fantasy easily became whimsy; complicated plots and subplots degenerated into forced crises and coincidences; pathos wobbled toward weepiness, as in the famous death of Little Nell in *The Old Curiosity Shop*. In *A Tale of Two Cities*, therefore, Dickens set out determinedly, not to purge the chief characteristics of a lifetime's work (which would have been impossible in any case), but to purge the excesses to which he had often let them run. The result, in the *Tale*, is that we have a plot complicated but fast-moving, stark at times like a Greek tragedy, dispensing with subplot yet managing to weave in surprises, coincidences, and late revelation of the meaning of earlier events. In the double arrest of Charles Darnay, for example, or the ride of the Marquis with his murderer-to-be accompanying him unseen; or again, in the dramatic announcement of Madame Defarge's motivation from years gone by and in her death at the hands of an unexpected but fitting agent—in such moments we have the essential Dickens but distilled to a new quintessence. Similarly, description and background, a great feature of Dickens's, are reduced to functional or symbolic effect, and characterization likewise is minimized; so that perhaps more than with any other novel he wrote, the author himself recedes into the distance, and the story seems to tell itself, or to be unfolding, with only his guidance rather than his usual manipulation.

Such handling of his material appears to have been personally significant to Dickens in the sense that he was showing his audience, and himself, that he could function as well in the art of the novel—better, to judge from the statements quoted above—without the trappings, devices, and lavish coloration of the past. "I set myself," he says,

> the little task of making a *picturesque* story, rising in every chapter, with characters true to nature, but whom the story itself should express, more than they should express themselves, by dialogue.[2]

[2] Letter to John Forster, August 25, 1859, in *Letters*, III, 118.

In the phrase, "I set myself," we see something of the sense of challenge he felt in attempting this particular task, which turned out to be bigger than he had anticipated. There were greater and more personal challenges behind it, too. Critics have often noticed that Dickens's career moves from condemnation of specific social ills, like the workhouse system in *Oliver Twist,* to condemnation of whole corrupt societies, like the mercenary world struggling for a trash heap in *Our Mutual Friend.* In the French Revolution he found a subject worthy of his broadest conceptions: a great nation ripening its own destruction—literally France, of course, but by implication England, too, and any other nation having ingrained feudal privileges with their inherent abuses. The very breadth of that prospect may well be responsible for the deliberate tightening and narrowing of scope in the *Tale.* Avoiding the enormous sweep and drama of the Revolution in all its complexity, he tries to condense the basic threat and the basic lesson by showing the effects of the Terror—the vengeful side of that great event—on a small group of people variously involved.

In a yet more personal way, Dickens's undertaking of this work brings us to the boundary between fact and conjecture. He was going through perhaps the greatest crisis of his life as he approached it, a crisis peculiar in the way it resurrected memories and feelings from earlier crises, making this a compacted period of intense strain. To trace connections between an author's life and his works is always dangerous and uncertain since it plays down the role of the controlling artist; and no work of Dickens's is more controlled. At the same time, the material the artist controls comes, at some stage, from a level of personal experience and feeling; and we can understand better, or be better pointed toward understanding, the finished form of the novel if we look briefly at the roots of some of its themes and their illustrations.

More than most works of Dickens's, this book needs at the present time to be approached thematically. Its special moments and descriptions stand out so unforgettably for most of us—the implacable grimness of Madame Defarge; the sudden upsurge of the mob (a kind of preview of their later quest for blood) when the wine is spilled; the calm heroism, above life and death alike, of Sidney Carton—that they tend to obscure some of the larger and deeper of Dickens's themes—larger and deeper than, for example, social injustice, revolutionary violence, or even individual self-sacrifice. These last, of course, are what the book is "about" in an important sense that we must not slight. But they are obvious themes, themes of statement, themes which lend themselves easily to the merely visual apprehension of its events, hence to the stage and movie career the novel has enjoyed to the detriment of its appreciation as a work of literary art—though, as Dickens's comments make clear, it was as art that he wanted it appreciated. The

larger and deeper themes, on the other hand, lead us in more profitable directions. First of all backward—to a view of Dickens's childhood and early life. Then forward—toward a more modern judgment of this strangely "modern" book.

I

We can see the personal themes of Dickens's writing beginning to emerge early in his boyhood, blending with each other in sometimes curious ways, and becoming re-emphasized by later happenings. His first childhood experiences, he makes clear, became associated with dramatic fantasy and rhetoric through his father, who, although a conscientious naval clerk by day, was a kind of Falstaff when off duty, full of elaborate gesture and high-flown speech. One early memory, for example, was of a fine house at Gad's Hill near Rochester, which his father told him he might own, if he worked very hard, when he grew up—an idea with which his imagination continued for a long time to play. Later, these fantasies took on a new dimension when he learned that this was the area where Falstaff had had his night adventures with Prince Hal and the practical jokers who robbed him. Still later—years later—when he accidentally learned of the availability of this house on the market, and bought it and moved there, he felt, as he had so often in his life, the perilous thinness of the boundary between fantasy and fact.

When Dickens was only twelve, another side of the Falstaffian personality—improvidence—sent his father to debtor's prison and left the son to long hours of drudgery in a blacking warehouse. Ever flamboyant, his father remarked when he left for prison: "The sun has set upon me forever!" The son, too, with no way of knowing when or whether he might escape the warehouse, believing indeed that he never would, felt equally lost. More specifically, he felt betrayed by both parents, first by his father for his failure to provide, and later, as if they were taking turns, by his mother for her failure to care what happened to him and to his early talents. As he put it to his friend and later biographer, John Forster, he felt that he, who had been a quick and sensitive and promising student, had been in an instant "thrown away"; and he spoke of his shock when, his father having been released after an unexpected legacy and the question of his own future coming up, he realized that his mother wanted him to stay on indefinitely at the warehouse instead of going back to school: "I never afterwards forgot, I never shall forget, I never can forget, that my mother was warm for my being sent back." [3] He was released, however,

---

[3] These and other details of the prison and warehouse episode, and Dickens's feelings about it, are given by Edgar Johnson in *Charles Dickens: His Tragedy and Triumph,* 2 vols. (New York: Simon and Schuster, Inc., 1952), I, iii, now the standard biography and the chief source of the biographical material in this volume.

and did go back to school, where his former buoyancy and mental agility quickly returned. But his bitterness and sense of betrayal, tinged with the desolate and depressive feelings that the uncared-for child inevitably experiences, remained and were to remain all his life. The whole experience had also given another twist, we can easily conjecture, to his sense of the intermingling of reality and fantasy. Not only were the realities of the occasion so surprising and painful that they had the effect of fantasy—in this case, nightmare—on his childish feelings and imagination; there was also a double betrayal, the falling back from one support to another only to find that too giving away; and there was a confused apprehension of the meaning of what would prove to be one of his repeated overt themes, prison and imprisonment. For he had more reason to feel a prisoner and an outcast than his father did. Life in debtors' prison was a kind of communal arrangement then, and prisoners could have their families with them. John Dickens, always energetic and talkative, soon became the friend and adviser of many of the other prisoners and was made chairman of the committee that provided for their needs. He was an individual and a leader even in those restricted circumstances. Many years later, Charles remembered this anomalous role of his father's when he created William Dorrit, who in *Little Dorrit* served twenty-five years in debtors' prison (Dickens's father served only a few months), and rose to a position that gave him the title—ironic, and perhaps to Dickens bitter in memory—of "master of the Marshalsea." Charles, meanwhile, was neither leader nor individual, was but one sweated boy among many, doing machinelike work, leaving his personal mark on nothing; and it is not hard to imagine this as the beginning of his lifelong feeling that more than one institution can become a prison, and that imprisonment, in the sense of being shut off from others, can occur in many ways and under many circumstances. This feeling returns in several of his novels, culminating in *A Tale of Two Cities,* where, as we shall see, almost everybody is in some kind of prison.

A new world opened to Dickens after this dark early period, which now seemed forever lost in the past. His spirits bounded forward as he embraced his new prospects one after another. On finishing school, he first became a clerk in a law firm, then a newspaper reporter, then a parliamentary correspondent, having brought his shorthand to a peak of skill which surpassed that of all his older rivals. As if all this were not sufficiently taxing he began to write, in his leisure time, little vignettes, character studies, observations of London eccentrics, which he shortly published under the title *Sketches by Boz* (his brother's childhood mispronunciation of Moses, a family nickname). They brought him immediate success and the promise of an income.

On the strength of this achievement he married, and in one great year (1836–37) seemed to be started toward a brilliant literary career

and a happy, fulfilling domestic life. But though the literary career did indeed become brilliant, the domestic life was marred and threatened from the start. It was, to begin with, partly the result of rebound. A four-year courtship of a pretty, empty-headed, frustrating coquette had left him with memories both bitter and passionate. Maria Beadnell, model for Dora the child-bride who dies young in *David Copperfield,* had in a sense also died young to Dickens, not only because she married another but because she was never fully alive to him, even during their courtship: she was a kind of porcelain doll, either untouchable or cold when touched. Whether in spite of this quality or because of it, Dickens remembered her with a romantic longing that is hard for us, over a century later, to give its proper credit.[4] Even twenty years after his marriage, when he heard from her again, all the old yearnings were reawakened. It was as if distance (and in this case time) lent the true enchantment to his ideal of femininity. He was to say of himself, partly in jest: "I don't like . . . Realities except when they are unattainable," and this seems to have been particularly true in his relations with women.[5] The reality he did attain with his wife Catherine Hogarth was a disappointment and frustration almost from the start. Their marriage eventually culminated in a crisis and then collapsed during the year preceding his work on *A Tale of Two Cities.*

With the advantages of hindsight, we can see a further way in which his marriage was marred and threatened, or at least oddly insecure; and this too is owing to his curious capacity for attachment to the unattainable, as well as his early and profound sense of "bereavement," of youth wasted and "thrown away." With the young couple when they moved into their first home had gone, for reasons which we do not know, Catherine's sister Mary Hogarth, beautiful, virtuous, intelligent, and gay, who within a year died very suddenly at the age of seventeen.[6] It was to Dickens an event at once fantastic and frighteningly real; and his reaction was extraordinary. "So perfect a creature never breathed. . . . She had not a fault. . . ." Laid to rest, she was "a silent but solemn witness that all health and beauty are but things of the hour. . . ." Finally, and strangely: "Thank God she died in my arms, and the very last words she whispered were of me. . . ." He took a ring from her finger and put it on his own, and never removed it; years later he was hoping to be buried next to her.

[4] He tells Forster that the intensity of his nature is "desperate"; that he had seen Maria, when they were young, in a unique light; that no one could imagine "in the most distant degree" the pain of recollecting her in *David Copperfield*; and finally that to see or hear her now is to wander away "over the ashes of all that youth and hope in the wildest manner." John Forster, *The Life of Charles Dickens,* ed. J. W. T. Ley (New York: Doubleday Doran, 1928), p. 49.
[5] Huntington Library MS, Dickens to Mrs. Watson, December 7, 1857. Quoted in Johnson, II, 911.
[6] The known facts are related in Johnson, III, ii.

We are told that sentimentalizing of children and idealizing of women are Dickens traits: but his experiences and reactions suggest something deeper. V. S. Pritchett has said of Dickens's characters that they are distinguished by their solitariness—"they do not talk to one another; they talk to themselves"—and counters the view of E. M. Forster that they are external caricatures ("flat" in Forster's famous designation) by his own view that their posturing, their soliloquies, their eccentricities reveal "fragments of inner life." [7] Elsewhere Mr. Pritchett refers to the "weary pieties of realism that lie between us and a comprehension of Dickens." [8] If we couple such acute observations as these with our own analysis of the man at the crises of his life (including one more, the greatest, which we have yet to see), we discover in *A Tale of Two Cities* a writer who is struggling to present a kind of psychic overlay of fantasy on reality, a ghostly yet real heightening of experience, and a symbolic residue within even his most realistic characters. We become conscious of determining contrasts of light and shade in an innocent sunrise as Mr. Lorry looks out over a ploughed field after the fogs and ruts of the Dover road, or in a blood-red sunset on the stony face of the Marquis; we sense a Revolution that is as much an encroaching weave of footfalls and whispers as an historical fact; we see characters whose identity is more than half-symbolic and whose relationships are allegorical made secure nonetheless, through sheer circumstantiality and fine particulars, within a credible world of everyday experience—as when Sidney Carton, the great emblem of the outsider, quips in contemporary slang and drinks brandy with the spy Barsad. Dickens's feelings run deeper than we think, and his struggles often take him beyond the literary terms and conditions of his period: he manages a realistic tale of adventure that is at the same time fantastic, almost dreamlike, in its imaginative sway over the reader.

It is not only from women and children that Dickens often seems detached, though these as representatives of innocence and gentleness in a brutal world are always symbolically expressive.[9] He has a certain detachment from all his characters, placing them on high as it were; and, as Mr. Pritchett has noted, detaching them from each other as well as from himself. At the same time, no writer ever noted

---

[7] "Edwin Drood," in *The Living Novel and Later Appreciations* (New York: Random House, Inc., 1964), p. 86. Forster's opinions are in *Aspects of the Novel* (New York: Harcourt, Brace, 1927), pp. 67ff.

[8] "The Shocking Surgeon," in *The Living Novel*, p. 20. This is an essay on Smollett, whose work was a chief influence on Dickens.

[9] The pressure of his obsession with the death of young innocence may be reflected in what, in his description of Charles and Lucie's early years of marriage, seems all but forced: the loss of their young son (II, xxi, "Echoing Footsteps"); but the event is partly redeemed, and partly made symbolical, by the child's connection with Sidney Carton, whom he remembers at almost the last moment of his life, and who is himself like a dying child, being forlorn and separated from all others.

detail so masterfully; and, because he also seems to note it imperson-
ally and inadvertently, the effect is to lend a kind of dramatic tension
to the total "feel" of his work. Nowhere was this ever more true than
in *A Tale of Two Cities,* as we have earlier suggested, where the author
becomes refined almost wholly out of existence, the story itself "expressing" the characters, as he says.[10]

Dickens's life in these early years, indeed his whole public life, seems
to belie assertions of his detachment, much more of his isolation or
estrangement, just as his novels, so full of his stage-manager presence,
seem to belie assertions of the author's absence. Yet *A Tale of Two
Cities,* coming as we have said at a time of crisis in his life and innovative by intention, unmistakably gives us the perspectives af alienation;
for his life did have a private, not to say a secret, side. True, no writer
ever had greater success, ever lived a more ebullient, hard-driving,
energetic, and gregarious public life. From *Boz* to *Pickwick* to *Oliver
Twist* his creativity not only climbed but rather soared, in a way ex-
ploded. He became an editor of various periodicals, attending personally to every detail, as accomplished in business as in letters. He
made an enormous number of friends, literary and nonliterary alike. He
was much invited as an after-dinner speaker. He engaged in amateur
theatricals and, again at about the time of *A Tale of Two Cities,*
launched a new and consuming career as a public reader of his own
works, in which he excelled as much as he had in authorship. He made
two trips to America, where he lectured on the need for an international copyright law and gave public readings for which long lines of
spectators patiently waited for hours; and he visited France and Italy
and took a walking tour of England with this friend Wilkie Collins.
Through all this his presence was always larger than life, always dramatic, always charged with an energy that remained inexhaustible.
After one of his incomparably busy days he would often walk about
London half the night, and he told Forster once that scaling all the
Alps in Italy would not assuage his restlessness. Yet clearly this energy,
hence this activity, was in part compulsive and hysterical, a sign of run-

[10] Some touches in the story which give a combined sense of nearness and detachment may be worth citing: one is the use made of the ploughed field mentioned above, a reminder of homely, workaday life, followed by Mr. Lorry's ex-
clamation: "Gracious Creator of day! To be buried alive [which is one theme of
the book, and one of Dickens's earlier titles for it] for eighteen years!"; another is
the Negro cupids which so extraneously intrude upon Mr. Lorry's first interview
with Lucie Manette; or there are the flies and the mirror, studiously observed by
Dickens in the first courtroom; or the revealing marks on the Marquis's nose, more
effective than a burst of rage; or the "shadow attendant on Madame Defarge"
which falls on Lucie and her child. This same "shadow" is also a kind of dis-
embodied romantic revolutionary, an abstraction like Delacroix's *Liberty Guiding
the People,* another kind or level of reality, until reduced to still a third, that of
mere uppity hussy by the blunt Englishness of Miss Pross: "Well, I am sure, Bold-
face! I hope *you* are pretty well!"

ning from or to something, trying to fill some gap that would not be filled. Though we may be surprised when we first encounter Santayana's remark: "He was a waif himself, and utterly disinherited," [11] if we remember those early crises, which he himself describes in terms so extreme that they make us think of an eternity and infinity of lostness— we have to acknowledge that so it was. And we understand better why, again surprisingly, he one day turns to his friend Forster with a sudden confession of his loneliness, and specifically of his great longing for "one friend and companion I never made, one happiness I missed in life." [12] He was indeed two realities: the unbelievably successful man of the world, but likewise the outsider: Oliver or Jo the crossing-sweeper or Sidney Carton, always either below or above the normal requirements and standards of civilization, never a part of it.

In 1857, when he was forty-two, when three-quarters of his work was done, he suddenly had reason to feel that the friend and companion had been found and the missed happiness lay in sight. But the experiences of that and the next year, though a certain personal fulfillment came of them, also resurrected in odd fashion the feelings that had been planted and augmented by his childhood losses and the death of Mary Hogarth. For years now, his marriage had been deteriorating, and his nervousness and restlessness with the harmless Catherine had correspondingly mounted. By ironic coincidence he had become attached once more to a sister-in-law, Georgina, as untouchable, and nearly as perfect, as Mary. He invokes her with something of the tone of twenty years before when he calls her indispensable, "the active spirit of the house." [13] Then overnight came a startling change: he met Ellen Ternan, an eighteen-year-old actress. His subsequent behavior was scarcely to his credit, but it indicates more than words how obsessed he was. He who had so long suffered from separateness now imposed a walling-off on his wife Catherine, and inevitably on himself. He ordered the passage between his room and hers to be closed by a wooden door, and (surely an elaboration of cruelty and doubly symbolic) the recess to be filled up with shelves. By June of 1858 Catherine had left his London house; Ellen was set up in a separate establishment; and in the following year the London house itself was given up and Dickens had gone to live in the house of his boyhood dreams at Gad's Hill near Rochester. He lived on there for another twelve years, writing *Great Expectations* and other works including the unfinished *Mystery of Edwin Drood,* and apparently remained the old gregarious Dickens who kept a permanently open door for his friends. But he was increasingly occupied with his public readings, and increasingly performed them under a

[11] "Dickens," in *Soliloquies in England* (London, 1922), p. 59.
[12] Letter to Forster [January, 1855], in *Letters*, II, 621.
[13] Letter to M. De la Rue, October 23, 1857, Berg MS, Dickens to De la Rue. Quoted in Johnson, II, 909 and n.

strain, a kind of frenzy and self-destructiveness that alarmed his doctor and his family until their combined pressure forced him to give them up, only three months before his death in June of 1870. He had never during these years been in touch with Catherine, and Ellen was at Gad's Hill when he died. He had presumably attained the unattainable: but the evidence suggests that not Ellen, but something deeper, farther away, more lost and mysterious, was his goal, and that he remained as unfulfilled and obsessed with his loneliness as ever.[14]

II

It was in the midst of this last great personal struggle that he began *A Tale of Two Cities.* He had long wanted to combine his bent toward social criticism and warning with the technique and point of view of the historical novel; and, further, he needed to find an escape from the torments of his struggle that would be at the same time a way of expressing it. Thus he would retain the experience, but he would remove it to a distance, an aesthetic distance. Only once before, in 1841 with *Barnaby Rudge,* had he attempted a historical novel; and the special difficulties and partial failure of that undertaking (an unaccustomed experience for him) had perhaps steered him back to contemporary scenes. But in 1857 and 1858, everything suddenly seemed transformed, and so he tried again, with various special helps he had not had before. One problem had been to combine the breadth of historical panorama with the particular, even eccentric or grotesque, observation that was his stock-in-trade. Another was to combine the truth of history with the "truth"—psychological, moral, dramatic—

[14] The best study of Dickens's relationship with Ellen Ternan is Ada Nisbet's *Dickens and Ellen Ternan* (Berkeley: University of California Press, 1952).

On Dickens's dramatic gesture of rejection, Professor Johnson comments that "the closing of that door after twenty-one years of married life was, in the tragedy of Dickens, symbolically as significant as Nora's slamming of the door in *A Doll's House.*" Symbolically, and ironically: the effect on Dickens was only a parody of freedom. He was the more a prisoner: of a society not framed to accommodate his separation and the illicit arrangement with Ellen (a further discreditable and revealing act was his printing of a public explanation); of his own emotions and passions, not to be quelled by any external events; perhaps most cruelly of disappointment, since the remark, "I don't like Realities except when they are unattainable," probably reflects the deepest truth of his mental life and of his creative force. Professor Johnson adds, on the subject of his hysterical pursuit of exhausting public readings: "Perhaps Dickens would have felt shocked had he been accused of a deliberate effort at suicide. . . . But he had ceased to care what happened. All his fame had not brought him the things he most deeply wanted." He also suggests that the enchantment Dickens had felt in Maria had never been there, but had been imposed all along by "the radiant hallucination of youth" (Johnson, II, 911 and n., 1104; II, 835). We shall see later a different use of the idea of "hallucination" to explain Dickens's peculiar vision of life as it appears in his novels.

of literary expression. Still another was to imagine characters who would have a both public and private, historical and personal interest and to house them in a story that itself had this double kind of relevance. And finally, there was always in Dickens's case, especially in his impending crisis, the need to weave in and make relevant special themes and interests out of his most personal, intimate, psychological history. To reach all these objectives in a single, unified work was doubtless impossible, even for a genius of Dickens's surpassing powers. But if we know something of the many motives and materials he was working with, we shall better understand both the successes and the partial failures of the *Tale*.

The reality-fantasy "mix" runs through all Dickens's work.[15] In the *Tale*, the plot seems to bring us merely a straightforward story of adventure, danger, and suspense, with a certain amount of commentary, characterization, and atmosphere added. But without violating "reality," Dickens has managed to give everything—including the plot—a coloring of fantasy. The basic "detail"—the basic fact—of the whole enterprise is the Revolution itself. But it is the effect of the Revolution, its immediate and shocking effect, on individuals that suits Dickens's metamorphosizing imagination best, hence its horrific and terrific aspects, its nightmare side in the Terror and in its prelude, the September, 1792, Massacre. His treatment of historical event in *Barnaby Rudge* shows the same tendencies. On the one hand, he is interested in a moment of history—the anti-Catholic riots inspired by the half-mad Lord Gordon in the late eighteenth century. On the other, it is its

[15] Although *A Tale of Two Cities* does not, in its economy, show as often as some of his novels his tendency to give life and feeling to inanimate objects, it does produce a dream-like effect at important points—the forays of the mob, the burning of the chateau, the Carmagnole, the counting of heads—which illustrates the blend. Dickens's strong sense of a kind of hallucinatory participation in the works of his fancy was, as it happens, noted in his time, but not always with critical approval (see Forster's comments, pp. 716ff, on a review of Dickens's work at large published after Dicken's death by George Henry Lewes). Of the idea of this work, chiefly no doubt of the sacrifice of Sidney Carton, he says in his preface, ". . . it has had complete possession of me; I have so far verified what is done and suffered in these pages, as that I have certainly done and suffered it all myself."

For further comment on this subject, with illustrations from other novels of Dickens's, see Dorothy van Ghent, "The Dickens World: A View from Todgers's," originally published in the *Sewanee Review*, LVIII (1950), 419–38; and John Bayley, *"Oliver Twist:* 'Things as They Really Are',' originally published in *Dickens and the Twentieth Century*, ed. John Gross and Gabriel Pearson (London: Routledge & Kegan Paul, Ltd., 1962; Toronto: University of Toronto Press, 1962), both reprinted in the *Twentieth Century Views* volume *Dickens: A Collection of Critical Essays*, ed. Martin Price (Prentice-Hall, Inc., 1967), pp. 24–38 and 83–96 respectively. For the form which this feature of Dickens's mind takes in *A Tale of Two Cities*, see the selections in this volume from Professor Taylor Stoehr's *Dickens: The Dreamer's Stance* (Ithaca: Cornell University Press, 1965).

bloodiness, violence, and insanity that attracts him, countering the rationalism and rigor that Victorian society in general, and his own personal life in particular, so full of demands and obligations, thrust upon him.[16] Outward fact and psychic impulse here probably served each other.[17]

Madness is thematic also in the *Tale*. Dr. Manette is mad, or so disoriented as to be mad in effect, when his daughter Lucie is first led to him. He is mad from his senseless imprisonment of eighteen years—or, worse than senseless, the imprisonment to which he is condemned as the result of an accidental discovery made while performing a virtuous act. After he is rescued, he is brought back to health through love and care. But then the pressure of outside events—the fear of having to enact the whole nightmare over again, either in his own person or in that of others he loves—forces his madness to return. And this time it is a true madness: a doubling of the original condition, a sense that one is never to be free. Doubling in this sense, and in many senses, plays a role in the significant structure of the book. It is not of course the same thing as madness: but it is related in the sense that

[16] Mr. Pritchett, referring to Edmund Wilson's earlier comment on this quality in Dickens, mentions "the twin strains of rebel and criminal in his nature." ("Edwin Drood," in *Living Appreciations*, p. 87). And Forster tells of how he talked Dickens out of his original intention of having the riots led by actual maniacs. But Dickens makes much of *comparing* the actions of the mob to those of maniacs, thus keeping part of the point: he describes how one dabbles in fire as if it were water, how another melts his own head under a stream of molten lead, etc. George Orwell says of these events that "Dickens . . . delights in describing scenes in which the 'dregs' of the population behave with atrocious bestiality. These chapters are of great psychological interest, because they show how deeply he had brooded on this subject. The things he describes can only have come out of his imagination, for no riots on anything like the same scale had happened in his lifetime" (Forster, p. 168; Orwell, "Charles Dickens," in *Dickens, Dali and Others* [New York: Reynal and Hitchcock, 1946], pp. 11–12).

[17] A hideous and curious example—curious in that Dickens both included it and yet had to be so reticent about it that it hardly makes sense as it stands—and a kind of epitome of the reality-fantasy-nightmare identity is an instance of historical allusion apparently put in for those who had read Carlyle's *French Revolution*. It is the farthest reach of shocking affront offered to Marie Antoinette, when one of the murderers of the Princesse de Lamballe fashions a mustache of pubic hair and flaunts it under the Queen's window. Carlyle's comment is Dickensian in its joining of horror with grandeur of feeling, and was perhaps meant by Dickens to be part of the specific allusion: "She was beautiful, she was good, she had known no happiness. Young hearts, generation after generation, will think with themselves: O worthy of worship, thou king-descended, god-descended, and poor sister-woman! why was not I there . . . ?" (*French Revolution*, III, i, 4). Dickens says only, and as it stands perplexingly: "False eyebrows and false moustaches were stuck upon them, and their hideous countenances were all bloody and sweaty, and all awry with howling, and all staring and glaring with beastly excitement and lack of sleep." Which of course, even without the specific allusion, makes for something of the effect of fantasy becoming real.

when anything is doubled, neither half can be said to make up the whole reality so that each alone is incomplete, a deficiency or distortion: though both together, in a specific situation, may only mean a reinforcement of nightmare. Thus Charles Darnay's double arrest, thus the sudden casting of Dr. Manette in the role of accuser, an especially apt irony since he had earlier been cast in the role of injured innocence. These have been criticized as forced or rigged: but equally they can stand, symbolically, as instances of the contradictory nature of subjective experience, even of the self, in relation to events. Certainly Dr. Manette had as much reason, or more, to curse the house of Evrémonde, as to honor and protect his son-in-law; and one basic lesson of the Revolution was that as it gathered strength it turned on itself. This at least seems to have been Dickens's feeling.

Doubling of one kind and another, whether as indication of madness or simply as a prime technique of symbolism in the fantasizing of reality, recurs throughout the book. The most obvious example is the physical resemblance of Charles Darnay and Sidney Carton—which looks on the surface like a trick, a plot device that hurts both theme and characterization. Yet if we move away from the realistic and literalistic, we can see this form of doubling as a representation of two worlds, the social or collective on the one hand, the individual or subjective—or, in Freud's terminology, "instinctual"—on the other. This second cannot live with the first; its way is the way of the outsider, the creature of waste places: but at moments of crisis it can save the first. Charles Darnay, the admirer of George Washington, is the "new man" of his time, unable to speak with his immovable uncle, the representative of the old regime, a gargoyle whom only the fire of revolution can melt or move; but in a way he is as immovable as his uncle, immovably virtuous and democratic, socially conscious. Sidney Carton, his counterpart, the outsider, is on the contrary moved from extreme to extreme: from an emptiness, desolation, and uncaring that place him below the norm of the collective, to a willed love and sacrifice that lift him above it. He is always isolated: but his isolation at first rejects society, at last embraces it, as when he says, "I see a beautiful city and a brilliant people rising from this abyss. . . ."

One of the best touches of counterrealism in the book is Dickens's refusal to account for Sidney Carton's isolation and emptiness; he is, at first, a jackal lurking out of nowhere. With Madame Defarge, perhaps wrongly, Dickens attempts a compromise, one of the indications of his struggle to bring together disparate materials. She too is a lonely stalking animal, a deadly counterpart of Lucie Manette, the two of them representing opposite versions of the forever untouchable woman in Dickens's longing imagination. At first, she is unmotivated, a creature of pure malignancy like Claggart in Melville's *Billy Budd,* or like

Iago: a cold monomaniac whose whole identity lies in hate and the meditation of revenge.[18] To be sure, the general oppression of the regime forms a general motivation; but she towers above the general world by virtue of her inflexible obsession, inhabiting a world of her own as much as the Marquis, a self-defining world. Surprisingly, toward the end, Dickens yields to realism and gives her a specific and credible motivation. This is jarring. At this point, both the Marquis and Sidney Carton, the one with a generalized motivation, the other with none at all, come off better. Yet she remains an instructive instance of Dickens's attempt throughout this novel to identify fantasy with reality —as in his own life at this momentous crisis he was likewise attempting to do.

Prison and imprisonment also color this novel and remove our thoughts from motivation. More perhaps than any other work by Dickens—though there are prisons and imprisonment in plenty elsewhere —this one is about people trapped in some kind of vise, consequently shut away from others, or susceptible of shutting others away. The Marquis is pent up by the logic of his world—only death can reach him. So, at an opposite pole, is Madame Defarge. Dr. Manette returns compulsively to shoemaking at a moment of crisis, the prisoner of past suffering and solitude; and he finds later in the story that his accusations as a prisoner return to thwart his new and larger acceptance of life. Lucie Manette's imprisonment is in passive purity, always likely to be crushed between mighty opposites; and Charles Darnay, courageous but helpless, is rendered a prisoner by his own probity. In a way the whole outlook is pessimistic, individual frailty pitted against public insanity, with salvation coming only accidentally and at the cost of yet another life. Even Sidney Carton's self-sacrifice has been depressed in value by some critics, who offer the opinion that when he gave up his life he gave up only what had been adjudged by the author and himself to be nearly worthless.

On the negative side, such considerations suggest that the novel discloses Dickens's despair at the choices before him: imprisonment, or, as the price of breaking out, madness and death. More positively, it reveals his ability to give his personal concerns an artistic shape. Despite its shortcomings, the work's effect is finally powerful and centralized. It escapes from the pull of excessive detail and plotting to a level of symbolic action as entrenched power, destructive revenge, thwarted love, isolation, and reconciliation play out their drama. And it is Dickens's closest approximation to the effect of tragedy. The significance of Sidney Carton's life is his growth to a new awareness and new love, a love perhaps higher than Dickens himself could

[18] Orwell says of her that she is "certainly Dickens's most successful attempt at a *malignant* character" ("Charles Dickens," p. 15).

achieve but one that he could—and it is all we ask of a writer—vividly imagine and record. Hence, in one way, this is Dickens's most personal novel, where he purged himself of one part, at least, of his distress; while in another way, it is his most impersonal, the grand objectivity of the historical events it springs from, the steady movement of its action, and the economy and integrity of its details keeping him at a workmanlike distance from his materials, and enabling him to achieve a purer effect at the close than he had ever achieved before.

III

This very purity caused concern when the novel first appeared. The author's friend and great admirer, John Forster, became altogether apologetic when, after Dickens's death, he analyzed it in his biography:

> . . . there is no instance in his novels, excepting this, of a deliberate and planned departure from the method of treatment which had been preeminently the source of his popularity as a novelist. To rely less upon character than upon incident, and to resolve that his actors should be expressed by the story more than they should express themselves by dialogue, was for him a hazardous, and can hardly be called an entirely successful, experiment.[19]

Then, as if to save the book from his own faint praise, he turns to its nobility at the end: "Dickens speaks of his design to make impressive the dignity of Carton's death, and in this he succeeded perhaps even beyond his expectation." [20] Forster thus takes the high road of moral feeling in judging the book and quotes enthusiastically the American critic, Grant White, for his lavish praise of Sidney Carton's last moments. The grandeur of this episode, along with the uncluttered theatricality of the main characters and the main action, formed for many years the chief points of emphasis for critics of the novel and its chief ground of popularity with the public.[21]

Some contemporary and later opinion remained adverse. A severe attack appeared in the *Saturday Review*, a Tory journal hostile to many reformist ideas, by Sir James Fitzjames Stephen, an attorney and judge who had been angered by Dickens's satirical treatment of legal and court procedures in *Bleak House*. It is an early example of wrongheadedness in criticism of this novel, yet occasionally shrewd enough

---

[19] Forster, p. 731.
[20] *Ibid.*
[21] A play of the time, *The Dead Heart*, by Watts Phillips, is an early reflection of the dramatic values of *A Tale of Two Cities*, as is Freeman Wills's play, *The Only Way* (1890), popular in both England and America; not to mention the MGM movie classic of the 30s, or the recent report that still another film version is to be made in the 70s.

to provoke an answer.[22] It was shortly answered [23] by a review in the periodical *The Press,* which made the point that the French Revolution is, to the greater effectiveness of "the storyteller's art," not allowed to intermingle in the action save as a *Deus ex machina;* that though the book runs the risk of morbidity in its first descriptions of Dr. Manette's insanity, it is saved by "the admirable account" to which his character is turned in the denouement; that Sidney Carton, "whether or not we admit that so peculiar a compound of opposites be humanly possible," represents the highest "poetical" reach of Dickens's genius; and that the book's few faults are chiefly faults of style: his "inveterate formalism," and (oddly harsh phrase) the "malicious affectation aforethought in which he wilfully and perversely insists upon dressing his best and his worst thoughts alike, as in the stiffest Prussian uniform." ("It was the best of times, it was the worst of times. . . .") But neither this piece nor Stephen's finds a level sufficiently above the work to see the whole, or sufficiently near it to see the contribution of the details. This effort was left to modern criticism.

Though Dickens hoped it was his best story, many moderns and near-moderns have named it his worst.[24] George Saintsbury, George Gissing, and Arnold Bennett found it unimpressive, an anomaly among Dickens's work, though Gissing had the perception to see that Dickens had produced "something like a true tragedy." [25] Another disappointed group was made up of those who preferred the Dickens of *Pickwick*; still another, of those who found the presentation of French culture and manners distorted or defective; and yet a third, of those who questioned Dickens's optimism in his portrayal of a beautiful city with a brilliant people and a Rousseauistic peasantry. There has also, more pertinently, been complaint about the mixture of realism with contrivances of suspense, coincidence, and sensationalism. Here Dickens himself had some opinions worth noting. He liked to observe that life is full of odd ties of circumstance and fortune, and of the *Tale* he says specifically:

[22] It contains such phrases as: "The broken-backed way in which the story maunders along. . . ." "The whole art is to take a melancholy subject, and rub the reader's nose in it . . ." and ". . . this is the very lowest of low styles of art." The whole review has been reprinted in *The Dickens Critics,* ed. George H. Ford and Lauriat Lane, Jr. (Ithaca: Cornell University Press, 1961), pp. 38–46.

[23] Without mention of the *Saturday Review* or of Stephen; but John Blackwood writes to George Eliot on December 25, 1859: "Look at the Press this week and you will see our friends of the Saturday Review as pleasantly flayed as you could wish for their insolent attack upon Dickens" (*The George Eliot Letters,* ed. Gordon Haight [New Haven: Yale University Press, 1954], III, 237).

[24] The chief source of the following summarized information is a very thorough and documented survey by Professor Heinz Reinhold, "Charles Dickens Roman *A Tale of Two Cities* und das Publikum," *Germanisch-romanische Monatsschrift,* XXXVI (1955), 319–37.

[25] *Charles Dickens: A Critical Study* (London, 1904), p. 67.

I am not clear . . . respecting that canon of fiction which forbids the interposition of accident in such a case as Madame Defarge's death. Where the accident is inseparable from the passion and emotion of the character; where it is strictly consistent with the whole design, and arises out of some culminating proceeding on the part of the character which the whole story has led up to; it seems to become . . . an act of divine justice. And when I use Miss Pross . . . to bring about that catastrophe, I have the positive intention of making that half-comic intervention a part of the desperate woman's failure; and of opposing that mean death, instead of a desperate one in the streets, which she wouldn't have minded, to the dignity of Carton's. Wrong or right, this was all design. . . .[26]

This may not justify Dickens's use of coincidence to the taste of every reader: but it shows that he held it to be more than mere contrivance, either because it was in fact realistic or had thematic relevances beyond the claims of realism.

A final point of attack has always been the high romanticism of Carton's sacrificial death, which is seen as an outcropping of Dickens's insensitivity to psychological nuance. Placed beside George Eliot and Flaubert, he can indeed be made to look a caricaturist. But there are other perspectives on his work which show us, through all his apparent flatness and simplicity, a "vision" unique in fiction, one in which the caricatures, the plot tricks, and the large, blunt emotions lock in, as behind a series of floodgates, a vast expanse of mythic contemplation involving mysterious figures (Sidney Carton, Madame Defarge), fateful journeys (the Marquis to his death, Darnay to his survival, Carton to his salvation), and a world in flames or darkness, yearning for the light. Modern criticism is trying to provide the appropriate keys for these locks, keys that will fit.

The essays and parts of essays reprinted here represent a body of modern criticism that shows the wide range of approaches possible in interpreting *A Tale of Two Cities.* Generally, they fall into three groups: (1) those that consider the work mainly as an expression of Dickens's personal obsessions and torments during the years just before its composition; (2) those that deal with its sources, of which there is a surprising variety, ranging from sensational literature to Bulwer Lytton's novel *Zanoni,* itself a handling of the theme of spiritual regeneration during the French Revolution but with mystical and magical overtones such as Dickens eschews; and (3) those that attempt a definitive assessment by examining the elements of the work itself. Earle Davis and Jack Lindsay discuss circumstances and sources, the first concentrating on literary and editorial matters, the second on the relevance of Dickens's personal life to his workmanship. The late

[26] Letter to Forster [August, 1859], in *Letters,* III, 117.

William H. Marshall takes up the neglected topic of symbolism and rhetoric, tracing patterns of image structure, a theme on which John Gross comments more broadly, assessing image-idea relationships and their expressive function. Such approaches are continued at greater length and with greater specialization by Taylor Stoehr, who argues persuasively that the structure of the novel is dreamlike in its pattern of association, its use of metonymy, and its grand pervasive metaphors. G. Robert Stange differentiates the actual *Tale* from the "tale" category by showing that it has a wholeness rich in detail, image, and thematic implication. Among the *View Points,* Bernard Shaw's provocative comment tries to make us believe in a vulgarized Dickens, an entertainer without a moral core; George Orwell, taking predictably a political-historical approach, nevertheless makes acute and surprising observations on Dickens's eye for detail and his ability to evolve an atmosphere—sinister, haunting, unforgettable; Sergei Eisenstein writes excitingly of the "overlay" or "montage" effect in Dickens, with examples chiefly from *Oliver Twist,* yet suggestively touching on the *Tale;* A. O. J. Cockshut strikes a Shakespearean note in surveying the whole achievement: ". . . in the end . . . the vivid journalist, the entertainer, and the artist are triumphantly at one"; and Taylor Stoehr, in a second excerpt, extends his treatment of Dickens's special powers of organization, particularly the power of giving life to objects, and of conjoining realism and metaphor to produce the effect of myth.

Interpretations

A Tale of Two Cities

by John Gross

A Tale of Two Cities ends fairly cheerfully with its hero getting killed; Dickens's previous novel, *Little Dorrit,* ends in deep gloom with its hero getting married. Violence offers Dickens a partial release from the sense of frustration and despondency which crept over him during the eighteen-fifties; the shadow of the Marshalsea lifts a little with the storming of the Bastille, and everyone remembers *A Tale of Two Cities* above all for the intoxication of its crowd-scenes. In fact they take up less space than one supposes in retrospect, and for the most part the atmosphere is every bit as stifling as that of *Little Dorrit.* Dickens originally thought of calling the book *Buried Alive,* and at its heart lie images of death and, much less certainly, of resurrection: themes which foreshadow *Our Mutual Friend.*

The story opens with the feeblest of resurrections, the recall to life of Doctor Manette. His daughter is afraid that she is going to meet his ghost, a fear that is almost justified when she actually sees his spectral face and hears his voice, so faint and lacking in life and resonance that it is "like the last feeble echo of a sound made long and long ago . . . like a voice underground." (Bk. I, Ch. 6.) The whole novel is thronged with ghosts; from the mist moving forlornly up the Dover Road "like an evil spirit seeking rest and finding none" to the gunsmoke which as it clears suggests Madame Defarge's soul leaving her body, there are scores of references to spectres, phantoms, and apparitions. The penniless émigrés haunt Tellson's like familiar spirits; Lorry sees the likeness of the Lucie whom he once knew pass like a breath across the pier-glass behind her; the fountains of the château show ghostly in the dawn—but it would be tedious to compile a catalogue.

Reprinted, with permission, from Dickens and the Twentieth Century, *ed. John Gross and Gabriel Pearson (Toronto: University of Toronto Press; London: Routledge & Kegan Paul, Ltd., 1962), pp. 187–97. Copyright © University of Toronto Press and Routledge & Kegan Paul, Ltd.*

Such ghostliness suggests, first of all, a sense of unreality, of the death in life to which men are reduced by imprisonment, psychological or actual. To Darnay, the prisoners in La Force, going through the motions of elegance and pride in the midst of squalor, are ghosts all, "waiting their dismissal from the desolate shore," and the scene simply "the crowning unreality of his long unreal ride." (Bk. III, Ch. 1.) But ghosts are also the creatures of false or, at any rate, imperfect resurrection: the grave gives up its dead reluctantly, and the prisoner who has been released is still far from being a free man. The inmates of the Bastille, suddenly given their liberty by "the storm that had burst their tomb," are anything but overjoyed: "all scared, all lost, all wondering and amazed, as if the Last Day were come, and those who rejoiced around them were all lost spirits." (Bk. II, Ch. 21.) Even the phlegmatic Darnay, after his Old Bailey acquittal, "scarcely seems to belong to this world again." As for Doctor Manette, he has been as deeply scarred by his prison experience as William Dorrit. Lucie's love is not enough in itself to stop him from retreating into his shoe-making, and it takes a symbolic act of violence to complete the cure; he is fully restored to himself only after Mr. Lorry has hacked to pieces his cobbler's bench, "while Miss Pross held the candle as if she were assisting at a murder." (Book II, Ch. 19). But by this time the centre of interest in the book has shifted unmistakably to Sydney Carton.

The prison and the grave are linked in Dickens's mind with the idea that "every human creature is constituted to be that profound secret and mystery to every other." We live in essential isolation; in each heart there is, "in some of its imaginings, a secret to the heart nearest it. Something of the awfulness, even of death itself, is referable to this . . . In any of the burial-places of this city through which I pass, is there a sleeper more inscrutable than its busy inhabitants are, in their innermost personality, to me, or than I am to them?" (Bk. I, Ch. 3.) On his journey to greet the newly released Manette, Mr. Lorry feels as if he is going to unearth a secret as well as dig up a dead man; in his dream the grave is confused with the underground strong-rooms at Tellson's, and he fancies himself digging "now with a spade, now with a great key, now with his hands." In his hotel room, the two tall candles are reflected on every leaf of the heavy dark tables, "as if *they* were buried in deep graves of dark mahogany, and no light to speak of could be expected of them until they were dug out." (Bk. I, Ch. 4.)

This oppressive sense of mystery generates suspicion and fear. "All secret men are soon terrified," Dickens tells us in connection with Barsad, the police spy; but we are in a world where everyone is a secret man, a world of whispers and echoes. On the Dover Mail "the guard suspected the passengers, the passengers suspected one another and the guard, they all suspected everybody else"; when Darnay returns to

France, "the universal watchfulness so encompassed him, that if he had been taken in a net, or were being forwarded to his destination in a cage, he could not have felt his freedom more completely gone." (Bk. III, Ch. 1.) Even in the haven established for Doctor Manette near Soho Square there is foreboding in the air, in the echoes which Lucie makes out to be "the echoes of all the footsteps that are coming by and by into our lives." An accurate enough premonition of the noise of feet and voices pouring into the Paris courtyard which first draws her attention to the bloodstained grindstone, or of the troubled movement and shouting round a street-corner which herald the Carmagnole. Carton's last impression, too, is to be of "the pressing on of many footsteps" on the outskirts of the crowd round the guillotine. Footsteps suggest other people, and in *A Tale of Two Cities* other people are primarily a threat and a source of danger. The little group around Doctor Manette is as self-contained as any in Dickens, but it enjoys only a precarious safety; the emblematic golden arm on the wall at Soho Square is always capable of dealing a poisoned blow.

A Tale of Two Cities is a tale of two heroes. The theme of the double has such obvious attractions for a writer preoccupied with disguises, rival impulses, and hidden affinities that it is surprising that Dickens didn't make more use of it elsewhere. But no one could claim that his handling of the device is very successful here, or that he has managed to range the significant forces of the novel behind Carton and Darnay. Darnay is, so to speak, the accredited representative of Dickens in the novel, the "normal" hero for whom a happy ending is still possible. It has been noted, interestingly enough, that he shares his creator's initials—and that is pretty well the only interesting thing about him. Otherwise he is a pasteboard character, completely undeveloped. His position as an exile, his struggles as a language-teacher, his admiration for George Washington are so many openings thrown away.

Carton, of course, is a far more striking figure. He belongs to the line of cultivated wastrels who play an increasingly large part in Dickens's novels during the second half of his career, culminating in Eugene Wrayburn; his clearest predecessor, as his name indicates, is the luckless Richard Carstone of *Bleak House*. He has squandered his gifts and drunk away his early promise; his will is broken, but his intellect is unimpaired. In a sense, his opposite is not Darnay at all, but the aggressive Stryver, who makes a fortune by picking his brains. Yet there is something hollow about his complete resignation to failure: his self-abasement in front of Lucie, for instance. ("I am like one who died young . . . I know very well that you can have no tenderness for me . . .") For, stagy a figure though he is, Carton does suggest

what Thomas Hardy calls "fearful unfulfilments"; he still has vitality, and it is hard to believe that he has gone down without a struggle. The total effect is one of energy held unnaturally in check: the bottled-up frustration which Carton represents must spill over somewhere.

Carton's and Darnay's fates are entwined from their first meeting, at the Old Bailey trial. Over the dock there hangs a mirror: "crowds of the wicked and the wretched had been reflected in it, and had passed from its surface and this earth's together. Haunted in a most ghastly manner that abominable place would have been, if the glass could ever have rendered back its reflections, as the ocean is one day to give up its dead." (Bk. II, Ch. 2.) After Darnay's acquittal we leave him with Carton, "so like each other in feature, so unlike in manner, both reflected in the glass above them." Reflections, like ghosts, suggest unreality and self-division, and at the end of the same day Carton stares at his own image in the glass and upbraids it: "Why should you particularly like a man who resembles you? There is nothing in you to like: you know that. Ah, confound you! . . . Come on, and have it out in plain words! You hate the fellow." (Bk. II, Ch. 4.) In front of the mirror, Carton thinks of changing places with Darnay; at the end of the book, he is to take the other's death upon him. Dickens prepares the ground: when Darnay is in jail, it is Carton who strikes Mr. Lorry as having "the wasted air of a prisoner," and when he is visited by Carton on the rescue attempt, he thinks at first that he is "an apparition of his own imagining." But Dickens is determined to stick by Darnay: a happy ending *must* be possible. As Lorry and his party gallop to safety with the drugged Darnay, there is an abrupt switch to the first person: "The wind is rushing after us, and the clouds are flying after us, and the moon is plunging after us, and the whole wild night is in pursuit of us; but so far, we are pursued by nothing else." (Bk. III, Ch. 13.) *We* can make our escape, however narrowly; Carton, expelled from our system, must be abandoned to his fate.

But the last word is with Carton—the most famous last word in Dickens, in fact. Those who take a simplified view of Dickens's radicalism, or regard him as one of nature's Marxists, can hardly help regretting that *A Tale of Two Cities* should end as it does. They are bound to feel, with Edgar Johnson, that "instead of merging, the truth of revolution and the truth of sacrifice are made to appear in conflict." A highly personal, indeed a unique crisis cuts across public issues and muffles the political message. But this is both to sentimentalize Dickens's view of the revolution, and to miss the point about Carton. The cynical judgment that his sacrifice was trifling, since he had nothing to live for, is somewhat nearer the mark. Drained of the will to live, he is shown in the closing chapters of the book as a man

courting death, and embracing it when it comes. "In seasons of pestilence, some of us will have a secret attraction to the disease—a terrible passing inclination to die of it. And all of us have like wonders hidden in our breasts, only needing circumstances to evoke them." (Bk. III, Ch. 6.) It is Carton rather than Darnay who is "drawn to the loadstone rock." [1] On his last walk around Paris, a passage which Shaw cites in the preface to *Man and Superman* as proof of Dickens's essentially irreligious nature, his thoughts run on religion: "I am the Resurrection and the Life." But his impressions are all of death: the day comes coldly, "looking like a dead face out of the sky," while on the river "a trading boat, with a sail of the softened colour of a dead leaf, then glided into his view, floated by him, and died away." (Bk. III, Ch. 9.) His walk recalls an earlier night, when he wandered round London with "wreaths of dust spinning round and round before the morning blast, as if the desert sand had risen far away and the first spray of it in its advance had begun to overwhelm the city." (Bk. II, Ch. 5.) Then, with the wilderness bringing home to him a sense of the wasted powers within him, he saw a momentary mirage of what he might have achieved and was reduced to tears; but now that the city has been overwhelmed in earnest, he is past thinking of what might have been. "It is a far, far better thing that I do, than I have ever done"—but the "better thing" might just as well be committing suicide as laying down his life for Darnay. At any rate, he thinks of himself as going towards rest, not towards resurrection.

By this time the revolution has become simply the agency of death, the storm that overwhelms the city. Or rather, all the pent-up fury and resentment that is allowed no outlet in the "personal" side of the book, with Carton kow-towing to Stryver and nobly renouncing Lucie, boils over in revolutionary violence: Dickens dances the Carmagnole, and howls for blood with the mob. Frightened by the forces which he has released, he views the revolution with hatred and disgust; he doesn't record a single incident in which it might be shown as beneficent, constructive or even tragic. Instead, it is described time and again in terms of pestilence and madness. Dickens will hear nothing of noble aspirations; the disorder of the whole period is embodied in the dervishes who dance the Carmagnole—"no fight could have been half so terrible." Confronted with the crowd, Dickens reaches

[1] Darnay, who only comes to life in the face of death, is nevertheless obsessed with the guillotine. He has "a strange besetting desire to know what to do when the time came, a desire gigantically disproportionate to the few swift moments to which it referred; a wondering that was more like the wondering of some other spirit within his, than his own." (Bk. III, Ch. 13.) Carton's spirit, perhaps; through the exigencies of the plot, Dickens has got the wires crossed.

for his gun; he looks into eyes "which any unbrutalized beholder would have given twenty years of life, to have petrified with a well-directed gun." (Bk. III, Ch. 2.) That "well-directed" has the true ring of outraged rate-paying respectability, while the image seems oddly out of place in a book which has laid so much stress on the stony faces and petrified hearts of the aristocracy.

Dickens can only deal with mob-violence in a deliberately pictur-esque story set in the past. But *A Tale of Two Cities,* written by a middle-aged man who could afford a longer perspective at a time when Chartism was already receding into history, is not quite analogous to *Barnaby Rudge.* There, however contemptible we are meant to find the world of Sir John Chester, the riots are an explosion of madness and nothing more. But the French Revolution compels Dickens to acquire a theory of history, however primitive: "crush humanity out of shape once more, under similar hammers, and it will twist itself into the same tortured forms." (Bk. III, Ch. 15.) The revolutionaries return evil for evil; the guillotine is the product not of innate depravity but of intolerable oppression. If Dickens's sympathies shift towards the aristocrats as soon as they become victims, he can also show a grim restraint; he underlines the horror of Foulon's death, strung up with a bunch of grass tied to his back (how his imagination pounces on such a detail!), but he never allows us to forget who Foulon was. Nor does he have any sympathy with those who talk of the Revolution "as though it were the only harvest under the skies that had never been sown," although he himself is at times plainly tempted to treat it as an inexplicable calamity, a rising of the sea (the gaoler at La Force has the bloated body of a drowned man, and so forth) or a rising of fire: the flames which destroy the château of St. Evrémonde "blow from the infernal regions," convulsing nature until the lead boils over inside the stone fountains. But cause and effect are never kept out of sight for long; Dickens is always reminding himself that the Revolution, though "a frightful moral disorder," was born of "unspeakable suffering, in-tolerable oppression, and heartless indifference." Society was diseased before the fever broke out: the shattered cask of wine which at the out-set falls on the "crippling" stones of Saint Antoine is scooped up in little mugs of "mutilated" earthenware.

But to grasp a patient's medical history is not to condone his dis-ease, and Dickens is unyielding in his hostility to the crowd. The buzzing of the flies on the scent for carrion at the Old Bailey trial and the mass-rejoicing at Roger Cly's funeral are early indications of what he feels. The courtroom in Paris is also full of buzzing and stirring, but by this time the atmosphere has become positively cannibalistic; a jury of dogs has been empanelled to try the deer, Madame Defarge

"feasts" on the prisoner, Jacques III, with his very Carlylean croak, is described as an epicure.

Whatever Dickens's motives, a good deal of this is no doubt perfectly valid; morbid fantasies can still prompt shrewd observations, as when we are shown Darnay, the prisoner of half an hour, already learning to count the steps as he is led away to his cell. In particular, Dickens recognizes the ways in which a period of upheaval can obliterate the individual personality; there is no more telling detail in the book than the roll-call of the condemned containing the names of a prisoner who has died in jail and two who have already been guillotined, all of them forgotten. Insane suspicion, senseless massacres, the rise to power of the worst elements: in the era of Gladstonian budgets Dickens understands the workings of a police state.

But it would be ludicrous to claim very much for the accuracy of Dickens's account of the French Revolution as such. There are scarcely any references to the actual course of events, and no suggestion at all that the revolution had an intellectual or idealistic content, while the portrayal of fanaticism seems childish if we compare it even with something as one-sided as *The Gods are Athirst*. For the purposes of the novel, the revolution is the Defarges, and although Carton foresees that Defarge in his turn will perish on the guillotine, he has no inkling of how the whole internecine process will ever come to a halt. As for Madame Defarge, she is as much driven by fate as the stony-hearted Marquis, with his coachmen cracking their whips like the Furies: the time has laid "a dreadfully disfiguring hand upon her." Her last entry is her most dramatic. Miss Pross is bathing her eyes to rid herself of feverish apprehensions, when she suddenly appears—materializes, one might say—in the doorway:

> The basin fell to the ground broken, and the water flowed to the feet of Madame Defarge. By strange stern ways, and through much staining blood, those feet had come to meet that water. (Bk. III, Ch. 14.)

We are reminded, by rather too forcible a contrast, of the broken cask of red wine which prefaces Madame Defarge's first appearance in the novel. Her element, from the very start, is blood.

• Still, *A Tale of Two Cities* is not a private nightmare, but a work which continues to give pleasure. Dickens's drives and conflicts are his raw material, not the source of his artistic power, and in itself the fact that the novel twists the French Revolution into a highly personal fantasy proves nothing: so, after all, does *The Scarlet Pimpernel*. Everything depends on the quality of the writing—which is usually one's cue, in talking about Dickens, to pay tribute to his exuberance

and fertility. Dickens's genius inheres in minute particulars; later we may discern patterns of symbolism and imagery, a design which lies deeper than the plot, but first we are struck by the lavish heaping-up of acute observations, startling similes, descriptive flourishes, circumstantial embroidery. Or such is the case with every Dickens novel except for the *Tale,* which is written in a style so grey and unadorned that many readers are reluctant to grant it a place in the Canon at all. Dickens wouldn't be Dickens if there weren't occasional touches like the "hospital procession of negro cupids, several headless and all cripples," which Mr. Lorry notices framing the mirror in his hotel (or the whitewashed cupid "in the coolest linen" on the ceiling of his Paris office, which makes its appearance three hundred pages later). But for the most part one goes to the book for qualities which are easier to praise than to illustrate or examine: a rapid tempo which never lets up from the opening sentence, and a sombre eloquence which saves Carton from mere melodrama, and stamps an episode like the running-down of the child by the Marquis's carriage on one's mind with a primitive intensity rarely found after Dickens's early novels, like an outrage committed in a fairy-tale.

But it must be admitted that the *Tale* is in many ways a thin and uncharacteristic work, bringing the mounting despair of the eighteen-fifties to a dead end rather than ushering in the triumphs of the 'sixties. In no other novel, not even *Hard Times,* has Dickens's natural profusion been so drastically pruned. Above all, the book is notoriously deficient in humour. One falls—or flops—back hopefully on the Crunchers, but to small avail. True, the comic element parodies the serious action: Jerry, like his master, is a "Resurrection-Man," but on the only occasion that we see him rifling a grave it turns out to be empty, while his son's panic-stricken flight with an imaginary coffin in full pursuit is nightmarish rather than funny. As comic characters the Crunchers are forced and mechanical; such true humour as there is in the book is rather to be found in scattered observations, but settings and characters are colourful rather than grotesque. Obviously Dickens's humour is many things, but it is usually bound up with a sense of almost magical power over nature: to distort, exaggerate, yoke together or dissolve is to manipulate and control external reality. In Dickens people are always taking on the qualities of objects with which they come into contact, and *vice versa:* a basic Dickensian trick of style, which makes its appearance as early as the opening pages of *Sketches by Boz,* where there is a fine passage ("Our Parish," Chapter VII) on the "resemblance and sympathy" between a man's face and the knocker on his front door. Such transformations are not unknown in *A Tale of Two Cities*—there is the obstinate door at Tellson's with the weak rattle in its throat, for example—but they occur less fre-

quently than in any other Dickens novel, and there is a corresponding lack of power for which a neatly constructed plot is small compensation.

Contrary to what might be expected, this absence of burlesque is accompanied by a failure to present society in any depth. *A Tale of Two Cities* may deal with great political events, but nowhere else in the later work of Dickens is there less sense of society as a living organism. Evrémondes and Defarges alike seem animated by sheer hatred; we hear very little of the stock social themes, money, hypocrisy, and snobbery. Tellson's, musty and cramped and antiquated, makes an excellent Dickensian set-piece, but it is scarcely followed up. Jarvis Lorry, too, is a sympathetic version of the fairy-godfather, a saddened Cheeryble who repines at spending his days "turning a vast pecuniary mangle," but this side of his character is only lightly sketched in. He may glance through the iron bars of his office-window "as if they were ruled for figures too, and everything under the clouds were a sum," but he is more important as a protective, reassuring figure: in times of revolution Tellson's mustiness becomes a positive virtue.

The lack of social density shows up Dickens's melodrama to disadvantage. This is partly a question of length, since in a short novel everything has to be worked in as best it can: Barsad will inevitably turn out to be Miss Pross's long-lost brother, Defarge has to double as Doctor Manette's old servant, and so forth. But there is a deeper reason for feeling more dissatisfaction with the artificial plot here than one does with equally far-fetched situations elsewhere in Dickens. Where society is felt as an all-enveloping force, Dickens is able to turn the melodramatic conventions which he inherited to good use; however preposterous the individual coincidences, they serve an important symbolic function. The world is more of a piece than we suppose, Dickens is saying, and our fates are bound up, however cut off from one another we may appear: the pestilence from Tom-all-Alone's really will spread to the Dedlock mansion, and sooner or later the river in which Gaffer Hexam fishes for corpses will flow through the Veneering drawing-room. In a word, we can't have Miss Havisham without Magwitch. But without a thick social atmosphere swirling round them, the characters of *A Tale of Two Cities* stand out in stark melodramatic isolation; the spotlight is trained too sharply on the implausibilities of the plot, and the stage is set for Sir John Martin-Harvey and *The Only Way*. So, too, the relentless workings of destiny are stressed rather clumsily by such a bare presentation; Madame Defarge points the finger of fate a little too vigorously, and there is a tendency towards heavy repetitions and parallelisms, brought out by the chapter-headings, "A Hand at Cards" and "The Game Made," "Dusk" and "Darkness," and so forth.

Yet despite the dark mood in which it was conceived, the *Tale* isn't a wholly gloomy work; nor is the final impression which it leaves with us one of a wallow of self-pity on the scaffold. We are told of Darnay in the condemned cell (or is it Carton?) that

> his hold on life was strong, and it was very, very hard to loosen; by gradual efforts and degrees unclosed a little here, it clenched the tighter there; and when he brought his strength to bear on that hand and it yielded, this was closed again. There was a hurry, too, in all his thoughts, a turbulent and heated working of his heart, that contended against resignation. (Bk. III, Ch. 13.)

And near the end, as Miss Pross grapples with Madame Defarge, Dickens speaks of "the vigorous tenacity of love, always so much stronger than hate." The gruesome events of the book scarcely bear out such a judgment, yet as an article of faith, if not as a statement of the literal truth, it is curiously impressive. For all the sense of horror which he must have felt stirring within him when he wrote *A Tale of Two Cities*, Dickens remained a moralist and a preacher, and it was his saving strength. But if the author doesn't succumb with Carton, neither does he escape with Darnay. At the end of the book "we" gallop away not to safety and Lucie, but to the false hopes of Pip, the thwarted passion of Bradley Headstone, the divided life of John Jasper. Nothing is concluded, and by turning his malaise into a work of art Dickens obtains parole, not release: the prison will soon be summoning him once more.

From *The Flint and the Flame*

by *Earle Davis*

Between the writing of *Little Dorrit* and of *A Tale of Two Cities* several important personal experiences affected Dickens' creative attitude. *A Tale of Two Cities* is a completely different kind of novel from any he had previously attempted, to a certain extent unlike his usual composition. It is odd that because this is the Dickens work that has been generally assigned for reading, generations of high school students have known Dickens mainly through this untypical novel. *Great Expectations* is also representative of experimental narrative technique, somewhat unlike his previous custom. One must look to Dickens' life for some light on this shift from the complex, interlocking-plot method and the careful dependence on symbolic reference he had developed in the great novels of his dark period.

When he broke with his wife and got involved in disagreement with the backers of *Household Words,* he decided to start a new magazine. *All the Year Round* needed to establish itself in the public eye, and it had to attract subscribers. It was natural for him to feel commercial pressure and to desire to re-establish his reputation with the reading public. He decided to write a novel for the new magazine which would "sell," and he wanted a subject which would attract attention. He would have to write it in weekly installments, and he recalled how much trouble he had experienced with his panoramic plan in *Hard Times.* Therefore he abandoned the multiple-plot technique and chose a subject completely different from his usual concerns. Accordingly, he did not aim at anything like the breadthwise cutting attempted by Tolstoi in *War and Peace* or by Thomas Hardy in *The Dynasts,* as one might have expected from the example of *Bleak House* and *Little Dorrit.*

From The Flint and the Flame: The Artistry of Charles Dickens, *by Earle Davis* (Columbia: University of Missouri Press, 1963), Chapter XII, "Recalled to Life" pp. 238–54. Copyright © 1963 by The Curators of the University of Missouri. Reprinted by permission of The University of Missouri Press. [This is the excerpted central section of the chapter, with some introductory and transitional remarks omitted.]

His usual rule for aiming at commercial success in fiction was to emphasize excitement, sentiment, and humor. Yet nothing was certain, and you could not foretell success or failure. He had reached sudden fame with *Pickwick,* had sold in the neighborhood of 100,000 copies for each issue of *The Old Curiosity Shop,* had dropped down to 20,000 for *Martin Chuzzlewit,* had gone back up with *Dombey and Son,* had fallen with *David Copperfield,* and had reached about 35,000 for *Bleak House* and *Little Dorrit.* Several conclusions derive from these figures. One of them is that his public did not comprehend the theses of his novels; his violent attacks on Victorian society did not materially affect his popularity and the money he received. A second conclusion is that his mature artistry was not generally understood or appreciated, since his most popular books sold best for reasons which were ephemeral or illogical. *Martin Chuzzlewit* and *David Copperfield* made him the least money of all his novels in monthly part form. From a commercial standpoint it is easy to see that Dickens might have been puzzled about his relationship to his audience. It is certain that his language, his tone, and his choice of material were influenced many times by his efforts to adjust his fiction to his readers, not only from a financial but from an artistic standpoint. Therefore he wrote *A Tale of Two Cities,* his latest attempt to compose a "popular" novel.

The new book was to be "historical." His only previous experimentation with history had been in *Barnaby Rudge.* But this time he was vitally interested in the history and convinced of its importance in relation to his own times. A number of sources supplied the inspiration for his story of the French Revolution. In the background for these influences was Carlyle's *French Revolution,* which Dickens claimed to have read over and over. In this book he felt he had a perfect source book for the primary historical scenes and events he would need.

His basic plot idea derived from the play written by Wilkie Collins, *The Frozen Deep.* The action of this play centers upon rivalry in love, one man at the last sacrificing himself to save the life of the other, who has won the girl. The main characters are Richard Wardour, Frank Aldersley, and Lucy Crayford. When Lucy decides to marry Frank, Richard volunteers for a dangerous sea voyage to the frozen North, and later Frank is assigned to the same expedition. When the exploring party is shipwrecked and marooned, two of the survivors are chosen by lot to attempt to get back to civilization and bring aid. Richard and Frank are—naturally—the two chosen. Frank becomes exhausted, and it appears that Richard may leave him to die. The final scene, however, shows Richard carrying his rival to safety, after which Richard collapses and dies. Dickens acted the role of Richard, and

Collins was Frank in the performance which brought Ellen Ternan eventually into Dickens' life.

The idea of one man sacrificing himself for another who had won the girl beloved of both also implied that the better man deserved the girl. Dickens had often studied the character who did not make the most of his capacities: Martin Chuzzlewit, Steerforth, Richard Carstone, and Henry Gowan show weakness in overcoming their environmental obstacles. Out of this type evolved Sidney Carton, man of great ability and charm, drifting with the tide, but atoning for his weaknesses by a grand gesture at the last—sacrificing himself that the girl he loves might be happy with the man she marries, the man whose life he saves at the cost of his own. Dickens was correct; this kind of story would sell.

The Frozen Deep does not resemble *A Tale of Two Cities* except for the central triangle-sacrifice theme. Dickens took this idea and set it in the time and events of the French Revolution. His main inspiration for the transposition was a novel by Bulwer-Lytton called *Zanoni,* which had been published in 1845. *Zanoni* is full of Rosicrucian dogma and concerns the initiate who has achieved earthly immortality; he lives for centuries. One of the requirements for reaching this magical state is the renunciation of all earthly passions, including love. Zanoni falls in love with a beautiful singer, Viola, and is faced with the choice between temporary happiness and earthly immortality. The theme of the novel is Zanoni's passion; he eventually sacrifices his own life to save Viola's, although she dies too and makes his attempt unavailing.

The early events of *Zanoni* take place in Italy, but the action moves to Paris and the Revolution for its climax. Here Viola is sentenced to the guillotine, and all efforts to help her prove abortive. Suspense rises as Zanoni realizes that the only way to save her is to die for her. Since he is theoretically able to live forever if he will abandon her, he has to make the supreme gesture to prove his love. His substitution for her in the condemned group is relatively simple. The number to die is eighty. Zanoni takes Viola's place and attempts to arrange the disguise and forged passports for her escape with Glyndon, a young man who also loves her. Zanoni then goes to his death by guillotine:

On to the Barrière du Trone. It frowns dark in the air,—the giant instrument of murder! One after one to the glaive,—another and another and another! Mercy! Oh, mercy! is the bridge between the sun and the shade so brief,—brief as a sigh? There, there! *His* turn has come. "Die not yet; leave me not behind. Hear me, hear me!" shrieked the inspired sleeper. "What! and thou smilest still!" They smiled—those pale lips— and *with* the smile, the place of doom, the headsman, the horror van-

ished! With that smile, all space seemed suffused in eternal sunshine. Up from the earth he rose; he hovered over her,—a thing not of matter, —an IDEA of joy and light! Behind, Heaven opened, deep after deep; and the Hosts of Beauty were seen, rank upon rank, afar; and "Welcome," in a myriad melodies broke from your choral multitude, ye People of the Skies,—"Welcome, O purified by sacrifice, and immortal only through the grave,—this it is to die." And radiant amidst the radiant, the IMAGE stretched forth its arms, and murmured to the sleeper, "Companion of Eternity! This it is to die!"

Comparison with Dickens' eventual death scene for Carton is interesting indeed; the younger author must have wanted to surpass this stylistic monstrosity, and he rose to the occasion.

The Frozen Deep and *Zanoni* combined to provide in the creative mind of Dickens the sacrifice of one lover for another, with the French Revolution and the guillotine providing the scene for death. When Dickens began planning the action which would lead up to this climax, he must have felt that a more dramatic means of substituting one lover for the other would have to be worked out. Previous novelists, including Collins, had written stories in which one main character resembled the other, resulting in confusion. Collins had just done this in *Hide and Seek,* and he was to do it in *The Woman in White* soon afterward. So Dickens seized upon the idea of having Darnay and Carton resemble each other.

The fact that Collins had been writing stories about the French Revolution had something to do with turning Dickens to this historical background. Two of these tales, *Gabriel's Marriage* and *Sister Rose,* were printed in *Household Words.* The latter tale introduces characters named Trudaine and Sister Rose who are denounced by Rose's villainous husband because they aided the escape of a victim of the revolutionary party. They are tried, sentenced, and would have gone to their deaths but for the help of a certain Lomaque, a worthless character who atones for his shameless life by saving them. He does it by painting an erasing liquid over their names on the death list, timing this to coincide with the fall of Robespierre, when all prisoners were released. Lomaque is a spy, and like Barsad in *A Tale of Two Cities,* he is in a position to effect a substitution of prisoners before the march to the guillotine. Dickens got Barsad into his novel early, because he knew he would have to supply a convincing way of putting Carton in Darnay's place at the climax. The general nature of this inspiration from Collins is apparent.

With a broad sketch of his proposed novel securely set in his mind, Dickens had a few definite ideas for narration: sacrifice of one lover for another; substitution before the guillotine; the French Revolution as his scene. He needed a reason for his hero's being sentenced to die.

Those who died were generally aristocrats; Darnay becomes an aristo-
crat, but a good one. He accordingly disagrees with the evil principles
of his class, principles which Carlyle had categorically insisted caused
the Revolution, and long before the Terror, Darnay emigrates to England. This allowed Dickens to balance the action between the two
countries, and his idea for his title followed naturally. Darnay could
fall in love in England, win his suit for Lucy against Carton, and later
be caught in the Terror's net in Paris, setting up the closing scenes.

At what point his actual reference to Carlyle occurred does not
matter for our purposes. Perhaps it was previous to some of the points
discussed or coincident with them. Carlyle does not tell lurid stories of
the atrocious deeds of the aristocrats in the days before the Revolution.
Dickens understood the conclusions of Carlyle very well. Lack of concern, pity, brains, understanding, and leadership among the aristocrats
had driven the downtrodden lower classes to rise in desperation. Any
ruling class needed to pay more than it was *forced* to pay in wages or
living conditions for its underlings, or it courted revolt. This point had
been the essence of Carlyle's warnings in *Chartism* and *Past and
Present*. But for his story Dickens needed a striking example of the
criminal incapacity and intolerance of the ruling classes.

When he asked for help in discussing his proposed tale with Carlyle,
the latter confused his own scholarly practice with Dickens' simple
needs and sent down a cartload of books which he had used in preparing *The French Revolution*. These books must have looked very
imposing and uninviting to the novelist, but he selected from them
the ones he thought would do him the most good. Forster says that
Dickens found Mercier's *Tableau de Paris* a useful source for many incidents and ideas incorporated in the novel. Actually, all Dickens got
from it was an atrocity or two.

Mercier provided a meticulous rendition of the years which preceded
the Revolution. His several-volume history covered the entire story
and gave Carlyle important parts of his data. Among Mercier's facts
and rumors of fact were instances of the feudal privileges once held by
the lord over his serfs. These included the notorious custom which
permitted the lord to take temporarily any woman in his domain from
her family or husband, the so-called *droit du seigneur*. Many tales
have been founded on this custom, particularly when some rebellion
occurred against it. The man who refused to give up his newly wed
wife was often roughly treated, sometimes tortured or killed when
he resisted or attempted vengeance. Dickens decided to use this spectacular example of evil aristocratic privilege in his novel.

Forster pointed out later, when Dickens had supplied it as the reason for Dr. Manette's confinement in the Bastille, that such feudal
customs had disappeared long years before the time Dickens covered

in *A Tale of Two Cities*. The author seems somewhat nettled in his reply:

> I had of course full knowledge of the formal surrender of the feudal privileges, but these had been bitterly felt quite as near to the time of the Revolution as the Doctor's narrative, which you will remember dates long before the Terror. With the slang of the new philosophy on the one side, it was not unreasonable or unallowable on the other, to suppose a nobleman wedded to the old cruel ideas, and representing the time going out as his nephew represents the time coming in. If there be anything certain on earth, I take it that the condition of the French peasant generally at that day was intolerable. No later inquiries or provings by figures will hold water against the tremendous testimony of men living at that time. There is a curious book printed at Amsterdam, written to make out no case whatever, and tiresome enough in its literal dictionary-like minuteness; scattered up and down the pages of which is full authority for my marquis. This is Mercier's *Tableau de Paris*.

In Carlyle's history, as part of his description of the fall of the Bastille, there is reprinted a letter found in the paper archives of the old prison. Dated October 7, 1752, it reads:

> If for my consolation Monseigneur would grant me, for the sake of God and the Most Blessed Trinity, that I could have news of my dear wife; were it only her name on a card, to show she is alive! It were the greatest consolation I could receive; and I should forever bless the greatness of Monseigneur.

This letter intrigued Dickens. It became his device for revealing the secret of Dr. Manette's imprisonment, elaborated into an account of the whole story of the woman appropriated by Monseigneur, brought to death along with her protesting brother. Dr. Manette, called in a medical capacity to attend the dying woman and her brother, later writes a letter to the King about what he had seen, and is therefore put in the Bastille by Monseigneur through a *lettre de cachet*. The letter quoted by Carlyle furnishes the ending of Dr. Manette's document, found by Defarge in Manette's empty cell in the Bastille when it is stormed:

> If it had pleased God to put it in the hard heart of either of the brothers, in all these frightful years, to grant me any tidings of my dearest wife—so much as to let me know by a word whether alive or dead—I might have thought that He had not quite abandoned them.

Mention of the prisoner's wife suggests the existence of a child. Dickens needed the girl for whom Carton would die. What better idea than that she should be Dr. Manette's child, sent to England after her mother's death and her father's imprisonment, ignorant of his fate?

That Darnay, nephew of Monseigneur and son of the brother who was involved in the affair which led to Dr. Manette's imprisonment, should also go to England, love and marry Lucy Manette, appealed to Dickens as another dramatic source of emotion. This circumstance would set the stage for Manette's Parisian and revolutionary friends to take revenge on all the descendants of Monseigneur for his past evil deeds, and it would provide the excuse for Darnay's death sentence.

In planning his novel, Dickens also took account of the difficulties he had previously encountered in the shorter installments. His solution was a simple one, but he had never tried it before: long novel—complex plots; short novel—one plot. All he really needed was the Darnay-Manette-Carton intrigue, with a dependent subplot to provide for the detail of exchanging his principals in prison before the guillotine. This is where Barsad came in, the spy whose scheme to fake the death of his fellow spy, Roger Cly, would be discovered by Jerry Cruncher, the body snatcher. Later in Paris this information is used by Carton to put pressure on Barsad and force his help in replacing Darnay with Carton on the guillotine list. A further narrative device occurred to Dickens in adapting his tale to shorter installments. This idea was to eliminate excessive dialogue, change his practice of developing his story by conversation, and describe more of the action. Forster did not like this idea at all. He says:

> To rely less upon character than upon incident, and to resolve that his actors should be expressed by the story more than they should express themselves by dialogue, was for him a hazardous, and can hardly be called an entirely successful, experiment.

The result, however hazardous it seemed to Forster, did contribute one thing to the final effect: It automatically eliminated many opportunities for melodramatic excesses, and by substituting description Dickens produced a tighter, faster-moving story than usual. What he lost was characteristic humor and entertaining speech. He had difficulty in selecting the scenes he wished to use from the many which occurred to him. He did not like restraint. He complains in his letters, "the small portions drive me frantic," but he was interested in the story and in the possibilities of his tragic action: "Nothing but the interest of the subject, and the pleasure of striving with the difficulty of the form of treatment . . . could else repay the time and trouble of the incessant condensation."

To the modern reader Dickens' way of developing all his novels is dramatic, since he normally uses dialogue more than any other device and designs his scenes as if for the stage. For *A Tale of Two Cities* he planned the course of action in direct imitation of the way it would be done for the theater, even though he had resolved to limit his dialogue.

He says: "How as to a story in two periods—with a lapse of time between, like a French Drama?" The reference to French drama is significant. He was thinking of the type of French tragedy which started its action with a prologue before the main acts, the conflict of motives being seized at some interesting point, back action thereby revealed, and the stage prepared for the main intrigue. The action which followed was usually in two acts which were carefully balanced in effect. Dickens decided to use as a kind of prologue the journey of Mr. Lorry to France to bring to England the recently released prisoner, Dr. Manette, to restore him to his daughter who had grown up in safety in England while he was confined in the Bastille. This opening scene introduced the mystery of what the doctor had done to cause his confinement. Then Dickens was ready to leap into his main story. *A Tale of Two Cities* is divided into three books as it is printed, but the first is really the prologue, shorter than the other two, which are balanced in length and action.

The practice of the historical novelist requires some specific knowledge of the history involved. Carlyle is Dickens' authority for the scenes in Paris before and during the Terror. There are three kinds of inspiration in the references Dickens makes to Carlyle. These are direct borrowings of description and scene, indirect use of characters and events, and suggestions which Dickens transfers to different characters or combines into new forms for fictional purposes.

For example, in the section in which the Bastille is stormed Dickens transposes many of Carlyle's own words:

> . . . the living sea rose, wave on wave, depth on depth, and overflowed the city to that point. Alarm-bells ringing, drums beating, the sea raging and thundering on its new beach, the attack begun . . .

> . . . behold, . . . how the multitude flows on, welling through every street; tocsin furiously pealing, all drums beating the *générale:* the Suburb Saint-Antoine rolling hitherward wholly, as one man! . . .

The second example is Carlyle's. The historical source gives many details which Dickens omits or concentrates, but the entire description is quite similar up to Defarge's journey to Dr. Manette's old cell to hunt for the document hidden there—the document which will later doom Darnay at the time of his trial.

Further direct borrowings are evident in the following chapter, which tells of continued killings and hangings to the *lanternes*. The murder of old Foullon who had once been injudicious enough to say of the third estate, "Let them eat grass!" is similar in both books. Smaller resemblances are numerous. Carlyle always talks of the suburb of Saint-Antoine as a sort of symbol of the third estate. It is here that the worst rioters, known as Brigands, operate. Dickens naturally puts

the Defarges and their wine shop in this section. The conduct of the trials, prison procedures, the tumbrils, and the guillotine come from Carlyle. The dancing of the Carmagnole finds its place in the novel as Lucy watches the prison where her husband lies. When Darnay is temporarily released he puts his name over the door of his residence in accord with the custom noted by Carlyle. The third volume of *The French Revolution* was an extremely convenient source book for all the details Dickens needed, and the novel gives the effect of authenticity for this reason.

Defarge and his wife come indirectly from Carlyle. The history presents Santerre, a brewer, living in Saint-Antoine, who became a leader of the revolt, and Carlyle makes casual mention of the president of the Jacobin Society, whose name was Lafarge. A certain Usher Maillard was active in the storming of the Bastille, doing most of what Defarge did in Dickens' narrative. "Defarge" combines from these originals whatever the novelist needed for his action. Carlyle also devoted eleven chapters in his history of the early rioting to "The Insurrection of the Women." One of his female leaders, a black Joan of Arc, was Demoiselle Théroigne, a striking and spectacular mob captain. In the fight at the Tuileries, Carlyle describes her as *Sibyl* Théroigne: "Vengeance, *Victoire ou la mort!*" Mme. Defarge is not "small-waisted," but she performs as mob leader, being much more ruthless than her husband. Dickens also invents a character, a companion of Mme. Defarge, whom he designates only as The Vengeance. He took what he wanted from Carlyle, changed and concentrated, it, and dressed up the details of his story from the historical record.

Carlyle attributes the worst excesses of the mob to the Jacobins, or the *Jacquerie*. Dickens creates types of revolt leaders from the lowest classes, giving them the names of Jacques One, Jacques Two, Jacques Three. The insignia of the French Revolution was patterned in threes —witness the tricolor and the slogan, "Liberty, Fraternity, and Equality." The Jacobin women were especially prominent at the guillotine, too, and the stories of their knitting while watching the executions were famous. Carlyle describes them at the executions, and Dickens applies this graphic bit of data to Mme. Defarge's knitted record of victims, handwork in which the names of the doomed were entwined with vengeance in her own variety of shorthand. The women are there knitting when Carton dies.

Names occasionally wander from one book to the other, perhaps in some entirely different connection from the original, showing merely that the name remained in Dickens' mind and was appropriated because the novelist needed some kind of cognomen. The hated *gabelle*, France's salt tax, turns up as the name of Darnay's agent on Monseigneur's estate, the man whose letter to Darnay begging his assistance in

his trial is the excuse for tempting Darnay back to France and his capture. Carlyle casually mentions Thelusson's Bank, where the great
Necker was once a clerk. Dickens, needing a name for the agency
which served to bring Lucy Manette and later her father from France
to England, shifted the establishment to Tellson's Bank, with branches
in Paris as well as London.

Carlyle's description of the butchery which went on outside La
Force Prison in the September Massacres of 1792 is about as horrible
as anything in his chamber of hyperbolic horrors. Wanton and brutal
slaying in the streets with axe and sword is much more forthright than
death under the guillotine. Dickens describes the great grindstone in
the yard outside the quarters of Tellson's Bank in Paris where the mob,
shirts and clothing dripping with the blood of their victims, comes to
sharpen weapons blunted in the awful slaughter.

Much of this transposition is the routine custom of the historical
novelist, taking his details from a reputable source and supplying his
facts where they are needed in his story. Of more interest to the critic
of narrative technique are the instances in which only a suggestion is
in the source, Dickens' expansion adding to the picture or the characterization which becomes an important part of his story. Dr. Manette,
for example, lost his mind in the long years of confinement. He learned
the shoemaker's trade in prison, and although nursed back to health
and sanity upon coming to England, he suffers lapses of memory and
reverts to his prison occupation whenever he is seriously troubled.
This regression happens when Lucy marries Darnay and again when
all seems lost and Darnay is sentenced to die.

Louis XVI was the king who mismanaged the governmental treatment of all parties in the days before the Terror. Without ability
at the proper moment, he was often a pitiable figure as he became
more and more enmeshed in problems beyond his scope. Occasionally
he escaped from the world of his troubles with the tools of a smith,
finding perfect release and forgetfulness while fashioning something
purely mechanical. The leap from this account in Carlyle to Dickens'
brilliant use of the shoemaker's tools by Dr. Manette shows his genius
in action; it is the trait which makes Dr. Manette the unforgettable
person he is.

The whole picture of Carton's death is traceable to bits of inspiration from Carlyle. Maton de la Varenne tells of his own narrow escape
from death when the haphazard trials were at their height. His terror
and the wild events during the time he spent in prison are recounted
in a pamphlet called "Ma Résurrection." Dickens seized upon the
idea of the resurrection as a symbol for Carton's death and intensified
it in other parts of the story. The connection with Christ's death and
the doctrine of the atonement was an easy transference. Dickens pre-

pares for his use of the resurrection theme by having Carton remember, on the night before Darnay is sentenced, how he had followed his father to the grave, and the preacher had read: "I am the resurrection and the life."

Mme. Roland, a brave and noble lady, was another individual sentenced to die. Carlyle tells her story:

> And now, short preparation soon done, she too shall go her last road. There went with her a certain Lamarche, "Director of Assignat-printing"; whose dejection she endeavoured to cheer. Arrived at the foot of the scaffold, she asked for pen and paper, "to write the strange thoughts that were rising in her"; a remarkable request; which was refused. Looking at the Statue of Liberty which stands there, she says bitterly: "O Liberty, what things are done in thy name!" For Lamarche's sake, she will die first; show him how easy it is to die: "Contrary to the order," said Samson.—"Pshaw, you cannot refuse the last request of a Lady"; and Samson yielded.

That Dickens referred to this passage is clear from his epilogue, where he records what Sidney Carton might have been thinking had he been able to do what Mme. Roland wanted to do. Says Dickens:

> One of the most remarkable sufferers by the same axe—a woman—had asked at the foot of the same scaffold, not long before, to be allowed to write down the thoughts that were inspiring her. If he had given utterance to his, and they were prophetic, they would have been these: . . .

The thoughts follow, ending with the lines:

> "It is a far, far better thing that I do, than I have ever done; it is a far, far better rest that I go to than I have ever known."

Mme. Roland's friend Lamarche had been timid about dying. The inspired idea of giving Carton the little seamstress to comfort—a completely new character in the story—follows from this hint. There is one other influence. It comes from the account in Carlyle of the manner in which Elizabeth, sister of Louis, and the "once timorous" Marchioness de Crussol went to the scaffold. They embraced before they walked up the steps to the guillotine. And so the little seamstress waits her turn, and as she goes to her death, "she kisses his lips, he kisses hers."

A Tale of Two Cities is the one book of Dickens in which the student can see his artistry in some detail, since the sources can be compared more accurately and completely than usual. His practice of noting and transforming anything he could use shows also to advantage. His climactic chapter depicting the death of Carton is his best experiment with sensation, and it reaches tragic intensity. The curtains of

trite melodrama have fallen away; dissection of his narrative devices shows how far he had come from the pure sentimentalism of Little Nell's death.

The novel, excellent as it is in certain respects, presents a number of problems. It is different from Dickens' usual narrative style, and this difference does not utilize every resource which we are accustomed to associate with his artistry. Farce and caricature are either absent or underplayed. The only effective farce character is Jerry Cruncher, the body snatcher who robs graves and objects to his wife's praying while he is at work. Mr. Lorry is described in the old manner of caricature, Mr. Stryver is a stupid ass, and Miss Pross as Lucy's maid has some eccentric moments. No remarkable speech mannerisms are given to any of the characters, unless Jerry may be considered to have one. In a sense Dr. Manette's "far away" voice is such a device, and it is appropriate to his long confinement in the Bastille. The development of action by dialogue is not completely replaced by description, for there are a few rare moments when Dickens reverts to his old habits. Examples are the scenes in which Jerry talks to his wife, or Carton almost proposes to Lucy.

The development of the plot is generally expert. In Book Two Dickens alternates action between England and France, managing to balance the events which introduce the Defarges and the scene in which Monseigneur is assassinated after he has run over a child, with the story of Lucy and Dr. Manette in London, building up to Lucy's marriage with Darnay. Dickens also carefully contrasts the two trials for Darnay's life, the first showing him acquitted on the false charge of spying brought by Barsad and Cly. Carton saves him by calling attention to the remarkable resemblance they have for each other, and thus confuses the witness and the jury. The second trial, in Book Three, gives Carton another opportunity for saving Darnay, but only after sentence is passed.

The weaknesses of the novel derive partially from Dickens' need to have something exciting happen in each installment. It is a shock to read the Bastille chapter and find the authentic surging action come to its crest when Defarge goes to Dr. Manette's cell. It is almost as if, for the purposes of the plot, the whole taking of the Bastille is important only because a fatal private document is hidden there. This is a question of emphasis, yet the novel is the tale of Carton, Darnay, and Lucy, not of the larger implications of the Revolution itself. In his dark novels Dickens had used his plots to illuminate the largest issues he could imagine. In this book he does not try to make the story of the Manettes symbolize the deepest meanings of French history.

Wilkie Collins was not quite satisfied with the way in which Dick-

ens handled his plot. In addition to suggesting that the story of Dr. Manette might be revealed early, he apparently felt that the device of the document which leads to the conviction of Darnay was weak or unlikely. Perhaps the doctor might have been able to write such a detailed and lengthy account of his wrongs and secrete it in his cell; it is improbable that the entire record would be read in the trial at this date in Paris. Dickens certainly imitated the practice of French drama in his alternating trial sequence, in which the hero's concerns prosper at first, then are suddenly reversed. Stage and motion-picture versions of the double trial usually combine events of the two days and speed up the action. In this and in several other moments which develop Dickens' intrigue there is the suggestion of overelaborate complication.

A few sequences have little motivation. Why does Carton go to Paris? Darnay goes to help Gabelle escape a death sentence, although what happens to Gabelle is lost in Darnay's own difficulties. Carton supposedly goes because Lucy is in trouble. Of course, Darnay spends a long time in prison before his trial, Dickens rapidly passing over months in his narrative. Carton could hardly know when he leaves London that he will be called upon to sacrifice his life for Darnay. In this kind of novel, such coincidence is generally accepted by the average reader, but it must be taken into account by the particular and critical ones.

The substitution of Carton for Darnay calls for more manipulation. Dickens' readers would hardly retain respect for Darnay if he easily permitted Carton to die for him; therefore he must be tricked into escaping. Dickens solved this problem by having Darnay drugged with some form of anesthetic so that he will be far from Paris before he wakens to learn what has happened. The exact nature of the anesthetic remains doubtful, since such drugs were not in general use at the time. Dickens reached into the misty realm of alchemy to find the mysterious potion which could secure the necessary effect. This point is easily accepted by the modern reader because he is used to the general properties of anesthesia and knows about Mickey Finns from modern detective novels.

The symbolism used by Dickens in this novel is of a different order from the fog of *Bleak House* and the prison atmosphere of *Little Dorrit*. It centers about the "recalled to life" hint in Carlyle and extends itself to the general implication of resurrection. Dr. Manette's release is a form of resurrection, and "Recalled to Life" is the password of the Prologue or Book One. Jerry Cruncher introduces a grotesque variation of this theme when he steals bodies to sell to medical students. Carton's death is a form of spiritual resurrection at the same time that

Darnay's release is to life from the sentence of death. Carton also carries some sense of atonement into his sacrifice, and the symbol works its way into the great climax.

This climax is prepared for and built up in a more concise fashion than in any other novel. The last three chapters are chronologically adjusted for this effect. In Chapter XIII Carton substitutes himself for Darnay, and the drugged man is hurried from the city by Mr. Lorry, Lucy, and Dr. Manette. Enough is told to assure the reader that they escape, and then they are lost to the narrative. Chapter XIV recounts the death of Mme. Defarge at the hands of Miss Pross, then goes on to show that she and Jerry Cruncher escape too. In Chapter XV Carton goes to the guillotine, and that is the end. In other novels Dickens had sometimes added chapters and incidents to take care of the future of almost every character in the story. In *A Tale of Two Cities* Carton dies, and the story is finished except for his imaginary thoughts at the scaffold.

The thesis of the novel is: *Revolution can happen in England too!* The aristocrats in France were stupid and hardhearted; they were responsible for spurring the people to revolt; England's ruling classes were also being stupid and hardhearted. Dickens joins with Carlyle in showing the reasons for what had happened in France, although he does not try to bring in a panoramic view of historical characters like Mirabeau, Lafayette, Robespierre, or Napoleon. Nor is there any attempt to do what Tolstoi might have attempted: show the struggles of the government for money in time of depression, the difficulties of parliament, the pathetic story of Marie Antoinette, the philosophical thinking behind the movement. Dickens centered on saying of the French Revolution just what he had said concerning the economic crises which were happening in England. In the first part of his novel he sympathizes with the downtrodden people; but at the last these people are the villains. Extreme injustice leads to violence; see what happened in the days of the Terror. If British employers insist upon the selfish laissez-faire doctrine, workers will eventually rise to protect themselves. A catastrophe like the French Revolution could easily happen elsewhere.

The implied comparison is not quite valid. Modern research shows that the French Revolution was a much more complex affair than Carlyle and Dickens judged. But the effect of Dickens' novel is intentionally limited in scope. The book is not *War and Peace*. His tale remains the account of one small group of characters who suffered in the course of the cataclysm which surged about them and went on to historical, political, and economic developments completely beyond the purposes of the tale. On a small and relatively selective scale within

the limits defined it is a dynamic historical novel, even though it does not call upon all the technical resources at Dickens' command. He sacrificed solidity for the spectacular, the large scene for the single vivid flash, but he got it.

The Method of *A Tale of Two Cities*

by William H. Marshall

"Knitted, in her own stitches, and her own symbols, it will always be as plain to her as the sun." So Ernest Defarge describes the meaning which his wife imposes upon her art. We are tempted at first to regard the words as a description of Dickens's method in *A Tale of Two Cities,* but in the novel the result is far more subtle than a private allegory. It is commonplace to recognize the popularity of this work, the difference between it and other Dickens novels, and the successful use of what would usually be hackneyed devices, such as the opening with a lost-and-found scene, with which many novels close, and the closing with a switch of doubles, with which many open. Prolepsis and antithesis are characteristically associated with Dickens's method, but here we have a pattern involving the explicit and obvious use of these for structural purposes and the implicit and indefinite use for symbolic purposes. In the fusion of these we find the method of *A Tale of Two Cities.*

There are many obvious parallelisms in the novel, which because of the restricted number of characters, never become confusing or distracting. The contrast is explicit in the title, as in the opening chapter, "It was the best of times, it was the worst of times" (I, i). Mr. Lorry's journey to Paris and his recall of Dr. Manette to life in the beginning of the story foretell the flight from Paris and the rescue of Charles Darnay toward the end. Darnay's one trial in London foreshadows the two in Paris. The First Book ends with Dr. Manette's release from prison and the Second with Darnay's beginning the journey that will lead him to prison. The differences are as obvious as the similarities in a comparison between Mr. Lorry's professional activities and Jerry Cruncher's other trade. Manette and Darnay, both Frenchmen, the principal persons "Recalled to life," present a kind of

"The Method of A Tale of Two Cities," *by William H. Marshall. From* The Dickensian, *LVII, part 3, no. 335 (September, 1961), 183–89. Copyright © 1961 by* The Dickensian. *Reprinted by permission of* The Dickensian. [*This article appears in modified form as a part of Chapter VII of the author's book,* The World of the Victorian Novel (*South Brunswick and New York: A. S. Barnes and Co., Inc.; London: Thomas Yoseloff, Ltd., 1967*).]

opposition which becomes comprehensible only as the story unfolds; and Lorry and Carton, the recallers to life, represent mutually exclusive areas in the British character. Dr. Manette and Sydney Carton are both concerned with fusing the split personality. And always there is present the comparison between the mob of London and the mob of Paris and, derivatively, between the few and the many.

These more easily recognized parallelisms are usually structural, that is, they are concerned with the action of the work and in themselves may frequently be meaningless. It is, however, those parallelisms which are part of the descriptions, the themes, and the moods of *A Tale of Two Cities,* those which are implicit in the work as an artistic creation, frequently possessing limited structural value, which give the work the basis of its appeal and its power. They are essential to the full meaning of the novel, but because of their nature and function—they constitute a complex of symbolism rather than sheer allegory—the full meaning is indefinite, elusive, and uncertain.

To pursue this line of criticism with regard to *A Tale of Two Cities* may be to suggest to many readers that Dickens is here more profound or complex—more "metaphysical" or "poetic"—in his meaning than they have been accustomed to admit. This is certainly not my intention, but it is apparent that many readers have sacrificed the image of Dickens as a thinking being and a conscious artist to the insistence on his commonplace practicality. They have confused the quality of the point of view, obvious and somewhat simple, which Dickens establishes for his readers, with the craft that he employs, subtle and at times complex, to develop such a point of view. Regarded objectively, *David Copperfield* may be taken to have a meaning, that simple goodness and intelligence ultimately bring happiness; or *A Tale of Two Cities* may convey the proposition that love conquers hate. Both are simple meanings, but their nature does not require that the method of projecting them, of constructing the novels through which they are presented, need also be simple. Reduced to a statement, the objective meaning of *A la Recherche du Temps perdu* or *Portrait of the Artist as a Young Man* may be quite simple, but few, if any, would suggest that the method of Proust or of Joyce is simple. The comment of Professors Wellek and Warren on the results of analysis of philosophic content is as applicable to novels as to poetry: "we frequently discover mere commonplaces concerning man's mortality or the uncertainty of fate."

Such is the case of *A Tale of Two Cities.* The phrase "Recalled to Life," the title of the First Book, reveals at once that the novel is about the relation between life and death, that it embodies the rebirth theme. The developing situation involves the desire of a people for political and social regeneration, and the principal characters in

the novel dramatize the means by which love alone can bring about rebirth. Dr. Manette is the first "recalled to life." Then Charles Darnay is once "recalled" from death under English Law and twice under French Terror. Throughout the novel the meaning of the phrase is implicit in incidents. Miss Pross discovers her brother alive, and even Madame Defarge is "recalled" in that she reveals herself as the one surviving member of the peasant family injured by the brothers Evrémonde. 'At all times life and death are juxtaposed to give the structure and meaning of the novel. Related to this juxtaposition is the antithesis between the worlds of reality and of dream—in the chapter "Echoing Footsteps"; in the reference to "the shadows of the actual Bastille thrown upon him [Dr. Manette] by a summer sun, when the substance was three hundred miles away" (II, iv); and in the picture of Darnay, alone in his cell, dreaming that he is home again and yet, when Carton comes to rescue him, incapable of accepting this situation as reality. In terms of the antithesis between reality and dream we grasp the significance of the silent interplay of eyes and hands in the action—the watching and the knitting—of Madame Defarge, for whom reality becomes not the world of flesh which she records in her work, but that record itself. The central dramatic parallelism of the work, the contrast-in-similarity between Charles Darnay and Sydney Carton, fuses the life-death and thence the reality-dream juxtaposition. "Indeed, I begin to think we are not much alike in any particular you and I," Carton remarks to Darnay after the English trial, the outcome of which arose from their apparent similarity (II, iv). Each represents what the other might have been. Carton admits to himself that he dislikes Darnay because "he shows you what you have fallen away from, and what you might have been!" (II, iv). Carton dislikes the image of that with which in life he would but cannot identify himself, that which he can become only in death. The meaning of *A Tale of Two Cities* is concerned with irony, the perceived difference between essence and appearance, in this instance the coming of life from death.

The method of the novel, originating within but transcending the meaning, is the development of the life-death antithesis—with its implication that every object has its shadow and every being its alternate —into a pattern of images, whose value, though frequently structural, is always symbolic; but the significance of the symbol in any given instance is sufficiently inconclusive that the imaginative faculty of the reader, though stimulated to relate this symbol to others in the work, is not inhibited by a fixed allegorical equation. The method of the novel amplifies its meaning: we know that *A Tale of Two Cities* is about rebirth through death, the essential Christian paradox, but we cannot reduce to a simple statement all that it says about this.

The method is most obvious in the opposition between symbols of life and death. These usually take the form of images of food and of destruction. Early in the novel the mill is explicitly the symbol of the system that grinds people unto death rather than of the peaceful production of food; it foretells the appearance of both the grindstone, with which the instruments of slaughter are to be sharpened, and the guillotine itself. And at this same early point we learn that amid hunger, "Nothing was represented in a flourishing condition, save tools and weapons" (I, v). In time, only the conditions of the latter will be "flourishing." But for the moment ferment exists just beneath the surface: "the time was to come, when the gaunt scarecrows of that region should have watched the lamplighter, in their idleness and hunger, so long, as to conceive the idea of improving on his method, and hauling up men by those ropes and pulleys, to flare upon the darkness of their condition" (I, v). In the ceremony of taking chocolate, "the leprosy of unreality disfigured every human creature in attendance upon Monseigneur" (II, vii). The fountain in the country recalls that in the town, and though both would ordinarily be symbols of life, each becomes a scene of death—in the city a child lies under the wheels of the carriage of the Marquis, and much later in the country the body of the murderer of the Marquis remains hanging on the gallows near the fountain. "It is frightful messieurs. How can the women and children draw water! Who can gossip of an evening under that shadow!" remarks the mender of roads to Defarge and the three Jacques. "When I left the village, Monday evening as the sun was going to bed, and looked back from the hill, the shadow struck across the church, across the mill, across the prison—seemed to strike across the earth, messieurs, to where the sky rests upon it!" (II, xv). And in time the shadow becomes reality of course, and the fire that destroys the chateau of the Marquis becomes so intense that "molten lead and iron boiled in the marble basin of the fountain; the water ran dry" (II, xxiii). The massacre "was to set a great mark of blood upon the blessed garnering time of harvest" (III, i). During the second French trial of Darnay, Madame Defarge, looking on the face of the hated one who is to be condemned, is described as "feasting" (III, ix). And the tumbrils, instruments of death, are compared to plows as they cut through the crowds (III, xv). There are other examples, but in all instances the symbols of death seem to triumph over the symbols of life—only to give greater emphasis to the resolution of the work when it comes.

The most significant images of life and death are those of blood, wine, and stone. In the beginning the relation is indicated by the incident of the man writing the word *blood* with wine spilled on the stone before Defarge's shop. "Is there no other place to write such words

48 William H. Marshall

in?" Defarge asks (I, v). The question is rhetorical, and the answer lies in the remark of one of the three Jacques standing in the wine shop: "It is not often . . . that many of these miserable beasts know the taste of wine, or of anything but black bread and death" (I, v). Wine is traditionally a beneficent symbol, the food for life, as blood is the sustainer of life; but when either is spilled, it becomes a maleficent symbol—of hate, waste, and death—and on this value rests much of the development of the method of the work. The wine mars the stone with what seems to be a death-like permanence, which will not yield to supposedly purifying force of water. Regarding the "terrestrial scheme," Sydney Carton remarks: "As to me, the greatest desire I have, is to forget that I belong to it. It has no good in it for me—except wine like this—nor I for it" (II, iv). His wine, explicitly red wine, recalls that spilled in front of Defarge's shop and foretells the fall of blood, the only means by which Sydney Carton can fulfill his death-wish, but also much more.

The image of stone is potentially the symbol of life, as in the stone used in a mill to grind grain; but through much of the novel stone symbolizes death, at times explicitly so, as in the report of the murder of the Marquis, "that there was one stone face too many, up at the chateau" (II, ix). In the description of the village at night, as the body of the murderer hangs from its scaffold, the life-death symbols as they have appeared to this point are brought together: "Chateau and hut, stone face and dangling figure, the red stain on the stone floor, and the pure water in the village well—thousands of acres of land—a whole province of France—all France itself—lay under the night sky, concentrated into a faint hair-breadth line" (II, xvi). The blood-wine relation is again explicit in the contrast between the security of Lucie's life in England and the threat to her happiness which the mob unconsciously prepares in France: "Now, Heaven defeat the fancy of Lucie Darnay, and keep these feet far out of her life! For, they are headlong, mad, and dangerous; and in the years so long after the breaking of the cask at Defarge's wine-shop door, they are not easily purified when once stained red" (II, xxi). Defarge's shop has become the center for the spilling of blood. The grindstone, anticipated by the mill and foretelling the guillotine in its lifeless substance and deathly function, is a kind of unifying central symbol; as two men turn at it, "some women held wine to their mouths that they might drink; and what with dropping blood, and what with dropping wine, and what with the stream of sparks struck out of the stone, all their wicked atmosphere seemed gore and fire"; in the silence, when the stone was again still, it "stood there in the calm morning air, with a red upon it that the sun had never given and

would never take away" (III, ii). And the blood of the daily group of her victims is "the day's wine to La Guillotine" (III, xv).

The association of blood and wine is probably archetypal but certainly, within the Christian tradition, orthodox. The Eucharistic suggestions should be quite apparent, despite a possible tendency to minimize the traditional element in Dickens's own background and in the culture in which he and his readers lived. But the use of these images as part of the action would seem to be ironic, for, in immediate appearances at least, the blood-wine correspondence portends evil— the stone remains stained. Man's evil, feeding on hatred, would seem to produce only further evil, and the journey into the shadow of death would appear to bring no rebirth. But for this thesis of action there is an antithesis of symbol, first suggested perhaps in the description of the calm that came to Dr. Manette following the emotional intensity of his reunion with Lucie—"emblem to humanity, of the rest and silence into which the storm called Life must hush at last" (I, vi)—and finally made fully explicit in the presumed thoughts of Sydney Carton in the moment before death. From the beginning of the work to the conclusion, despite all appearances, the meaning emerges, that ultimately good and love will destroy evil and hate. To state this as I have done is to recapitulate the essential teaching of Christian ethics, but it is also to repeat a cliché: it carries no more emotional force in itself than the mere assertion that Miss Pross possesses "the vigorous tenacity of love, always so much stronger than hate" (III, xiv); it is forceful only because it emerges from the story and, more significantly, from the scheme of images which become the symbols of redemption running through the novel.

Evil engenders evil; terror creates terror. In Defarge and his wife we find what has happened to France, what could happen to any nation, to any man: if we hate, we become what we hate. But eventually hatred, though intense, is self-destructive, and of this assertion the image of the rack is an emblem: "the last drop of blood having been extracted from the flints, and the last screw of the rack having been turned so often that its purchase crumbled, and it now turned and turned with nothing to bite" (II, xxiii). Madame Defarge, to be destroyed by her own pistol, so surprises Miss Pross that the English lady drops the basin in which she has been washing her eyes, and it "fell to the ground broken, and the water flowed to the feet of Madame Defarge. By strange stern ways, and through much staining blood, these feet had come to meet that water" (III, xiv). In the opening lines of the final chapter the narrator remarks, "Crush humanity out of shape once more, under similar hammers, and it will twist itself into the same tortured forms." And Carton, about to die, is presumed

to foresee that in years ahead "this place" will be "fair to look upon, with not a trace of this day's disfigurement" (III, xv).

But before this, as he has resolved upon his plan, Sydney Carton, the man who would die rather than live but has had the compelling motivation to do neither, recalls the "solemn words, which had been read at his father's grave" but now have for him the meaning held only for the reborn: "I am the resurrection and the life, saith the Lord: he that believeth in me, though he were dead, yet shall he live: and whosoever liveth and believeth in me shall never die" (III, ix). Carton's need for real motivation to live and his wish to die have been apparent from the beginning, but now they are fused and to be fulfilled within the context made clear by the allusion. The "solemn words" are most familiar perhaps in the service for the burial of the dead, but they are first those of Christ in *St. John* (xi, 25), spoken after Lazarus has been recalled to life; as the recall of Lazarus in the Gospel anticipates the resurrection of Christ and the salvation of Man, so the recall of Darnay through Carton's sacrificial death and the rebirth of the spirit of Carton prefigure the redemption prophesied in the final chapter.

The Christ-like image of Carton is now, though faint and uncertain, inescapable, and—aware of the significance of the blood and wine imagery—we look backward and forward seeking signs. The guilt of Darnay is not really his own but, like Original Sin, that inherited which he himself cannot remove and from the effects of which he must be saved by one who, closely resembling him in his physical being, will take upon himself through his own death the burden of guilt. The guillotine has become for the people what the Cross was formerly: "It was the sign of regeneration of the human race. It superseded the Cross. Models of it were worn on the breasts from which the Cross was discarded, and it was bowed down to and believed in where the Cross was denied" (III, iv). But by his death Sydney Carton makes the guillotine in reality what the people imagine it to be. Carton is clearly the agent through whom good destroys evil. Motivated by love, he undoes what Madame Defarge, who has been moved solely by hatred, has wrought; finally, as she lies dead in Lucie's deserted apartment, Madame Defarge has by all her efforts brought about only one fact, the inevitable death of Sydney Carton, which has become to him psychologically and spiritually necessary. Like one of the Fates, Madame Defarge involves in her incessant knitting the symbols for individual men, but of their death rather than their lives. She does not think; nor does she feel outside of her one destructive motivation, and here she might be said only to react: she becomes a further agent in the series of evil causes and effects which she herself attributes to destiny. At first it might appear that her antithesis is Lucie, who loves what

Madame Defarge hates, whose "weaving" with "the golden thread" of life (II, xxi) is in opposition to Madame's knitting, and whose Miss Pross, in fact, brings about the physical destruction of Madame Defarge. But her physical death is of no greater importance than that of Sydney Carton considered in itself. It is Carton himself who is her real antithesis. He rejects the one temptation to destroy her by force —when she gives him directions from the wine shop and her hand is on his arm—and destroys the corruption in her spirit and all its evil effects by allowing her to destroy him in the flesh. Where she is seemingly impersonal, he is obviously personal; where she controls herself and her surroundings, he apparently lacks control of either; where she is strong, he is weak. But it is Sydney Carton by his sacrifice, rather than Madame Defarge through her revolution, who shows the way to achieve that to which the French nation in its violence, or all mankind in fact, aspires.

But we must face the implications of the symbolism. Is there an equation to Christ in the person of Sydney Carton at the time of his sacrifice? Has Dickens put the story of Christ in a social and psychological context? I think not. The implication permeates the symbolic structure of *A Tale of Two Cities,* but the equation is never specific. Nor was it meant to be, for in the very inconclusiveness of Dickens's use of symbols—rather than in a contrived and ultimately meaningless allegory, which would leave the reader no room for the work of the imagination—lies the source of the effect of the work. In the case of Carton it is not an equation to Christ but the allusion to Christ which is significant. Acting in the image of Christ, Carton is, in his splendid sacrifice, the representative of the best achievement in Man. Darnay in his good faith with an old servant and in his love for his wife and child is the model of the more normal though less dramatic good in Man, as indeed the misguided French people themselves might become following their struggle for bread rather than death.

But these statements come dangerously close to meaning, and the meaning of the novel seen as a simple formula we know well enough. It is the method which is the source for power in *A Tale of Two Cities* —the suggestive yet inconclusive use of interacting images, upon which are built the reader's tensions, expectations, and imaginings.

A Tale of Two Cities

by Jack Lindsay

Charles Dickens was in a driven demoniac state of mind when the idea for *A Tale of Two Cities* came to him. The bracelet he sent to Ellen Lawless Ternan had fallen into the hands of his wife Kate; and he was determined to end his marriage and to seduce Ellen. But he was in the midst of the rehearsals which had finally brought himself and Ellen together; and he could not pause to think. Amid Kate's tears, Forster's disapproval and a generally unnerving situation, he carried on in his furious possessed fashion, determined to have his own way and yet to keep his hold on the public; and in the midst of this spiritually and physically racked condition, as he was holding back his agony of mind by acting and producing *The Frozen Deep*, the central idea of the novel burst upon him.

So much we know from his own statement. It is clear then that we should be able to find the imprint of his ordeal, his tormented choice, in the novel. One would expect writers on his work to concentrate on this problem; but so abysmally low is the standard of Dickens criticism that no one has even seriously raised the question at all.

I

Where then is the imprint of the situation to be traced? By solving this point we can begin to understand what the novel itself is about, and the part it plays in Dickens' development. One general aspect of the selection of theme is at once obvious. The deep nature of the breach he is making with all customary acceptances is driving him to make a comprehensive effort to grasp history in a new way. So far (except for *Barnaby Rudge*) he has been content to use certain symbols to define his sense of basic historical conflict and movement. Yet all the while the influence of Carlyle, both in his *French Revolu-*

tion and his prophetic works like *Past and Present*, has been stirring him with the need for a direct statement of the historical issue as well as a symbolic one; and now, as he is coming close to a full confrontation of his opposition to all ruling Victorian values, he feels the need to set his story of conflicting wills in a manifestly revolutionary situation: that on which he had so long pondered as holding the clue to the crisis of his own world.

He had read and re-read Carlyle's history, till its theme and material were richly present in his mind; and now he wrote to the master asking for a loan of the cited authorities. The story goes that Carlyle jokingly sent him all his reference-books, "about two cart-loads." And in the novel's preface Dickens wrote:

> It has been one of my hopes to add something to the popular and picturesque means of understanding that terrible time, though no one can hope to add anything to the philosophy of Mr. Carlyle's wonderful book.

But though this need to make a general reconsideration of the nature of historical movement and change was certainly central in the impulse that Dickens felt, he had to fuse the overt theme with a more immediately personal nexus of emotion and imagery before it could take full grip of him. In the midst of his domestic misery and frenzied play-acting he did not feel simply an intellectual need to revalue history. The desire to break through obstructions and to mate with Ellen could turn into the desire to write about the French Revolution only if some image or symbol made him feel a basic coincidence between his own experience and the Revolution. What then was this image?

It was that of the Imprisoned Man in the Bastille. The Lost Man who had been jailed so long that he has become an automaton of oppressed misery; who has forgotten even the source of his wrong, the cause of his dehumanizing misery; who needs to break out of the deadly darkness of stone in order to become human again, to learn the truth and regain love.

Here then is the core of the novel. The originally-intended title was *Recalled to Life*. Though Dickens dropped this for the whole novel, he kept it for the first part, and it expressed the originating emotion of the story. *A Tale of Two Cities* is built up from the episode of Dr. Manette's unjust imprisonment; and its whole working-out is concerned with the effects of that unjust deprivation of light and joy: effects which entangle everyone round the Doctor and recoil back on his own head in unpredictable ways. The Doctor's fate is thus for Dickens both a symbol of the Revolution, its deeds, causes, and consequences, and of himself, immured in a maddening cell of lies and

cruelties, and seeking to break through into the truth, into a full and happy relationship with his fellows. It was the demented sense of environing pressures, of an unjust inescapable mechanism, which caught Dickens up in the midst of his wild mummery and gave him a sense of release when he determined to write the novel.[1]

It has been pointed out (by T. A. Jackson) that there is a close underlying similarity between the plot of *A Tale* and that of *Little Dorrit* (the preceding novel in which Dickens had at last fully marshalled his condemnation of Victorian society). Both Dorrit and Manette are imprisoned for a score of years; both are released by forces outside their control and then continue tormented by their jail-experience. Dorrit is haunted by fear of social exposure, which comes finally in the collapse of Merdle (the exposure of the theft basic in the economic system). Dorrit thus from one angle embodies Dickens's deep fears of the past, fears of being exposed, fears of being driven back on the terrible moment of loss which therefore threatens to return in exacerbated form. He also embodies the bad conscience of a whole society which dares not contemplate truly its origins. But in Manette the symbolism goes much deeper. The experience of oppressive misery has not merely twisted him, as it twisted Dorrit; it has broken down the whole system of memory in his psyche. The problem then is: What can restore consciousness? what can connect the upper and the hidden levels of the mind again? Manette is kept going by a blind exercise of the craft learned in the cell of oppression, and only the intrusion of events from the Revolution can bring him back to an active consciousness and release him from his obsession. But the drama of objectifying in action the pattern of memory, the repetition-compulsion which must be broken, inevitably brings its shocks, its apparent evocation of forces as destructive as those working from the traumatic level. The test lies in the way that evocation is faced, the way it works out. So Manette finds that the bitterness engendered by his sufferings as an innocent wronged man has tangled him up in a net (inside a larger reference of social action and reaction, guilt and innocence) from which escape is possible only after a great sacrifice has been made. The old must die for the new to be born; man cannot attain regeneration without accepting its sacrificial aspect. In the story this appears in the struggle between Darnay and Carton for Manette's daughter, and the solution that mates Darnay and the girl, yet sends Carton to a regeneration in death.

---

[1] We must not forget that from the 1790's the people had called Poor Houses *Bastilles,* and often burnt them down in a memory of the Bastille-attack. The use of the symbol here has therefore its links with Dickens's deep hatred of the Poor Law which he identified with his own child-fear of loss and rejection (especially in *Oliver Twist*).

In this dire tangle of moral consequences we see Dickens confronting his own confused situation and trying to equate his own moment of painful compelled choice with the revolutionary moment in which a definite break is made with the old, amid violent birthpangs, and makes possible the rebirth of life, the renewal of love and innocence.

The lacerated and divided state of Dickens's emotions at this moment of choice is revealed by the device of having two heroes who are practically twins in appearance and who love the same girl. Both Carton and Darnay are generous fellows, but one is morally well-organized, the other is fecklessly a misfit. The latter, however, by his devoted death reaches the same level of heroic generosity as his rival; indeed goes higher. His gesture of renunciation completes the ravages of the Revolution with its ruthless justice, and transforms them into acts of purification and redemption, without which the life of renewed love would not be possible.

Thus, in the story, Dickens gets the satisfaction of nobly giving up the girl and yet mating with her. He splits himself in the moment of choice, dies, and yet lives to marry the beloved, from whom the curse born out of a tainted and divided society is at last removed. And at the same time he is Manette, the man breaking out of a long prison-misery, who seeks only truth and justice, and whose submerged memory-drama projects itself as both the Carton-Darnay conflict and the socially-impinging dilemma that disrupts and yet solves that conflict.

There are thus a number of ambivalences in the story; and Dickens shows himself divided in his attitude to the Revolution itself. His petty-bourgeois fear of mass-movements is still alive; but the fascination of such movements, which stirred so strongly in *Barnaby,* is even keener than the fear. On the one hand he clings to the moral thesis to defend the Revolution: the Old Regime was vilely cruel and bestialized people, it could not but provoke excesses in return as the bonds slipped. But this thesis, to which Carlyle had sought to give a grandiose religious tang, now merges for Dickens with a deeper acceptance:

> Crush humanity out of shape once more under similar hammers and it will twist itself into the same tortured forms. Sow the same seed of rapacious license and oppression over again and it will surely yield the same fruit according to its kind.
>
> Six tumbrils roll along the streets. Change these back again to what they were, thou powerful enchanter Time, and they shall be seen to be the carriages of absolute monarchs, the equipages of feudal nobles, the toilets of flaring Jezebels, the churches that are not my Father's house but dens of thieves, the huts of millions of starving peasants.

This passage begins with the simple moral statement; but the tum-

brils, conjured up as mere counterpoises to the feudal carriages, become emblems of a great purification sweeping away the reign of the old iniquity. They express a ruthless *transformation* of society and are far more than an allegory of cruel tit-for-tat. Rather, they appear as forces of triumphant righteousness.

Throughout the book there runs this ambivalent attitude to the Revolution, shuddering, yet inclining to a deep and thorough acceptance. Not a blank-cheque acceptance, but one based on the subtle dialectics of conflict revealed by the story of Manette. For that story, symbolizing the whole crisis and defining its tensions in the depths of the spirit, makes a serious effort to work out the process of change, the rhythms of give-and-take, the involved struggles with their many inversions and opposed refractions, the ultimate resolution in death and love, in the renewal of life.

The working-out of the clash of forces is in fact more thoroughly done than in any previous work of Dickens. The weakness lies in the comparative thinness of characterization. The strain of grasping and holding intact the complex skein of the story is too much for Dickens at this difficult moment of growth. But his instinct is, as always, right. He needed this strenuous effort to get outside himself: no other way could he master the difficult moment and rebuild his foundations. After it he could return to the attack on the contemporary world with a new sureness, with new thews of drama, with new breadths of comprehension. The great works, *Great Expectations* and *Our Mutual Friend,* were made possible. (I am not here dealing with those works; but it is interesting to note that the imprisonment-theme finds its completion in the contrasted and entangled themes of Miss Havisham and the old convict, the self-imposed prison of the traumatic moment and the socially-imposed prison of the criminal impulse, both merging to express the compulsions of an acquisitive society.)

A Tale is not a successful work like the two novels that followed it, but they would never have been written without it. An inner strain appears in the rigidity of tension between the thematic structure and the release of character-fantasy. Such persons as Manette, however, show a new persistence of psychological analysis, and the Defarges show what untapped sources of dramatic force Dickens could yet draw on. The final falsification of the book's meaning came about through the melodrama based on its material, in which the emphasis put on Carton sentimentalized away all the profundities.

Lucie is meant to represent Ellen Ternan; but at this stage Dickens knows very little about the real Ellen, and Lucie is therefore a stock-heroine. Charles Darnay, the winning lover, has the revealing initials *Charles D.* Dickens with his love of name-meanings can seldom resist leaving at least one or two such daydream-admissions among the names

of a novel. Ellen was acting as Lucy in *The Frozen Deep* at the time when the novel's idea came.[2]

II

This analysis, drawing its method from a study of the way in which Dickens uses symbol and allegory in his novels, has enabled us to get under the surface, on which discussion has so far played. We can at least see roughly why the themes of *A Tale* burst out so magically in the midst of his personal crisis. What are those themes? The theme of the man released from a long deforming prison-experience into a new life, who carries against his will into the new life a repetition-compulsion from the past, and who thus has to discover as completion of his release the way of ending that compulsion. And the theme of the sacrificial death, which ends the compulsion and transforms violence into its opposite; which ends the whole vicious circle of the curse.

By noting the sources from which Dickens to a considerable extent drew these themes, we get important sidelights on to his creative intention. For Dickens was so closely entangled with certain currents of symbol-development in his day that we cannot get right inside his work unless we continually relate it to these currents of influences. So far the study of Dickens has been quite superficial and has neglected this aspect of his work.

In seeking the spiritual impacts behind any turn of development in Dickens it is always safe to look at Bulwer-Lytton's work; for that writer throughout his novels drew powerfully on certain traditional imagery, carried on from folk-days in various forms of popular or semi-popular expression. He influenced Dickens at decisive moments again and again: for example, his *Paul Clifford* led on to *Oliver Twist,* his *Night and Morning* led on to *Martin Chuzzlewit.* The work of his which underlay *A Tale of Two Cities* was *Zanoni* (1842).

Zanoni's method links closely with that of *A Tale.* Bulwer is openly writing a symbolic account of the creative process, in which all the characters, one way or another, represent phases or forms, types or anti-types, of the creator in his movement to enlarged or constricted life. This method is more rationalized in *A Tale,* but it is present in a degree that Dickens would scarcely have reached without knowing Bulwer's book. Further, *Zanoni* takes the French Revolution as its scene, to merge the personally creative struggle with a social convulsion of change.

Dickens revives his memory of *Zanoni* because he now feels the need

[2] In view of the deep and ceaseless fantasy of word-play in names in Dickens's work, it is no accident that *Manette* reversed is *Tenam,* not so unlike *Ternan.* Lucie Manette = Lucy (Ellen) Ternan.

to grapple with his pangs of consciousness in a related way. Inevitably he brings the method down to earth more than Bulwer, and to some extent changes the method of symbolic representations into one of dramatic realization. But the travail of his spirit appears in the extent to which the allegorical substratum intrudes and prevents a fully concrete character-projection.

Bulwer's attitude is far from that of Carlyle. With his odd kind of Tory anarchism he politically abhors the Revolution and tries consciously to reduce it to a demented terrorism. But in the working-out of his allegory he cannot help giving it further values, which in the end achieve something like a full acceptance of its action at deeper levels than those of intellectual judgment. For, if the Revolution is the moment when the creative process reaches its intensest moment of conflict and union (as *Zanoni* implies), then the schematic political attitude falls away and sets free a quite different conception, in which revolution and stability, death and life, are equally accepted as aspects of process.

Zanoni, the idealizing and integrating art-activity, is opposed to old Melnour, the contemplative and analytic mind. But both these figures are opposed in turn to Glyndon, emblem of art-science which strives to rise above convention and stereotype, but is stricken down by the attack of fear on the threshold of adventure into the unknown (the human future, the unconscious). Both Glyndon and Zanoni compete for possession of Viola (love, the affective life, union); and the spiritual drama of their struggles is linked throughout with the tumults and clashes of the Revolution. Bulwer, despite his hectic denunciations of the Terror, finds himself willynilly in the position of identifying the innermost struggle of human and artistic values with the struggle of basic social change.

His Viola is arrested in Paris at the height of the Terror (through the jealous hauntings of Nicot and Fillide). Glyndon, whose contact with her was the direct cause of her danger, has fled; but Zanoni steps in and substitutes himself for her on the guillotine.

The derivation of *A Tale* from *Zanoni* is certain; for it appears both in method and theme. But in the years between 1842 and 1859, Dickens's mind has transmuted *Zanoni's* tensions and forms into something very different. The frankly and wildly symbolic tale has been rationalized and psychologized, but the undissolved structure is visible. Dickens like Bulwer wants to define the crucial moment of personal pang and growth in terms of the revolutionary situation and to find by these means the clue to human and artistic growth. In Bulwer the emblem of new life is the Child, in Dickens it is the United Lovers. In Bulwer Zanoni must sacrifice himself to save the new life, because the idealizing activity has gone too far and has lost human sympathy;

and Glyndon must flee, because he is the artist who cannot break through his fear into a renewal of art and life. But the total effect of all the unions and cleavages, possessions and renunciations, is to liberate the creative image, to beget the child. Out of the revolutionary pangs of birth comes the continuity of life, the fresh stabilization of the life-process. Therefore Viola dies at the same moment as Zanoni sacrifices himself, and (as the book ends) the People come bursting with freedom into the prison, to find a dead mother and a helpless babe.

> Even in the riot of their joy, they drew back in astonishment and awe. Never had they seen life so beautiful; and as they crept nearer, and with noiseless feet, they saw that the lips breathed not, that the repose was of marble, and the beauty and the ecstasy were of death. They gathered round in silence; and lo, at her feet there was a young infant, who, wakened by their tread, looked at them steadfastly, and with its rosy fingers played with its dead mother's arms.

The terrible moment of creation is ended. There is only the in-breaking movement of union and freedom, which meets a new life apparently quite cut away from all parentage. But in the working-out of that new life the struggle will revive, the innocence will become tainted, the freedom will reveal its limitations and tensions, and the struggle of process will start all over again. But not at the same level. The decisive moment of death and renewal has given a fresh-start as well as reestablished continuity.

In *A Tale,* with its less obvious allegory, and its more direct acceptance of social process, the romantic formulas of lovers-restored-to-one-another and the defeated-curse are used, and it is the rejected or excluded one who makes the sacrifice. But however differently the ingredients are mixed, the kinship of pattern remains; and a consideration of *Zanoni* helps us much further to an understanding of the passionate moment when Dickens felt that at last he could and must use the French Revolution as material and setting for a novel.

III

It happens that we can go yet further and find the direct link between *Zanoni* and *A Tale,* the work which revived Dickens's memories of *Zanoni* at the time when he was moving near to his domestic collapse. This work is *The Dead Heart,* a play by a minor playwright and artist, Watts Phillips.

Watts Phillips had been trained by Cruikshank at the time when that artist was illustrating *Oliver Twist;* he studied in Paris and was present during the February Revolution of 1848, when, though his political understanding was slight, he felt much sympathy for the insurgents; he also knew Carlyle's *French Revolution* well. His play in

part derived from an episode in Carlyle's book, which certainly lay also behind *A Tale*.

> I have a knowledge (from my long residence) of the French *people*, and know the literature of the revolution *well*. My only borrowing was from an incident related in Carlyle's history (concluding chapter of third volume) in which an old man, the Marquis de something, answers to the roll-call in place of his son (who is asleep) and takes *his place in the tumbril*.

But memories of 1848 certainly gave the vivifying touch. In letters from Paris during the upheavals Watts Phillips wrote:

> Glorious things are happening. Liberty *has* dawned on France. Hurrah . . .
>
> I came home last evening over the Pont Neuf, and stopped for some minutes to look at the crowd of buildings (the Cité) which formed the gloomy masses that stretched along the river's banks—the faint and flickering lights that shone on the dark waters—the tall towers of the various edifices, all so quiet and yet so grand in their indistinctness—when I was roughly disturbed in my meditations by crowds of fellows marching (from some banquet, I imagine) over the bridge and roaring the revolutionary songs. No sooner were they passed than a body of the Garde Mobile succeeded, their bayonets glistening in the moonlight.
>
> The *Ca ira* still ringing in my ears, I walked on, musing upon the scene, which might have been an extract from the drama of the First Republic; and when I looked up—standing in the old Place de la Révolution—I almost expected to see the tall, gaunt form of the guillotine, showing black against the sky, **and** blasting, like the upas with its hideous aspect, the passers by.

And at least once he seems to have been in some danger.

He composed *The Dead Heart* some three years before *A Tale*, though it was not produced till the year of the novel's publication, 1859. Boucicault had made an adaptation of Dumas's *Chevalier de la Maison Rouge*, in which the Bastille and the revolutionary crowd had appeared; and thus was the probable reason for the delay in staging Watts Phillips's play. In April, 1859, *A Tale* began its instalments, and Watts Phillips was at once dismayed:

> Of course they will make a play of Dickens's new tale, *The Two Cities*, and (if you have read it) you will see how the character of the man "dug out" of the Bastille will clash with the man in *The Dead Heart* written more than three years ago. . . . The tone of the resurrection from the Bastille ought to have been *fresh* in my play, not in his story. It's very heart-breaking. (2 June.)

As a result, a speedy effort was made to produce the play, which was

first acted on 10th November, 1859. Then the final instalments of the novel turned out to have used the same denouement as *The Dead Heart*—the substitution of one man for another at the guillotine in an act of self-sacrifice.

A single theme may be used accidentally by novelists or playwrights; but when two main themes coincide and entwine (the resurrection from the living-death of the Bastille and the sacrificial death), it seems more than likely that there is some direct contact. The death-substitution theme was certainly floating about. Dickens had *Zanoni* in mind, and something of the sort might have been suggested by Dumas's play. The motive had appeared also in a play *All for Her* by Palgrave Simpson and Merivale. It is the combination of this motive with that of return-to-life which is surprising.

And there seems little doubt that Dickens had heard or read *The Dead Heart* well before beginning *A Tale*. The biographer of Watts Phillips says:

> The author, indeed, went so far as to say that the piece was "seen by Dickens long ago." It seems that when he first sent the piece to [the manager] Webster, the latter took it down to Brighton, and there read it to two or three friends, one of whom was the novelist.

This statement was never contradicted; and we may therefore assume that Dickens knew the play and had been moved by its conception, which he revived in his own form to express the crisis of change he felt in breaking with Kate.

What exactly then did he get from *The Dead Heart* which he did not get from Carlyle and Bulwer? The name itself gives a first clue. The Bastille is in some sort the Dead Heart, which must break open with new life and love. And when we look at the play itself, we find that its hero Robert Landry is exactly the figure we require as the halfway-house between Zanoni and Manette-Darnay-Carton. He begins as a hopeful young artist, is horribly changed by the hell of twenty years' imprisonment, returns to life, becomes a resolved revolutionary leader, cannot resolve his love-problem, and finds release from his inner contradictions by a redeeming death of sacrificial substitution. Here we meet the implications I have discussed of the *Zanoni*-theme, brought to a level of more manifest unity and providing the basis for the new splitting-up that Dickens carries out. Landry is Manette, Darnay, and Carton all in one: the sufferer, the reborn, the accuser of social evil, the revolutionary leader, the rent lover, the hopelessly-divided romantic. Also, through the way in which for Watts Phillips, 1793 and 1848, are emotionally merged, we get the contemporary impact more obviously than in *A Tale*.

Through this play then we can underline the extent to which

Manette, Darnay, and Carton are all one person, Dickens. Here, as in
Zanoni, the emphasis is on the giving-way of the old before the claims
of the new. The revolutionary moment breaks open, the contradictions
which it has been perpetuating against its own will are abruptly
overcome, and only the new life remains. In *Zanoni* this theme was
embodied in the symbol of the Babe. Here it comes out in the fact that
Landry dies to restore to Catharine Duval her son: the play ends with
Catharine embracing the son and learning the truth about Landry
by looking through the window as he mounts the guillotine. (By a
stage-device the prison-walls slid away and the guillotine appeared:
thus the two aspects, death and renewal, were brought together.)

The romantic hero, at the end of his tether, gives way to the youth
who regains his mother. The hero is barred away and must go to
death. (Note that the lost wife-mother in the play chances to be a
Kate.) Thus the *Zanoni*-theme is redefined in a more rationally-mature
way, which is more assimilable to Dickens's own inner conflict. We see
that the Manette-Darnay-Carton complex holds a father-son conflict,
of the sort later to come out clearly in *Edwin Drood.* The romantic
artist, perverted by suffering and yet turned into a strong revolutionary
agent, finds his completion by making way for the young Baptiste.
Dickens feels himself confronted by the younger generation, Wilkie
Collins and Sala, who go easily into issues that are still baffling for
him; and by the young girls, his daughters and their friends, and Ellen
Ternan, who turn easily to the loves and laughters he has lost or
never had. But he refuses to accept the *Zanoni*-solution, the Babe
coming out of the cleft prison-stone or Baptiste finding his mother's
bosom again in safety. He wants desperately to share in the new life.
So he splits up the Zanoni-Landry figure, and gives to Manette the
horror and rebirth, the rigid accusation and the revolutionary conscience, and to Darnay and Carton the entangled conflict of love. Then
one half of him can lose, because the other half wins. Carton-Charles
goes down and renounces, but Darnay-Dickens takes the girl and finds
his place in society.

A Tale was dramatized, as Watts Phillips had feared, and the public saw the connection of the two stories:

> The plays caught on, and their resemblance to each other attracted
> universal attention, society divided itself unto two factions—the
> Celestites and Dickensites, the Websterites and Phillipsites. Then
> came accusations and recriminations as to coincidences and pla-
> giarisms, and bad blood arose on both sides. (Coleman.) [3]

[3] See *Watts Phillips: Artist and Playwright,* by E. Watts Phillips (1891), written
after *The Dead Heart* had been successfully revived by Irving. Phillips was an
attractive person of considerable intelligence and a quick witty draughtsman's eye.
There were many points of similarity between his outlook and Dickens's. He too

IV

An examination then of the inner movement of symbolism in *A Tale* and the relation of the symbolism to kindred contemporary trends makes sufficiently clear the potence of the image that burst on Dickens in the midst of his personal crisis. The examination reveals important subtleties that have been ignored or explained away in the general movement of falsification which has held appalling sway (except for the rare comments of a few critics such as Bernard Shaw and Edmund Wilson) in the realm of Dickens "criticism." *A Tale* is not a great work, though like almost anything written by Dickens it has great elements; but when it is seriously approached, it turns out to be a work of high interest, yielding some essential clues to the workings of Dickens's mind and of creative symbolism in general.

---

attacked the Victorian Sunday, loved Paris, wrote on a visit to the Morgue, respected French culture more than English-Victorian, and was fascinated by the London underworld. He wrote (1854–5) *The Wild Tribes of London,* describing the slum-folk.

Dickens and the Fiery Past:
A Tale of Two Cities Reconsidered

by G. Robert Stange

"But why waste time on Dickens when one can read Henry James?"
The sophisticated graduate student who asked the question did not
really want an answer; he wanted to provoke critical discussion. The
obvious reply is that life, thank God, is long enough to include both
these novelists, but the question's chief use is to define two permanent
poles of literary art. James, in his search for a flawless technique,
sustained control, and delicate effect, is worlds apart from the sprawl-
ing, uneven, essentially imperfect Dickens. In this respect, at least,
Dickens is like the "imperfect" Shakespeare; by dint of his extraordinary creative energy, the very scope of his art, he enters the rare category of writers who have ceased to be detached objects of contemplation, and become instead parts of everyone's past.

Seen under the aspect of eternity Dickens may not be a greater
novelist than James, but he can speak more easily than James could to
many more people. James could not have afforded to be vulgar as
Dickens was; he could not have allowed himself the artistic errors that
Dickens continually falls into; he could never have cried over his
characters so unabashedly, nor laughed so uproariously. When we read
the great fictional craftsmen we are impressed by the justness with
which they have *rendered* a character or an aspect of life; we approve
them by considering that they have been faithful to our experience of
the world. But the characters of Dickens' novels have an independent
existence; his world operates by its own laws, and after being immersed
in it we return to our world with heightened perceptions and a finer
sense of reality. In reading Dickens one tends to compare the characters of real life with those in his novels: no one ever praised Grand-
father Smallweed or Mr. Micawber or Mrs. Gamp for being faithfully
rendered; we find instead human beings who resemble *them*.

"*Dickens and the Fiery Past:* A Tale of Two Cities *Reconsidered," by G. Robert
Stange. From* The English Journal, XLVI (*October, 1957*), 381-90. Copyright ©
1957 by The National Council of Teachers of English. Reprinted with the permission of The National Council of Teachers of English and G. Robert Stange.

There are many reasons why Dickens' novels are the best kind of thing for young people to read. On the most general level, his great creative energy, the easy extensiveness of his work, help suggest to the young the joyful possibilities of all art. His sensitivity to the beauty and interest of the humblest aspects of life, his vibrant sympathy, are fine examples of responses that must inform any permanently significant literature. A novel by Dickens should be in every high school curriculum. But I have sometimes wondered why that novel has almost invariably been *A Tale of Two Cities.* Reflection suggests an initial advantage in its being the shortest—next to *Hard Times*—of Dickens' fourteen novels. However, I think there are other more worthy reasons, and some of them are good.

This particular novel was most widely accepted as a high school assignment about half a century ago. At that time, we must assume, it reflected contemporary literary enthusiasms. In the 1890's Freeman Wills' play, *The Only Way,* an adaptation of Dickens' novel, was an enormous success. I suspect that, for this reason, our pedagogical forbears found *A Tale* the most immediately relevant, the most "modern" of all Dickens' novels.

The fact that this novel is unlike most of Dickens' work may also have recommended it to teachers. There are more big scenes in it than in any of his other novels; there is less of the grotesque, fewer episodes and characters that the inexperienced reader might consider quaint or antiquated; and there is, almost uniquely in Dickens, a single plot that is unravelled with speed and concision, and which always dominates both the characters and their *milieux.* The novel's relatively simple construction makes it easy for the reader to get into and through the story; it invites an immediate and simple response. In addition to these not inconsiderable advantages conscientious teachers must have regarded the historical background of the novel as a kind of unearned dividend that could be drawn on at need. If one could get a little history in by the back door, so much the better.

Some of these reasons have lost their force over the last thirty or forty years. There may be some point in reconsidering the exclusive assignment of this novel (if I were choosing for a high school course I should pick *Great Expectations* or *David Copperfield*), but I do not think we need regard *A Tale of Two Cities* as a really bad choice. It may be—along with *Hard Times*—the least Dickensian of the novels, but no novel of Dickens is uninteresting; none can fail to enchant or to instruct us. The very weaknesses of Dickens are illuminating, and if in this novel he has, as I believe, failed to achieve his ambitious plans, the novel nevertheless has qualities which make it uniquely valuable.

In considering the general scheme of *A Tale of Two Cities* we can discern three main points of departure from which the conception obviously develops. Dickens tells us in his preface that the main idea of the story came to him while he was performing in an amateur production of Wilkie Collins' play, *The Frozen Deep*. This melodrama, which was much admired by Dickens and his friends, is about two men, Antarctic explorers, who are in love with the same girl. One of the heroes (played by Dickens) sacrifices his life to save his rival's, and by this sacrifice is morally regenerated. Dickens' comment on the play helps emphasize the fact that in the novel Sydney Carton's sacrificial death, and more important, the whole theme of violent death and regeneration, must be regarded as the "main idea."

Though *A Tale* ends with Carton's execution, its beginning and middle are dominated by the sufferings of Doctor Manette, the Bastille prisoner. Dickens had considered calling the novel "Buried Alive," or "The Doctor of Beauvais," and the theme of imprisonment runs darkly through it, second in importance only to the theme of rebirth. During the years to which *A Tale of Two Cities* belongs Dickens seems to have been obsessed by the notion of a prisoner buried alive, suddenly released to the light of everyday life, and having to re-form his connections with free men, to learn again the meaning of love and responsibility. Both *Little Dorrit,* which preceded *A Tale,* and *Great Expectations,* which followed it, develop the prison theme; one works out the comic and tragic conditions of prison life itself, the other treats with pathos and searing irony the ideas of innocence and guilt in terms of the bond between the convict and the "free" and "guiltless" men who judge and sentence him. "Recalled to Life" is the title of the first book of *A Tale.* Doctor Manette's story is not developed with irony or complication, but the narrative of his experiences is as much an inciting motif of the novel as is the story of Sydney Carton. Both lives are broadly conceived in the pattern of suffering, death (either real or symbolic), and regeneration. Both private lives reflect and mesh with the great public events which, we are to see, follow the same pattern.

From Thomas Carlyle's *French Revolution,* originally published in 1837, Dickens derived the account of historical events within which he could dispose his private dramas. He was devoted to Carlyle's history, "the book of all others," according to his American friend, J. T. Fields, "which he read perpetually and of which he never tired—a book for inexhaustibleness to be placed before every other book." In 1850 Dickens wrote to his friend and biographer, John Forster, that he was reading *The French Revolution* "again, for the 500th time," and he concluded the preface to his novel with the statement that "no one can hope to add anything to the philosophy of Mr. Carlyle's wonderful book."

Many of the details of Dickens' novel are drawn directly from Carlyle. Certain great scenes, such as the storming of the Bastille or the operation of the guillotine, are as firmly based on Carlyle's history as are such smaller details as the firing of the chateaux or, even, the four valets who help Monseigneur to dress. But in emphasizing these specific obligations one may overlook the more fundamental debt. Dickens' choice of the historical event which would be the subject of his novel, the ideas about history and man's relation to it which shape his treatment of that subject, all derive from Carlyle.

As Carlyle saw it, history evolved through successive stages of destruction and reconstruction. The study of the past had not so much an intellectual as a moral purpose: every fact of life is a matter of divine revelation; by scanning history, the inspired writer finds the prophetic truth that would guide the future. Fundamental to Carlyle's views was the belief that each new age was born like the phoenix out of the ashes of the past. The men of his time were entering, he felt, an age of reconstruction and rebirth; the preceding age of Revolution he interpreted as the period of apocalyptic fire out of which the new world would rise. In his book he only implied his moral judgments of the French Revolution; in conversation he was more direct, and described it as "the suicidal explosion of an old wicked world, too wicked, false and impious for living longer." His book was planned to emphasize the dramatic—and symbolic—aspects of the historical event: its three sections are concerned with the *ancien régime,* the Terror, and the building of the new society.

Two attitudes that emerge from Carlyle's view of history are particularly important to Dickens' fiction. First, though Carlyle was disgusted by the theories and practice of the revolutionists, he was able to welcome their fury as a cleansing flame. He observed the noble and vicious events of the catastrophe with a grim, religious certainly, never moved by revolutionary ardour, but never doubting the necessity of revolutionary violence. And second, he did not entertain the conception of the past as a subject of study in its own right. We of the twentieth century are so imbued with the notion of a "scientific," "objective" study of history that we forget how recent an idea it is. For Carlyle the past lay like a scripture which, being interpreted, revealed the eternal and inexorable laws of sin, expiation, and redemption. That a past time might be dispassionately reconstructed, or that it might be interpreted, not by the standards and beliefs of the present, but by its own systems of order and value, never occurred to the historian Carlyle, nor to his disciple Charles Dickens.

Both the general approach and the structure of *A Tale of Two Cities* are shaped by Carlylean doctrines. Dickens chose the French Revolution as his subject because he, too, saw it as the event which ushered

in the modern world. And then, his idea of the past led him to write historical fiction with a difference. By nature Dickens was contemptuous of the past: he had neither the patient enthusiasm of the antiquarian nor the curious eye of the scholar; he wished to regard history only from a moral (and preferably superior) standpoint. Consequently, we do not have in this novel the careful reconstruction of manners and morals which occasionally gives such richness to the novels of Scott or Thackeray. Dickens' reader is not made to feel that he has been projected into a bygone time. Instead, the novelist uses the condescending "in those days" formula; he continually reminds us that we have escaped from the trammels and superstitions of the past into a freer, better age: "But indeed, at that time, putting to death was a recipe much in vogue with all trades and professions, and not least of all with Tellson's." (Book II, Ch. 1.) Or we find him sneering at "dear old institutions," which turn out to be such things as the pillory, the whipping post, and blood money, all fragments of "ancestral wisdom, systematically leading to the most frightful mercenary crimes that could be committed under Heaven." (Book II, Ch. 2.)

Dickens, then, is encouraged by Carlyle's theory to regard the past primarily as a storehouse of lessons, a terrible moral drama. In constructing his novel—it seems clear—he conceived his problem as one of integrating the personal lives of his characters with the wider pattern of history. It is the principal scheme of the novel to show the individual fate mirroring and being mirrored by the fate of the social order. The lives of both Doctor Manette and Sydney Carton are, in a sense, parables of the Revolution, of social regeneration through suffering and sacrifice. The Doctor's return to life illustrates the stumbling course of the new order, released from its dark dungeon of oppression and misery, finding its place in a new and juster world. And Carton embodies both the novel's central narrative theme and its profoundest moral view: his past of sinful negligence parallels the past of eighteenth-century Europe; his noble death demonstrates the possibility of rebirth through love and expiation.

The web of moral interdependence is very closely spun. John Forster, who often echoed Dickens' own views, emphasized this aspect as the finest feature of the novel: "There is no piece of fiction known to me, in which the domestic life of a few simple private people is in such a manner knitted and interwoven with the outbreak of a terrible public event, that the one seems but part of the other." Indeed, in a work of serious historical interest it is necessary that the reader have a sense of his own connection with—even his own responsibility for—a social crisis. A modern example would be Ernest Hemingway's persuasive epigraph reminding the American or English reader that the knell that sounded the death of the Spanish Republic tolled also for him.

Dickens, in a similar manner, set himself the task of persuading his readers that they were not islands entire of themselves, but involved in the injustice that led to the Revolution and in the violence that it set loose. "The world," Dickens is reported to have said, "is so much smaller than we think it; we are all so connected by fate without knowing it; people supposed to be far apart are so constantly elbowing each other; and tomorrow bears so close a resemblance to nothing half so much as to yesterday."

This notion of reciprocity between private and public, England and France, past and present, imposes a pattern of parallelism on Dickens' novel. It had to be a tale of *two* cities, not just a story of revolutionary Paris. Every device that ingenuity suggested was used to connect the seemingly placid world of England with the upheaval in France. Symbolically the point is emphasized by the footsteps which echo on the quiet corner of Soho where Lucie lives with her husband and father. These echoes, becoming increasingly ominous, finally mingle with the "headlong and dangerous footsteps . . . raging in Saint Antoine afar off." (Book II, Ch. 21.) Mechanically considered, the novel is divided almost equally between the two countries: of the forty-five chapters, two recount the parallelism of events in England and France, nineteen are set in England, and twenty-four in France. The subject, however, did not permit a true balance of emphasis; all of Book III takes place in France, so that the movement of the novel is directed away from England toward the heart of the revolutionary strife.

In terms of action Dickens seems to have tried to establish a correspondence between the two nations, but not to have quite succeeded. Tellson's Bank is to some extent conceived as agent of the Old Order, and therefore as evidencing its guilt, but it turns out to be quite an attractive (perhaps because thoroughly English) place. The description of the London mob attacking the funeral procession of the Old Bailey spy (Book II, Ch. 14) must have been designed to balance the descriptions of French mob violence with a home-grown Fleet Street variety. But the episode seems irrelevant to the story, and is handled in an oddly perfunctory way, ending in a moralistic rather than a dramatic strain: ". . . the crowd gradually melted away, and perhaps the Guards came, and perhaps they never came, and this was the usual progress of a mob." Jerry Cruncher, the grave-robber, who for professional reasons joins the attack on the funeral, was probably conceived as an English counterpart to the implacable Defarge, but no significant parallel is established.

The process of doubling is observable in the treatment of the main characters. The shiftless Carton and the virtuous Charles Darnay are doubles. Darnay is tried as an enemy of the state both in England and

in France; in both cases he is unjustly accused, and in both is saved by Carton. Darnay has an original French name, D'Evrémonde, a coupling of the English word *every* and the French word *monde*. The association is with *tout le monde,* suggesting that Darnay is an Anglo-French Everyman. Lucie Manette, finally, is the child of an English mother and a French father.

The difficulty in this attempt to yoke the worlds of London and Paris by violence together is that Dickens had to forego his usual confident placing of English characters in English scenes. He was able to make use of a number of Englishmen, but he had to violate both fictional probability and historical possibility by transporting them all to Paris in the Year of Terror, 1792. Then, the absence of English backgrounds prevents, I think, the unhampered flowering of his comic spirit. The comedy that appears in *A Tale* is only a faint echo of the old Dickens. Mrs. Cruncher's "flopping" is purely verbal humor, and attached to a pathetic situation. There are some deft satirical strokes in the description of Darnay's first trial, and a droll description of the fresco of Cupid in Tellson's Paris office, "still to be seen on the ceiling in the coolest linen, aiming (as he very often does) at money from morning to night." But these touches are few and comparatively weak.

Dickens' comic spirit was, I am sure, inhibited by the nature of his material. Comedy is based on the familiar and the particular; the wide gestures of intense passion or suffering are far removed from the minute turns of comic vexation. For this reason comedy would obviously be inappropriate to a study of revolution. However, there is another reason for the gravity of *A Tale of Two Cities:* Dickens' best comedy is verbal; Mrs. Gamp (in *Martin Chuzzlewit*) is supremely comic because of the wild irrelevance of her speech, a speech which rises from the carefully perceived cadences of the vulgar language. Since Dickens rarely made good comedy out of the well-bred, it seems likely that in this novel, where he was pretty much confined to upper middle-class people, aristocrats, and foreigners, he was bereft of the native, colloquial speech upon which his genius fed. He was not up to creating comic French characters and, indeed, for reasons of historical consistency, the Frenchmen had to be a grim crew.

In the absence of the comic spirit other means had to be used to vivify the novel, so it is no surprise to find that Dickens spoke of setting himself "the little task of making a *picturesque story,* rising in every chapter, with characters true to nature, but whom the story should express more than they should express themselves by dialogue." It is one of the great weaknesses of the novel that Dickens attempted to rely on plot rather than on character, but it is one of its strengths— as well as its most distinctive feature—that it became a novel of *pic-*

tures. So marked is the painterly quality of *A Tale* that one's memory of it is dominated by a series of *tableaux vivants,* scenes without dialogue, but with a composition so clear that one tends to see them within the limits of a frame.

The most memorable scenes are charged with symbolism and become a primary means of shaping the reader's judgment of the Revolution. The first glimpse of France that the novel provides is the scene of the broken wine cask in Chapter Five. The two paragraphs in which this is contained are so purely visual that they might almost stand for the description of a painting called—let us say—"The Broken Cask." To this the novelist has added a notation of sound effects, "a shrill sound of laughter and amused voices," and a final sentence that sends the participants back to their usual tasks, and rounds out the scene. The great paragraph which describes the Carmagnole is another *tour de force* of word painting (Book III, Ch. 5), as is the picture of the men sharpening their bloody "hatchets, knives, bayonets, swords" at the grindstone (Book III, Ch. 2). These episodes are peculiarly interesting in that they are imagined to exist in the spatial dimensions of picture rather than in the temporal flow of narrative or verbal description. Dickens concludes his picture of the grindstone, for example, by saying: "All this was seen in a moment, as the vision of a drowning man, or of any human creature at any very great pass, could see a world if it were there." These three most elaborate pictures serve to create an intense emotional impression of the historical action of the novel. Each is a scene of passion and violence, each is presented with the clarity and overcharged feeling of a vision in delirium. This frenzy, Dickens would have us conclude, *is* the Revolution. It is through picture that he chose to control our responses: "It has been one of my hopes," so runs the preface, "to add something to the *popular and picturesque* means of understanding that terrible time, though no one can hope to add anything to the philosophy of Mr. Carlyle's wonderful book." (The italics are mine.)

Though there are no other pictures as highly wrought as these I have mentioned, the tableau technique is the ruling method of the book. Dickens tends throughout to make important episodes into set-pieces which are more visual than strictly dramatic. Since such passages are obviously separable from the surrounding matrix of narrative, the unity of tone in the novel suffers, but in his use of the stylized image Dickens developed a method that owes nothing either to the theatre (the source of much of his technique) or to the fiction of his predecessors and contemporaries. There is a groping toward a new form of the literary picturesque, the creation of an image which derives more from the conventions of painting than of literature, but which makes

use in an impressionisic way of sound and movement. Dickens spoke justifiably of adding something to the "picturesque" means of understanding.

The general conception of *A Tale of Two Cities* is so grand that one is tempted to overlook the novel's technical faults. But faults there are, some of them unforgivable, many of them quite instructive. The elements of sentimentality and melodrama are no more persistent here than in some of the earlier novels, but as always, they are unpalatable to the modern reader. Lucie Manette's heart-rending reunion with the father she has never known is simply not prepared for:

> "And if, when I shall tell you of my name, and of my father who is living, and of my mother who is dead, you learn that I have to kneel to my honored father, and implore his pardon for having never for his sake striven all day and lain awake and wept all night, because the love of my poor mother hid his torture from me, weep for it, weep for it!" (Book I, Ch. 6.)

The illustrious analogue here is the reunion of Cordelia and Lear, but to define the differences between the two scenes is merely to become impatient with Dickens.

Similarly, Sydney Carton's declaration of love to Lucie is entirely possible, even noble, but it is undermined by sentimentality.

> "In my degradation, I have not been so degraded but that the sight of you with your father, and of this home made such a home by you, has stirred old shadows that I thought had died out of me.
>
>   .   .   .
>
> "Will you let me believe, when I recall this day, that the last confidence of my life was reposed in your pure and innocent breast, and that it lies there alone, and will be shared by no one?" (Book II, Ch. 13.)

What is wrong in this passage is not so much the emotional situation, which we could be persuaded to believe in, as the language: there are too many dreams, and souls, and homes, and innocent breasts.

Some of Dickens' characteristic mannerisms grew all out of bounds in *A Tale*. Repetition was an endemic Victorian rhetorical device of which Dickens was always fond, but in no other novel is it so obtrusive. Observe the opening paragraph: "It was the best of times, it was the worst of times, it was the age of wisdom, it was the age of foolishness, it was the epoch of belief, it was the epoch . . . ," etc. Perhaps some of the repetitions and parallels were intended to emphasize the interconnections of twin realms of the novel, but too often the device becomes merely a trick. It does not add to the reader's experience to find the titles of chapters in balanced pairs, "The Fellow of Delicacy" followed by "The Fellow of No Delicacy," and "Knitting" followed

by "Still Knitting." These verbal devices evidence a curious lack of control, a tendency to depend for effect on mere smartness.

One stylistic problem that Dickens did not quite overcome was the challenge of rendering the quality of foreign speech. Many novelists (and more dramatists) have been defeated in their efforts to make foreigners sound really foreign; on the whole Dickens has done pretty well. He was for the most part content to give the French dialogue a slightly stilted quality, the result usually of a literal translation of French idiom. M. Defarge's first statements are illustrative: " 'Say, then, my Gaspard, what do you do there?' . . . 'What now? Are you a subject for the mad-hospital?' " This, at least, sounds exotic without suggesting that the speaker has an imperfect grasp of his own language, but the method of rendering idioms literally can easily become absurd. One bit of dialogue runs, " 'One can depart, citizen?' 'One can depart,' " and French readers have been particularly annoyed by such solecisms as "the Bridge of the Pont-Neuf." However, clumsy as these locutions are, it is profitable—and to Dickens' advantage—to compare his efforts with Hemingway's valiant attempt to render the spirit of Spanish speech in *For Whom the Bell Tolls.* Hemingway's earthy Spaniards sound as queer as Dickens' Parisians.

But if there are weaknesses in Dickens' technique, there is also strength in many of the smaller touches which give richness to the novel. Much of the effect of *A Tale* is a result of artful patterns of imagery. The pervading image of the road, for example, runs through the whole book. The first chapter, which opens with a general description of the period, ends with a reference to the figurative road along which all men will be carried in the years ahead of them. The second chapter, which begins the narrative, makes the figure of speech literal: "It was the Dover road that lay, on a Friday night late in November. . . ." When, in the course of the novel, we encounter many roads upon which the characters drive or ride, none, thanks to the explicitness of the opening chapter, is without metaphorical significance.

Sometimes the imagery is allegorical. In the scene of the broken wine cask, which I have already mentioned, Dickens makes it obvious that the wine symbolizes blood, and the multiple meanings of wine and blood are then developed. Defarge's wineshop is the center of revolutionary action; we are led to reflect that the fellowship of blood and wine has many guises. Affecting the reader, however, on a more instinctual level are the images—which tend to run together—of fountains, flood, and fire. The fountain which is the center of the life of Saint Antoine becomes a symbol of the irrepressible force of humanity welling up against repression. After the wicked Monseigneur's carriage has run down a child, the novelist tells us, "The water of the fountain ran, the swift river ran, the day ran into

evening, so much life in the city ran into death according to rule . . . all things ran their course." (Book II, Ch. 7.) The Saint Antoine fountain has its rural counterparts: "The fountain in the village flowed unseen and unheard, and the fountain at the chateau dropped unseen and unheard—both melting away, like the minutes that were falling from the spring of Time." In the passages that follow, the water of the chateau fountain seems to turn to blood, and the village fountain becomes the rallying place for the populace, the symbol of their common humanity, of the force of life that cannot be put down. In the chain of imagery the fountain images give way to a flood, a sea, and the sea is succeeded by fire. The flowing water may be curbed or checked, but it cannot be stopped, and it can soon turn from a beneficent to a destructive force.

One of the powerful features of Dickens' art which should not go unmentioned is his strong sense of the lusts and guilts and passions which lie under the surface of human consciousness. It is notable that his treatment of the Revolution is free of sentimental notions as to the essential goodness of man. The Terror is conceived as both a cleansing and polluting force, but men are shown to be attracted to violence for its own sake. There is also a deal of deep psychological understanding in the treatment of Charles Darnay's attraction by the "Loadstone Rock" of the Revolution. And for us who live in a world of concentration camps, of political betrayals, and inexplicable confessions there is something almost prophetic in Dickens' analysis of the prisoner's state of mind:

> Similarly, though with a subtle difference, a species of fervor or intoxication, known, without a doubt, to have led some persons to brave the guillotine unnecessarily, and to die by it, was not mere boastfulness, but a wild infection of the wildly shaken public mind. In seasons of pestilence, some of us will have a secret attraction to the disease—a terrible passing inclination to die of it. (Book III, Ch. 6.)

This is not only brilliant psychology; it has turned out to be good history. It is in its grasp of its subject that the power and brilliance of this novel are finally seen to lie. The novel's chief weaknesses are the results of its excessive artificiality: its construction constantly calls attention to itself. But in reacting against these smaller details we must not forget that Dickens' main intention was to present a view of, to "add something" to our understanding of the French Revolution. And the more I consider this novel as an interpretation of that event, the more successful it seems to me. One may quarrel with this or that detail of documentation but the historical view, in its broad outlines, is a sound one. Dickens suggested that "this terrible Revolution" was an inevitable response to injustice, but he showed also how revolutionary

ardor produced its own forms of injustice. Carton, describing the Revolution as a dark phase in the development of modern history, saw "the evil of this time and of the previous time of which this is the natural birth, gradually making expiation for itself and wearing out." This view of history was temporarily out of fashion, but there is some evidence that historians are now returning to it. Experience of the revolutionary era of our own century has led more influential writers to see the French Revolution as the critical event of modern history, as a cataclysm whose effects are still with us.

A Tale of Two Cities is a profoundly thoughtful, if not a theoretical book. It is the sort of novel that should be enormously *usable* for young people and for their teachers. Its technical weaknesses are of a kind that can illustrate the nature and problems of fiction, but what is much more important, its conception can vivify for us the meanings of the past, can offer us a reading of history, humane and deep, by a great artistic intelligence.

The Style

by Taylor Stoehr

Dickens' style has a characteristic flavor. It is, as specialists sometimes say, Dickensian. The following analysis is not intended as a comprehensive study of his style, but is rather an attempt to isolate some outstanding features of it which seem to me to produce its characteristic flavor, especially (1) Dickens' use of detail as an active ingredient in setting and plot, (2) his use of rhetorical devices such as anaphora and metonymy to order and connect these details, and (3) the effect of such usages on Dickensian characterization and plotting. As the reader will see, particularly in the treatment of Dickens' principle of ordering, I am not so much concerned with any single instance of his use of detail or rhetoric as I am with the general nature of these elements; consequently, terms like "anaphora" and "metonymy" should be interpreted very broadly in this context, as designating tendencies of method in Dickens' work rather than specific tricks in his bag of artistic expedients.

Because I want to ground my study in close analysis of stylistic features and their inner consistency and integrity, I concentrate here on a single novel. In later chapters, as the argument progresses, there will be more and more reference to other novels, but in the beginning *A Tale of Two Cities* must serve as a representative text. The *Tale* will be familiar to almost any reader I can expect to reach, including those who are not specialists in the field; yet it is a novel which, unlike most of the major works in the Dickens canon, has not received the critical attention it deserves from our generation. The *Tale* provides familiar material about which readers are likely to have fewer critical preconceptions than they have about other Dickens novels—an obvious advantage in presenting a new reading of an old master.

A Tale of Two Cities has sometimes been thought atypical of Dickens; if this were true, of course, it would not be suitable for the kind of representative analysis offered here. In some ways the *Tale* is special

and unusual, but its peculiarities do not prejudice the case any more than the specialness of *Bleak House* or *Great Expectations* would. Each of Dickens' novels differs from its predecessors and sequels, because Dickens was a serious artist, who learned something from each book he wrote. Yet always much persisted of his style and manner, and it is what persists that we think of as Dickensian, the essence of his art. *Pickwick, Oliver Twist, Martin Chuzzlewit, David Copperfield, Hard Times, Little Dorrit*—it is hard to name a novel that does not seem unrepresentative of the canon in one respect or another, and yet they are all quite Dickensian too. In *A Tale of Two Cities* Dickens is perhaps at his most rhetorical; but he is always a highly rhetorical writer, and the heightening that may be seen in the *Tale* is not un-Dickensian so much as it is ultra-Dickensian. For stylistic analysis, this has not seemed to me a drawback but rather an advantage.

Unnecessary Detail

Like other novelists, Dickens has his stylistic ups and downs, his moments of brilliance and his lapses into self-parody. In his best writing and in his worst, the habits that constitute his style persist, and here as in the work of other great stylists these habits call attention to themselves, regardless of the success or failure of particular passages. Nevertheless, the passages of greatest excellence—what in poetry used to be called the "beauties"—deserve our closest attention, for we are interested in Dickens' style, after all, only because it is so often brilliant.

Dickens lovers and scholars have always been disposed to praise those parts of *A Tale of Two Cities* in which the revolutionary scene predominates—the Wine-Shop chapter, the murder of the Marquis, the storming of the Bastille—so it seems natural to begin with these. Nothing is more typical than the way the Wine-Shop chapter opens:

> A large cask of wine had been dropped and broken, in the street. The accident had happened in getting it out of a cart; the cask had tumbled out with a run, the hoops had burst, and it lay on the stones just outside the door of the wine-shop, shattered like a walnut-shell.

The beginning of interest lies in the concrete object, the thing; Dickens sets the scene, almost cinematically, by focusing on such particulars. Here the effect is that of a high-angle view, centered on the splintered cask, slowly moving down on the square. As we are brought closer, description slides into narration, still determined by the objects in the setting:

> All the people within reach had suspended their business, or their idleness, to run to the spot and drink the wine. The rough, irregular

stones of the street, pointing every way, and designed, one might have thought, expressly to lame all living creatures that approached them, had dammed it into little pools; these were surrounded, each by its own jostling group or crowd, according to its size.

Everything "run[s] to the spot"; people are mere adjuncts of the stones and wine. It is the scene that sticks in the memory. Places, buildings, all kinds of physical objects take up most of the available space in the Dickensian world. Later, when the revolutionary characters are introduced and made to come alive in their dazzling way, we discover that even in the delineation of character Dickens depends on the physical setting, the *mise-en-scène*, the concrete object, for his favorite effects. In the passage quoted it is the objects that have character, that exist "expressly to lame all living creatures that approached them"; in other passages the people derive much of their special kind of life from the things which invariably accompany them: Madame Defarge and her knitting, Doctor Manette and his cobbler's bench, Jerry Cruncher and his spiky hair, Gaspard and his nightcap are typical examples. This insistence on the bits and pieces of physical reality has attracted the attention of most of Dickens' readers in one way or another. George Orwell, perhaps the most interesting of the critics who discuss the problem, has even suggested that the abundance of "unnecessary detail" is "the outstanding, unmistakable mark of Dickens's writing." Orwell likens such details to "florid little squiggle[s] on the edge of the paper"—and he includes among them not merely physical objects given in the setting, but also bits of narrative, scraps of dialogue, all the trivia of plot and character. "Everything is piled up and up, detail on detail, embroidery on embroidery," and the result, concludes Orwell, is like a wedding cake, as much beyond criticism as the rococo—"either you like it or you do not like it."

The notion that the details in Dickens are "unnecessary" is not as simple as it sounds, for Orwell does not mean that the "little squiggles" do not function in the work; otherwise he would not have said that "it is by just these details that the special Dickens atmosphere is created." But exactly how do the details operate in the total impression? In what way are they both necessary and unnecessary? . . . That the details in Dickens are unnecessary from a certain point of view does not mean that they fail to contribute to the total effect. Indeed, from another point of view they *are* the effect. (Similarly, Victorian society might be usefully contemplated as merely the embodiment of that taste for objects and things which, as we say, characterized it.) Thus is the apparently superfluous detail indispensable simply by virtue of being a prominent part of the whole.

One can go further than this, however, in specifying the function of detail in Dickens' novels. He himself gives something of his

views on the use of setting and props in a letter of advice written to a would-be contributor to his magazine:

> Suppose yourself telling that affecting incident in a letter to a friend. Wouldn't you describe how you went through the life and stir of the streets and roads to the sick-room? Wouldn't you say what kind of a room it was, what the time of day it was, whether it was sunlight, starlight, or moonlight? Wouldn't you have a strong impression on your mind of how you were received, when you first met the look of the dying man, what strange contrasts were about you and struck you? I don't want you, in a novel, to present *yourself* to tell such things, but I want the things to be there.

Such injunctions might come from any writer of fiction, but Dickens' suggestions are particularly interesting because they so very exactly describe his narrative method in the Wine-Shop passages. He begins with the larger situation, given in concrete detail yet suggesting the whole framing context. He moves next to some unit already mentioned in the description of the larger context (the sickroom, the sharp stones). Finally characters are introduced, in some close relation to the objects. The emphasis throughout is on things, not so much things that happen, that can be recounted (though they are important too, obviously enough), as things that are *there*, in the novel and in the novel's world. Once the scene has become a human one, the narrative continues to be organized around the bits and pieces of the physical context:

> Some men kneeled down, made scoops of their two hands joined, and sipped, or tried to help women, who bent over their shoulders, to sip, before the wine had all run out between their fingers. Others, men and women, dipped in the puddles with little mugs of mutilated earthenware, or even with handkerchiefs from women's heads, which were squeezed dry into infant's mouths; others made small mud embankments, to stem the wine as it ran; others, directed by lookers-on up at high windows, darted here and there, to cut off little streams of wine that started away in new directions; others devoted themselves to the sodden and lee-dyed pieces of the cask, licking, and even champing the moister wine-rotted fragments with eager relish.

Here, as in the passages already quoted, the details of the setting seem to determine the movement of the narrator's eye: the wine is sipped and dipped, squeezed out and dammed up and cut off; mugs and handkerchiefs, mud and fragments of wood, figure more prominently than the people handling them. Even the dramatic feeling—the passion and despair of the characters, the meanness of their daily lives—is given through these vulgar objects and their uses.

It is worth pressing this point, for by just such means do we feel the

pressure of atmosphere which is so powerful in Dickens, the impression that the world is thick with moods and presences, that will affect the course of events and drive the characters to their fate. The "unnecessary details" and "needless ramifications" fill up this world, and whether needless or not they constrain and determine action as the pebbles of a gravelly soil at once guide and hinder the searching roots.

Furthermore, Dickens only seems to pack his world full to bursting with the merely incidental and fortuitous; more often than not the apparently needless and accidental details form part of a meticulous weaving which, as the novel progresses, leaves less and less to chance. Consider the following passage, which occurs after all the wine has disappeared from the street:

> The man who had left his saw sticking in the firewood he was cutting, set it in motion again; the woman who had left on a door-step the little pot of hot ashes, at which she had been trying to soften the pain in her own starved fingers and toes, or in those of her child, returned to it; men with bare arms, matted locks, and cadaverous faces, who had emerged into the winter light from cellars, moved away, to descend again; and a gloom gathered on the scene that appeared more natural to it than sunshine.
>
> The wine was red wine, and had stained the ground of the narrow street in the suburb of Saint Antoine, in Paris, where it was spilled. It had stained many hands, too, and many faces, and many naked feet, and many wooden shoes. The hands of the man who sawed the wood, left red marks on the billets; and the forehead of the woman who nursed her baby, was stained with the stain of the old rag she wound about her head again. Those who had been greedy with the staves of the cask, had acquired a tigerish smear about the mouth; and one tall joker so besmirched, his head more out of a long squalid bag of a night-cap than in it, scrawled upon a wall with his finger dipped in muddy wine-lees— BLOOD.
>
> The time was to come, when that wine too would be spilled on the street-stones, and when the stain of it would be red upon many there.

When one first comes upon it in the novel, this passage foreshadows little more than the explicit prophecy of the last sentence, but as we read further we find that the little details thrown out so lavishly, and as it were so casually, have their echoes throughout the story. We meet the same woodsawyer again, and we begin to connect him with the "Woodman Fate" of the opening chapter. We see and hear the stained feet again—the echoing footsteps in Lucie's life, the dancing feet of the Carmagnole, the cruel foot of Madame Defarge as she steadies the governor's head for her knife. The "tigerish smear about the mouth" is our first introduction to the "life-thirsting, cannibal-looking, bloody-minded juryman, the Jacques Three of St. Antoine." The tall citizen in the night cap is Gaspard, who has in him still an-

other note, also to be "scrawled," after the murder of the Marquis: *"Drive him fast to his tomb. This, from* JACQUES.*"*

The whole narrative is webbed with such interconnections, based always on the foreshadowing or echoing detail. Such repetitions have the obvious function of promoting the unity and probability of the novels, but an even more important result is the creation of a density of atmosphere beyond the power of mere verisimilitude or circumstantiality to achieve: we are presented with a cosmos everywhere interdependent, so that even objects in the landscape contribute to the sense of an interlocking system. With their multiple linkages, the "unnecessary detail" and "needless ramifications" of Dickens' style and plot provide the very fiber and fabric of his tightly knit world. The notorious coincidences of his novels are not the weak expedients of melodrama, but have behind them this same cosmic rationale. Thus Dickens' friend and biographer John Forster reports:

> On the coincidences, resemblances, and surprises of life, Dickens liked especially to dwell, and few things moved his fancy so pleasantly. The world, he would say, was so much smaller than we thought it; we were all so connected by fate without knowing it; people supposed to be far apart were so constantly elbowing each other; and to-morrow bore so close a resemblance to nothing half so much as to yesterday.

Again and again, Dickens' stories depend on the "unnecessary," coincidentally related details of this small world . . . In the typical Dickens novel, then, the concrete detail not only gives a framework for the movement of the narrative (as in the Wine-Shop passages) and a medium for the establishment of unity and coherence in the total action of the plot (by means of foreshadowing and other devices based on repetition), but also creates, in its very abundance and multiplication, the characteristic Dickensian atmosphere, a world in which all seemingly trivial, unrelated objects, people, and events finally mesh in an intricate and self-contained pattern.

The Principle of Ordering

Dickens' extravagant fondness for enumerating the flotsam and jetsam of life (one way of viewing the needlessness of the detail) is combined with a similarly extravagant passion for order (so that the details must be made necessary). Every new impulse to expand and amplify is accompanied by a corresponding desire to curb and control. Thus generalized, of course, the paradox is recognized as a central fact of all art, and we must look further in order to discover anything of special relevance to our understanding of Dickens. We must consider the particular character of Dickens' materials, how he chooses them, orders

them, and so forth; and this in turn will lead us into questions about Dickens' vision of the world and the choices it offers to any man.

Let us approach the problem in terms of *A Tale of Two Cities* itself. As is his usual practice, Dickens begins by mystifying us. We are rushing along the Dover Road, in the dead of night, to what distant event we know not. Later we discover the purpose of that journey, but for each solution to a mystery some new and even more tangled puzzle is introduced. Why was Doctor Manette imprisoned? Who is Charles Darnay? Why is Doctor Manette so disturbed by him? Whose are the footsteps that echo in Lucie's chamber? What did Defarge find in his search of 105 North Tower? By the end of the novel every question has been answered, but meanwhile the world presented to us is a rather strange one. It is not so much mysterious, even, as it is peculiarly discontinuous. We are offered, to be sure, a sequence of events: one thing leads to another, time passes, the ground goes by under foot. But there seems to lurk behind the façade of normal occurrences some secret meaning, every now and then intruding itself as though in warning of imminent catastrophe. These intrusions are woven into the pattern of ongoing events in such a way that the train is never broken, but they strike us differently, as isolated bits of another story somehow underlying the one that takes up the actual time and space of the narrative. The denouement consists of the discovery that these apparently disconnected elements are in fact related, and even form a logical sequence—the true action of the story that we have been reading. . . .

. . . In Dickens, both . . . insistent circumstantiality and the larger, subtler pressure of fate may be discerned, but neither is a mark of his style. The essence of his style is not found in the kinds of details, or the general direction in which they seem to lead, but in the principle that governs their disposition in particular sentences and paragraphs. To see what this principle is and how it works, let us return to the Wine-Shop chapter; Dickens is describing Saint Antoine and its citizens, who have now lapped up all they can of the spilled wine:

> The children had ancient faces and grave voices; and upon them, and upon the grown faces, and ploughed into every furrow of age and coming up afresh, was the sign, *Hunger*. It was prevalent everywhere. *Hunger* was pushed out of the tall houses, in the wretched clothing that hung upon poles and lines; *Hunger* was patched into them with straw and rag and wood and paper; *Hunger* was repeated in every fragment of the small modicum of firewood that the man sawed off; *Hunger* stared down from the smokeless chimneys, and started up from the filthy street that had no offal, among its refuse, of anything to eat. *Hunger* was the inscription on the baker's shelves, written in every small loaf of his scanty stock of bad bread; at the sausage-shop, in every dead-dog preparation that was

offered for sale. *Hunger* rattled its dry bones among the roasting chestnuts in the turned cylinder; *Hunger* was shred into atomies in every farthing porringer of husky chips of potato, fried with some reluctant drops of oil. [my italics]

There is much that will bear analysis in this passage, but for our present purposes what is interesting is the articulation of the narrative and descriptive materials by the use of the rhetorical device of *ana-phora,* the repetition of the key word "Hunger" to introduce and mark off the successive items of the presented scene. This device, which may be seen at work very frequently in Dickens—for instance, in the Wine-Shop passages already quoted—epitomizes Dickens' method of ordering his imagined world. The details of the scene are not merely piled up, one upon another; rather, there is a kind of logic in their arrangement. Everything here is mentioned because it is a concomitant of hunger, because it is a familiar result or cause or symptom or contingency of that condition. Observation and report are controlled, selection is determined, by the key word. One cannot, however, argue the converse, that what is given in the scene necessitates the choice of the word "Hunger," for it is the word which tells the reader what to notice, how to take the descriptive elements. Substitution of another word— say, "Poverty" or "Misery"—would result in a different set of mean-ings for the same reported observations. Thus the principle of *relevance* in the passage seems to be determined by the choice of the anaphoric expression. But the principle of *order* in the passage seems to be dif-ferently derived. The reader is presented with a cinematic rendering of continuous space in continuous time, the narrator functioning as a camera-eye; details make their appearance according to their position in the imagined scene, one thing next to another, and still another next to that. We are invited to attend to the houses, to the clotheslines stretched from their windows, to the man sawing firewood in front of the houses, to the chimneys which show no sign of wood being burned inside, and back again to the street and its shops and shop signs, its chestnut stand, costermongers and their wares. Although the selection of details is determined by the anaphora, the ordering seems to be given by the scene itself, by the mere contiguity of things. Of course, one can discover other principles of order here—for instance, the gradual movement of the attention toward what little food there is— but the description is handled in such a way that these other principles of arrangement seem to be mere corollaries of the physical arrange-ment of the actual scene, as if one could not avoid seeing things in this order. Indeed, the camera-eye effect, the rendering of continuous space in continuous time, seems to imply a strict necessity to report every-thing just as it is; and if Dickens actually had been under such a necessity, there could be no order at all except the "natural" order of

the observed scene. Such is, in fact, the impression one often gets in reading his descriptions. He manages this effect, without seeming to wander aimlessly and endlessly over the scene, by means of the same rhetorical device that allows him to exercise selectivity. The obligation to record everything is avoided by the use of anaphora, which acts as a delimiting device, a kind of lens and shutter marking off selected bits of the scene, moving the reader's attention from representative sample to representative sample, and thus building an impression of the whole from the enumerated parts. The rhetoric controls the time and space of perception and report by opening (and, at each new opening, also thereby closing) the windows of the linguistic medium, our access to the author's world.

Anaphora, then, seems to give Dickens his means both of exercising selectivity and of presenting a scene as if he were exercising no selectivity at all, as if he were merely reporting what is there to be seen, without any authorial influence or distortion. Clearly enough, this is not a use of rhetoric merely for its own sake. The flavor of the passage is not rhetorical at all; what one notices is the vehemence of gaze which so impressed Taine:

> The imagination of Dickens is like that of monomaniacs. To plunge oneself into an idea, to be absorbed by it, to see nothing else, to repeat it under a hundred forms, to enlarge it, to carry it, thus enlarged, to the eye of the spectator, to dazzle and overwhelm him with it, to stamp it upon him so firmly and deeply that he can never again tear it from his memory,—these are the great features of this imagination and style.

The cumulative process by which the word-idea *Hunger* becomes a distinctive figure against the background of the street scene, a whole to which all the parts contribute and cling, is analogous to the mechanism of visual perception: a series of ocular fixations (with corresponding eye-movements) is essential to the perception of even the simplest figure, and, within limits, the vividness of the image depends on the number as well as the "intensity" of fixations and movements. In the passage from the Wine-Shop chapter the vividness of the description may be partially accounted for by the anaphoric construction, each repetition of the word "Hunger" acting as a signal for "fixation" on that part of the whole which follows it. . . .

. . . Two kinds of order may be seen at work [in the Wine-Shop passage —ED.]—the order by juxtaposition given in the details themselves, and the directionless order superimposed by the anaphora. Contiguity determines both arrangements: on the one hand, the movement from detail to detail; on the other, the schematizing repetition and emphasis of the rhetorical frame. The details attract the eye and provide the continuity of a contiguous world. The anaphora marks

off these details, or groups of them, one by one, drawing attention to the juxtaposition; but here the effect is not so much an emphasis on continuity as it is the opposite, a sort of discontinuity—a rhetorical net in which the details are caught in motion, like the arrested activity of a snapshot. Because the anaphora is neutral, in that it suggests no *particular* progression in the elements it frames, and yet at the same time does very strictly impose *some* order, the whole scene is thrown into a kind of relief. To borrow another cinematic concept, the effect is like that of a montage-cluster, a series of detail shots juxtaposed in time, as for example in the Odessa Steps sequence in *Potemkin*—or, perhaps even closer to Dickens' montage, the collocation of stills-in-sequence which Barnaby Conrad edited for his remarkable "movie," *The Death of Manolete* (others have borrowed the technique, as viewers of American television commercials can testify). In such models, it almost seems as if one thing does not lead to another; everything exists at once, juxtaposed, superimposed, articulated in the consciousness by the anaphoric pattern. The details are both isolated from and joined to each other by the rhetorical boundaries. The isolation in time and space—the caught moment—exactly identifies the photographic realism that is characteristic of Dickens' treatment of detail. Similarly, it is the articulation, the juxtaposition, the superimposition of such details that gives, by its combination of order and disjunction, the strangely unreal effect which we also associate with Dickens, the sense of a world all in pieces, where every fragment is nonetheless intimately and mysteriously involved with every other fragment.

Metonymies of Character and Plot

Sometimes the "montage-clusters" of details which Dickens invents seem to take particularly strong hold on his mind, and he repeats them, or parts of them, in other contexts. Anaphora and other schematizing devices can have the effect of freezing the separate units together in the memory as an associational whole, and thus provide the basis for still another metonymic principle of connection between the larger parts of a novel. For example, Kenneth Burke has explained how any part of such an "associational cluster" may do synecdochic duty for the whole:

And as regards our speculations upon the nature of "clusters" or "equations," would it not follow that if there are, let us say, seven ingredients composing a cluster, any one of them could be treated as "representing" the rest? In this way such an image as a "house" in a poem can become a "house plus," serving as proxy for the other ingredients that cluster about it (e.g., for the beloved that lives in the house, and is thus "identified" with it). Usually, several of these other ingredients will appear surrounding the one temporarily featured.

The cluster of details that forms the basis of a structural synecdoche like this may derive its original cohesiveness in several ways. Positional contiguity—the fact that the elements first occur in close proximity to each other, often strongly marked by anaphoric devices—may determine the connection. Then again, the pattern need not be set up in a single paragraph or even a single chapter. Take the example of the Stone Face cluster in *A Tale of Two Cities*: throughout several chapters of Book 2 various ingredients are associated through their connection (again, by contiguity) with the Marquis St. Evrémonde's face. The Marquis is introduced in Chapter VII of the second book:

> He was a man of about sixty, handsomely dressed, haughty in manner, and with a face like a fine mask. A face of a transparent paleness; every feature in it clearly defined; one set expression on it. The nose, beautifully formed otherwise, was very slightly pinched at the top of each nostril. In these two compressions, or dints, the only little change that the face ever showed, resided. They persisted in changing colour sometimes, and they would be occasionally dilated and contracted by something like a faint pulsation; then, they gave a look of treachery, and cruelty, to the whole countenance.

In the same chapter, after running down a child with his coach, the Marquis betrays his anger through this physiognomical peculiarity:

> "You dogs!" said the Marquis, but smoothly, and with an unchanged front, except as to the spots on his nose: "I would ride over any of you very willingly, and exterminate you from the earth."

Chapter IX begins with a description of the Marquis' château, and introduces the image of the stone face:

> It was a heavy mass of building, that château of Monsieur the Marquis, with a large stone court-yard before it, and two stone sweeps of staircase meeting in a stone terrace before the principal door. A stony business altogether, with heavy stone balustrades, and stone urns, and stone flowers, and stone faces of men, and stone heads of lions, in all directions. As if the Gorgon's head had surveyed it, when it was finished, two centuries ago.
>
> The great door clanged behind him, and Monsieur the Marquis crossed a hall grim with certain old boar-spears, swords, and knives of the chase; grimmer with certain heavy riding-rods and riding-whips, of which many a peasant, gone to his benefactor Death, had felt the weight when his lord was angry.

Later in the chapter, the Marquis' face begins its transformation to stone:

> Every fine straight line in the clear whiteness of his face, was cruelly, craftily, and closely compressed, while he stood looking quietly at his nephew, with his snuff-box in his hand.

In the Marquis we have a perfect model, almost a prototype, for the well-known Dickens caricature, complete with social mask, hidden motives, and an exaggerated oddity—the nose—which provides the necessary key to the connection between the apparent and the real character. The cluster of information about the Marquis—his cold indifference (to the child's death), his heritage of cruelty (the riding-whips), his crafty hatred (of Darnay, his nephew)—circles persistently about the central image of his masklike face with its pinched and dinted nose. Everything comes back to that mask, that nose, and those dints, which finally take on more life than the Marquis himself. . . .

As Burke points out, there is a special advantage to these circling yet fixed patterns of association, in that a single part of any cluster may be used synecdochically to suggest the whole. Typically in Dickens there is some pivotal detail that serves in this way; the image of the stone mask with its pinched nose sets off the train of associations. Thus at the end of Chapter IX, where Dickens sums up all the Marquis' sins and their punishment, he returns to this dominant image:

> The Gorgon had surveyed the building again in the night, and had added the one stone face wanting; the stone face for which it had waited through about two hundred years.
>
> It lay back on the pillow of Monsieur the Marquis. It was like a fine mask, suddenly startled, made angry, and petrified.

The mask has usurped the field; nothing else of the cluster remains. The Marquis has been totally dehumanized, and exists only as a stone face. Taine has pointed out this dehumanizing effect of Dickens' caricature:

> The tenacity of your imagination, the vehemence and fixity with which you [that is, Dickens] impress your thought into the detail you wish to grasp, limit your knowledge, arrest you in a single feature, prevent you from reaching all the parts of a soul, and from sounding its depths.

But Taine short-changes Dickens' genius. This static, almost staring effect in the characterization of the Marquis, the fascination with his nose, accounts for the vividness of the characterization, just as the repetitive, "fixing" devices such as anaphora account for the vividness of the scenes. Actually Taine's complaint has to do with the lack of conventional realism in Dickens—we do not see "all the parts of a soul," the contradictory motives, the paradoxes of behavior that give an illusion of depth. But Dickens' verisimilitude is of another sort: the static quality is necessary to the photographic precision and clarity, while the third dimension—apparent depth—is given in the *meaning* of the character, by the use of associational clusters circling round a central image.

Dickens' iconography is in no sense unsophisticated or unpsycho-
logical. In the example of the Marquis' nose, the Marquis' defining
quality is not ordinary anger but rage, habitually suppressed and therefore white-hot. In the stone mask with the pinched, pulsating dints
in the nose, Dickens manages to express both the fury and its suppres-
sion. Moreover, while the Marquis' nose gives us the key to his character, other elements in the scene itself are used to elaborate this indirct
presentation. When the Marquis leaves the town house of Monseigneur,
furious because he is out of favor, the anger is allowed to show only
in his pulsating nose. But for once the image is not adequate to the
power of the feeling, which is actually expressed in the scene that follows, when the Marquis' *coach* runs down a helpless child—thus con-
veying, by a perfectly appropriate metonymy, the murderous rage that
possesses him. In general, the Marquis cannot be allowed to have any
direct contact with the fulfillment of his fiery desires, since it is his
character to suppress his feelings. His ancestors wielded the riding
whips, his coach acts out his fury, his nose betrays his hidden passion.

The extreme of his detachment is given in the vengeance he takes
for his own murder, for now he exists *only* as a stone mask with a dinted
nose:

> A rumour just lived in the village—had a faint and bare existence there,
> as its people had—that when the knife struck home, the faces changed,
> from faces of pride to faces of anger and pain; also, that when that
> dangling figure [of Gaspard] was hauled up forty feet above the fountain,
> they changed again, and bore a cruel look of being avenged, which they
> would henceforth bear for ever. In the stone face over the great window
> of the bed chamber where the murder was done, two fine dints were
> pointed out in the sculptured nose, which everybody recognised, and
> which nobody had seen of old. [2, xvi]

In Chapter xxiii of the second book, the Marquis' anger reaches its
climax when the revolutionaries have seized power and are destroying
his château. Appropriately enough, the Marquis is himself consumed
in his own rage, symbolized in the scene by the holocaust:

> The château was left to itself to flame and burn. In the roaring and
> raging of the conflagration, a red-hot wind, driving straight from the
> infernal regions, seemed to be blowing the edifice away. With the rising
> and falling of the blaze, the stone faces showed as if they were in torment.
> When great masses of stone and timber fell, the face with the two dints
> in the nose became obscured: anon struggled out of the smoke again, as
> if it were the face of the cruel Marquis, burning at the stake and con-
> tending with the fire.

Dickens says "as if it were the face of the cruel Marquis," but indeed
the Marquis' face has become stone, and we finally see him in his true

aspect, concealed so long behind the mask: "burning at the stake and contending with the fire."

The same synecdochic use of an image to express character or even theme occurs again and again in the *Tale* and in Dickens' other novels. . . . A Dickens novel is like a crossword puzzle, worked out temporally, one item at a time, but existing finally in space, all at once, in a network of interconnections. Joseph Frank has pointed out similar systems in other writers, where "relationships are juxtaposed independently of narrative progress; the full significance of the scene [in Dickens' case, one could say of the whole novel] is given only by the reflexive relations among the units of meaning." In such a novel, foreshadowing is only one part of the reflexive structure. Elements refer both forward and backward, and clusters of associations not only provide a context for new materials, but are themselves influenced by their repetition in varying circumstances, so that foreshadowing is modified in the memory by what it foreshadows. Consider, for example, the gradual accumulation of meaning in the successive reappearances of the Wine-and-Scarecrow motif introduced in the Wine-Shop chapter:

> Those who had been greedy with the staves of the cask, had acquired a tigerish smear about the mouth; and one tall joker so besmirched, his head more out of a long squalid bag of a nightcap than in it, scrawled upon a wall with his finger dipped in muddy wine-lees—BLOOD.

> A narrow winding street, full of offence and stench, with other narrow winding streets diverging, all peopled by rags and nightcaps, and all smelling of rags and nightcaps, and all visible things with a brooding look upon them that looked ill . . . every wind that blew over France shook the rags of the scarecrows in vain, for the birds, fine of song and feather, took no warning. [1. v]

> The rooms [of Monseigneur], though a beautiful scene to look at, and adorned with every device of decoration that the taste and skill of the time could achieve, were, in truth, not a sound business; considered with any reference to the scarecrows in the rags and nightcaps elsewhere (and not so far off, either, but that the watching towers of Notre Dame, almost equidistant from the two extremes, could see them both), they would have been an exceedingly uncomfortable business. . . . [2, VII]

> Saint Antoine had been, that morning, a vast dusky mass of scarecrows heaving to and fro, with frequent gleams of light above the billowy heads, where steel blades and bayonets shone in the sun. [2, XXI]

> Lovely girls; bright women, brown-haired, black-haired, and grey; youths; stalwart men and old; gentle born and peasant born; all red wine for La Guillotine, all daily brought into light from the dark cellars of loathsome prisons, and carried to her through the street to slake her devouring thirst. [3, v]

Rags, nightcaps, patched scarecrows, greedy drinkers of wine—all change, from signs of poverty, to causes of revolution, to effects of revolution. In this change a kind of temporal succession is implied; however, the meaning of these relations among the images finally exists not in a sequence but rather all at once, "spatially" configured. . . .

. . . [I]n *A Tale of Two Cities,* Chapter VI of the second book contains . . . a synecdochic foreshadowing, from which the lines of correspondence stretch out both forward and backward to encompass the whole novel. The passage, long as it is, must be quoted nearly in full to preserve its peculiar effect:

> The night was so very sultry, that although they sat with doors and windows open, they were overpowered by heat. When the tea-table was done with, they all moved to one of the windows, and looked out into the heavy twilight. Lucie sat by her father; Darnay sat beside her; Carton leaned against a window. The curtains were long and white, and some of the thunder-gusts that whirled into the corner, caught them up to the ceiling, and waved them like spectral wings.
>
> "The rain-drops are still falling, large, heavy, and few," said Doctor Manette. "It comes slowly."
>
> "It comes surely," said Carton.
>
> They spoke low, as people watching and waiting mostly do; as people in a dark room, watching and waiting for Lightning, always do.
>
> There was a great hurry in the streets, of people speeding away to get to shelter before the storm broke; the wonderful corner for echoes resounded with the echoes of footsteps coming and going, yet not a footstep was there.
>
> "A multitude of people, and yet a solitude!" said Darnay, when they had listened for a while.
>
> "Is it not impressive, Mr. Darnay?" asked Lucie. "Sometimes, I have sat here of an evening, until I have fancied—but even the shade of a foolish fancy makes me shudder tonight, when all is so black and solemn—"
>
> "Let us shudder too. We may know what it is."
>
> "It will seem nothing to you. Such whims are only impressive as we originate them, I think; they are not to be communicated. I have sometimes sat alone here of an evening, listening, until I have made the echoes out to be the echoes of all the footsteps that are coming by-and-by into our lives."
>
> "There is a great crowd coming one day into our lives, if that be so," Sydney Carton struck in, in his moody way.
>
> The footsteps were incessant, and the hurry of them became more and more rapid. The corner echoed and re-echoed with the tread of feet; some, as it seemed, under the windows; some, as it seemed, in the room; some coming, some going, some breaking off, some stopping altogether; all in the distant streets, and not one within sight.

"Are all these footsteps destined to come to all of us, Miss Manette, or are we to divide them among us?"

"I don't know, Mr. Darnay; I told you it was a foolish fancy, but you asked for it. When I have yielded myself to it, I have been alone, and then I have imagined them the footsteps of the people who are to come into my life, and my father's."

"I take them into mine!" said Carton. "*I* ask no questions and make no stipulations. There is a great crowd bearing down upon us, Miss Manette, and I see them—by the Lightning." He added the last words, after there had been a vivid flash which had shown him lounging in the window.

"And I hear them!" he added again, after a peal of thunder. "Here they come, fast, fierce, and furious!"

It was the rush and roar of rain that he typified, and it stopped him, for no voice could be heard in it. A memorable storm of thunder and lightning broke with that sweep of water, and there was not a moment's interval in crash, and fire, and rain, until after the moon rose at midnight.

In the first paragraph the still developing relations among the characters are sketched: Doctor Manette, his loyal daughter, her future husband, and, removed from them all, Carton, in a characteristic posture. The mention of "spectral wings" suggests that what follows may not be merely what it seems. And indeed almost every detail— even bits of the syntax—reaches outside the scene. The triad "large, heavy, and few," which Doctor Manette uses to describe the rain, gives place by the end of the scene to "fast, fierce, and furious," and this in turn looks forward to the phrase "headlong, mad, and dangerous," which later in the novel will be used to describe the outbreak of the revolutionary storm. In accord with the quickening tempo implied in this sequence, the tempest begins slowly, if surely, as Doctor Manette and Carton observe. Their remarks parallel those of Defarge and his wife, as they too await the "tempest" and its lightning, in Chapter XVI of the second book:

"It is a long time," repeated his wife; "and when is it not a long time? Vengeance and retribution require a long time; it is the rule."

"It does not take a long time to strike a man with Lightning," said Defarge.

"How long," demanded madame, composedly, "does it take to make and store the lightning? Tell me."

But Defarge has not long to wait, nor does the little group in Soho. The footsteps that echo in the dark room are in a hurry, pounding into their lives. They are the footsteps of the wine-stained feet in St. Antoine, of the blood-stained feet yet to come. Ironically it is Darnay (through whom the others are all involved in the Revolution) who

asks whether the footsteps are coming to them as a group or individually. In the end, of course, they are coming not for Lucie or Darnay, but for Carton, and his voluntary acceptance of whatever they may bring exactly forecasts his final acceptance of another's fate. Finally the tempest is upon them. The description looks forward, with its "rush and roar," its "thunder and lightning," to the Revolution scene:

> Saint Antoine had been, that morning, a vast dusky mass of scarecrows heaving to and fro, with frequent gleams of light above the billowy heads, where steel blades and bayonets shone in the sun. A tremendous roar arose from the throat of Saint Antoine, and a forest of naked arms struggled in the air like shrivelled branches of trees in a winter wind: all the fingers convulsively clutching at every weapon or semblance of a weapon that was thrown up from the depths below, no matter how far off.
>
> Who gave them out, whence they last came, where they began, through what agency they crookedly quivered and jerked, scores at a time, over the heads of the crowd, like a kind of lightning, no eye in the throng could have told. [2, xxi]

The "crash, and fire, and rain" also match the three chapters that describe the Revolution: "Echoing Footsteps," "The Sea Still Rises," and "Fire Rises." But most precise of all is the foreshadowing "sweep of water" which, in its rush, "stopped" Carton. Compare his last moments on the scaffold:

> The murmuring of many voices, the upturning of many faces, the pressing on of many footsteps in the outskirts of the crowd, so that it swells forward in a mass, *like one great heave of water,* all flashes away. [italics mine]

Even Carton's final resurrection is hinted in the rising of the moon which ends the storm. In fact, no major movement of the novel is without its reflection in this scene—the introduction of characters and of the relations between them; the awaiting of the tempest, the listening to approaching footsteps; the breaking of the storm; Carton's sacrifice, his death, his resurrection.

The basis of the elaborate structural synecdoche we have just been examining is to be found in Dickens' use of details, especially details of setting, as means of establishing clusters of meaning and feeling—which, in this novel, finally resolve themselves into two great polar loci, London and Paris, the tales of the little house in Soho and the streets of St. Antoine. *A Tale of Two Cities* displays in its very title this tendency of all Dickens' later work to polarize into two main locales, around one or the other of which all the action centers. This geographical organization is at the heart of each novel's structure, and on it too depends the powerful sense of atmosphere that is one of Dickens'

trademarks. Thus is the "unnecessary detail" of the novels crucially significant in their overall effect. Similarly, the principle of combination and connection that holds these details together in their clusters and larger configurations is contiguity. Metonymically and anaphorically controlled patterns dominate the structure, keeping the materials ordered in what, from one point of view, might seem a rather rigid and artificial rhetorical frame. This same principle may be seen operating on every level of the style, articulating sentence and paragraph, episode and plot; characters are built on it, and setting is everywhere determined by it. Artificial as Dickens' rhetoric may sometimes seem, it allows him to command effects which are out of the question for most writers, at once realistic in kind and in quantity of detail, and almost allegorical in the schematization and intensity of rendering. The blend is dreamlike, hallucinatory, super-real. Dickens seems to have tapped a source of imaginative truth which, although it surely corresponds to modes of perception and feeling in all men, has rarely been exploited for literary purposes with any success, and has still more rarely given rise to so full and elaborate a fictive world.

View Points

George Bernard Shaw: From the Preface to
Man and Superman

That the author of Everyman was no mere artist, but an artist-philosopher, and that the artist-philosophers are the only sort of artists I take quite seriously, will be no news to you. Even Plato and Boswell, as the dramatists who invented Socrates and Dr Johnson, impress me more deeply than the romantic playwrights. Ever since, as a boy, I first breathed the air of the transcendental regions at a performance of Mozart's Zauberflöte, I have been proof against the garish splendors and alcoholic excitements of the ordinary stage combinations of Tappertitian romance with the police intelligence. Bunyan, Blake, Hogarth, and Turner (these four apart and above all the English classics), Goethe, Shelley, Schopenhauer, Wagner, Ibsen, Morris, Tolstoy, and Nietzsche are among the writers whose peculiar sense of the world I recognize as more as less akin to my own. Mark the word peculiar. I read Dickens and Shakespear without shame or stint; but their pregnant observations and demonstrations of life are not co-ordinated into any philosophy or religion; on the contrary, Dickens's sentimental assumptions are violently contradicted by his observations; and Shakespear's pessimism is only his wounded humanity. Both have the specific genius of the fictionist and the common sympathies of human feeling and thought in pre-eminent degree. They are often saner and shrewder than the philosophers just as Sancho Panza was often saner and shrewder than Don Quixote. They clear away vast masses of oppressive gravity by their sense of the ridiculous, which is at bottom a combination of sound moral judgment with lighthearted good humor. But they are concerned with the diversities of the world instead of with its unities: they are so irreligious that they exploit popular religion for professional purposes without delicacy or scruple (for example, Sydney Carton and the ghost in Hamlet!): they are anarchical, and cannot balance their exposures of Angelo and Dogberry, Sir Leicester Dedlock and Mr. Tite Barnacle, with any portrait of a prophet or a worthy

From the Preface to Man and Superman *by George Bernard Shaw (1903) in* The Complete Prefaces of Bernard Shaw (*London: Paul Hamlyn Ltd., 1965*), *pp. 161–62. Copyright © by The Society of Authors. Reprinted by permission of The Society of Authors, for the Bernard Shaw Estate.*

leader: they have no constructive ideas: they regard those who have them as dangerous fanatics: in all their fictions there is no leading thought or inspiration for which any man could conceivably risk the spoiling of his hat in a shower, much less his life. Both are alike forced to borrow motives for the more strenuous actions of their personages from the common stockpot of melodramatic plots; so that Hamlet has to be stimulated by the prejudices of a policeman and Macbeth by the cupidities of a bushranger. Dickens, without the excuse of having to manufacture motives for Hamlets and Macbeths, superflously punts his crew down the stream of his monthly parts by mechanical devices which I leave you to describe, my own memory being quite baffled by the simplest question as to Monks in Oliver Twist, or the long lost parentage of Smike, or the relations between the Dorrit and Clennam families so inopportunely discovered by Monsieur Rigaud Blandois. The truth is, the world was to Shakespear a great "stage of fools" on which he was utterly bewildered. He could see no sort of sense in living at all; and Dickens saved himself from the despair of the dream in The Chimes by taking the world for granted and busying himself with its details. Neither of them could do anything with a serious positive character: they could place a human figure before you with perfect verisimilitude; but when the moment came for making it live and move, they found, unless it made them laugh, that they had a puppet on their hands, and had to invent some artificial external stimulus to make it work.

George Orwell: From "Charles Dickens"

Dickens deals with revolution in the narrower sense in two novels, *Barnaby Rudge* and *A Tale of Two Cities.* In *Barnaby Rudge* it is a case of rioting rather than revolution. The Gordon Riots of 1780, though they had religious bigotry as a pretext, seem to have been little more than a pointless outburst of looting. Dickens's attitude to this kind of thing is sufficiently indicated by the fact that his first idea was to make the ringleaders of the riots three lunatics escaped from an asylum. He was dissuaded from this, but the principal figure of the book is in fact a village idiot. In the chapters dealing with the riots Dickens shows a most profound horror of mob violence. He delights in describing scenes in which the "dregs" of the population behave with atrocious bestiality. These chapters are of great psychological interest, because they show how deeply he had brooded on this subject. The

From "Charles Dickens," in Dickens, Dali, and Others by George Orwell (New York: Reynal and Hitchcock, 1946), pp. 10–16. Copyright © 1946 by George Orwell. Reprinted by permission of Harcourt Brace Jovanovich, Inc.

things he describes can only have come out of his imagination, for no riots on anything like the same scale had happened in his lifetime. Here is one of his descriptions, for instance:

> If Bedlam gates had been flung open wide, there would not have issued forth such maniacs as the frenzy of that night had made. There were men there who danced and trampled on the beds of flowers as though they trod down human enemies, and wrenched them from their stalks, like savages who twisted human necks. There were men who cast their lighted torches in the air, and suffered them to fall upon their heads and faces, blistering the skin with deep unseemly burns. There were men who rushed up to the fire, and paddled in it with their hands as if in water; and others who were restrained by force from plunging in, to gratify their deadly longing. On the skull of one drunken lad— not twenty, by his looks—who lay upon the ground with a bottle to his mouth, the lead from the roof came streaming down in a shower of liquid fire, white hot, melting his head like wax. . . . But of all the howling throng not one learnt mercy from, or sickened at, these sights; nor was the fierce, besotted, senseless rage of one man glutted.

You might almost think you were reading a description of "Red" Spain by a partisan of General Franco. One ought, of course, to remember that when Dickens was writing, the London "mob" still existed. (Nowadays there is no mob, only a flock.) Low wages and the growth and shift of population had brought into existence a huge, dangerous slum-proletariat, and until the early middle of the nineteenth century there was hardly such a thing as a police force. When the brickbats began to fly there was nothing between shuttering your windows and ordering the troops to open fire. In *A Tale of Two Cities* he is dealing with a revolution which was really *about* something, and Dickens's attitude is different, but not entirely different. As a matter of fact, *A Tale of Two Cities* is a book which tends to leave a false impression behind, especially after a lapse of time.

The one thing that everyone who has read *A Tale of Two Cities* remembers is the Reign of Terror. The whole book is dominated by the guillotine—tumbrils thundering to and fro, bloody knives, heads bouncing into the basket, and sinister old women knitting as they watch. Actually these scenes only occupy a few chapters, but they are written with terrible intensity, and the rest of the book is rather slow going. But *A Tale of Two Cities* is not a companion volume to *The Scarlet Pimpernel*. Dickens sees clearly enough that the French Revolution was bound to happen and that many of the people who were executed deserved what they got. If, he says, you behave as the French aristocracy had behaved, vengeance will follow. He repeats this over and over again. We are constantly being reminded that while "my lord" is lolling in bed, with four liveried footmen serving his chocolate and

the peasants starving outside, somewhere in the forest a tree is growing which will presently be sawn into planks for the platform of the
guillotine, etc. etc. etc. The inevitability of the Terror, given its causes,
is insisted upon in the clearest terms:

> It was too much the way . . . to talk of this terrible Revolution as
> if it were the only harvest ever known under the skies that had not been
> sown—as if nothing had ever been done, or omitted to be done, that had
> led to it—as if observers of the wretched millions in France, and of the
> misused and perverted resources that should have made them prosper-
> ous, had not seen it inevitably coming, years before, and had not in
> plain terms recorded what they saw.

And again:

> All the devouring and insatiate monsters imagined since imagination
> could record itself, are fused in the one realisation, Guillotine. And yet
> there is not in France, with its rich variety of soil and climate, a blade,
> a leaf, a root, a sprig, a peppercorn, which will grow to maturity under
> conditions more certain than those that have produced this horror. Crush
> humanity out of shape once more, under similar hammers, and it will
> twist itself into the same tortured forms.

In other words, the French aristocracy had dug their own graves.
But there is no perception here of what is now called historic necessity.
Dickens sees that the results are inevitable, given the causes, but he
thinks that the causes might have been avoided. The Revolution is
something that happens because centuries of oppression have made
the French peasantry sub-human. If the wicked nobleman could somehow have turned over a new leaf, like Scrooge, there would have been
no Revolution, no *jacquerie,* no guillotine—and so much the better.
This is the opposite of the "revolutionary" attitude. From the "revolutionary" point of view the class-struggle is the main source of progress,
and therefore the nobleman who robs the peasant and goads him to
revolt is playing a necessary part, just as much as the Jacobin who
guillotines the nobleman. Dickens never writes anywhere a line that
can be interpreted as meaning this. Revolution as he sees it is merely
a monster that is begotten by tyranny and always ends by devouring
its own instruments. In Sidney Carton's vision at the foot of the guillotine, he foresees Defarge and the other leading spirits of the Terror
all perishing under the same knife—which, in fact, was approximately
what happened.

And Dickens is very sure that revolution *is* a monster. That is why
everyone remembers the revolutionary scenes in *A Tale of Two Cities;*
they have the quality of nightmare, and it is Dickens's own nightmare.
Again and again he insists upon the meaningless horrors of revolution
—the mass-butcheries, the injustice, the ever-present terror of spies,

the frightful bloodlust of the mob. The descriptions of the Paris mob —the description, for instance, of the crowd of murderers struggling round the grindstone to sharpen their weapons before butchering the prisoners in the September massacres—outdo anything in *Barnaby Rudge*. The revolutionaries appear to him simply as degraded savages —in fact, as lunatics. He broods over their frenzies with a curious imaginative intensity. He describes them dancing the "Carmagnole," for instance:

> There could not be fewer than five hundred people, and they were dancing like five thousand demons. . . . They danced to the popular Revolution song, keeping a ferocious time that was like a gnashing of teeth in unison. . . . They advanced, retreated, struck at one another's hands, clutched at one another's heads, spun round alone, caught one another, and spun round in pairs, until many of them dropped. . . . Suddenly they stopped again, paused, struck out the time afresh, forming into lines the width of the public way, and, with their heads low down and their hands high up, swooped screaming off. No fight could have been half so terrible as this dance. It was so emphatically a fallen sport—a something, once innocent, delivered over to all devilry.

He even credits some of these wretches with a taste for guillotining children. The passage I have abridged above ought to be read in full. It and others like it show how deep was Dickens's horror of revolutionary hysteria. Notice, for instance, that touch, "with their heads low down and their hands high up," etc., and the evil vision it conveys. Madame Defarge is a truly dreadful figure, certainly Dickens's most successful attempt at a *malignant* character. Defarge and others are simply "the new oppressors who have risen on the destruction of the old," the revolutionary courts are presided over by "the lowest, cruellest and worst populace," and so on and so forth. All the way through Dickens insists upon the nightmare insecurity of a revolutionary period, and in this he shows a great deal of prescience. "A law of the suspected, which struck away all security for liberty or life, and delivered over any good and innocent person to any bad and guilty one; prisons gorged with people who had committed no offence, and could obtain no hearing"—it would apply pretty accurately to several countries to-day.

The apologists of any revolution generally try to minimise its horrors; Dickens's impulse is to exaggerate them—and from a historical point of view he has certainly exaggerated. Even the Reign of Terror was a much smaller thing than he makes it appear. Though he quotes no figures, he gives the impression of a frenzied massacre lasting for years, whereas in reality the whole of the Terror, so far as the number of deaths goes, was a joke compared with one of Napoleon's battles. But the bloody knives and the tumbrils rolling to and fro create in his mind

a special, sinister vision which he has succeeded in passing on to generations of readers. Thanks to Dickens, the very word "tumbril" has a murderous sound; one forgets that a tumbril is only a sort of farm-cart. To this day, to the average Englishman, the French Revolution means no more than a pyramid of severed heads. It is a strange thing that Dickens, much more in sympathy with the ideas of the Revolution than most Englishmen of his time, should have played a part in creating this impression.

Sergei Eisenstein: From *Dickens, Griffith, and the Film Today*

The visual images of Dickens are inseparable from aural images. The English philosopher and critic, George Henry Lewes, though puzzled as to its significance, recorded that "Dickens once declared to me that every word said by his characters was distinctly *heard* by him. . . ."

We can see for ourselves that his descriptions offer not only absolute *accuracy of detail,* but also an absolutely *accurate drawing of the behavior* and actions of his characters. And this is just as true for the most trifling details of behavior—even gesture, as it is for the basic generalized characteristics of the image. Isn't this piece of description of Mr. Dombey's behavior actually an exhaustive regisseur-actor directive?

> He had already laid his hand upon the bell-rope to convey his usual summons to Richards, when his eye fell upon a writing-desk, belonging to his deceased wife, which had been taken, among other things, from a cabinet in her chamber. It was not the first time that his eye had lighted on it. He carried the key in his pocket; and he brought it to his table and opened it now—having previously locked the room door—with a well-accustomed hand.

Here the last phrase arrests one's attention: there is a certain awkwardness in its description. However, this "inserted" phrase: *having previously locked the room door,* "fitted in" as if recollected by the author in the middle of a later phrase, instead of being placed where it apparently should have been, in the consecutive order of the description, that is, before the words, *and he brought it to his table,* is found exactly at this spot for quite *un*fortuitous reasons.

From "Dickens, Griffith, and the Film Today," in Film Form by Sergei Eisenstein, edited and translated by Jay Leyda (New York: Harcourt, Brace and Company, Inc., 1949), pp. 211–16. Copyright © by Harcourt Brace Jovanovich, Inc. and reprinted with their permission.

In this deliberate "montage" displacement of the time-continuity of the description there is a brilliantly caught rendering of the *transient thievery* of the action, slipped between the preliminary action and the act of reading another's letter, carried out with that absolute "correctness" of gentlemanly dignity which Mr. Dombey knows how to give to any behavior or action of his.

This very (montage) arrangement of the phrasing gives an exact direction to the "performer," so that in defining this decorous and confident opening of the writing-desk, he must "play" the closing and locking of the door with a hint of an entirely different shade of conduct. And it would be this "shading" in which would also be played the unfolding of the letter; but in this part of the "performance" Dickens makes this shading more precise, not only with a significant arrangement of the words, but also with an exact description of characteristics.

> From beneath a heap of torn and cancelled scraps of paper, he took one letter that remained entire. Involuntarily holding his breath as he opened this document, and 'bating in the stealthy action something of his arrogant demeanour, he sat down, resting his head upon one hand, and read it through.

The reading itself is done with a shading of absolutely gentlemanly cold decorum:

> He read it slowly and attentively, and with a nice particularity to every syllable. Otherwise than as his great deliberation seemed unnatural, and perhaps the result of an effort equally great, he allowed no sign of emotion to escape him. When he had read it through, he folded and refolded it slowly several times, and tore it carefully into fragments. Checking his hand in the act of throwing these away, he put them in his pocket, as if unwilling to trust them even to the chances of being reunited and deciphered; and instead of ringing, as usual, for little Paul, he sat solitary all the evening in his cheerless room.

This scene does not appear in the final version of the novel, for with the aim of increasing the tension of the action, Dickens cut out this passage on Forster's advice; in his biography of Dickens Forster preserved this passage to show with what mercilessness Dickens sometimes "cut" writing that had cost him great labor. This mercilessness once more emphasizes that sharp clarity of representation towards which Dickens strove by all means, endeavoring with purely cinematic laconism to say what he considered necessary. (This, by the way, did not in the least prevent his novels from achieving enormous breadth.)

I don't believe I am wrong in lingering on this example, for one need only alter two or three of the character names and change

Dickens's name to the name of the hero of my essay, in order to impute literally almost everything told here to the account of Griffith.

From that steely, observing glance, which I remember from my meeting with him, to the capture *en passant* of key details or tokens—indications of character, Griffith has all this in as much a Dickensesque sharpness and clarity as Dickens, on his part, had cinematic "optical quality," "frame composition," "close-up," and the alteration of emphasis by special lenses.

Analogies and resemblances cannot be pursued too far—they lose conviction and charm. They begin to take on the air of machination or card-tricks. I should be very sorry to lose the conviction of the affinity between Dickens and Griffith, allowing this abundance of common traits to slide into a game of anecdotal semblance of tokens.

All the more that such a gleaning from Dickens goes beyond the limits of interest in Griffith's individual cinematic craftsmanship and widens into a concern with film-craftmanship in general. This is why I dig more and more deeply into the film-indications of Dickens, revealing them through Griffith—for the use of future film-exponents. So I must be excused, in leafing through Dickens, for having found in him even—a "dissolve." How else could this passage be defined—the opening of the last chapter of *A Tale of Two Cities:*

> Along the Paris streets, the death-carts rumble, hollow and harsh. Six tumbrils carry the day's wine to La Guillotine. . . .
> Six tumbrils roll along the streets. Change these back again to what they were, thou powerful enchanter, Time, and they shall be seen to be the carriages of absolute monarchs, the equipages of feudal nobles, the toilettes of flaring Jezebels, the churches that are not my Father's house but dens of thieves, the huts of millions of starving peasants!

How many such "cinematic" surprises must be hiding in Dickens's pages!

However, let us turn to the basic montage structure, whose rudiment in Dickens's work was developed into the elements of film composition in Griffith's work. Lifting a corner of the veil over these riches, these hitherto unused experiences, let us look into *Oliver Twist.* Open it at the twenty-first chapter. Let's read its beginning:

Chapter XXI [1]

1. It was a cheerless morning when they got into the street; blowing and raining hard; and the clouds looking dull and stormy.

The night had been very wet: for large pools of water had collected in the road: and the kennels were overflowing.

---

[1] For demonstration purposes I have broken this beginning of the chapter into smaller pieces than did its author; the numbering is, of course, also mine.

There was a faint glimmering of the coming day in the sky; but it rather aggravated than relieved the gloom of the scene: the sombre light only serving to pale that which the street lamps afforded, without shedding any warmer or brighter tints upon the wet housetops, and dreary streets.

There appeared to be nobody stirring in that quarter of the town; for the windows of the houses were all closely shut; and the streets through which they passed, were noiseless and empty.

2. By the time they had turned into the Bethnal Green Road, the day had fairly begun to break. Many of the lamps were already extinguished;
a few country waggons were slowly toiling on, towards London;
and now and then, a stage-coach, covered with mud, rattled briskly by:
the driver bestowing, as he passed, an admonitory lash upon the heavy waggoner who, by keeping on the wrong side of the road, had endangered his arriving at the office, a quarter of a minute after his time.

The public-houses, with gas-lights burning inside, were already open.
By degrees, other shops began to be unclosed; and a few scattered people were met with.
Then, came straggling groups of labourers going to their work;
then, men and women with fish-baskets on their heads:
donkey-carts laden with vegetables;
chaise-carts filled with live-stock or whole carcasses of meat;
milk-women with pails;
and an unbroken concourse of people, trudging out with various supplies to the eastern suburbs of the town.

3. As they approached the City, the noise and traffic gradually increased;
and when they threaded the streets between Shoreditch and Smithfield, it had swelled into a roar of sound and bustle.
It was as light as it was likely to be, till night came on again; and the busy morning of half the London population had begun. . . .

4. It was market-morning.
The ground was covered, nearly ankle-deep, with filth and mire;
and a thick stream, perpetually rising from the reeking bodies of the cattle,
and mingling with the fog,
which seemed to rest upon the chimney-tops, hung heavily above. . . .
Countrymen,
butchers,
drovers,
hawkers,
boys,
thieves,
idlers,
and vagabonds of every low grade,
were mingled together in a dense mass;

5. the whistling of drovers,
the barking of dogs,
the bellowing and plunging of oxen,
the bleating of sheep,
the grunting and squeaking of pigs;
the cries of hawkers,
the shouts, oaths and quarrelling on all sides;
the ringing of bells
and roar of voices, that issued from every public-house;
the crowding, pushing, driving, beating,
whooping and yelling;
the hideous and discordant din that resounded from every corner of
the market;
   and the unwashed, unshaken, squalid, and dirty figures constantly
running to and fro, and bursting in and out of the throng; rendered it a
stunning and bewildering scene, which quite confounded the senses.

How often have we encountered just such a structure in the work
of Griffith? This austere accumulation and quickening tempo, this
gradual play of light: from burning street-lamps, to their being extinguished; from night, to dawn; from dawn, to the full radiance of
day (*It was as light as it was likely to be, till night came on again*);
this calculated transition from purely visual elements to an interweaving of them with aural elements: at first as an indefinite rumble,
coming from afar at the second stage of increasing light, so that the
rumble may grow into a roar, transferring us to a purely aural structure, now concrete and objective (section 5 of our break-down); with
such scenes, picked up *en passant,* and intercut into the whole—like
the driver, hastening towards his office; and finally, these magnifi-
cently typical details, the reeking bodies of the cattle, from which the
steam rises and mingles with the over-all cloud of morning fog, or
the close-up of the legs in the almost ankle-deep filth and mire, all
this gives the fullest cinematic sensation of the panorama of a market.

A. O. J. Cockshut: From *The Imagination*
of Charles Dickens

In *Barnaby Rudge* and in *A Tale of Two Cities* Dickens caused
two of the dominating images of his literary life to clash. The crowd
makes war on the prison. In these passages we are aware of a very
deep excitement in the author, as if this was his own private version
of the meeting of irresistible force and immovable object. If examined

From The Imagination of Charles Dickens, *by A. O. J. Cockshut (New York:
New York University Press, 1962), pp. 32–36, 81–83, 185–86. Copyright © 1961 by
A. O. J. Cockshut. Reprinted by permission of New York University Press.*

in association with *Oliver Twist,* the prison chapters [in *A Tale of Two Cities*] read almost like a reply to the superficiality of Fagin's death scene. If prison is only the temporary detention of the innocent boy, who is sure to be saved in the end, or the horrible but just punishment of the thoroughly evil man, much of its terror disappears. But in *A Tale of Two Cities* it is a great deal more than this. Manette has been released from "105 North Tower," the royalist prison, and is living in the house of the revolutionary plotter, Defarge. He is free, but his freedom means nothing to him. He is always alone, and can scarcely bear visitors. He requires to be locked in his room, "because he has lived so long locked up, that he would be frightened—rave, tear himself to pieces—die—come to I know not what harm, if his door was left open."

He has forgotten his name, but remembers perpetually the number of his prison room, and he still occupies himself with the manual work he did in prison. But worse, he has not only forgotten himself as a human being, he has been virtually forgotten by his benefactors. Defarge does not pity him as a kind of dead trophy or example to stir up revolutionary feeling. So influential is Defarge's view of him that it momentarily infects even Manette's daughter.

"I am afraid of it."

"Of it? Of what?"

"I mean of him . . . of my father."

We miss the point if we read this merely as a description of callous perversity. On the contrary, when the prisoner is described by the author, he appears in much the same light. "He, and his old canvas frock, and his loose stockings, and all his poor tatters of clothes, had, in a long seclusion from direct light and air, faded down to such a dull uniformity of parchment-yellow, that it would have been hard to say which was which." Here is Dickens's ultimate in misery, a suffering that cannot be relieved, pitied or understood, that is not aware of itself, and to the question "I hope you care to be recalled to life?" can only answer "I can't say."

And to make us universalise the picture, and apply it to the suffering world in general, Dickens placed at the end of the chapter this image: "Beneath that arch of unmoved and eternal lights; some, so remote from this little earth that the learned tell us it is doubtful whether their rays have even yet discovered it, as a point in space where anything is suffered or done. . . ."

In this chapter, Dickens achieved something new. He used the image of the prison for a steady gaze, without self-pity or hysteria, at the general miseries of life. For although Manette can recover his wits and his human dignity, the prison is lurking within him, ready

to regain control, when a new emotional crisis occurs. At the time of his daughter's marriage he goes back to his unconscious shoemaking. Perhaps this incident has a somewhat unreal and contrived air. But its importance in the author's development is nevertheless considerable. Dickens was, as we have seen, exceptionally aware of external objects; his imagination was extraordinarily literal; his psychological grasp, which was eventually to become formidable, was slow to develop. His natural tendency, therefore, was to blame all the misery he observed on circumstances, on tyrants, on social conditions. So it was bound to take time for him to comprehend that the prison he was endlessly seeking to describe and understand was, in part, the mental creation of the prisoner, that to strike away the chains and fetters could not solve all the prisoner's problems. Having now realised this, having arrived at his own version of the discovery:

> O the mind, mind has mountains; cliffs of fall
> Frightful, sheer, no-man fathomed.

he was eventually able to develop it in the case of Miss Havisham into a deep psychological study.

But it may be objected that all this special pleading does not improve the quality of the actual scene in which Manette returns to his shoemaking, if, as I have suggested, that is deficient. And, of course, that is true. Dickens was, in his way, a great artist, but he was never a pure artist. Aspects of his mind, interesting in themselves, but structurally irrelevant, are always liable to break in. But sometimes, as here, we can have the satisfaction of feeling that the imperfections contribute to the making of later and better works.

The consequences of Manette's hopeless misery are very instructive. When the Revolution comes, his long years of imprisonment under the old régime entitle Manette to a privileged position. He can use his influence on behalf of his accused son-in-law; and he can even say "It all tended to a good end, my friend; it was not mere waste and ruin." When these hopes seem to be fulfilled, he is a proud and happy man. But the release of Evrémonde is only temporary. He is once again denounced and sentenced to death. The melodramatic ending in which Evrémonde is saved by the substitution of Carton, cannot obscure the significance of this. For Evrémonde's second condemnation is occasioned by the reading of a document written by Manette in prison. The supposed utility of those long years in prison ends in disillusionment. And at this point, with sombre appropriateness, Manette returns, as Dorrit had done so much more convincingly, to the imbecile mode of consciousness which possessed him in his prison years.

So the direct and tangible value of prisoners' suffering is implicitly

denied. But there is still a strange dignity in the prison, which comes to Evrémonde as a surprise:

"In the instinctive association of prisoners with shameful crimes and disgrace, the newcomer recoiled from his company. But the crowning unreality of his long unreal ride, was, their all at once rising to receive him, with every refinement of manner known to the time, and with all the engaging graces and courtesies of life."

No doubt Dickens had read of some such scene in the French Revolution, but all the same, this dignity had personal significance also for him. It reduces the prison to a terror of manageable proportions. If it cannot be called a complete moral or artistic answer to the problem of the prison which he carried with him through his writing life, it at least contains no cheat or deception. He was making progress.

. . . It is not surprising, given Dickens's comparative immaturity at the time, and the degree to which his personal emotions were involved, that the end of *Barnaby Rudge* should be unsatisfactory. His deepest meditations on the prison would come many years later in *Little Dorrit,* while he would develop an interest in a different, more civilised type of crowd. In *Barnaby Rudge* there is a mighty clash, but no tragedy and no reconciliation.

It would be pleasant and convenient in this study where the main stress falls on Dickens's development, to point to a later work where this clash of great ideas led up to a satisfying climax and resolution. But no writer's career, certainly not the career of Dickens, is as neat and regular as critics are inclined to wish. In some ways, the crowd of *Barnaby Rudge* remains the most memorable that Dickens ever described. Yet there were developments, even if they were not all necessarily improvements. In *A Tale of Two Cities,* he contrived to give a keener impression of an invisible crowd, of mounting communal passions nursed in secret which must one day overthrow the government. Dickens had little of importance to say about the meaning of political revolution. But he was able, especially by the use of images of darkness, to convey a fine glimpse of slowly nurtured social forces coming to catastrophic fruition.

> Darkness closed around, and then came the ringing of the church bells and the distant beating of the military drums in the Palace Court-Yard, as the women sat knitting, knitting. Darkness encompassed them. Another darkness was closing in as surely, when the church bells, then ringing pleasantly in many an airy steeple over France, should be melted into thundering cannon. . . . So much was closing in about the women who sat knitting, knitting, that they their very selves were closing in around a structure yet unbuilt, where they were to sit knitting, knitting, counting dropping heads.

Dickens never repeated these vast spectacular crowd scenes. His mind turned to different versions of the crowd. In *Little Dorrit* and *Our Mutual Friend,* the crowds are only a background, the cheerful sufferers of Bleeding Heart Yard, the swarming inhabitants of those sad streets where Arthur Clennam walks on Sundays, and remembers the miseries of his youth.

The crowd and the solitary—there is nothing really surprising in the fact that the same man should concentrate on both. The friendless solitary feels as if the whole of society were an implacable crowd. And the dual preoccupation reminds us of what was missing in Dickens. He did not understand, or at any rate, did not effectively portray family relationships. Like every novelist, of course, he described many families; but did he ever give us a convincing portrait of a marriage? On the subject of the parent-child relationship he is more lucid, but still apt to be perverse. He tends to reverse the roles. Little Dorrit is a mother to her father, not a daughter. The doll's dressmaker in *Our Mutual Friend* is a stern and terrifying stepmother to her father. Even friendship tends to develop into an unreal jollity.

Now, of course, Dickens is, or was once, a great author for family reading. And he was revered in his time, and has sometimes been attacked since, as a fanatical celebrator of the family affections. But this is deceptive. The Dickens family is not the fundamental Christian and Freudian family of father, mother and children. It is a covey of aunts, and cousins and relatives by marriage. His favorite family celebration is Christmas. That is, in England, just when the basic Christian and Freudian family is least itself, when it is a confused jumble of three or four generations, in fact, when it becomes a *crowd.*

So it is that the idea of the crowd (and the corresponding idea of the solitary) are fundamental for Dickens. They are the key to his unrivalled strength as a portrayer of industrial society, the home of crowds. They are the source of his weakness in presenting deep personal relationships. And since the deepest human affections, if denied proper expression, will become muddled and distorted, his sentimentality also can be referred to the same source. . . .

Nearly all the most popular literary works of the nineteenth century were melodramas. *Murder in the Red Barn, Lady Audley's Secret,* Carlyle's *French Revolution* and Macaulay's history differ widely in quality, no doubt, but they were all very popular, and all intensely melodramatic. Now, as we have seen, one of Dickens's leading ideas, involved with some of his best, and some of his worst devices of plot, was that we are members one of another. Solemnly consecrated though this idea is by religious tradition, in literary terms it is very

closely related to melodrama. Coincidences, long-lost sons, buried wills, hidden relationships—all these are crude statements of the idea that we are linked much more closely than we realise with people we have never seen. Vulgar in his tastes, and towering in imagination, Dickens seized eagerly upon the ridiculous paraphernalia of English melo-drama. He enjoyed over-obvious comparisons, like the wine running through the gutters and foreshadowing the blood bath of the Revolu-tion in *A Tale of Two Cities.*

But the melodrama Dickens at first so carelessly copied was capable of enormous development, for its simple stock of ideas has very deep psychological roots. What could be more naïve and melodramatic, and at the same time more subtle and serious than the following pas-sage from *Great Expectations?* The child Pip is watching the terrify-ing convict depart:

> As I saw him go, picking his way among the nettles, and among the brambles that bound the green mounds, he looked in my young eyes as if he were eluding the hands of dead people, stretching up cautiously out of their graves, to get a twist upon his ankle and pull him in.

We have all read articles about the influence of heredity on crime. But this idea, which we associate, perhaps rather wearily with "social science," here plunges down to a far deeper mental level, the level at which artistic appeals are made. And the means by which it reaches this point of depth is very near to the traditional macabre and childish melodrama. Dickens was at the same time a rather naïve conservative-liberal reformer, a lover of the fantastic, and an original artist fash-ioning new symbolic equivalents for our most inarticulate emotions. It is in this cluster of contradictions that much of the fascination of his work resides.

His slowness to grasp general ideas did not prove a handicap to the kind of achievements for which he was best fitted. Symbolic meanings seep slowly through the mass of accumulated detail, the wonderful topographical intimacy, the jostling contemporary problems. Gigantic failures like Melville's "Pierre" bear witness how ill-fitted the novel is to bear a condition where the idea triumphs and the fact is defeated. The ambiguities of Dickens's river in *Our Mutual Friend* or the slowly-developing meaning of the sea in *Dombey and Son* are only tolerable because they merge hesitantly out of an undeniable physical reality.

So, in the end, his lack of intellectual consistency, already casti-gated in these pages, and the neurotic instability of the man's feelings, hardly matter, because the vivid journalist, the entertainer and the artist are triumphantly at one.

Taylor Stoehr: From *Dickens: The Dreamer's Stance*

In a "realistic" novel—say Jane Austen's *Emma*—the selection and ordering of details is what we might call "socially" or "conventionally" determined; many details seem to have been omitted, as irrelevant or uninteresting ("unnecessary" in Orwell's terms); and those actually selected seem to be arranged and presented with a view to expressing a particular attitude, a notion of what is important—all of which gives rise to the reader's feeling that things "add up," that one thing leads to another in an organic way. Thus, appropriate as it may seem to call her method "realism," Jane Austen's contriving intelligence is in evidence at every point, shaping and arranging things with careful artifice. We feel her presence in the abstraction and orientation. It is, in fact, essential to the realistic effect that we be aware of the narrator in reading *Emma* or *Pride and Prejudice.* With Dickens the situation is quite different. There is little apparent abstraction (and thus little apparent choosing), and the ordering is of a very peculiar sort—artificial in such a way as to strike us as even mechanical. The order given in devices such as anaphora is imposed from above, like the grid used in interpreting an aerial photograph, so that the elements do not seem to add up or move in a particular direction, but rather to exist all at once, articulated without being integrated, ordered without being organized. The detail is not presented according to principles that foster a sense of growth and change in time, the essence of realistic plot and character. Instead, the method involves a halting of time, a freezing of the scene to allow "photographic accuracy" in the representation of life-going-on. This is exactly comparable to the timeless quality of the present-tense narrative in *Bleak House,* with its immediacy and detachment, and its impassive camera-eye narrator.

Of course there is some direction and progress in even the most ornamental of Dickens' scenes. But this orientation rarely arises from the rhetorical ordering; it is usually embedded in the details themselves, which only *seem* to be accidental and unchosen. Thus in the Hunger passage, emotional organization is implied in the way the scene develops, first from Hunger "pushed out of the tall houses, in the wretched clothing," to the Hunger "shred into atomies," then from the "wild-beast thought of the possibility of turning at bay" to the "murderous" gunstocks and "crippling stones of the pavement." This

From "The Vision of Reality," Chapter II of Dickens: The Dreamer's Stance (Ithaca: Cornell University Press, 1965) pp. 59–65. Copyright © by Cornell University. Used by permission of Cornell University Press. [Numbered footnotes acknowledging Professor Stoehr's scholarly references have been omitted.]

movement is not inherent in the scene itself (though it appears to be), but is a movement of the narrator's perception, or of his attitude toward what he perceives, as he reads more and more violence into the details before him. The bias of the narrator's intelligence may thus be exposed to our view, but the emotion works only as an undercurrent, subverting the structure of the rhetoric rather than following it. And in any case, the feeling seems to have less to do with the narrator than with the independent existence of the scene itself, with the objects which present themselves because *there they are,* already quivering with life. . . .

When Dickens uses metaphor, we must recognize that he is intruding in the scene. The metaphors of the Hunger passage—the comparison of the street lamps to sea-lamps on a ship, or the comparison of the darkness surrounding the lamps to the darkness of man's condition—clearly show Dickens the narrator stepping in, to comment on the story. Both these metaphors are part of the overt prediction (as distinguished from mere foreshadowing) which Dickens feels so often compelled to introduce in his tales ("For, the time was to come . . ."). It might even be argued that metaphors are invariably to be found in those passages traditionally condemned for their "editorializing" tone, where Dickens sentimentally or angrily or bitterly inserts his own opinion of the world he has created. Such is the basis, for example, of the metaphoric passage in the last chapter of the *Tale:*

> Crush humanity out of shape once more, under similar hammers, and it will twist itself into the same tortured forms. Sow the same seed of rapacious licence and oppression over again, and it will surely yield the same fruit according to its kind.

The oratorical tone that is so unpleasant here marks the author's withdrawal from the story in order to grind his own axe, his rather conventional moral indignation, a declaration of authorial intentions.[1]

And yet, even in metaphor, Dickens' narrative perspective is often maintained in its detachment. The "lamp-light" metaphor in the

---

[1] The problem of irony is not so easily dealt with as that of metaphor. Does the presence of irony necessarily remind us of the narrator? Take the case of *Moll Flanders,* where we are frequently presented with what must be regarded as "unintentional irony." Instances of this sort surely make us aware of the narrator's (Defoe's, not Moll's) presence; but it is not so obvious that *intended* incongruities between states of affairs "expressed" and "implied" will have this effect. The ironic conception of Doctor Manette's part in the denunciation of his son-in-law does not produce any special awareness of the narrator as we read; on the other hand, the harsh, satirical treatment of Stryver may remind us that we are being told a story, by a narrator who has his own thoughts and opinions. Perhaps we could say that Dickens' detachment (and hence the usual narrative perspective) collapses only when the irony veers toward sarcasm, tantamount to a loss of control much as in Defoe's "unintentional irony."

Hunger passage is a good example, for here the setting—basis of most of his metonymies—predominates as usual, so that the comparison seems less invented than stumbled upon. The motion of the lamps seems like the swaying of ship-lanterns at sea, which in turn reminds us of tempest, ship, and crew (connection by contiguity), and from these we are referred back again metaphorically to the state of France, its being at sea and in danger of tempest. Dickens' tendency is to extend his metaphors, chiefly by metonymic attachment of the related circumstances, until the original comparison becomes almost mythic, often with something like a plot line relating the separate elements of the expanded correspondence. Consider, for example, the further development of this "lamp-light" metaphor, which becomes a full-fledged "sea" metaphor in Dickens' description of the Revolution (2, XXI):

> As a whirlpool of boiling waters has a centre point, so, all this raging circled round Defarge's wine-shop, and every human drop in the caldron had a tendency to be sucked towards the vortex. . . .
>
> With a roar that sounded as if all the breath in France had been shaped into the detested word ["Bastille"], the living sea rose, wave on wave, depth on depth, and overflowed the city to that point. Alarm-bells ringing, drums beating, the sea raging and thundering on its new beach, the attack begun.
>
> . . . Suddenly the sea rose immeasurably wider and higher, and swept Defarge of the wine-shop over the lowered drawbridge, past the massive stone outer walls, in among the eight great towers surrendered!
>
> So resistless was the force of the ocean bearing him on, that even to draw his breath or turn his head was as impracticable as if he had been struggling in the surf at the South Sea. . . .
>
> . . . So tremendous was the noise of the living ocean, in its irruption into the Fortress, and its inundation of the courts and passages and staircases. All around outside, too, it beat the walls with a deep, hoarse roar, from which, occasionally, some partial shouts of tumult broke and leaped into the air like spray.
>
> The sea of black and threatening waters, and of destructive upheaving of wave against wave, whose depths were yet unfathomed and whose forces were yet unknown. The remorseless sea of turbulently swaying shapes, voices of vengeance, and faces hardened in the furnaces of suffering until the touch of pity could make no mark on them.

The completeness and inner consistency of the metaphor, as it is extended and expanded to constitute a world in itself, seem to lift the figure out of the realm of metaphor altogether. We believe in the metaphor as though it were not a metaphor at all. The power of such

figures to compel belief is beyond rhetoric, as Ernst Cassirer has suggested in *Language and Myth:*

> For mythic thinking there is much more in metaphor than a bare "substitution," a mere rhetorical figure of speech; . . . what seems to our subsequent reflection as a sheer transcription is mythically conceived as a genuine and direct identification.

All of Dickens' major metaphors—the widely discussed symbols which lie at the center of his didactic concerns in the novels—have this "mythic" quality. Pestilence and tempest, court and prison, factory and slum, these are more than mere metaphors for aspects of society; they *are* aspects of society. The dust-heaps in *Our Mutual Friend* do not merely represent wealth, nor is their function simply to establish the psychological relation between money and excrement: rather an *identity* is posited—money is excrement, "gold-dust." Similarly the sea-mob in *A Tale of Two Cities,* the scarecrow-citizens of Saint Antoine, the blood-wine on the cobblestones—in varying degrees these figures have transcended metaphor to become dreamlike amalgams of object and feeling. The effect is weirdly hallucinatory, rather more like dream than myth. Objects are exhaustively described with the vividness of detail characteristic of dream; the "meanings" of the objects are also dreamlike, so that things count as passions yet remain things too, in a way that is rarely felt in waking life. Taine made the point brilliantly a century ago:

> An imagination so lucid and energetic cannot but animate inanimate objects without an effort. It provokes in the mind in which it works extraordinary emotions, and the author pours over the objects which he figures to himself, something of the ever-welling passion which overflows in him. Stones for him take a voice, white walls swell out into big phantoms, black wells yawn hideously and mysteriously in the darkness; legions of strange creatures whirl shuddering over the fantastic landscape; blank nature is peopled, inert matter moves. But the images remain clear; in this madness there is nothing vague or disorderly; imaginary objects are designed with outlines as precise and details as numerous as real objects, and the dream is equal to the reality.

Juggle the last clause and you have it precisely: the reality is that of dream.

Chronology of Important Dates

	Dickens	The Age
1812	Charles Dickens born February 7, at Portsea near Rochester.	Luddite riots: knitting machines smashed by hand-workers in several shires; death penalties imposed.
1814	Dickens family moves to London.	
1815		Final defeat of Napoleon and restoration of Bourbon dynasty. Corn Law passed to support British wheat prices.
1819		Queen Victoria born. "Peterloo Massacre," armed opposition to assemblage of workers in St. Peter's Fields, Manchester.
1824	John Dickens imprisoned in the Marshalsea for debt; Charles works for a few months in Warren's Blacking Warehouse.	
1824–26	Dickens finishes his schooling at Wellington House Academy.	
1827–28	Works as attorney's clerk, learns shorthand.	
1829–32	Law reporter for Doctor's Commons; general and parliamentary reporter for the *True Sun* and the *Mirror of Parliament*.	
1832		First Reform Bill passed, extending suffrage.

Dickens   The Age

	Dickens	The Age
1833	First publication, a sketch entitled "A Dinner at Poplar Walk," in the *Monthly Magazine*.	Factory Act places restrictions on child labor.
1834	Reporter for the *Morning Chronicle*.	
1836	*Sketches by Boz. Pickwick Papers* begun in monthly parts. Dickens assumes editorship of *Bentley's Miscellany*. Marries Catherine Hogarth.	
1837	*Oliver Twist* begun in monthly parts. First child, Charles, born. Sudden death of Mary Hogarth.	Accession of Queen Victoria. Publication of Carlyle's *French Revolution*.
1838	*Nicholas Nickleby* begun.	Chartism, chiefly a movement to reform parliament and electoral procedures, develops.
1840–41	*The Old Curiosity Shop* and *Barnaby Rudge* published in *Master Humphrey's Clock*.	
1842	Travels and lectures in the United States. *American Notes* published.	Female and child labor in mines prohibited.
1843	*Martin Chuzzlewit* and *A Christmas Carol* published.	Publication of Carlyle's *Past and Present*.
1844–45	Travels in Italy and France. Beginning of amateur theatricals.	
1846	*Dombey and Son* begun.	Corn Laws repealed.
1847		Publication of Thackeray's *Vanity Fair* and J. S. Mill's *Political Economy*.
1848		Revolutions break out all over Europe. Chartist demonstration and petition in London. Collapse of Chartist movement because of divided leadership and gradually improving working conditions.

	Dickens	**The Age**

1849–50	*David Copperfield;* Dickens establishes the weekly periodical, *Household Words.*	
1851	Performs with an amateur company before the Queen.	Judicial reforms to improve equity and efficiency of courts begun in a series of parliamentary acts.
1852–53	*Bleak House.*	
1854	Visits Preston to observe effects of a strike in the cotton mills; returns to publish *Hard Times* in *Household Words.*	Crimean War begins; Preston strike ends.
1855	Meeting with Maria Beadnell, his early love (now Maria Winter), excites a flood of anticipation followed by severe emotional disappointment. *Little Dorrit* begun.	
1856	Buys Gad's Hill Place, near Rochester, which will remain his home until death.	Bernard Shaw born.
1857	First public reading from his works. Wilkie Collins's play, *The Frozen Deep,* first performed, with Dickens in the role of the self-sacrificing Richard Wardour. A later performance given for the Queen. Partially recast for still later performance in Manchester; among new participants is Ellen Ternan.	Divorce Act. Publication of *Madame Bovary.*
1858	Announces separation from Catherine, and publishes a statement of explanation on the front page of *Household Words.*	
1859	Brings *Household Words* to a close. Begins new periodical, *All the Year Round,* with *A Tale of Two Cities* in weekly parts (April 20–Nov. 26).	Darwin's *Origin of Species* published.

Dickens	The Age

	Dickens	**The Age**
1860–61	*Great Expectations* published in *All the Year Round*. Public readings become more fervent.	
1864–65	*Our Mutual Friend*. Severe shock of railway accident breaks his nerve and leads to decline in health and stability.	
1866		Publication of *Crime and Punishment*.
1867		Second Reform Bill extends suffrage to most wage earners, exclusive of rural laborers. Publication of *Das Kapital*.
1867–68	Immensely successful reading tour of the United States brings about exhaustion and near-collapse.	
1869	Begins The *Mystery of Edwin Drood*.	
1870	Ends public reading; received by the Queen; retires to Gad's Hill. Suffers a stroke and dies on June 9. Buried in Westminster Abbey on June 14. *Edwin Drood* left unfinished.	

Notes on the Editor and Contributors

CHARLES E. BECKWITH, Professor of English at California State College, Los Angeles, is a contributor to the forthcoming Oxford edition of the works of John Gay.

A. O. J. COCKSHUT, fellow of Hertford College, Oxford, is the author of *Anglican Attitudes* and *The Unbelievers,* a study of the religious controversies of the nineteenth century.

EARLE DAVIS, Chairman of the English Department at Kansas State University, has written various articles on Dickens, several textbooks and volumes of poetry, and *Vision Fugitive: Ezra Pound and Economics.*

SERGEI EISENSTEIN (1898–1948), director of *Potemkin* and *Ivan the Terrible,* was, like D. W. Griffith, one of the great innovators in film as art work.

JOHN GROSS, who has taught at the Universities of Cambridge and London and is now a freelance writer, has published an edition of Gissing's *New Grub Street,* a monograph on James Joyce, and *The Rise and Fall of the Man of Letters,* a study of the role of reviewers and reviewing in the nineteenth and early twentieth centuries in England.

JACK LINDSAY is a historian, novelist, poet, archaeologist, and critic, whose many books include lives of Bunyan, Cézanne, and Cleopatra, besides works on ancient alchemy and an edition of the poems of Marx and Engels for a forthcoming collection of their works.

The late WILLIAM H. MARSHALL was Professor of English at the University of North Carolina, Chapel Hill, and author of *The World of the Victorian Novel,* of which the earlier article here reprinted forms part of Chapter VII in modified form.

GEORGE ORWELL (1903–1950), whose work as a whole has been obscured by the fame of *Animal Farm* and *1984,* has now been represented in his full range by a four-volume collection of his essays, journalism, and letters.

GEORGE BERNARD SHAW (1856–1950), whose remark that *Little Dorrit* was a more seditious book than *Das Kapital* is characteristically excessive, was nevertheless early in his perception of the revolutionary thrust that lay beneath the sentiment and moralizing of Dickens.

G. ROBERT STANGE, Chairman of the English Department at Tufts University, is author of *Matthew Arnold: the Poet as Humanist* and numerous articles on nineteenth century literature.

TAYLOR STOEHR, Professor of Literature at the University of California at Santa Cruz, is a historian of nineteenth century culture who has written a number of articles on nineteenth century American figures and movements.

Selected Bibliography

Bodelson, C. A. "Some Notes on Dickens' Symbolism." *English Studies*, XL (1959), 420–31. Asserts the greater importance of symbolic pattern— exemplified in *A Tale of Two Cities* by contrasts of light and dark, recurrent color effects, journeys toward a catastrophic goal—than plot pattern, an importance not recognized in Dickens's time, even by Dickens.

Brain, Russell. "Dickensian Diagnoses." In *Some Reflections on Genius*. New York: J. B. Lippincott, Co., 1960. Praises Dickens's psychological insight, chiefly shown in his treatment of Dr. Manette as a multiple personality whose old identity is tied to the symbol of the shoemaker's bench, and who can achieve his new or "real" self only when the old controlling symbol is destroyed.

Collins, Philip. *Dickens and Crime*. London: Macmillan & Co., Ltd., 1962. Contains no separate section on *A Tale of Two Cities,* but remarks *passim* are of special interest, such as that the idea of showing the effects of live burial came from Dickens's experience in visiting prisons, including American prisons, where he observed the deadly effects of solitary confinement and imposed silence, and asked himself if ghosts were one of the terrors of gaols.

Falconer, J. A. "Sources of *A Tale of Two Cities.*" *Modern Language Notes,* XXXVI (1921), 1–10. Studies several borrowings and parallels from a variety of sources, such as Mercier's *Tableau de Paris,* an anecdote from Carlyle's *French Revolution,* and Scott's *Rokeby,* revealing something of the range of threads from Dickens's reading that are woven into *A Tale of Two Cities.*

Fielding, K. J. "Separation—and *A Tale of Two Cities.*" Chapter X of *Charles Dickens: A Critical Study*. London: Longmans, Green, & Co., Ltd., 1958. A brief but full narrative of Dickens's separation, his relations with his wife's parents, and the beginning of *All the Year Round,* along with some discussion of the novel which names Lucie as the central figure and Dr. Manette, the imprisoned one who feels a compulsive need for action, as the figure with whom Dickens feels the greatest identification.

Gregory, Michael. "Old Bailey Speech in *A Tale of Two Cities.*" *Review of English Literature,* VI (1965), 42–55. A linguistic study, applying some

newly defined categories of speech to Darnay's first trial, attempting to show the appropriateness of the various forms to the various moments in the trial, hence Dickens's dramatic control on even so meticulous a level as "vocal and aural potential."

Jackson, T. A. "The *Tale of Two Cities.*" In *Charles Dickens: The Progress of a Radical.* New York: International Publishers, 1938. An offering of the "Marxist" Dickens which designates the adverse criticism of the time as bourgeois hostility contriving to let the story pass as a moral tale in which Carton's sacrifice redeems the horrors of the Revolution, whereas the real force of the story lies in Dickens's approach, "nearer than ever," to a positive assertion of revolution as man's only hope.

Johnson, Edgar. "The Tempest and the Ruined Garden." Chapter iii, Part IX, of *Charles Dickens: His Tragedy and Triumph.* 2 vols. New York: Simon and Schuster, Inc., 1952. A uniformly sensible survey of the book, scotching the biographical literalness of some criticism while acknowledging the characters and their situations as representative of various aspects of Dickens's emotional dilemma, which he expresses with "new and flaming power" even though in the book at large the themes of love and revolution do not satisfactorily mix, each tending to blur the other.

McMaster, R. D. "Dickens and the Horrific." *Dalhousie Review,* XXXVIII (1958), 18–28. Asserts that Dickens's obsession with ghastliness is constant and profound, part of the very fiber of his web. Points out as a source of the gossip at the well about the punishment of Monseigneur's murderer the torture and execution of Damiens, attempted murderer of Louis XV, as narrated in *The Terrific Register; or, a Record of Crimes, Judgments, Providences, and Calamities,* a sadistic journal read by Dickens as a boy.

Milley, H. J. "Wilkie Collins and *A Tale of Two Cities.*" *Modern Language Review,* XXXIV (1939), 525–34. Suggests that the French Revolution and Carlyle's book are not so influential as Collins's play about self-sacrifice, in which Dickens acted, *The Frozen Deep;* and his *Sister Rose,* a long tale of regeneration through self-sacrifice during the Revolution, which was first printed in *Household Words* in 1855.

Monod, Sylvère, "Dickens as Historical Novelist: *A Tale of Two Cities*" and "The Evolution of Dickens' Art in *Hard Times* and *A Tale of Two Cities.*" Sections iii and iv of Chapter XXV of *Dickens the Novelist.* Norman: University of Oklahoma Press, 1968. A shrewd weighing of Dickens's talents and equipment for historical fiction, found wanting in the larger application but excellent in the creation of atmosphere and emotion, though often with exaggeration, distortion, and rhetorical repetition, flaws which in turn are balanced by the book's firm and symmetrical construction.

Shannon, Edgar F. "The Dramatic Element in Dickens." *Sewanee Review,* XXI (1913), 277–86. An early study of the instinct for drama so strong in Dickens from the beginning, which contrasts the melodramatic treatment